Youth, Music and Creative Cultures

Also by Geraldine Bloustien

GIRL MAKING: A CROSS-CULTURAL ETHNOGRAPHY ON THE PROCESSES OF GROWING UP FEMALE

THE HAWKE LEGACY (*co-edited with B. Comber and A. Mackinnon*)

MUSICAL VISIONS: MUSIC AS SOUND IMAGE AND MOVEMENT

RE-VISIONING ETHNOGRAPHY

Also by Margaret Peters

SONIC SYNERGIES: MUSIC, TECHNOLOGY, COMMUNITY, IDENTITY (*co-edited with G. Bloustien and S. Luckman*)

Youth, Music and Creative Cultures

Playing for Life

Geraldine Bloustien

Margaret Peters

© Geraldine Bloustien and Margaret Peters 2011

All rights reserved. No reproduction, copy or transmission of this publication may be made without written permission.

No portion of this publication may be reproduced, copied or transmitted save with written permission or in accordance with the provisions of the Copyright, Designs and Patents Act 1988, or under the terms of any licence permitting limited copying issued by the Copyright Licensing Agency, Saffron House, 6-10 Kirby Street, London EC1N 8TS.

Any person who does any unauthorized act in relation to this publication may be liable to criminal prosecution and civil claims for damages.

The authors have asserted their rights to be identified
as the authors of this work in accordance with the Copyright,
Designs and Patents Act 1988.

First published 2011 by
PALGRAVE MACMILLAN

Palgrave Macmillan in the UK is an imprint of Macmillan Publishers Limited, registered in England, company number 785998, of Houndmills, Basingstoke, Hampshire RG21 6XS.

Palgrave Macmillan in the US is a division of St Martin's Press LLC,
175 Fifth Avenue, New York, NY 10010.

Palgrave Macmillan is the global academic imprint of the above companies and has companies and representatives throughout the world.

Palgrave® and Macmillan® are registered trademarks in the United States, the United Kingdom, Europe and other countries.

ISBN 978–0–230–20058–6

This book is printed on paper suitable for recycling and made from fully managed and sustained forest sources. Logging, pulping and manufacturing processes are expected to conform to the environmental regulations of the country of origin.

A catalogue record for this book is available from the British Library.

Library of Congress Cataloging-in-Publication Data
Bloustien, Gerry.
   Youth, music and creative cultures: playing for life / Geraldine
   Bloustien, Margaret Peters.
     p.   cm.
   Includes index.
   ISBN 978–0–230–20058–6 (alk. paper)
   1. Music–Social aspects.   2. Music and youth.   I. Peters, Margaret,
   1951–   II. Title.
   Ml3916.B56 2011
   780.835—dc23   2011020959

10 9 8 7 6 5 4 3 2 1
20 19 18 17 16 15 14 13 12 11

Printed and bound in the United States of America

Contents

List of Figures and Table	vi
List of Illustrations	vii
Acknowledgements	viii

1	Music is Youth and Youth is Music	1
2	Reflections on Theory and Method	43
3	'Everyone Wants to be a DJ'	83
4	Creating Spaces	123
5	Money Matters: Government Policy, Funding and Youth Music	165
6	Becoming Phat: Youth, Music and Micro-Enterprise	206
7	Taking Flight: Creative Cultures and Beyond	233
	Appendix: Our CBOs at a Glance	257

Notes	263
References	274
Index	294

List of Figures and Table

Figures

1.1	Diagrammatic representation of the Playing for Life methodology	16
1.2	Map of our CBO research sites in Berlin	38

Table

2.1	Berlin districts 2004: comparison of researched districts	54

List of Illustrations

DJ Lady Lick in Thailand. © Tuesday Benfield		xi
1.1	Row in the studio. © Geraldine Bloustien	1
1.2	Shep in action. © Helen Page	30
2.1	Kyle prepares for a rave (video still). © Kyle D'Andrea	43
2.2	'It's a bit like making a *Big Brother* movie!' (video still). © Vanessa Cussack	75
3.1	Everyone wants to be a DJ! © Kyle D'Andrea	83
3.2	Da Klinic promotional flyer. © Adrian Shepherd	88
3.3	Totally Stressed in performance. © Sandra Wildeboer	95
3.4	Watch that line! Vaky breakdancing photo. © Adrian Shepherd	106
3.5	Mix Master Mike creates a journey. © Alex Parardes	112
3.6	Watching the dance floor. © Alex Parardes	113
4.1	Tuesday's practice space (video still). © Tuesday Benfield	123
4.2	On the air at *Youth Revolutions*. © The City of Salisbury, South Australia	137
4.3	Carclew. © Jaclyn Bloustien	147
4.4	Interchange Studios and Weekend Arts College. © Jaclyn Bloustien	148
4.5	The Tabernacle. © Jaclyn Bloustien	148
4.6	The Palais Royale. © Jaclyn Bloustien	149
4.7	Save our Loft! Campaign poster. © Julie Pavlou-Kirri	154
4.8	Open youth venue, Norwich. © Jaclyn Bloustien	160
5.1	Remains of The Disco space at Statthaus Bocklerpark. © Anna Steigemann	165
5.2	Entrance to the Pie Factory. © Alexis Johnson	171
5.3	Pie Factory music room, whole room. © Alexis Johnson	172
5.4	Michael and his self-made didgeridoos. © Anna Steigemann	178
6.1	Katie Williams in performance. © Davi Matheson	206
6.2	Row and HOD at Phatbeats studio. © Geraldine Bloustien	213
6.3	Patterns in Static: integrated marketing. © Alicia Woodrow	223
6.4	Buttons for Patterns in Static. © Alicia Woodrow	224
7.1	Taking flight. © Adrian Shepherd	233
7.2	Mural, Pie Factory music room. © Alexis Johnson	234
7.3	Alexis on her boat. © Geraldine Bloustien	243
7.4	On the street set of Passport 2 Pimlico. © Alexis Johnson	245
7.5	Christmas (W)Rapping Float. © Adrian Shepherd	252

Acknowledgements

Undertaking a project this complex over such a long period of time means that inevitably we have a very large number of people to thank and to whom we continue to be grateful. Neither the original research project nor this book would have been possible without the support, encouragement and assistance of a great many people but we want to mention some in particular.

We are indebted to Felicity Plester and Christabel Scaife at Palgrave Macmillan as our commissioning editors, both of whom also became our friends, for their unflagging enthusiasm for the project and their patience and insights along the production process. Together with their superbly efficient production team at Palgrave, Felicity, Christabel and Catherine Mitchell have made the process of publishing this book amazingly painless and even enjoyable. Particular thanks must go to Kate Leeson at the Hawke Research Institute, University of South Australia, for her painstaking care, patience and precise editing skills. As ever her expertise is greatly valued and appreciated. Thanks too to the institute for Kate's time and all the administrative and in-kind support at all stages of the research and publication process.

For overall encouragement and critical insights we wish to thank Graeme Turner, Sheila Whiteley, Larry Grossberg, Shirley Brice Heath, Henry Jenkins, Anne Cranney-Francis, Jane Kenway, Claudia Mitchell, Jane Davidson, Hartmut Häußermann and David Buckingham – all of whom at different times read, discussed and offered insightful comments on the project design, analysis and publication drafts and gave us the confidence to proceed.

Australian funding for the project was from three grants: an Australian Research Council Discovery Grant (2003–5), an Australian Research Council International Linkage Fellowship (2004–6) and a University of South Australia Visiting Fellowship (2004). The non-Australian partners and their institutions provided supporting cash and in-kind funding, with particular generosity from Humboldt University for the extended onsite visits for many of the team members. The academic research team comprised (at the time of the fieldwork) Assoc Prof Geraldine Bloustien and Assoc Prof Margaret Peters (University of South Australia), Associate Professor Shane Homan (University of Newcastle, NSW), Dr Sarah Baker (ARC Post Doctoral Research Fellow 2003–5, University of South Australia, Prof Andy Bennett (University of Surrey, UK). Dr Bruce Cohen joined us from Humboldt University, Germany with the 2003 International Linkage Fellowship, noted above, enabling him to work onsite with the Australians during 2004–6. Prof Tommy DeFrantz and Prof Henry Jenkins (Massachusetts Institute of Technology) joined us from the USA, completing the team. The main Australian research assistants were Julie Pavlou-Kirri (University of Newcastle, NSW) and Danni Nicholas-Sexton (University of South Australia). David van der Hoek, Peter Dutton, Mia Bennett, Nikolas de Masi, Mari Kain, Anna Steigemann and Jaclyn Bloustien provided additional research assistance, with Jane Broweleit admirably undertaking the administrative tasks. Bruce Cohen, Jessica Terruhn and Anna Steigemann translated our audio-visual and printed materials from the German.

International advisers to the project were Prof Shirley Brice-Heath (Brown University, USA), Prof Henry Jenkins (Massachusetts Institute of Technology, USA), Prof David Buckingham (University of London, UK), and Prof Hartmut Häußermann (Humboldt University, Germany). The Playing for Life website was created by Andrew Plummer of Scenestealer and maintained at different stages by Stuart Dinmore and Paul Wallace, Hawke Research Institute, University of South Australia.

The main fieldwork period started before 2003 and in many ways it is still continuing to date. We are still in regular contact with so many of our wonderful young co-researchers and their mentors. Clearly our greatest debts of gratitude belong to the generosity, patience and tolerance of all of the youth, their families, friends and wider social networks whose narratives of their ongoing passion for music fill these pages. Their openness and acceptance of what must so often have felt like intrusion into their worlds and their willingness to share so much of their everyday lives, their moments of quiet reflection as well as of exuberant fun cannot be overstated. We learnt so much from them – far beyond the scope of this study. We believe all of the initial academic team at different times learnt to shed their initial embarrassment and adult inhibitions to participate with the youth in particular moments of fun, including joining the on-air team at the *Youth Revolutions* radio show; DJ Roland Samuel's Phatbeats UK garage online radio program; Rowland's and Tuesday's garage and R&B events or Katie's rock gigs in London; the Heavy Metal gig at Wutzkyalle in Berlin and the live-in all-girls music weekend at Köpenick in Berlin; the Kandinsky Sessions in Adelaide; the Beats and Rime and Breakers workshops and hip hop battles in Newcastle, New South Wales and the similar exciting events held by the Da Klinic crew in Adelaide, South Australia. Many of the team also attended a number of music festivals and events where we watched our young talented co-researchers perform confidently to ever larger audiences and test themselves in ever more competitive situations. Possibly, however, we were most affected as we watched many of the youth in the Brighton Treatment Center, a juvenile detention facility in Boston, develop. Before our eyes, they grew from angry, disaffected, troubled young men into individuals who felt they could gain new levels of competence, confidence and creativity through the music lessons opportunities offered by Juri and her team in the Genuine Voices Program. Here we saw the quintessence of what musical engagement can and does offer in the everyday lives of some of our most troubled youth.

Thank you to the directors, youth workers, teaching staff, trainers and advisers from all of the organisations that participated in our study. Over the past seven years we have been privileged to gain the friendship of these very committed people and of even more young people and their social networks from each of the four international sites we worked in. Again the generosity of time and confidences cannot be overestimated. We are certainly in awe of the considerable talent and openness of all the young people we spent time with.

Without doubt, our ongoing gratitude has to go to our families and close friends who lived alongside this work for so many years. Our respective children, David and Jacki Bloustien and Nick and Matthew Peters, now young adults themselves, frequently offered valuable insights and corrective criticism of our interpretations from their own everyday and eminently sensible perspectives. Because he also became so well known to many of the young people in our research, Mark Bloustien was often invited as an additional 'guest' by the youth to many of the gigs and social evenings in which we participated, particularly in Australia and in London. While he was often our additional photographer, onsite technician and an extra sounding board for the youth themselves, he clearly enjoyed the rock concerts, the garage events and hip hop battles as much as we did.

Certain parts of this book have appeared in various forms in other collections as we developed, clarified and fine-tuned our thoughts and ideas. Material from Chapters 2, 3 and 4 has been developed from Bloustien's earlier published work on play including material expanded from various chapters in *Girl Making: A Cross-Cultural Ethnography on the Processes of Growing up Female* (New York and Oxford: Berghahn Books, 2003). Material from Chapters 5 and 6 appeared in Chapters 8 (by Bruce Cohen), 14 and 16 of our 2008 edited collection *Sonic Synergies: Music, Technology, Community, Identity*, edited by Bloustien, Peters and Luckman (Aldershot, Hampshire: Ashgate). All have been published with kind permission of the respective publishers. The illustrations listed above are reproduced here with kind permission of their respective creators.

Geraldine Bloustien
Margaret Peters

DJ Lady Lick in Thailand. © Tuesday Benfield

1
Music is Youth and Youth is Music

Global music, local identities: in the beginning

Photo 1.1   Row in the studio. © Geraldine Bloustien

> The man that hath no music in himself,
> Nor is not moved with concord of sweet sounds,
> Is fit for treasons, stratagems and spoils;
> The motions of his spirit are dull as night
> And his affections dark as Erebus:
> Let no such man be trusted.
>   (William Shakespeare, *Merchant of Venice*, act 5, scene 1)

If your looking for a good start to your bank holiday weekend (or in the local area) and want some proper vybes to get you in the groove then look no futher than No.8 Bar/Nightclub in Willesden High Road NW10 where I'll be dropping the best in classic Rap/R'n'B and House + Garage vybes from 11pm–2am. (Rowland, email alert, May 2008, spelling as in the original)

Just a quick update on Aviator Lane's upcoming shows in Adelaide and Melbourne. Also, Really Good In Theory is back for its 3rd year and I will once again be having a stall. Details later in this email . . . (Alicia, email alert, May 2008, spelling as in the original)

From his home in North London, the then 28-year-old Rowland, pictured above, sent out an email through Facebook, a popular digital social networking site, to alert his friends and fans about his latest DJ gig. Across the world in Adelaide, South Australia, 26-year-old Alicia also sent out an alert through email and her personal social networks about her latest music ventures.[1] What is particularly fascinating about these two electronic advertisements is their differences in location, style and linguistic argot and yet their similarities in aim, approach and tone. Even more importantly, stylistically, in tone and in purpose, they are far from unique to these two young people. The activities described here and the method of dissemination are increasingly common and significant to young people's networks around the globe. Rowland, Row to his friends but DJ Roland Samuel (without the 'w') to his fans and professional networks, was born in Antigua but lives now in North London. He has been involved with the UK garage scene[2] ever since we first met him, which is now about seven years ago, and we still receive personal updates of his activities and shows regularly through Facebook (his personal and fan pages) and email. He endlessly practises and fine-tunes his DJ skills, performs weekly on internet and pirate radio and aims to develop his event management opportunities after and in between work commitments. Row's day job is assistant store manager at a syndicated health store, a job he finds boring but it pays the bills – just!

Alicia now works full time as an administrative assistant at a private girls' school in Adelaide but like Row it is a 'marking time' job so that she can support her music commitments. Until recently, these were her performance in a band, Aviator Lane, her independent label Patterns in Static and her music event management business. Sometimes it all gets too much and Alicia decides to 'leave off her music and event management for a while'. More information about Row and Alicia will follow but for now it is important to stress that they are but two of the determined, talented and enterprising young people we discovered in our three-year international project, Playing for Life, from all walks of life, all socio-political, economic backgrounds and across four countries.[3] We detail and reflect on all their stories below.

The study began in 2002 with a germ of an idea – a hunch, a nagging thought, based on our everyday encounters with young people. As two academics with substantial track records of working with young people, particularly those from disadvantaged backgrounds (Peters, 1993, 1994a; Bloustien, 1996, 1998, 1999, 2002), former high school teachers and parents of teenage children ourselves, it was our view that the ubiquitous negative media accounts of young people as disaffected, disillusioned, societal freeloaders (Matthews, 2001; Newburn, Shiner and Young, 2005) just did not align with our personal experiences. In fact from our own, though perhaps limited, perhaps subjective, professional and personal perspectives as parents, teachers and concerned adults, it seemed as though there was an almost hidden aspect of young people that was not getting sufficient airing. That was their total and often passionate involvement with music and related arts – as performers, musicians, audience members and promoters. What we saw was what some years later Axel Bruns was to describe as the development of 'produsers' (Bruns, 2008, p. 2), a term that

> highlights that within the communities that engage in the collaborative creation and extension of information and knowledge... the role of 'consumer' and even that of 'end user' have long disappeared and the distinctions between producers and users of content have faded into comparative insignificance. (Bruns, 2008, p. 2)

And then there were the implications of perceiving this voluntary involvement with and production of a shared knowledge base. We had heard and read the stories and reports and knew first hand of young people dropping out from formal education and refusing to take up opportunities of possible regular employment, when and if they were available (perhaps because they did not consider the opportunities of regular employment were 'creative' enough). We were aware of the usual discourses about the lack of 'staying power' and commitment from the young but such accounts did not fit with the ways we saw many of the youth engaging with a range of complex music activities, many observed from our own teaching and professional experiences. In these circumstances the so-called 'apathetic' teenager revealed the type of tenacity and focus that would make any educator and employer sit up and take notice. We saw young people forming their own social networks, voluntarily mentoring and training others, and acquiring appropriate business acumen and technical and professional skills. We also saw some teenagers getting disheartened and frustrated by the lack of support, scarcity of resources and opportunities to develop their talents.

So, with such burning questions and yet a glaring disparity of images in mind, we set about developing a project that would help answer some important questions. Firstly, we wanted to understand more about why music and related activities seemed to mean so much to young people around the globe, for we were already aware that our preliminary observations were not simply limited to Adelaide, South Australia. Secondly, if music were as important an activity as we assumed, then we wanted to know what was needed to ensure that engagement with music activities could serve as a vehicle or pathway for a broader sense of social inclusion for young people who were materially and psychologically on the margins of their societies. If others thought this way too and were possibly already working on such a model, what evidence was there of its success already in place in different locales and communities across the world? Was this a broad, idealistic and difficult task? Perhaps, but one we felt was more a question of revealing what was already there and needing to be exposed and articulated.

In summary, then, we began with the premise that popular music is globally acknowledged as affectively and culturally central to many young people. Secondly, we believed it is perhaps particularly so for those who feel that they are materially and psychologically marginalised from the broader resources and opportunities of society. It provides a rich medium for storytelling, oral exchange and sharing of experience. Increasingly combined with new digital technologies, it also becomes the central way in which young people inform, entertain and express themselves. Furthermore, we had already seen and documented how music could often provide strategic pathways to employment and socio-economic inclusion (Grossberg, 1984; Attali, 1985; Back, 1988; Cohen, 1991; Cross, 1993; Fornäs, Lindberg and Sernhede, 1995; Thornton, 1995; Brewster and Broughton, 2000; Flew et al., 2001; McRobbie, 2002a; also see additional references in Bloustien, 2003b; Bloustien, Peters and Luckman, 2008).

Previous studies had shown that music itself was central to the cultural identity of all cultures, to the night-time economy of both developed and Third World counties, contributing to their leisure, hospitality, entertainment and tourism industries (Comedia, 1991; Bianchini, 1995; Chatterton and Hollands, 2002; Florida, 2002; Jayne, 2004). Because of the inevitable link between night-time economy, alcohol abuse and crime (Thomas and Bromley, 2000; Winlow and Hall, 2005; Roberts, 2006; Roberts et al., 2006) the strategic potential of music in this context to underpin cultural cohesion and sustain community development is still grossly under-realised by most government agencies and social policy developers. This is so even though the value of arts programs themselves for disadvantaged youth and young people at risk, especially those offered out of school time through community-based organisations (CBOs), has been well documented (Weitz, 1996; Heath, Soep and Roach, 1998; Heath and Roach, 1999; Heath and Smyth, 2000; Heath 2005; Delgado, 2004; McLaughlin, 2000; Wilson, 2005). Or, as Lori Hager has argued, 'Community youth arts are, as yet, uncomfortably situated in the nexus of prevention, reform, enrichment, the arts and social and economic development' (2008, n.p.).

Our second premise based on previous studies and our own observations was that the ways in which young people engage with popular culture, and in particular popular music, as a means of agency and as a way of negotiating marginalisation, often in the face of immense political and economic hurdles, were far from simple (Richards, 1998; McCarthy et al., 1999; Dimitriadis, 2000; Bennett, 2001; Dimitriadis and Weis, 2001; Green, 2001; Jenkins, 2001; see also Grossberg, 2005 for some of the additional political challenges, he argues, youth particularly face in contemporary America's 'war on kids'). This also involved an understanding of the seriousness and complexity of the concept of 'play', access and performance (see Handelman, 1990; Schechner, 1993). In turn, this led us to consider how the concept of serious play is itself enabled and facilitated through the creation of private spaces and often through a complex negotiation of public place. We already realised that public space is not available to everyone – young people are particularly vulnerable and targeted to being moved on and excluded by official authorities and policies (Bessant and Hil, 1997; Heyward and Crane, 1998; Crane, 1999; Delany, Prodigalidad and Sanders, 2002; Childress, 2004).

Thus the unique combination of research and pedagogic questions provoked a further set of issues to be investigated, including ethical issues of reciprocity. We were very anxious not to replicate the sense of disempowerment for the young people we were attempting to work with. So our research questions were, firstly, what were the specific learning practices that marginalised and disadvantaged young people acquire and develop in their local and vernacular music practices, and how do these practices reflect and depend on global technological change? Secondly, in what ways are alternative learning sites and community-based organisations, particularly those based within specific ethnic and minority communities, effective in facilitating youth agency? In what ways do they offer opportunities of access into formal and informal employment, economies and professional music and creative industries? What are their limitations? What ways could they be aided to be more effective and valued? And, thirdly, what are the implications for other youth development and training programs and current cross-cultural practices concerning marginalised youth? Finally, how do we untangle these issues using an ethical, transparent and completely reciprocal methodology? What other issues of place, programming, funding and pedagogy do these issues raise? We will outline these components within our frameworks one at a time in the sections below, beginning with an overview of using what we argue is the main value: a participatory methodology.

Reciprocal and reflexive methodologies: young people as co-researchers

Implicit in our preliminary questioning and discussions was the aim to document the nature of the relationship between young people and the resources that help them achieve a sense of agency through popular music and related arts production. We started to realise that our study findings could elaborate upon an emerging body of research on community-based organisations as alternative learning sites, already acknowledged as enhancing the development of young people's sense of self-esteem and agency. To study this comprehensively we would need to understand the roles of mentoring, pedagogy and networking and felt this would be best achieved through integrating a quantitative and a qualitative methodology but particularly by foregrounding an auto-ethnographic research method. That is, we understood we needed to encourage a research dialogue between youth and adults by inviting the young participants and their mentors/significant adults to be *genuinely co-researchers* in the project. In these ways, in our preliminary discussions and through our conceptual frameworks and methodology, we aimed to investigate the best practice models of cross-generational mentoring and researching 'communities of practice' (Wenger, 1998) that could be established, where the categories of learner and expert, observer and observed can be shown to be flexible and mutually informing (Hawkey, 1997; Kamler et al., 2000; Schultz, 2001; Wallace, 2009).

We saw this as having three central aims and processes for this project which we describe in more detail in the following chapters: the establishment of real long-term, mutually rewarding relationships with the young people in question; the creation of an interactive website as a means for them to document, reflect on and share their learning processes and disseminate musical artefacts, if they chose to, across all of the research sites; ensuring that their voices and viewpoints in any resulting academic publications, including in this book, should be equally and accurately represented and heard and not subsumed by the academic discourses. We acknowledge that just one of these aims alone is ambitious and problematic. Inevitably for example, in this volume intended mainly for an academic audience, the language is greatly at odds with the way the youth would normally communicate. Our highlighted text boxes therefore are an attempt to present a parallel discourse, and ensure that the voices and viewpoints of the youth and their mentors are embedded in the text and that we do not simply (mis)represent them through our own discourses.

We had already recognised that young people materially, educationally, sociologically and psychologically 'at risk', in other words, disadvantaged and often disaffected, were frequently in regions where very few socio-economic resources for employment and leisure existed. Yet many had already developed informal strategies, networks and opportunities for themselves. The youth who were interested in music-related activities did this by utilising a range of multidimensional skills such as web design, turntable mixing, sound engineering, and emergent entrepreneurial skills, usually drawing upon particular places and expertise in their local communities and social networks to learn and develop these skills further – although clearly with varying degrees of success. So we decided to design our project reflexively to investigate this wealth of what was usually informal, extra-mural knowledge and praxis, from the ground up. Furthermore, because we were concerned to protect the participants' copyright and intellectual property (IP) rights over their own creative products[4] and thereby to protect our own ethical and reciprocal ideals, our resulting framework had to be one formed together with the young practitioners themselves, and their peers and mentors as co-researchers.

Auto-ethnography in context

The complexity of ethnography is not usually acknowledged or understood, beyond an often naive assumption of 'empowerment' felt to be embedded in the research strategy itself. While many disciplines share a concern and interest in ethnographic methodologies what is understood as 'ethnography' is often considered to be self-explanatory, perceived as carrying its own 'truth effect' (McEachern, 1998, p. 252). So 'doing ethnography' is often assumed to deliver evidence of opposition, subversion and resistance to 'dominant ideologies' simply because the subjects of the research are offered a chance 'to speak in their own voices'. Yet, in so many studies, the more complex analyses of the cultures under study then become subsumed under a canopy of 'suppressed politics' (McEachern, 1998, pp. 260–1). What is often left out of such research is a detailed account and analysis of the supporting cultural context, the 'messy' or 'lived' framework from which those voices and views have emerged and which allows the voices and views of the researched to be more fully understood. In contrast, Pierre Bourdieu argued that a fuller research strategy is required, which he termed 'social praxeology' or the study of particular microworlds within broader macro social and cultural contexts (Bourdieu and Wacquant, 1992). Such an approach provides the necessary theoretical frameworks to unravel and expose the complexities of everyday life but also demands revisiting and challenging some of the more simplistic ways of understanding ethnographic methodology.

This returns the discussion to our use of participatory video, more specifically referred to as auto-video-ethnography in this project. It is important to consider how this type of innovative ethnographic methodology relates to practitioner research and knowledge production. Our methodological aim was to conduct ethical research *with* rather than *about* people. In other words, we aimed to engage the targeted people and communities of our research, usually understood as subjects or respondents, as co-researchers or participants who could speak with their own voices. This was particularly important to us as we intended that the majority of our proposed participants were to be young people, many under the age of eighteen years and most from disadvantaged backgrounds. These young people would, we hoped, form the basis for an informed cross-generational international research community, deliberately blurring the lines between researcher and researched, theorist and practitioner (Schultz and Hull, 2002. See also Schneider, 2002; Burawoy, 2003; Crowe, 2003; Russell, 2005; Pack, 2006;

Mitchell, Pithouse and Moletsane, 2009). Complementing, and in some cases anticipating, Australian, British and US national agendas for addressing unequal outcomes of educational achievement and the consequences for marginalised youth, our project made the young practitioners central to the research process itself; central to unravelling the perceptions of social exclusion and youth disaffection. In the UK, for example, the Every Child Matters Policy of 2003 recognised that special attention should be placed on developing youth provision, opportunity and activity for

a. young people from black minority ethnic (BME/BAME) groups who continue to face poverty through poor education and employment;
b. those 'hard to reach' young people, including vulnerable young people living in insecure accommodation or at risk of dropping out of learning and of isolation and abuse;
c. the particular requirements of faith groups.

In the UK, the Respect Action Plan of 2006, which set out an approach for tackling the causes of disrespect and anti-social behaviour, included positive support for responsible behaviour in cultural and sports activities, citizenship and the community. The aim of this strategy was to empower young people in order that they can achieve a successful transition to adulthood, and to recognise perceptions of alienation and disaffection. International government policies and community programs have often sought to redress the problems of youth and community disaffection in this way, through a wide range of social, educational and employment programs, so far with limited success. In the UK educational reform, the Implementation Plan of the Department for Education and Skills (DfES) in 2005, together with the Department for Children, Schools and Families (DCSF) Schools' White Paper, were considered to be ground-breaking initiatives in developing a new enriched curriculum that recognised the necessity to engage marginalised young people from primary to university level. They did this by delivering a new inclusive curriculum that addressed cultural heritage (which included music) and citizenship. Specialist arts colleges, city academies and centres of vocational excellence are now delivering formal education in partnership with creative industries through new 14–19 vocational qualifications, while the Creative and Cultural Sector Skills Council is also leading the way on modern apprenticeships (for example in the Creative Apprenticeship initiative: www.ccskills.org.uk), offering learning in the workplace. In 2007 the London Development Agency piloted a Supporting Talent to Enterprise Programme (STEP) which recognises the role of non-formal learning providers (voluntary and community sector) in providing an alternative route to education and social inclusion by engaging and supporting the progression of marginalised groups in London through music and youth culture.[5]

Alas, as elsewhere around the world, funding cuts in the last few years have stymied initiatives such as these in the UK. Since the Conservative government was elected, youth arts workers in the UK have been feeling increasingly disheartened and concerned. Their worst fears were confirmed after the release of the Spending Review, in October 2010. The drastic cuts to the public purse have included the withdrawal of huge amounts of local authority support, the abolition of the UK Film Council and a 30 per cent cut to the Arts Council of England (ACE). Aside from its internal cuts, this also means that the ACE has had to stop funding to a number of arts advocacy and development programs such as the educational program Creative Partnerships.

In an open letter signed by a number of leading British arts practitioners, and published in the *Observer* and *Guardian* newspapers, actor Jeremy Irons protested the cuts stating

> These cuts are deep and will affect not just those working and training in regional theatre, independent arts, the BBC, UK film, festivals, dance or theatre in education, but also those who access the arts through outreach and education programmes, community and youth groups and social care.[6]

The 'Big Society' was the key focus.[7] It was the flagship policy idea of the 2010 Conservative Party general election manifesto and forms part of the legislative program of the Conservative/Liberal Democrat Coalition Agreement. Prime Minister David Cameron relaunched the initiative on 19 July 2010 at Liverpool Hope University in Liverpool. Flagship community projects are to be established in Liverpool, Eden Valley in Cumbria, the London Borough of Sutton, Windsor and Maidenhead ('David Cameron Launches', 2010). The aim is 'to create a climate that empowers local people and communities, building a big society that will "take power away from politicians and give it to people"' (Prime Minister's Office, 2010). *The Times* described it as 'an impressive attempt to reframe the role of government and unleash entrepreneurial spirit' ('The Big Society', 2010). The plans, which include setting up a Big Society Bank and introducing a national citizen service, also include the following priorities:

- give communities more powers;
- encourage people to take an active role in their communities;
- transfer power from central to local government;
- support co-ops, mutuals, charities and social enterprises;
- publish government data (Cabinet Office, 2010).

Most of the British mainstream media seem to share the same anxieties. *The Guardian* expressed concerns that 'the effect will be a more troubled and diminished society, not a bigger one' (Coote, 2010). *The Telegraph* stated: 'The sink or swim society is upon us, and woe betide the poor, the frail, the old, the sick and the dependent' (Riddell, 2010). *The Times* agreed, stating:

> It isn't hard to see what will happen with all these Big Society initiatives. It's all very well to have the bright idea of the locals running their own bus route...The trouble is that running a bus route is a professional job, not for a group of local enthusiasts. How many bets that five years down the line, the enthusiasm has run out and there is no more bus route. (Beard ('Cassandra'), 2010)

The immediate result, however, is uncertainty. Many programs have been cut and no one is sure as to what, if anything, will replace them other than an underfunded patchwork of charities and business, if indeed that happens.

To these initiatives, both potentially exciting and alarming, we add the findings of this study, providing on-the-ground information, with our major focus on the perspectives of young people themselves and the invaluable social networks on which they depend and through which they survive – and for some thrive.

The role of the camera: constituting whose world, vision and voice?

But what role did the camera play? How did we envisage undertaking ethical research that attempted to ensure that the perspectives and voices of the researched were not subsumed or subordinated by the dominant academic discourse and narrative – and how realistic was our aim? Participatory video, or auto-video-ethnography, is a deliberate reflexive and innovative strategy of inviting the respondents, in this case mainly young people, to record and represent themselves on video, enabling their own perceptions and embodied experiences to underpin the research. It is an attempt to ameliorate in part the slippery ethical issues of reciprocity, voice and intellectual property by placing the use and control of cameras and other recording instruments of representation in the hands of the people who are usually the subjects of such research. That means not only allowing the youth to film whatever they chose but also to *select* what they chose to portray and how they wished to frame and narrate their stories. What will they include and what will they refrain from including? What will be the reasons for their choice? At the same time, a reflexive analytical framework around these representations is created through the collaborative engagement of all the co-researchers: the youth themselves, their mentors and the university researchers. Inevitably the outcome cannot be a closed text but rather results in a polyvocal experience that provides a number of interpretations and perspectives side by side. In this framework the university researchers can also learn what the youth and mentors decided *not* to represent, and the reasons for the gaps and omissions.

The authors of this book also aimed to reflect their co-authorship in the design of the volume by including frequent text boxes in order to provide the perspectives of the other participants alongside our own and to offer their own unique and sometimes contesting views and challenges to our narrative.[8] As they read the various drafts of the manuscript, the other 'players' in this narrative were then able to add their own affirmation and sometimes their own corrective to our version of events and to our own stylistic lapses from our intended approach. The text box below, for example, demonstrates the thoughtful reflections of Julie, one of our research assistants, as she reviewed a preliminary draft that incorporated some of her fieldwork comments and notes:

> I am particularly concerned regarding research methods, that any of my observations are not woven into any authorial discourse that is vastly different to both the intentions and conditions of their writing (e.g., a particularised description of a discrete occasion being articulated in terms of representative discourse) – I must admit that after reading the Newcastle section of your draft chapter I felt like I and the breakers, rather than being co-researchers, had been subjected to research discourse, which I know is not at all your intention.
>
> (Julie, email correspondence, 15 March 2010)

The result of Julie's corrective and intervention was that we then attempted to address her issues and to rewrite the draft collaboratively – and hopefully succeeded – but in the interest of transparency we retained her justified concerns in the main narrative, as above. Of course, as Julie is pointing out, the language and observations of her field notes as an adult and an academic researcher were very different from the ways the youth were able or chose to communicate their passion for their music practices to us. While many of the youth workers, educators and mentors did use 'research discourse' in some of their discussions with us, the young people tended to use their own style, vocabulary and language to express their views and ideas.

Central to our methodological aim, then, was to incorporate all the participants, but especially the youth themselves, fully into the cross-generational community of co-researchers in the process of collection, reflection, interpretation and publication of the data. As far as possible, our intention was that the youth and their mentors would be equal members of the research process and acknowledged co-authors of the insights and findings. While we are aware that such an aspiration is complex and in some ways seems even theoretically naive, we struggled to design and realise a transparent project and make overt the complexities of the researcher–researched relationship. For the most part, previous definitions of participatory media research have derived from studies conducted with adults or with school students and it is still a developing and relatively under-analysed field (see Pithouse, Mitchell and Moletsane, 2009 for some of the latest work on these issues in relation to health literacy and education). The participation in the research process itself can give adolescents and their mentors (who are often not included in this final process of academic research) real opportunities to speak and be heard and to negotiate the traditional hierarchical and asymmetrical power relationships that remain in such studies and informal learning situations more successfully.

An additional aim of our team of researchers, which we believed and hoped our methodology would highlight and elucidate, was to counter the ways youth (music) 'cultures' are so often still seen as unitary and reified. That is, they are often represented as a neat package, particularly through the media themselves, in terms of the musical style, fashion, connected activities and the argot. Hip hop is a particularly good example of this, for many of the young affiliates themselves often pick up on and re-circulate the same academic and media discourses, talking about their music and 'scenes' in the same language as the professional critics and journalists. They readily articulate what it means to be 'in the scene' or to feel one is an 'authentic' member of the group or 'subculture' as opposed to being a fake or a 'try hard' – even if that distinction is not so clear to an outsider (see Nilan, 1992; Bloustien, 1996, 2003b). In these ways, musical praxis and talk about and around those activities, incorporating taste, engagement, production and consumption, become central to the ways that youth speak about, reflect on, negotiate and create this sense of cultural self. The young people themselves see the engagement with music not simply as an activity and pastime but as a recognisably open and powerful resource of symbolic capital and personhood. Rowland, introduced above, waxed lyrical recently in the middle of a discussion, recognising the importance of music to many of his contemporaries, even those outside his own social group: 'Music belongs to everyone. It's like water, it's like air – it's free.' Perhaps even more poignant are the comments that several of Juri Ify Love's[9] students, residents at the Brighton Treatment Center at the time,[10] made about music and the music program on the evaluation sheets:

> It brightened up my day a lot. I was feeling down and now I am happy. (youth, 15)
>
> It had a good effect because even though I am locked up it made me happy when I did music. (youth, 17)

I shared my lyrics with someone to let them know how I express myself inside. I showed my talent with somebody else and enjoyed it. It made me feel good. I shared my lyrics and you shared your skill with me and we both understood each others way of living [sic]. (youth, 17; all quotations gained from Genuine Voice's evaluation sheets, also cited in Baker and Homan, 2007, pp. 465–6)

Close ethnographic studies can move beyond accepting such statements at face value to unravel some of the deeper expectations and beliefs. They can also illustrate that, while such music practices can be political, pointing to larger social injustices, they are rarely about youthful resistance to all adult values and worlds. Indeed we would argue that engagement with music as 'serious play' is far more about learning to accommodate and become an adult in ways that are meaningful within one's own microworld (see Finnegan, 1998; Green, 2001) than challenging adult mores. Rather, we claim, music can provide an essential vehicle for young people negotiating their way between the past and the present, negotiating the best psychic fit. As we shall see in later chapters, this was also true for the young men in the Brighton Treatment Center.

Within our methodological framework, then, we argue that the participatory video allowed access to the everyday microworld of the young people as a 'core social context', sometimes facilitating access to places, spaces and situations where it would be difficult or totally inappropriate for an adult researcher to go. It also demonstrated the significance of this microworld as the research developed through what the participants decided to photograph and to video – and also, sometimes, through what they chose to avoid or ignore. The participants' photographs and films were thus always a foreground to a much wider complex background, two interconnected parts of one whole. It can be seen as a particular framing perspective, so that the young people in our research project inevitably place specific conceptual frames around their own understandings of their lives in their self-conscious reflexivity.

As we were introducing access to a video camera into the mix, we realised as the study progressed that our approach was perhaps not so completely novel after all. The concept of such self-representation is increasingly common amongst the young – and indeed even the not so young now. With the advent and broad take-up and acceptance of digital networking sites such as Facebook and MySpace, together with new mobile technologies such as mobile phones, individuals are regularly recording and sharing images of themselves and their activities. This reflexivity is particularly highlighted as the participants make choices of representation in their photographs and videos. As suggested above, however, sometimes these choices are not self-conscious. Sometimes they are taken-for-granted, non-reflexive ways of seeing their world; ones that can only be perceived when looked at against a less subjective backdrop of cultural expectations and social constraints. The resultant insights also highlight the particular and the local, demonstrating the deficiency and inappropriateness of talking about 'youth culture' as though it were uniform and global. As Bourdieu reminds us, 'Merely talking about "the young" as a social unit, a constituted group, with common interests relating these interests to a biologically defined age, is in itself an obvious manipulation' (Bourdieu, 1993, p. 95). How much more so in our project when we consider the ways in which young people see themselves over a long period of time and in comparison to similar communities in other countries!

It is essential, however, to keep in mind that, of course, the visual representations have to be understood as just that: 'representations' and 'identity work' in process. They can never be assumed to encapsulate the 'truth' of a young person's world, simply illustrating what the young person says they do. Rather they facilitate and capture several processes in snapshot, as it were, which have been previously considered in the social sciences to be ethically difficult to document, specifically because of issues of access, voice and reciprocity. Even when considered on a cursory level, it is clear that the use of the cameras and other recording instruments in the hands of the participants can ameliorate some potential inequities of power in the fieldwork arena. Here is an opportunity for the young people to explore, reflect and comment on and constitute their own worlds. They can choose what they want to record, how it is recorded and what may be offered for public viewing. Undoubtedly, this is one of the main reasons that Bloustien discovered in her previous work that the use of cameras and other recording devices was taken up with such alacrity by the youth participants (see 1998, 2003a, 2003b; see also Baker, 2001). The young people clearly saw it as a way of exploring their own worlds 'at one remove', an opportunity to engage in 'serious play' (Handelman, 1990; Schechner, 1993). Clearly, too, this play with image, identity and representation allows each young person the opportunity to explore and express their world non-verbally, testing out boundaries in ways previously not foreseen (see Bloustien, 1998, 2003b for a more detailed account of this process).

At the same time, we were always aware that the resulting images and the participants' explanation and interpretation of them can be also 'read' in terms of what is not filmed or photographed. That is, this contextualising of the images is required to expose the gaps that appear between the real life experiences and the images. It can reveal what has been regarded as too commonplace, too banal or even too threatening to record on camera in the first place. It can reveal what is recorded and then edited out of the image. It can also draw attention to what is filmed or recorded in a deliberately exaggerated way, indicating not so much serious play but rather a deliberate distancing strategy. Michael Taussig (1993) calls this process 'mimetic excess'. When it becomes threatening or menacing, it echoes the phenomenon that Handelman and Schulman described as 'dark play' – where anxiety and the pressures of reality become so intense that the distancing device of humour is no longer possible, for 'Play and terror are always confrontations of being, with questioning the nature or shape of self identity' (Handelman and Schulman, 1997, p. 52).

It is important to stress again that our analysis of the filmic images or the photographs is not simply subjective. As indicated above, the overall analysis requires a three-way contextualisation. Firstly, the individual's views of their lived experiences, the material conditions of their everyday lives and the processes of production of the ethnography itself – the young people's personal experiences – are directly observed by the researcher and set alongside the participants' own descriptions and accounts of these processes. Secondly, these accounts are contextualised within the specific material living experiences that the young people face – including the observed effects and understandings of class, gender and ethnicity (see Skeggs, 1997 for a complex account of this layering). This area of the research inevitably incorporates a close look at the processes of production of cultural texts, including their musical forms, in these worlds and how they emerge to become meaningful.

Such an analysis requires an unravelling of terms that may be taken for granted by the researcher and the participants themselves; for example, how members of a particular grouping or scene use the term 'community'. Or how they define the meaning of 'underground' or 'mainstream' music, and the ways in which those words are differently nuanced for members of a particular grouping. Or again, a consideration of what terms individuals take for granted and how they (re)adjust their definitions to suit their worlds.

Thirdly, we were anxious to highlight our equally rigorous reflexive concern with the research process itself – for the researcher too is a historically constituted subject. Questions about the university researchers' presence have to be explored within the narratives and their analysis. How do the young people acknowledge and negotiate our adult/outsider presence? What is important to them about our interest in their music production and play?

All of these areas of questioning and analysis can reveal the taken-for-granted constraints and values (that which cannot be said) as well as the more obvious concerns and issues that are talked about and challenged. As indicated above, the result is a dialectic, an understanding of 'the double reality of the social world…(weaving together) a "structuralist" and a "constructivist" approach' (Bourdieu and Wacquant, 1992, p. 11). When applied to the worlds of young people, this double analysis can also lead to a greater awareness of the 'immediacy' of their social reality. While young people are obviously enmeshed in the process of socialisation, in becoming adults, they are also actively involved in that process. From the perspective of youth, the 'now' of their worlds is more important than that of the future.

To conceptualise these worlds in any other way is to render youth as passive, 'as standing idly by awaiting to be filled with adult knowledge' (Caputo, 1995, p. 290).

The stories narrated in this book thus move beyond the personal views of the youth. Rather they are contextualised within a three-layered, interlocking framework that examines the local and global infrastructures that underpin and support the young people's music-making. As the stories unfold it will be clear that our analysis focuses simultaneously on the people (mentors, youth workers, practitioners, adult artists and peers) who provide education, training and support for the young people in their career pathways; the organisations and programs that provide access and skills development for the use of new technologies and related services; and, thirdly, the educational, art and youth policies that support and fund young people's art. In the middle are the overlapping consequences of these three elements observed and analysed in our perceptions and engagement by a community of researchers (academic and practitioners, young and older) in the field.

This methodology draws on Pierre Bourdieu's concept of social praxeology (Bourdieu and Wacquant, 1992; see also Bloustien, 2003b; Bloustien, Peters and Luckman, 2008) and in so doing creates a reflexive ethnography, which highlights a great deal about the ethnographic process itself. It produces a deliberate and informative tension between the creative subjects, the institutions within which they generate and consume their music and the policies that shape and fund their activities. Figure 1.1 illustrates this interrelated concept.

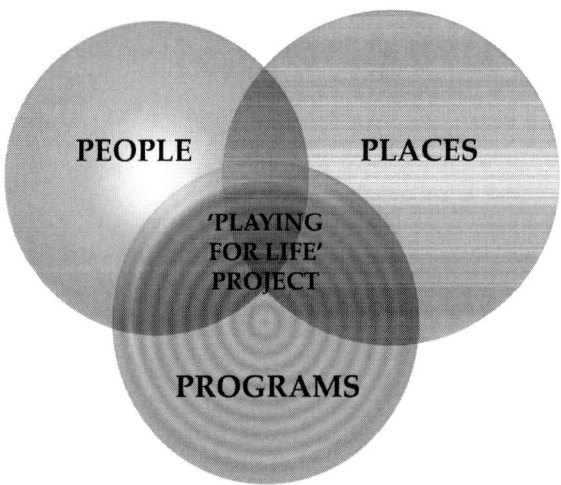

Figure 1.1 Diagrammatic representation of the Playing for Life methodology

The result is both an active, self-conscious, reflexive exploration of the complexities of ethnographic methodologies (Marcus, 1980; Marcus and Fischer, 1986) and, simultaneously, a focus on the process of the ways the young people engaged in 'identity work' (Wexler, 1992), their search for a sense of authenticity (Giddens, 1991; Lewin and Williams, 2009) through the continuous 'art' of self-making (Battaglia, 1995) and the role of 'serious play' (Turner, 1982; Schechner, 1985, 1993; Handelman, 1990), especially through their social networking and social relationships (Crossley 2011). In the following pages, the academic researchers reflect on their own involvement in the project together with the young people who struggle to develop their skills and music career pathways despite financial and socio-economic constraints and other structural hurdles.

At the same time, a salutary caveat! We do recognise that despite our best efforts and intentions the unequal power relationship between the youth and the adult university researchers is still inevitable. There was, for example, the large gap between intellectual and educational capital that was already present, which could not easily be overcome, however well-meaning and well-considered the methodologies were in terms of ethics, responsibility and reciprocity. Inevitably too, there would arise major issues of intellectual property and copyright, especially as the young people were being asked to reflect on their own skills, talents and performances. The best we can do, as we struggle to obtain our goal, is to highlight and reflexively comment on these issues as part of the process of research documentation and our analysis.

Gathering the 'crew'

With all of these thoughts in mind and in constant discussion, the team of academic and professional expertise was assembled. The Australian team consisted of Geraldine Bloustien and Margaret Peters (the principal authors of this book), from the Hawke Research Institute, University of South Australia, together with Dr Shane Homan (formally from the Cultural Industries and Research Practices Centre, University of Newcastle, NSW).[11] The British team consisted of David Buckingham, from the Centre for Children, Youth and Media, London Institute of Education and Andy Bennett, then from the Institute of Social Research, Surrey University, UK. In the United States, Tommy De Frantz, from the Center for Comparative Media, Massachusetts Institute of Technology, Boston, joined us and from Berlin, Bruce Cohen, a British scholar at that time attached to the Institute of Social Science, Humboldt University. A young postgraduate, Sarah Baker, from the University of South Australia, completed the team as the postdoctoral fellow whose main task was to work with all of the researchers for periods of time in their own countries at their various field sites. Each site had particular research assistants who assisted with the data collection. Of particular note are Julie Pavlou Kirri (hereafter Jules) and Danni Nicholas-Sexton (Danni), who worked with great sensitivity and insight with the young people and mentors at the Newcastle and Adelaide CBOs respectively. In the final stages of the project, Anna-Marie Steigemann from Humboldt University assisted with exit interviews and additional clarification for the German context while Mari Kain and Jacki Bloustien also competently and patiently assisted with cataloguing and organising the large quantity of visual, audio and printed data.[12] Added to this large cast of primary investigators were an even larger contingent of young co-researchers and their mentors and advisers, as will be explained in more detail below.

Building on pilot work, which she had already undertaken in London in 2001, Geraldine Bloustien initially compared ideas and fieldwork notes with Andy Bennett and Bruce Cohen, the two British colleagues named above, who had been undertaking related projects in England and Germany. In this way, the seeds for the Playing for Life project were formed. Indeed, the original plan was hatched in the lounge room of a small London flat as the three researchers excitedly compared notes and thought about ways to extend and compare their own work with what young people were doing in Australia, the UK, Europe and the USA.

This small team of three considered the implications of earlier studies that showed that materially disadvantaged and disaffected youth often drop out of traditional education before they reached the age of sixteen.[13] In fact, even before what is in most Western countries the legislated minimum age for leaving school, many young people had expressed their disaffection by regular absenteeism, leaving their formal schooling early without recognised skills, job or career path to go to. This meant, of course, that the local authorities saw many youth as perpetrators of property crime or damage, gang behaviour and violence, vagrancy and drug and alcohol abuse. They often also had a record of school avoidance or regular truancy. For this reason we too selected the sites with recognised 'social problems'. That is, in the Playing for Life project, each particular locale studied had previously been identified as a 'problem' area with the young people there regarded as being 'at risk'. The usual resolution taken by state and local policy-makers was to build on existing youth activities and attempt to use them as a basis for developing new pathways and positive role models for the youth. As Baker, Bennett and Homan point out in their earlier publication from the project:

> In each case, the presented solution had been to take existing forms of youth musical practice and to channel these via dedicated projects and/or outreach resources as a means of combating social exclusion (as determined through national/regional policy initiatives) experienced by young people and 'reinvigorating' those social spaces in which the targeted youth are situated. (2009, p. 152)

One of the problems that arises in such a policy framework is that inevitably such spaces and places become 'landscapes of power' (Zukin, 1991), being at once both the testing ground for a range of top-down spatio-cultural discourses oriented around buzzwords such as 'creativity' and the sites for more spontaneous forms of cultural practice grounded in established local knowledge of space and place (Baker, Bennett and Homan, 2009, p. 152). In this book, we focus on both of these 'landscapes of power', analysing how such power sites support and/or constrain the creative music-making practices of young people.

As Meyers (2008, p. 2) has stated 'Creativity is a complex construct, and it too frequently serves as a catch-all label for a diverse range of habits of mind indelibly associated with the arts.' We agree that nurturing creative capacity is not the sole province of 'the arts' and we also acknowledge both the complexity, as well as the futility, of attempting to find a one-size-fits-all definition of 'creativity'. Our research therefore has focused on the creative music practices and activities of the young people with the aim of engaging with, and further understanding, their creative music practices and activities and learning more about what creative music-making meant to them, and to their mentors, tutors and staff in youth-based community-based organisations. We discuss in later chapters the tensions that emerge between competing agendas in relation to the ways in which the concept of creativity is constructed and nurtured against a backdrop of local, state and national youth policies with their mix of funding opportunities and constraints.

The authors particularly felt that what has been so often overlooked in similar studies of youth 'at risk' was that these young people had not stopped learning or attempting to increase their skills, particularly in areas that were particularly meaningful to them. Indeed, in the social worlds of most of these young people, skills associated with music and performance – such as rapping, rhyming, writing, graphic design, dance, DJing, turntabling and sampling – were highly valued forms of cultural capital. However, such skills also need development, support and resourcing – equipment is expensive, sites for rehearsal and performance have to be found, mentors and tutors have to be cultivated. So where and how were these young people successfully developing these skills? What networks and resources were they using and what could we as cultural critics, educators, youth workers and policy-makers learn from these strategies? What implications do such insights and observations have for current knowledge and criticism about the burgeoning worlds of the cultural, creative and entertainment industries (Leadbeater, 1999; Florida, 2002; McRobbie, 2002a, 2002b; Hartley, 2005, 2009)?

Clearly, our first step was to link up with similar work being done in Australia, Britain, Europe and in the USA and plot together a theoretical framework that we all felt acceptable and valuable from within which to investigate these questions more fully in a transnational context. Just as the young people do among their own friends and acquaintances, the first three members of the future research team formulated in the UK first drew on our networks and formed our own 'crew', strategically extending the number of project leaders. We invited other colleagues in Britain, Australia and the USA, as named above, to join us. The skills of each person in the team deliberately complemented the others, so for example Margaret Peters is internationally known for her research on organisational communication incorporating socio-linguistics, play and gender. Within this field of enquiry, her work combined with Geraldine Bloustien's to explore cross-cultural identities, narratives, myths, rites, rituals and symbolic play (Peters, 1993, 1994a, 1994b). Shane Homan had spent a significant number of years working in the music industry as a musician. His previous academic research examined youth leisure activities, media portrayals of youth and their music-related activities, and historical perspectives on youth centres and similar institutions in the provision of alternative sites of music performance and music education (Homan, 1999, 2002a, 2002b). He brought historical knowledge about youth, music practices and their governance with a broader awareness and insights into wider cultural policy (Homan, 1999, 2003).

David Buckingham together with some of his colleagues had also published a number of influential books and articles on these issues (Buckingham and Sefton-Green, 1994; Buckingham, 2000; Buckingham and McFarlane, 2001; Buckingham and Scanlon 2003; see also Buckingham and Willet, 2009, for more recent work) with some challenging observations on the role of 'creativity' in UK cultural and educational policy. As one of the UK's leading researchers in the field of children, youth and media, David Buckingham had conducted several major research projects in this field (see, for example, Buckingham, 2000), many funded by transnational organisations such as the Economic and Social Research Council, the Broadcasting Standards Commission, the Gulbenkian Foundation, the Arts Council of England and the Spencer and Nuffield Foundations. It was at his invitation that Geraldine Bloustien had become a visiting research fellow at the London Institute of Education during 2001 and 2002 and it was during this time that the pilot studies were discussed with Andy Bennett (University of Surrey). These pilot studies complemented some earlier investigative studies that the Centre for the Study of Children, Youth and Media had explored. Bloustien's own particular expertise lay in her development of auto-video-ethnographic methodologies, based on a systematic use of auto-video-ethnography together with participant observation and incorporating the views and voices of the participants as co-researchers (Bloustien, 1996, 1999, 2002, 2003b). This culturally sensitive methodology, recognised by experts in the field for its creative potential to reveal new anthropological and sociological insights and for its incorporation of a clear ethical and reciprocal stance, had been emulated in other Australian and international studies. Henry Jenkins, who at the time of our project was Director of the Centre for Comparative Media, MIT, described the innovation of this work, which expands the more traditional forms of ethnography, as 'remarkable because of the extraordinary level of intimacy Bloustien achieved with her young collaborators and the emotional honesty with which she writes about their experiences' (Jenkins, 2003, p. ix).[14] It was through Jenkins' invitation to Geraldine Bloustien to visit his centre in Boston that Tommy De Frantz learned about the Playing for Life research team and was invited to join.

Tommy De Frantz's interest in this project built upon his interests in African-American expressive culture, and the global reach of hip hop culture. On a previous visit to the National Aboriginal Islander Skills Development Association (NAISDA) in Australia in 2001, De Frantz was struck by the degree to which the young artists had been influenced by hip hop, and how hip hop dance shaped their sensibility of which traditional Islander dances to preserve and which to enhance. As his particular focus area was the social and cultural politics of dance (De Frantz, 2001, 2004) he was well positioned to work with youth on the relationship of kinaesthesia and social dance practice to music production and cultural identity.

In these ways, the project was formed to bring together key academic overseas researchers with some of Australia's most creative researchers and practitioners in productive ongoing dialogue. The aim was to enable cross-cultural comparative insights to emerge based on the particular geographical, material and social contexts in which the young people lived, grew and developed. Furthermore, the eclectic though complementary nature of the researching team was deliberately intended to allow a myriad of disciplinary and theoretical perspectives to emerge. The group believed that one of the strengths (as well as one of the ongoing challenges) of the project was that they brought together particular knowledge forms from anthropology, education, psychology, sociology, cultural media and performance studies as well as particular insights and nuances from their own cultures and social systems. The innovation of the study was that, in creating this collaborative cross-generational and cross-cultural research community, we would be able to explore the phenomena longitudinally, in detail and across three continents. We built upon and provided fresh insight into three important interrelated interdisciplinary areas. Firstly, we focused on the causes and effects of alienation, disaffection and social exclusion on youth in technologically advanced societies (Miles, 2000). Secondly, we explored the complexity of the ways in which young people engage with popular culture, and in particular popular music, as a means of agency and as a way of negotiating marginalisation (Richards, 1998; McCarthy et al., 1999; Dimitriadis, 2000; Bennett, 2001; Dimitriadis and Weis, 2001; Green, 2001; Jenkins, 2001). Thirdly, our investigation delved into the role of community-based centres or CBOs as 'free spaces' (Boyte and Evans, 1992) or 'urban sites of possibility' (Fine and Weis, 2000), alternative learning spaces where young people seem particularly able to develop their own sense of creativity and cultural meaning (Bennett, 1997, 1998; Fine and Weis, 1998, 2000). The CBOs we identified as such places in our project are defined as alternative learning sites that are used by youth voluntarily to meet a range of skills-based needs. They encompass youth clubs and special programs for youth within performing arts, community, detention and church centres as well as some organisations and programs stemming from local council initiatives, such as Playford or Salisbury City Councils, South Australia or from the initiatives of private individuals, such as Adrian Shepherd (Adelaide) or Juri Ify Love (Boston).

The innovative research and pedagogic models embedded in this project inevitably raised new questions to be investigated. Firstly, what specific learning practices do young people at risk through marginalisation, disaffection or material disadvantage require, acquire and develop in and through their local and vernacular music practices, and how do these practices reflect and depend on global technological change? Secondly, in what ways can alternative learning sites and community organisations, particularly those based within specific ethnic and minority communities, become effective in facilitating youth agency? In what ways do they offer opportunities of access into formal and informal employment, economies and professional music and creative industries? Finally, what are the implications for other youth development and training programs and current cross-cultural practices concerning marginalised youth?

Integrated into the project design was the aim to document the nature and process of the relationship between young people and the human, spatial, political and technological resources that help them achieve a sense of agency through popular music and related arts production. The research team believed their findings would elaborate upon an emerging body of research on community organisations as alternative learning sites, noted above, for the development of young people's sense of self-esteem and agency. In these ways, the project aimed to address other significant gaps in the literature on youth development. It highlighted the roles of alternative learning practices, such as mentoring and networking, in the way young people gain knowledge and expertise from their peers and from significant adults in their everyday music activities (Hays, 1998). As indicated above, the project was also underpinned by an innovative auto-ethnographic research method – detailed in the following chapter – establishing a research dialogue between youth and adult by inviting the young participants and their mentors/significant adults themselves to be co-researchers not subjects in or objects of the project (Hawkey, 1997; Kamler et al., 2000; Schultz and Hull, 2002; Bloustien, 2003a, 2003b).[15]

The significance of place: CBOs as alternative learning spaces

To facilitate these aims, we decided that the research in all of the sites, both nationally and internationally, should be located primarily out of schools, focusing instead on the role of community-based organisations. While previous studies have suggested that CBOs frequently operate as alternative learning sites in the lives of young people, we need also to clarify that not all CBOs have the same origin or corporate structure. The common link is that all have close ties to their own communities; however, they exist on a continuum of government support with varying degrees of financial security. The difference in corporate structure can and does impact upon the way organisations function. For example, in Chapters 4 and 5, we discuss the community-based campaign to 'Save the Loft', a youth arts centre that emerged from the original Palais in Newcastle, Australia. This campaign was not only able to mobilise community and media attention but the involvement of Newcastle City Council (NCC) meant that there were/are 13 elected councillors who could be individually and collectively lobbied.

Over the past ten years or so, many studies, often considered controversial, have been conducted on the role of alternative, community learning sites in the USA (Heath and McLaughlin, 1993; Fine et al., 2000; Dimitriadis, 2001) and in Europe and Britain (see Bentley 2002). In Australia, however, where such detailed, empirical research was scarce or lacking, policy-makers depended primarily upon anecdotal evidence and government reports. Our work aimed to fill this gap by providing longitudinal comparative detail through detailed, grounded documentation and informed interpretation.

In Adelaide, South Australia and in Newcastle, New South Wales the research team identified at least four significant CBOs (amongst many possibilities) within our selected research sites. These were youth arts organisations, both government and privately funded, that we realised could be understood as alternative learning venues and so would be invaluable as primary case-study locales. In contrast, Germany offered a very different resource: 'youth clubs' or special CBOs for young people were numerous and, across Berlin particularly, they were seen as strategic tools in postwar government policy about the civic education and care of young people. In his study of Turkish migrant youth culture in Berlin, Levent Soysal described the German metropolis as the 'Holy City of youth organisations, clubs, cafes, recreational centers and sports associations'. He also noted that publications, job centres, mobile outreach programs and guides to local music production offered cross-cultural spaces where 'the teeming projects of youth culture are woven into the fabric of the spectacle called Berlin, the Cultural city' (Soysal, 2001, p. 10).

For this reason, under the initial direction of Bruce Cohen we were able to invite nine CBOs across Berlin to participate in this project, as detailed below. More detailed information follows about the sites, CBOs, the formal and informal learning centres in London and Kent and in Boston and Providence in the USA and their significance for social and cultural development for the youth in our study, particularly in Chapters 4, 5 and 6.

Simultaneously, what we were discovering in our preliminary scoping exercise was that there seemed to be a fascinating social, cultural and digital networking system, where resources and information were shared within and across (international) communities of young people via various digital networking systems such as Facebook and MySpace, through particularly enterprising and innovative individuals, despite bureaucratic hurdles and very poor financial support. This project was thus the first longitudinal international study concerning youth music and leisure activities in alternative learning venues that incorporated comparative, ethnographically informed research and that attempted to explore exactly how this network of support develops and is maintained.

The other important scaffold for this project lay in the wealth of sociological and anthropological literature pointing to the significance of music as a vehicle for the development and maintenance of cultural identities (Frith, 1992; Shepherd and Wick, 1997; Clarke and Davidson, 1998; Whiteley, Bennett and Hawkins, 2004). Many recent studies have further highlighted the central role of music-based youth cultures in the development of a sense of cultural belonging, agency and self-esteem in the lives of many marginalised youth in post-industrial societies (Bennett, 2001; Green, 2001).

Even more importantly perhaps, and in keeping with these conceptual frameworks, we argue that the music practices of youth should not be understood as separate from adulthood but rather should be interpreted as facilitating pathways into adult cultural activities. It is this that we saw as the most significant finding of our study. Furthermore, with the advancement of and access to new technologies, young people themselves often see these pathways as offering opportunities on a global scale. These technologies enable them to 'situate themselves historically, culturally and politically in a much more complex system of symbolic meaning than is available locally' (Frith, 1992, p. 77; see also Bennett, 2001). As this project was both longitudinal and comparative, it mapped this trajectory of access and opportunity across several cross-cultural, international locales.

Defining youth

So far, we have briefly introduced two of the young participants to this project, Rowland and Alicia. We will return to their stories in more detail and introduce some of the many other young people in the study, but firstly it is important to explain how we came to understand the concept of youth.

On their recently updated website the Australian Clearinghouse for Youth Studies (ACYS) defines the period of youth as spanning the ages from 10 to

24. While this definition is one shared by the Australian Medical Association and the World Health Organization, it varies a great deal from those used by other organisations and other countries. In her editorial introduction to a special issue on youth in 1999, Sheila Allison elaborated on this anomaly as follows:

> The by-laws of the Youth Development Association in the Federated States of Micronesia, for example, define youth as between the ages of six and 35 (or more than 70% of their population). The Southern African Zonal Youth Forum recently extended their 18–26 youth age range to 18–30 years, reasoning that all their existing youth organisations had an upper age limit of 30 or 35 and the school-leaving age was 20.... Another term – teenage – which I would have thought was self-defining too is open to interpretation. A 1996 Canadian report defined youth in three categories – young teens, teens, and young adults – and described 'young teens' as aged 10 to 14 (no doubt pleasing countless 10- to 12-year-olds). Concepts of age in regard to legal rights and responsibilities is another area open to anomaly. The various states of the United States exemplify this, such as Oklahoma where the law allows a 16-year-old to be sentenced to death but not to buy alcohol until the age of 21. (Allison, 1999, p. 2)[16]

While unfortunately Allison did not cite the particular 1996 Canadian report she was referring to concerning the ways youth are defined, an article by Lerner from the same year (1996) similarly summarises the dilemma of defining adolescence in Canada at that time. Over ten years later, it seems that the problems of definition have become even more complex.[17] Another, later policy report also from Canada still indicated the same difficulty of reaching a consensus on exactly what is meant by the term 'youth', pointing out:

> There is no consensus about how to define 'youth'. Defining youth primarily by the criterion of age is increasingly less appropriate in a context in which young people's life trajectories are becoming more diverse and complex, because it assumes that within a given age bracket all youth are similar. In fact, youth face a multiplicity of realities and there are increasing numbers of possible pathways to adulthood. Some youth leave school or have children in adolescence while many others extend their education, make their transition to the labour market and start a family in their late 20s or early 30s. Legal definitions of rights and responsibilities based on age – for example, the legal age for driving or voting – also underline the difficulty of using a biological criterion such as age. Defining youth by identifying certain target groups (for example, delinquent youth, homeless youth, handicapped youth, young entrepreneurs, etc.) assumes that youth categories can be reduced to functions or, even worse, to pathologies. (Franke, 2010, n.p.)

The report goes on to suggest that there are two preferable ways in which to define youth. Firstly, as it is increasingly clear that youth can no longer be defined based on an age criterion alone, the notion of transitions is also no longer useful so that 'leaving the parental home, living with a partner and having stable employment are no longer sufficient markers for understanding the passage to adulthood if they refer strictly to individuals' social situation or material independence' (Franke, 2010, n.p.). A far more effective framework, the author argues, would be to focus on and reflect the other forms of reality experienced by youth today such as 'a period of life marked by multiple, reversible transitions of variable length and uncertain outcomes, and secondly, as a process for developing autonomy, in which young people are launched on trajectories that lead them progressively to take on roles considered by society to be those of adulthood' (Franke, 2010, n.p.; see also Evans and Furlong, 1997; Statistics Canada, 1999, 2001; European Group for Integrated Social Research (EGRIS), 2001; Jones, 2002; Cicchelli and Martin, 2004; Arnett and Tanner, 2005; Bynner, 2005; Chisholm, 2006; Coles, 2006; Mitchell, 2006; Beaujot and Kerr, 2007; Clark, 2007 for some of the ongoing debates and recurring issues, discussed in recent Canadian, US and European literature and reports).

Part of the aim of our methodology was to tap into this way of conceptualising youth and understanding their worlds as 'a period of life marked by multiple, reversible transitions of variable length and uncertain outcomes' and as a series of 'trajectories that lead them progressively to take on roles considered by society to be those of adulthood'. More examples of our central research method of auto-video-ethnography in action are detailed in the next chapter and in the following pages.

Recruiting from the ground up

In order to address the issues outlined above, to disrupt any preconceived assumptions and to bridge this gap, we started by looking at 'the grassroots'. At the start of the project, the adult investigators in each locale began the task of seeking out and introducing themselves and the project to young people in their assigned areas. For some investigators that meant building on their previous knowledge and networks of the CBOs and/or young people they had had previous professional relations with. For others, it meant learning far more about programs and young people in their area that they had previously not known much about. The initial contact was achieved either by following leads about individuals through word of mouth with some of the young people we already knew (ground up) and sometimes by contacting key organisations and especially CBOs that we knew worked with young people in each of the communities we were targeting (top down). This then led to a snowball effect of gathering up people and places willing to participate in our study. So, for example, in attempting to find out about the ways young Aboriginal people were learning about and using hip hop in Adelaide, South Australia, we asked a number of young Nunga people we already knew. All told us to contact DJ Shep and Da Klinic (see below), an individual and CBO we would not have known about without this inside knowledge. DJ Shep introduced us to Kyle, one of the non-Aboriginal young men who was honing his DJ and breakdancing skills through Da Klinic workshops. On the other hand, we learnt about the Kandinsky Group of young people through youth workers and educators at the group's own community resource, Carclew Youth Arts Centre. Similarly, we learnt about the radio program *Youth Revolutions* through youth workers from Playford Council, one of the local city councils that had originally funded and supported the radio program initiative.

What we describe below are five located 'clusters' of activities, which took place in particular parts of the urban landscapes in which we were operating. Out of these clusters emerged a number of young individuals whom we had the privilege to know and work with and who decided to join the project as co-researchers. We will take one cluster and one location at a time, outlining the locale and naming some of the main youth and their mentors, although more will be introduced as we unfold details of each site in the coming chapters. It is important to stress that not every site offered us the opportunity to work closely and longitudinally with individual young people. We were interested in the range of resources that the young people of the various cultural communities drew upon to develop musical ambitions. Most of these were CBOs of one form or another, offering varying degrees of structure, access to equipment, mentoring and networking.

Cluster 1: South Australia

Carclew Youth Arts Centre

In Adelaide, South Australia we looked to see what youth arts activities were being publicised that we could attend and learn more about. Initially at least, all roads of enquiry seemed to take us to Carclew. Carclew is an innovative and dynamic youth arts centre situated in a Victorian mansion in a leafy, affluent part of North Adelaide, just on the fringe of the city of Adelaide. It was here that we first came across some of the key young people. We learned about a program called the Kandinsky Sessions (2003/4 Annual Report South Australian Youth Arts Board (SAYAB)), which had attracted a number of young people. This project emerged out of the direct requests from young people who were keen for opportunities to engage actively with 'the live music scene' through creating and learning the event management and business side of live music – programming, promoting, managing and facilitating events for young performers and all-ages audiences in popular live music venues within the city. A team of twelve young people came together, funded by Carclew, and were given the task of coordinating five free independent 'music events' over a five-month period. During this time, the group arranged and coordinated live music events throughout Adelaide, profiling a total of 56 young performers. The team named themselves the Kandinsky Sessions, referencing the Russian artist Kandinsky and his implicit connections between colour and sound.[18] Their own planned events deliberately matched genres of music performance with colours, so they named and promoted their 'gigs' with names such as: 'Acoustic Yellow', 'Purple Electronica', 'Punk Orange', 'Indie Green' and 'Fluorescent Incandescent'. As members of the team, the young people learnt to scout, recruit and promote young bands and musicians into free all-ages gigs in popular city venues. They fine-tuned their skills in negotiating deals with the venue owners (obtaining free venues and subsidised equipment in exchange for sales of non-alcoholic and alcoholic drinks at the bar) and learned to develop and coordinate innovative promotion strategies. As the events were designed for underage patrons, they also had to plan and negotiate security, legal issues and risk assessments. The initial Kandinsky members included Alicia Woodrow, Michelle Mitollo and Vicci Marsh, who all accepted our invitation to become participants in the Playing for Life project over the three years from 2003 to 2005.[19]

Alicia and her close friend Michelle were both about 20 years old when we met them. Both had initially become involved with the Kandinsky group because they had become friends through their involvement in Carclew's Off the Couch program. Alicia, though, already saw herself as a musician as she was a founding member and bass guitarist of the indie band Paper Tiger formed in Adelaide in July 2003. After initial success with performance and airplay on community radio stations across Australia, Paper Tiger disbanded and a new band was formed called Aviator Lane of which Alicia was still a member in 2009. The Kandinsky's main mentor was Clare De Bruin, Contemporary Music Programs Manager at Carclew Youth Arts Centre.

The Peachey Belt and *Youth Revolutions*

Carclew is situated in an affluent part of the city (even though its programs and clientele reached far beyond its home base), and the team were also looking to see what youth arts programs and activities other local councils were offering young people. Our enquiries inevitably took us to the 'Peachey Belt', an area of notorious material underprivilege but also an area of amazing resilient community spirit and social capital. The City of Playford was born through the amalgamation of the two local councils of Elizabeth and Munno Para in the 1990s. The 'Peachey Belt' is an area within Playford that is defined by a 2 kilometre stretch of road, Peachey Road, running through the centre of the three suburbs contained in the 'belt'.

Approximately 40 kilometres north of Adelaide, Elizabeth was established as a satellite town in the 1950s attracting many British migrants through the development of what was then a booming local industry, particularly the car manufacturing plant of General Motors Holden. In recent years the closure of local businesses and of many locally based social and public services has led to a severe downturn in employment opportunities resulting in the Peachey Belt in particular being recognised as one of the areas of highest disadvantage in Australia, based on the SEIFA index and Australian Bureau of Statistics figures.

It was in this setting that we learnt about *Youth Revolutions* (YR), a radio program on PBA-FM created by a number of young people in the area. The program was originally funded by Playford City Council but later supported by Salisbury Council. Its aim was to provide a forum to play music and showcase local bands while at the same time facilitating informed discussion about issues that mattered to their peers. 'We talk about the stuff that young people have to deal with in our community', explained Michael in a local print media publication. Michael, aged 17 when we first met him, was one of the founders of the program. As we got to know the young people behind the program, attending their official meetings, accepting invitations to go on air and seeing them in their other social contexts, our team of young co-researchers for the project from the northern areas of Adelaide grew to five: Michael (17), Monique (16), Vanessa (16), Bret (17) and Will (18). Their main mentor was Lilly Buvka, the Playford Council's Youth Development Officer.

Da Klinic and Adelaide's hip hop scene

The third group of young people in South Australia stemmed from our meeting with a vibrant young individual known around the city as DJ Shep. Adrian Shepherd, or Shep, was already a seasoned media personality. He has been interviewed several times on two arms of Australian public radio – the Australian Broadcasting Commission (ABC) and Special Broadcasting Service (SBS) radio – and his comments and image have been documented widely in various print media.

He is a well-known Adelaide DJ, rapper and inline skater in the local hip hop scene but is increasingly becoming known as a youth entrepreneur through his integrated media business, Da Klinic, consisting of a retail outlet, skills workshops and an event management business.

Some years earlier, he and his business partner Jeff redeveloped and refurbished their hip hop retail/workshop outlet, including leasing the space above the original basement shop in the heart of Adelaide. The effect was to double the floor space and add a new level of sophistication and professionalism. The retail shop above ground is now light, modern and open, stocked with a wide range of hip hop clothes, music and accessories for breakdancing, skating and graffiti art. It now also takes advantage of e-commerce developments, allowing his customers to purchase face-to-face or online. Such strategies together with his multilayered website (www.daklinic.com) have had an impressive effect in attracting new clients, including local

Photo 1.2   Shep in action. © Helen Page

youth, and educational and corporate clients. His speciality, he feels, is being able to bring together innovative and complex ideas to give people 'a retail experience' they have never seen before.

We first heard about Shep and his enterprise through word of mouth. Every time we asked young people in Adelaide about either the hip hop scene or about where urban Aboriginal young people went to practise their music skills we tended to be directed to Da Klinic. As Shep became a regular contributor to the research project we learnt a great deal about the other resources that the teenagers and often the pre-teens used across the city to develop their technical skills and social networks and also about Da Klinic's outreach, educational and commercial programs, which developed extensively during the period of our research (see particularly Chapters 5 and 6). It was also through Da Klinic that we learnt about one of his 'clients' and hip hop enthusiast 17-year-old Kyle. Kyle had first become interested in receiving 'training' in music skills such as DJing and 'breaking' (breakdancing), after seeing Shep DJ at a Da Klinic performance at an auto show in Adelaide. He had attended a Christian secondary school at South Plympton but had finished school early so that he had not completed Year 12, finding the school ethos too conservative and intolerant of his music taste. Kyle's friends were all into dance music and DJing, he said. Aware that some of his close friends were also performing publicly and producing their own music (and earning good money for DJing), he also aspired to get a chance to perform in a commercial dance club by the time he turned 18 years of age.

Cluster 2: Newcastle, New South Wales

The second cluster in Australia was in Newcastle, New South Wales. There the investigators explored two main CBOs offering youth music activities: the Palais Royale Youth Venue, and the Newcastle Community Arts Centre (NCAC). The youth and mentors who were responsive to the researchers' enquiries were those who regularly attended or facilitated the Palais' music activities. These had included continuous weekly or fortnightly access or sessions as well as discrete one-off workshops in hip hop, DJing and related performances, music production and dance. These often were part of regular school holiday programs such as the 'Indent Music Committee', which took place irregularly on Thursday afternoons. The Indent Music Committee provided participants with skills development in event management, so that the participants could then go on to help promote local bands and develop opportunities for emerging music artists. Its principal activities were the selection and organisation of music gigs at the Palais. This aspect was facilitated by Michelle, the Activities Coordinator, and assisted by Dale, who also acted in the role of mentor to the young people and had a background in sound engineering. Two Indent Committee members who also showed interest in being part of the Playing for Life co-researcher cohort were Shaun (18 years) and Ryan (17 years).

Shaun, a member of the Palais Indent Committee was also a band member of XELX, as both a guitarist and singer. Shaun, a TAFE student in 2003, had been studying 'literacy, maths and computers' since 2001. After a motorbike accident in 2000 that damaged his right hand, Shaun had to relinquish his guitar playing and focus on his singing. Still keenly feeling the loss of guitar playing, he was keen to talk about heavy metal, the genre he particularly liked. He described it as meaningful in its lyric content, unlike what he described as 'chick music' where the lyrics are danceable or 'up' rather than having the developed narrative structure and content of heavy metal.

At the time of the initial fieldwork, Ryan (17 years) was a final year High School Certificate (HSC) student in Newcastle. He was keen to be in the accredited audio engineering course offered by the school but says he missed out by a year (i.e. he was in Year 12 when it started as a two-year program from Year 11). Like Shaun, he liked heavy metal and disliked what he called 'chick music'. Ryan was not a musician or singer, but was keenly involved in management and arranging gigs and CD production. We were to find many of our young people focused on that aspect of the broader music industry. Ryan managed XELX, the band in which Shaun sang. He also managed the band Immune, whose members described themselves collectively as having a unique musical approach forged from influences ranging from Silverchair and Muse to Deftones and The Butterfly Effect. Vocalist/guitarist Elliott Lewis, bassist Matt Walker, lead guitarist James Overend and drummer Cameron Overend manage to combine classical songwriting sensibilities with the more visceral impact of modern/alternative rock to create a sound and a style entirely their own.[20]

During the first year of our study, the Palais held regular breakdancing sessions on Wednesday evenings. This was nominally an 'open', informal session which people could attend to learn and share skills. The 'breakers' used the Palais auditorium dance floor for their activities and in 2003 there was no formal tutor, but rather a core group of four regulars. The regular breakers were Dave, also known as DJ Maths (29 years), Paul (19 years), Ali (22 years) and Sonya (22 years). Dave had about 15 years' experience in breaking and seemed very much the mentor, if not 'leader' in terms of the seeming consensual group deference to his experience, skills and sense of 'authenticity' (i.e. a consistent adherence to hip hop culture and breaking), although the participants themselves may have disputed this view of him. As a leader though, the researchers noted, he was sensitive and respectful of dedication to practice. The session was open to newcomers, in terms of the practical group dynamics, and Dave did his best to ensure inclusiveness despite there being the occasional adoption of the credo of 'paying your dues' or proving yourself worthy, which meant that some anxious newcomers could sometimes be made to feel a little less than welcome.

Another popular workshop, 'Beats and Rimes', at the Palais offered a further opportunity to get to know and engage some Newcastle young people in the research project. This activity offered skill development in 'hip hop, learning writing and performing program beats' on Mondays after school. The workshop had mainly male participants (the session included one female), which perhaps explained, and no doubt ensured the maintenance of, what was perceived by some as a hyper-masculine atmosphere. A regular participant was Azza (19 years), who also assisted Saul, the facilitator and mentor, in leading hip hop workshops. Azza also attended the Palais aerosol art workshops on Fridays. Azza's artwork offered both plusses and minuses for him: he was employed as a mentor in aerosol art at his old school, which was a great opportunity considering he had recently been in trouble with the law for his illegal street art around town. Seven years after the start of the project, Saul, Dale, Adam (Madman), Azza, Yanni and several of the others from Beats and Rimes, 'u write mate' (street art) and the breaking workshops are still keen to keep in touch with the project and keep us up to date with their latest music developments and activities.

> The participant make up has shifted to the Sudanese so it has changed again. Beats and Rimes was originally equipment access for these young people, regardless of whether or not they were socio-economically disadvantaged. Some of them were but it was open.

It was actually the first hip hop formal or at least semi-formal music workshop or space. There were some other people who were having, like, jams in warehouses but for a younger person these might not have been accessible because they may or may have not have contained alcohol or other substances. So this was a space where young people, to maybe the top 25 year olds, could come. It was also a place where people met but not just meeting, there were people out there who had the capability both equipment wise and talent wise except though they maybe just weren't inspired. There is that battle nature to hip hop even if you are not battling with your words, you still have to get up there, show and prove you are making good stuff. It is inspiring. That crew comes in and hears that other crew – and they think oh that was a really good song and it makes them want to write a really good song too. It might not be in a conflict nature but it formed that space where everyone came and developed. Like these guys are doing their best and I want to do my best. It was also an 'information share' like 'if I get this equipment all I need is this, this and this'. Or 'I have tried all of this equipment and tried this type of program'... Like there was this crew called Mojo's Lab – Azza is part of that as well as Nameless. And they came in and recorded a couple of songs and DJ Begsy, he had some equipment and some cables and he would talk to Madman about this particular program that Madman had become quite proficient in. Begsy was wanted to record mainly so he had technical liaison. So it really built the community for itself... And now it is building something for the Sudanese community and for the newly settled and their accessibility. They can't afford to buy this equipment but they can come here and use it because it is here. It's like it's evolved and now Newcastle hip hop is all the better for it. It got people together. People got to know each other. It gave a much better sense of community. Above all, the Palais and now the Loft is a central place for Newcastle hip hop where people could self-actualise.

Saul Standerwick, personal communication, 8 June 2009

Cluster 3: the UK

The sites in the UK were initially selected through the previous networks of both Geraldine Bloustien and David Buckingham, particularly through Weekend Arts College (WAC), situated in North London, which provides training in the arts for children and young people up to the age of 25. WAC has a national and international reputation for its pioneering work.[21] Three young people who had previously been students at WAC and who had remained in regular contact with Geraldine were eager to document their continuing skills and involvement with music and excited at the prospect of participating in this project. Apart from Rowland Samuel, whose promotional email heads this chapter, there is Tuesday Benfield and Katie Williams who are still communicating with the researchers about their music and career paths some seven years later through personal emails and Facebook. Tuesday and Rowland later worked with Alexis Johnson, Director of AKarts, a community-based organisation created to help young people develop their entrepreneurial skills through the arts (see below).

In October 2003, Sarah Baker, as the postdoctoral fellow in the project, began her own UK site observations and participations in a range of CBOs, working under the guidance of David Buckingham in London and Andy Bennett in Surrey. Three more research sites were added to the project.

The Tabernacle

The Tabernacle is an arts and arts education centre based in Notting Hill, North Kensington. Its aim is to support and extend the creativity of the community by supporting artists to make and present their work and to encourage all ages to step into learning. At the time of our initial fieldwork the Tabernacle particularly offered a range of musical activities for young people from Trinidad. The Tabernacle's director during our fieldwork was Karin Woodley, who has since left to head the Stephen Lawrence Charitable Trust and more recently become the Executive Director of ContinYou, one of the UK's leading community learning organisations.

AKarts

AKarts is a youth arts development organisation, created and maintained by a very young woman herself, Alexis Johnson, previously Head of Education at the London Institute of Contemporary Arts. AKarts specialises in combined media arts projects that explore issues pertinent to youth culture and society. The projects are developed and run on a 'bespoke basis' with experienced facilitators/mentors and artists/creative industry experts seconded to deliver the projects. Although the main objectives of AKarts have been across visual arts, creative writing and digital media including graphics, web design and film, the organisation frequently integrated – and where appropriate focused upon – dance and music. The organisation uses the arts to facilitate cultural and social understanding through creative expression and debate, aiming to 'also supply participants with the practical know-how and network to help them access careers in the creative industries if they choose' (Alexis, personal communication, 8 January, 2008. Also see http://www.akarts.co.uk/). During the three-year fieldwork period of Playing for Life, both Rowland and Tuesday gained significant mentorship from Alexis.

The Pie Factory

The Pie Factory was a youth arts centre, which was situated in Margate when we first started the fieldwork there, but which has now been relocated to Ramsgate. It was set up to manage the 'Thanet Youth Music Action Zone' (TYMAZ) funded by Youth Music. The Thanet District Council initiated the Thanet Youth Music Action Zone by Youth Music in April 2001 with an initial two-year budget of £316,000 to bring music to deprived areas in Thanet. TYMAZ then became Pie Factory Music, a charity set up to provide music and related arts workshops for young people across East Kent. The research team observed various programs at the Pie Factory in early 2003. Although, as was the case with the Tabernacle, we did not manage to attract any young people to be co-researchers, we did have some valuable conversations with the staff and mentors at both centres, providing us with important insights about their aims and their challenges. For example, the director of the Pie Factory stated that Thanet was predominantly a white population with few Asian and hardly any Afro-Caribbean residents. There were fluctuating numbers of Eastern European asylum seekers, who only resided in Margate temporarily before moving on to other places. The divide between socio-economic groups was perceived to be extreme. It was an area rapidly becoming gentrified and yet at the same time it was a place of high unemployment and material deprivation. The director noted that there was also a special school in the area for 'emotionally and behaviourally disturbed young people that no one else will have'. These young people also accessed the Pie Factory music projects.

Although it lacked the industrial history of two of our other sites, Playford and Newcastle, Thanet is in a very similar economic and social position. The following overview from Baker, Bennett and Homan (2009, p. 154) summarises the setting for the Pie Factory CBO:

> Unemployment in the region is high – currently running at around 9.8% ('London Worst Region in the UK for Unemployment' 2005) – as is the instance of alcohol and substance abuse and drug addiction. Additionally, Thanet has the highest teen pregnancy rate in Britain, while a recent influx of families from ethnic minority groups raises new issues of racism and cultural intolerance within what was once an all-White population. Roughly forming the shape of a triangle between the towns of Margate, Broadstairs and Ramsgate, the region's full name of the Isle of Thanet relates to its unusual geographical past. Historically, Thanet was a real island, separated from the mainland by a body of water known as the Wantsum Channel. During the middle ages, the Wantsum Channel began to close because of shingle deposits from the North Sea. Land reclamation by local monasteries also contributed to this process, with the result that by the early mediaeval period the Wantsum Channel

had been reduced to a stream and Thanet effectively became part of the mainland (Bolton, 2006). However, Thanet's once physical status as an island remains ingrained in local knowledge, with many indigenous residents of Thanet retaining something of an 'island mentality'. Thanet people rarely travel out of the region or even to the next town. As a result, strong local ties exist between individuals, especially among Thanet youth, who often exhibit a fierce territorialism. As a local youth leader explained, in cases where fighting breaks out at events organised for young people, this is frequently as a result of gangs and individuals from neighbouring towns coming together.

By November 2002 Pie Factory Music (PFM) had expanded its services to other areas of East Kent. As well as running music projects for young people, PFM now coordinates a variety of music-making activities in the Thanet region. It also established an artist management service, and at the time that we first got to know them they were in the process of establishing a record label. In 2003, PFM was supported entirely by grant money, although they quite quickly had to expand their focus to 5–25 year olds, as much of the funding they received was for projects targeting primary school age children.

Two types of DJ/music technology workshops were running in Margate at the end of 2003 when we first contacted the organisation with project leaders Matt Smyth (D'Expressions) and Darren Edney (Danehill Productions). The first was a series of six workshops held at Holy Trinity Church, Millmead for young people from 'The Estate'. The second program of workshops began in December at the temporary studio in the PFM building. This program, called The Zone, continued to be held fortnightly as intensive workshops for a small number of young people from East Kent interested in improving their DJ and music technology skills.

As with many similar organisations in our study Brian expressed how they were constantly seeking funding and this meant it was always difficult to make long-term plans. Their budget is based around the funding year, which seems to be October to September. Margate's young people rarely ventured out of Margate because of the poor public transport. So if PFM held a workshop in Ramsgate, for example, which is only a short distance away, only young people from Ramsgate would attend. He also puts this down to working-class parents being less likely to ferry their kids around in cars. He also mentioned the stark class divide in the area between the poor and the well-to-do, with very few from the middle strata of society.

The two directors or leaders of the centre at the time, Mike Fagg and Brian Spencer-Smith, informed us that the two project leaders of the workshops were 'musos' rather than youth workers. The issue of the mentors being music professionals or practitioners as opposed to youth workers or youth leaders was a hotly debated topic we came across at all centres and will be dealt with in more detail in the following chapters.

Brian's point about the music tutors being 'musos' was to emphasise the way we definitely had to spend a lot of time initially training and developing some tutors to think more in a business/job type way. Community music didn't have the profile and level of quality standards, training, expectations as it does now and some of the people used struggled a bit at first in terms of time keeping, record keeping, evaluating etc. I am pleased to say we have really installed a lot of development in the tutors we work with and this has been a huge benefit for our organisation and for them as freelancers or employees. I think the reference to tutors being musos was probably a mixture of talking about tutors as mentioned above and a reference to the young teenage participants. That is, we probably won't get much from them if we were just to get them to fill out questionnaires or write things down, as we were working with a lot of young people with low basic skills levels, some not being able to read or write.

Mike Fagg, Pie Factory Music, personal correspondence, 2010

Between 2005 and the present day, it seems that PFM has gone from strength to strength. In their new site in Ramsgate, which they are already outgrowing, they hold many workshops and concerts and manage several youth events for the area. There are now seven regular staff and large numbers of young people from the local area attending their sessions and taking advantage of their programs (www.piefactorymusic.com). Chapters 4 and 5 provide more detail about the impact of the physical spaces and programs on the learning itself and the long-term impact of the centre.

Cluster 4: Berlin

As with Newcastle, Berlin became a particularly rich research site for us in terms of its CBOs, particularly due to the German government's postwar policy on the role and significance of youth organisations as vehicles to teach and encourage democratic citizenship. Under the guidance of Bruce Cohen, all of the Australian researchers undertook participant observation at nine different youth organisations (see Figure 1.2) across East and West Berlin, talking to mentors, youth workers and German-born and migrant youth.

Detailed discussions with the staff at CBOs and some of the youth provided valuable information about the complex intersections of politics, gender and ethnicity concerning arts and music-based programs for youth development. Only one young person, Magda (17), and her band, Totally Stressed, chose to become co-researchers. She was keen to share with us her experiences with her all-girl band, providing a particularly important

Figure 1.2 Map of our CBO research sites in Berlin

gendered perspective on our study. The band began in January 2001 at a suggestion and with the help of a youth worker, their 'band leader', through an East Berlin/Lichtenberg youth club called 'Linse'. Linse had always been extraordinarily active in organising local concerts, particularly helping young musicians to make progress. In mid-2010 the band was still going strong despite a few changes in personnel over the years. The six original band members were still rehearsing twice weekly and performing regularly.

Cluster 5: Boston and Providence

Our final cluster emerged from Boston and Providence in the USA. Through Tommy De Frantz the team learned about the work of an enterprising young woman – a female music graduate named Juri Ify Love (previously known to us as Juri Panda Jones). Juri was the founding member and director of her own not-for-profit organisation which she named Genuine Voices, created to provide creative and potential career pathways to young people at risk or who were incarcerated in juvenile detention centres. We observed the centres and got to know several of the young offenders but because of their situation we could not invite them to be co-researchers. Only one young man joined our group in this capacity after he was released from the centre. However, Juri and her colleagues were able to provide detailed information from case studies through their own experience and valuable work.

This is an overview of the main CBOs we worked with during the period of our fieldwork. We did in fact visit several others whose names and histories will crop up during the narrative as we describe the particular resources that the youth drew on as they developed their music and entrepreneurial skills and experiences. Clearly though, for young people to find these resources accessible and effective, it is not simply the facilities themselves that are important but the accessibility, programs, ideologies and style of pedagogies at each site. We will investigate this issue and the impact of various types of programs in Chapters 3 and 5 as we explore the way different styles of learning and teaching affect the young people's progress and increase their opportunities.

Structure of the book

The structure of the rest of the book accords with our notion of exploration, from the intensely personal, subjective accounts of the young people, their mentors and their social contexts into widening circles of family, social networks and public institutions. The developing pattern of enquiry, we propose, might be conceived of as a spiral, as we observe, record and interrogate the young people's attempts to negotiate and constitute their sense of self through their music practices, both facilitated and constrained by their broader cultural and social environments. Each chapter will return to the same questions but each time with another layer and deeper comprehension of these negotiations and tensions.

For example, Chapter 2 provides a closer look at the unusual ethnographic method outlined above and its implications for our research and focuses particularly on the ethical issues and dilemmas of researching youth. It begins with the very personal and paradoxical account of the authors and the youth co-researchers being not only 'ethnographers at home' – in locales of both private and public spaces – but simultaneously people who are in a cultural field very different from their own. This section of the book also describes in detail the critical engagement that emerges from such a complex reflexive methodology. It details the ways the youth participants use cameras, computers and other devices as critical vehicles to reflect upon their own learning pathways. This methodology is both innovative and creative, highlighting a process that is attractive to young participants, and offers a reciprocal and ethical approach to new forms of ethnographic research. It also provides insights into the some of the products – on digital video, CD and online – that the young people agreed to share with the academic researchers partly to enable the publicity and distribution of their creative work.

In Chapter 3 the spiral returns to the youth themselves in terms of the variety of narratives of the young people and the form that these take, especially as documented through their own video footage, their conversations and shared email correspondence with us. We provide more detail of the social and educational backgrounds of the youth within their social, cultural and geographic contexts. We then focus on in-depth longitudinal case studies of a few of the co-researchers, as key members of their social and familial networks from the sites in UK, Australia and the USA. This chapter thus explores the ways in which creative and innovative self-making occurs through a variety of physical performances within social and cultural contexts using music and serious play as the primary vehicle. The voices of the youth and their mentors will be heard alongside the description and analysis of the academic researchers.

Chapter 4 investigates how these physical practices are facilitated or hindered by the particular places in which they occur. It focuses upon the relationship between place and play by exploring the ways 'private' space is created, and negotiated and 'carved out' in both private and public domains. Much of the 'self-making' (Battaglia 1995; Bloustien 2003b) through music that we document in this narrative has to take place in actual physical settings (the street, clubs, community centres, garages, bedrooms) even if the audio product or musical performance itself ultimately appears online. This means that we need to recognise that use of any place demands a particular sense of licence or framing in order for the activity to occur at all and in order for that place to become an accessible 'space'. Not all places are equally accessible to young people; not all young people feel able to access places that might on the surface appear to be open and accessible to all. This chapter takes the reader through the ways in which the youth in our study used both public and domestic arenas as spaces to experiment with a developing, creative sense of self. Sometimes these spaces are created through opportunity – access to programs and people via community-based organisations. Music activities can then be viewed as aspects of wider narratives of ethnic, gendered and social differences mapping across cities' spatial divisions. However, for some young people these arenas of opportunity are very narrowly circumscribed indeed, such as the space of a detention centre.

In Chapter 5 the voices of the youth are not privileged, as it is the community-based organisations and their funding mechanisms that take centre stage. Yet, it is acknowledged that it is the youth who co-shape the community organisation and its enterprise culture. CBOs are defined here as alternative learning sites that are used by youth voluntarily to meet a range of social and skills-based needs. They include youth clubs or special programs for youth within performing arts, community and church centres. As indicated above, here we see how CBOs can justifiably be understood as places where 'serious play' (Handelman 1990) and new possibilities of self-making can be explored and achieved. Here we specifically focus on a macro view of youth creative and cultural enterprise activities and some policy responses that aim to unlock marginalised youths' creative potential, particularly in relation to music and arts-related practices. Following this, we provide a closer view of the responses by several organisations in our study to this creative economy push. The argument posited here is that while these places are conceived of as much more than a designated creative and cultural 'safe space' for youth, they are increasingly viewed by policy-makers, youth workers and so forth, and often by marginalised youth themselves, as pathways to employment. CBOs are increasingly becoming strategically governmentally positioned as significant nodes within a broad socio-cultural, economic and political web of reflexive networks.

Chapter 6 then moves into other ways of thinking about identity, space and place to remind us that young people can be immensely innovative in the ways in which they can recreate imaginative possibilities in their worlds. We name this chapter 'Becoming Phat' since its focus is on the innovative ways in which some of the youth in our study have engaged, often successfully and internationally, in social entrepreneurship. Here we can see music and related practices used as a symbol of identity and of geographic and economic distance (see Cohen, 2007) as well as ways of realising new forms of cultural and social capital.

While this chapter brings us back to our original questions it also looks forward to the future, summarising our findings across the five international sites while noting the paths that the young people are treading now. For some, it is into successful examples of creative and innovative entrepreneurship; for others it is juggling several jobs to continue to perform or develop their musical skills. For yet others, musical activities are forced to take a back seat, temporarily shelved as they struggle to support themselves in an increasingly competitive environment. In the midst of these risky economic times, it seems that it is all the more imperative to create and support safe spaces where youth music and arts-related programs can help young marginalised people become managers of such risk.

The final chapter brings us full circle. Here we explore the significance of our findings in the larger framework of youth arts and education funding and resources across the four continents. We look at recent research into youth arts, creative industries and organisations that support our own observations, highlighting the best pathways and policies that have been undertaken internationally and areas that are still proving to be challenging. The thematic thread that links our ever-widening spiral of observation is the concept of identity as process and the resources that enable this to occur.

We argue that it is the notion of 'serious play' that facilitates this process. What we identify above all in this complex narrative is the importance of enabling and facilitating safe 'spaces to play' for all young people in our various cultures. Here we see the process of self-making in action through bodily praxis – a process that is symbolically bound through song, dance and performance to each young person's understanding of his or her world. This reflexivity, the ways in which each person constituted and negotiated their sense of self through their music practice, is particularly evident in the ways in which they engaged with the camera and with the research process, as demonstrated in the next chapter.

2
Reflections on Theory and Method

Photo 2.1 Kyle prepares for a rave (video still). © Kyle D'Andrea

The promise of these big ideas for those of us formally-known-as the-audience is that we will be recast as the viewers/producers of a new participatory culture. Well, what I say is: 'Bring it on'. (Meadows, 2006, cited in Hartley, 2009, p. 125)

Self and other, subject and object are categories of thought, not concrete entities. (Hastrup, 1992, p. 117)

It's a bit like making a *Big Brother* movie, isn't it? (Vanessa, Adelaide, direct to camera, 2004)

The previous chapter provided an overview of our study, including a brief introduction to the main youth who participated and provided their own images and voices to the narratives that we unfold here and in the following chapters. We also sketched a preliminary outline of the socio-cultural worlds in which the young people were embedded and of the community organisations and other resources that the young people drew on for material and financial help and mentoring as they developed and practised their music skills and cultural identities. Now we focus on the central aspects of this study that involve our participatory and multilayered methodology. To do this it is necessary first that we detail both the theoretical framework and examples of the practice from our study. As indicated earlier, the project was underpinned simultaneously by Pierre Bourdieu's concept of 'social praxeology', incorporating the notions of both 'field' and 'habitus' (1977, 1993), and also by a long literary history of the concept of the seriousness of play. The latter includes the work of Victor Turner (1982), Paul Willis (1990), Don Handelman (1990) and Richard Schechner (1993), their understandings of 'serious play' – which means that which could conceivably be real or possible in the worlds of each individual – and the concept of 'unreal play' or fantasy, meaning that which could not be real, such as moments of extreme exaggeration or mimetic excess. From there we will outline the methodology of auto-video-ethnography, or participatory video as it tends to be known now, before moving on to revisit some of the ways the young people used the camera in both domestic and public settings as a reflective teaching and learning tool and as a vehicle of promotion.

Underpinning all of this process was the seriousness of play. For the young people we got to know through our fieldwork, all aspects of play and fantasy constituted their self-making. These were the essential ingredients in reflexivity, experimentation and risk-taking as they explored the boundaries of their gendered, classed and ethnically based sense of personhood though their music practices. In this conception, however, it is important to remember that negotiation and constitution of identity and selfhood are not aspects of personhood that people tackle head on. Rather they are the result of the continuous tension between embodied play and fantasy – an exploration of representation, image and possibilities. For the youth participating in our project, it seemed that their creative image-making and self-making all particularly stemmed from their engagement with music. For the authors to understand and analyse this process of self-making (Battaglia, 1995) through play fully, we believed that it was necessary to develop and maintain an ethical and open methodology, driven by what Debbora Battaglia described as 'the ethics of the open subject: writing culture in good conscience' (1999, p. 114). In turn Battaglia took her perspective from Walter Benjamin's description of 'convergence with real' (1978, p. 177), arguing that

> Anthropologically, getting real means examining the cultural imaginary, as it is revealed and configured in cultural practice, in order to

determine the value of particular relationships to particular times and places. Getting real means finding the points of comparison and contrasts in these contingencies. It is grasping the pragmatism and imagination and feelings people reveal in their common and uncommon practices. It is recognizing oneself or an other's as anything but given. (Battaglia, 1999, pp. 114–15)

The term 'cultural imaginary' stems from the Lacanian notion of 'the imaginary', which in turn relates to the mirror stage of child development. In the broader cultural studies sense, however, it refers to the ways fantasy images and discursive forms intersect and enable cultural communities to reflect on and recreate themselves, both as individual members and as a way of shaping their collective identities (Lykke 2000).

Cultural historian Graham Dawson (1994, p. 48) defined 'the cultural imaginary' as 'those vast networks of interlinking discursive themes, images, motifs and narrative forms that are publicly available within a culture at any one time, and articulate its psychic and social dimensions'. He argues further that the 'cultural imaginaries furnish public forms which both organize knowledge of the social world and give shape to fantasies within the apparently "internal" domain of psychic life' (Dawson 1994, p. 48).

Arjun Appadurai (1996, p. 31) similarly describes a common form of cultural activity as the 'social imaginary' which is 'directing us to something critical and new in global cultural processes: the imagination as a social practice'. He goes on to note that

> the imagination has become an organized field of social practices, a form of work (in the sense of both labor and culturally organized practice), and a form of negotiation between sites of agency (individuals) and globally defined fields of possibility. The imagination is now central to all forms of agency, is itself a social fact, and is the key component of the new global order. (1996, p. 31)

Nick Crossley takes this argument further, defining agency as the outcome of intersubjectivity and the relations *between* social actors. He takes issue with Bourdieu's theory of practice (1977, 1992) and Giddens' (1991) structuration theory, for both, he argues, strip structure 'of its relational content' (2011, p. 127) and thereby reduce the 'agency' of the social actors themselves. To cite Crossley's analogy, which is particularly apt to our purposes, 'actors are portrayed as soloists and there is little sense that they ever jam' (2011, p. 130).

Limitations of space prevent a fuller critique of the debate between the different perspectives of social science, many of whom, such as Nick Crossley, feel that Bourdieu's work, in particular, obfuscated the impact and influence of 'actual relations in reality' and therefore limited the notion of free will or agency (Crossley, 2011, p. 26; for earlier critiques see also Gorder, 1980;

Giroux, 1982; Jenkins, 1982; Honneth, 1986; Lash and Urry, 1987; Gartman, 1991; Sullivan, 2002). However, within and across his vast output of publications, in both English and French, Bourdieu frequently addressed many of these criticisms. He argued that it was essential to understand his approach as not deterministic but a dialectic *between* structures and social agents and one that principally was concerned with process and relations, especially the relations that occur and motivate individuals within various social groupings.

> Habitus is not the fate that some people read into it. Being the product of history, it is an *open system of dispositions* that is constantly subjected to experiences and therefore constantly affected by them in a way that either reinforces or modifies its structures. (Bourdieu and Wacquant, 1992, p. 133, emphasis in the original)

From this perspective, the relation between the individual as a social agent and the world in which they live is one of mutual 'possession' (Bourdieu, 1989, p. 23) or, expressed in another way, 'the body is in the social world but the social world is in the body' (Bourdieu, 1982, p. 38).

As indicated earlier, the authors of this book found Bourdieu's notion of 'social praxeology', the reflexive weaving together of a 'structuralist and a constructivist approach' (Bourdieu and Wacquant, 1992, p. 11), particularly illuminating. Methodologically it afforded insights into the 'cultural' or 'social imaginary' of the people in our research sites. It provided access into understanding the broad range of dimensions underpinning the ways in which individuals see, express and constitute themselves through their cultural practices. It allowed us to be more aware of what they *did*, not just what they *said* they did. It meant primarily *not* taking representations, whether visual or aural, 'at face value' or 'as (a) given' but rather understanding that such representations were part of the 'cultural imaginary'. In other words, these were aspects of the self that were negotiated, explored and challenged through 'serious play'. Indeed, we saw 'play' as essential to the process whereby the young participants in our project reflected on, constituted and negotiated their sense of self. In this conception play needs to be understood not as trivial or childish behaviour that one outgrows (or *should* outgrow) as one gets older but rather as a process of representation and identification, which is a fundamental human activity (Goffman, 1970; Lévi-Strauss, 1972; Turner, 1982; Handelman, 1990; Dawson 1994; Bloustien 2003b). Bourdieu similarly refers in his work to the personal investment and strategy of negotiation that underpins all human experience as learning 'a sense of the game' (1977, 1993; see also Bourdieu and Wacquant, 1992). The game analogy is apt as it emphasises the arbitrary rules and regulations that we all adhere to and impose upon ourselves when we want to be considered 'serious players' in whatever activities, social fields and arenas of life we engage. Observance of these 'rules', which apply to clothing, mannerisms, argot, food and drink preferences and music, demonstrate to ourselves and to others that we are 'authentic' and 'legitimate' members of that particular segment of society, club or 'scene' to which we aspire. But of course the rules are not fixed – they only appear to be. Rather they are being constantly contested so that we spend our lives trying to make sense of allegiances by justifying our choices and (re)shaping our sense of self. We challenge, represent and (re)create as we go – striving to establish that elusive sense of selfhood, what we often struggle to conceive of as the 'real me'.

For all the young people in our study music was a central vehicle for doing this and, for many, a very successful pathway that provided a meaningful and valuable cultural identity. While this insight regarding the central role of music for young people is clearly not new (see, for example, Ross and Rose, 1994; Bennett, 2000; Huq, 2006) our own focus on participatory video together with new digital technologies helped us to demonstrate this cultural vehicle and relationship through the young people's own perspectives, as the youth documented and shared their experiences through these media.

The relationship between identity and new media technologies

For many people cultural identity has been in flux since the onset of new developments in information technology, a project continually and impossibly in the process of completion. Arguably, this is not a new claim nor is it limited to contemporary life: each new development of technology has had an impact on the way individuals and communities feel able to shape, reflect on and 'play' with the ways they see themselves and the ways they choose to represent themselves to others. What has particularly exacerbated this change we would argue is the possibility for broader, more rapid, global social networking in recent years. As Nick Crossley has recently and convincingly argued:

> Belonging to different social worlds develops our individuality. It allows different and perhaps conflicting dispositions to be given expression, nurturing them, and it affords us different vantage points upon ourselves, different generalised others from whose perspective to construct our 'me'. Each world affords us a perspective upon the others, relativising and affording us a control over our identities and the information flow which partially shapes them, affording us a sense of autonomy and of control over who and what we are... What is of more concern to us here, however, is the fact that actors who belong to different worlds constitute a tie between those worlds. (Crossley, 2011, p. 173)

Because of this linking between very different worlds, the digital camera, the computer and the internet have all increasingly demonstrated that what we understand as 'reality' and as capable of being 'objectively' comprehended, analysed and represented is in fact not so easily fixed and captured. Rather it is continually being constituted and reconstituted by its representations and therefore is conceptually slippery, multifaceted and impossible to 'pin down'. Like a butterfly caught, stretched out and pinned to a display board, the usual information about young people and their experiences is often seemingly scientifically, psychologically or sociologically validated, apparently informative, but yet lacks the essence of 'the real' that Benjamin and Battaglia were alluding to in the quotations at the start of this chapter. From this perspective, the usual economically determined models of class and gender become inadequate, and related concepts of subjectivity and personhood have to be re-evaluated. Rather, 'the self' that each person envisages as their quintessential being, the 'who' we feel we *are*, has to be constantly recreated, reconstituted and re-evaluated – and that involves very serious play indeed! The young people we worked with seemed to understand this instinctively. They frequently talked about the personal time and energy investment they understood were required to fulfil their sense of who they felt they were and wanted to be, especially through their music ambitions, as for example in Tuesday's and Kyle's comments below:

> I'm aiming to be a DJ full time, as I love it. I have to practice and work very, very hard to achieve this but as long as I am alive I will achieve my goals!
>
> (Tuesday (DJ Lady Lick), personal correspondence, 2009)
>
> I've now done two 'real' gigs, both 18 birthday parties, unpaid but, been official in the sense of not just for friends. Free gigs are an important way to gain experience and to get my name out there by word of mouth. I want to be a club DJ, so doing parties are a great way to get experience, reading a crowd, and getting feedback. If they don't like the music, they just go somewhere else. At parties you have to please the crowd.
>
> (Kyle (then DJ D'Andrea), personal communication, 2004)

It also explains why many of our participants, who were often mentors themselves, such as DJ Shep or DJ Maths, emphasised the importance of continual practice, perfection of moves and commitment (see the following chapters for more detail on forms of mentoring).

The young people also understood that they required particular forms of symbolic and cultural capital (Bourdieu, 1986) in order to be accepted as legitimate or 'authentic', 'real' or 'legit' within their particular social spaces or experiential communities. In the following chapters we shall illustrate how, for example, various forms of capital and notions such as 'authenticity', 'realness', 'old skool' and 'hardcore' are legitimised in the everyday but specific music practices of the young people. For example, when a particular grouping uses the concept of 'cool' or 'hardcore' or even 'wikkid' to underpin their notion of a form of symbolic capital, it will have differently refracted connotations according to the particular musical, social and cultural fields in which the youth are engaged.

Social fields also have to be understood as systems of power relations independent of the people whom these relations define (Bourdieu and Wacquant, 1992, p. 106). This means that inevitably individuals will be engaged in several fields (or 'games') at the same time. In turn their particular position in the field will change according to their particular investment in that specific state of play and according to which aspect of their self they choose or need to emphasise in that particular field. For example, the same young men practising their 'beats and rimes' at the Palais workshop in Newcastle will see themselves and behave differently from when they perform at a 'hip hop battle' outside of their immediate community or when they meet in another person's informal recording studio to 'lay down the tracks' of their own CD. In the performance arenas they may deliberately cohere to become part of the Nameless Crew as opposed to individuals competing within the home space. Similarly DJ Roland Samuel takes on a new cloak of 'authenticity' when he mixes and plays at the Phatbeats show, the UK online radio program (http://www.phatbeats.co.uk). In his regular 'day' job as assistant store manger at a pharmaceutical retailer, he often feels negatively aware of his West Indian background and heritage as he deals with difficult customers and bosses. As DJ Roland Samuel, Rowland takes on a new sense of pride, including ethnic pride in his cultural and musical heritage.[1] Note a 2010 Facebook call he made to his friends and fans:

> **DJ Roland Samuel:** Need you input, guys. What tunes do you want me to play on the show tomorrow??.
> **Various responses including:**
> *waiting for the day*
> *never say never*[2]
> **DJ Roland Samuel:** Don't play 2 step on the show bro so no Freek Your Mind by Smooth Kriminal aka Deano (will drop it in a few weeks time on my 2 step special lol).
> **Responses:** MJ Cole always a good choice and u could go oldskool funky with Earth, Wind & Fire...
> **DJ Roland Samuel:** Your lucky i have a house RMX of EWF's September Chezza
> **Responses:** Hey how about artful dodger, please don't turn me on!! Love that chooooooooooone!!

DJ Roland Samuel: Knew i should of put NO 2 Step somewhere on the main status i put up Its a 2 step free zone – just straight 4/4 House and G!!. Saying that i don't have the track anyway lol.

Rowland (DJ Roland Samuel) Facebook fanpage entry (16 October 2010)

It is also important to understand that DJ Roland is not just addressing the Facebook fan base for his radio show but simultaneously his local friendship base. His social field thus negotiates two 'games' at the same time. These are manifestations of nuanced distinction (Bourdieu, 1984) as DJ Roland demonstrates his knowledge and expertise in the particular field of '4/4 House and G(Garage)' music and at the same time good-naturedly attempts to accommodate the tastes of his friends.

An even more poignant example of how social fields interweave is the story of another young man we met.[3] The young New York musician Yitzchak Jordan, also known by his stage name of Y-Love, is an Orthodox Jewish rapper. Born to Black and Puerto Rican parents, he converted to Judaism in his early teens. Y-Love's music translates his faith into freestyle rhymes and danceable beats for diverse audiences. An early fan of heavy metal and punk rock, he first became interested in hip hop while studying at a yeshiva (religious institute of learning) in Israel. There in Jerusalem Jordan met a fellow student, David Singer, and the two began memorising Talmudic texts via rap. Singer said he advised Jordan not to hide his ethnic background or try to pass as a Yemenite Jew. 'I always tell him, part of your genius and your beauty is that you don't have to fit in', he said (personal communication, May 2010).

In his own Facebook biography Jordan says of himself, 'I do hiphop. I try to bring the revolution. I'm angry at many things, but hopeful about even more' (information collated from various websites and personal communication). Yitz Jordan is also a self-described 'Hip Hop activist', using his music and his blog to address social justice issues. His website states that he designed his blog 'to motivate positive social change. Change in the culture, change in the world. We in the urban music community are capable of far more than we think. Let's do this' (http://hiphopactivist.com). He reminds us of this through his blogs and 'call to action'.

Since the times of the civil rights movement, slavery and time immemorial, the call for justice has often found its voice in music.

From the oldest spiritual to the singer-songwriter movement of the '60s to the politically-charged hip-hop of today, the voice of the oppressed have often been heard on the stage from an artist on a stage hoping to change the world through his art. (hiphopactivist.com)[4]

Y-Love's story serves to remind us of the multilayering of social fields and the ways these are negotiated through the serious nature of play.

Play as strategy

Bourdieu's concept of the 'rules of the game' is underpinned by the notion of serious play. Closely tied to identity and notions of self, the concept of play here is a means of dealing with uncertainty. It is important to stress that contemporary concepts of play are still often aligned to notions of the 'unreal', the inauthentic, the false, and the invalid. Play is therefore often conceived of as 'light', 'trivial', 'free' activity in contrast to notions of 'heavy', 'obligatory', 'necessary' 'work' (Turner, 1982, pp. 33–5). Before industrialisation, however, even though a distinction was made between the sacred and the profane, there was no separation of the concept of work from leisure and work itself incorporated many elements of play (see Turner, 1982; Handelman, 1990). Yet in Western cultural traditions as we began to believe more rigidly in scientifically based certainties and in fixed and maintainable (symbolic) boundaries, the notion of 'play' became trivialised through rationalist understandings of the world. Play then became synonymous with non-work, with leisure. Indeed it has come to mean freedom from institutional obligations and also freedom to transcend structural boundaries and constraints; freedom 'to play with ideas, words, with fantasies... and with social relationships' (Turner, 1982, p. 7). Yet late modernity has awakened greater possibilities for play because those former boundaries are now perceived as less solid and fixed.

In this context, then, throughout this book we are arguing for a concept of embodied play as strategy, which is tightly entwined with the particular 'rules of the game' and the 'emotional investments' that the young people understand to underpin their social and cultural worlds. The concept of 'play as strategy' here indicates the attempt to work within perceived or internalised structural constraints. These constraints are used to 'designate the objectively orientated lines of action which social agents continually construct in and through practice' (Bourdieu and Wacquant, 1992, p. 129). As indicated above, we also use 'play' to describe a particular process of representation: strategies that incorporate, reflect on and depict the everyday experiences of these young people and the significance of their music-making and consumption.

The more we explored the meanings of play in this way, the more we found that this project confirmed the salient role that popular culture and in particular music hold in this process. They are the main vehicles through which self-identity is created and negotiated. This is because music, television, cinema, magazines and online worlds are increasingly sites of the production of such play and fantasy, not simply the means of consumption (Jenkins, Shattuc and McPherson, 2002; Bloustien, 2003b). In other words, the constitution and negotiation of identity through play, between what conceivably could be real and fantasy is a very active exploratory and reflexive process, for, as Shouse has pointed out, 'The power of many forms of media lies not so much in their ideological effects but in their ability to create affective resonances independent of content or meaning' (Shouse, 2005, n.p.; see also Grossberg et al., 2006, pp. 267–74).

We will shortly return to one particular aspect of these 'ideological effects' and of the affective process of self-making, which is the exploration and performance of identity that can occur through the lens of a camera. As we shall see, this can be especially intense and poignant when that process converges with new digital media formats (Jenkins, 2006a; Hartley, 2009). First, however, we need to consider the attendant issues and contradictions of our fieldwork, in particular the complexity of our own placement as adults in the worlds of the young people.

Into the (contradictory) field: relationships and representations

The use of participatory video certainly facilitated the ways we were able to gain access to the worlds and networks of the youth. It allowed us to record, document and understand the processes by which the young people from the four countries created, developed, shared and distributed their various music activities. It also allowed us to gain greater insights into the diverse social and cultural contexts within which these activities occurred. Yet, as we explain, the process is never straightforward or uncontroversial.

Our methodology was deliberately designed and developed to be participatory, reciprocal, ethical and multifaceted. We began our approach using the socio-science tools of 'mapping' the various communities and locales that we were about to encounter in order to understand the demographics, socio-economic backgrounds and social networks of each of our prospective young participants. So, for example, in Berlin, through the thoughtful preliminary work of Bruce Cohen, a member of our international academic team, we were able to gain an overview of the relationship between the demographics of each area of the city state and the types of music and resources available in that city. In his overview of the city, Cohen noted:

Given the static nature of spatial movement experienced in both halves of the city during the cold war (restricted by the wall in West Berlin and by governmental restrictions on where people could live in East Berlin) there has been a notable acceleration of social, cultural and economic fragmentation in the city... Together with the restitution of housing in the East and renovation of old eastern housing stock, this has led to some areas of the city being economically transformed for the better and other areas for the worse, sometimes with the local culture within the community changing quite dramatically. (Cohen, 2008, p. 91; see also Häußermann, 1997; Häußermann and Kapphan, 2001)

His outline of the socio-demographics of the city enabled the team to consider the potential links between the particular ethnic populations, the material effects of their neighbourhoods, including clear material disadvantage, and the type of music the young people were engaged in.

Table 2.1 shows some characteristics of the new political districts where our youth centres were based, in the context of understanding the socio-demographic and political problems of the city of Berlin as a whole (see the previous chapter for a parallel map of exactly where the CBOs were situated within these districts).[5] Cohen wrote in his report that

with a population of just under 3.4 million (more than the populations of Hamburg and Munich put together), Berlin has over 13% of its residents classified as 'foreign'. Although many of these people may have been born in Germany they also hold foreign passports. The largest single group of these inhabitants are Turkish. There are also large numbers of people from the former Yugoslavia, the eastern bloc countries, parts of the Middle East and the Mediterranean. In November 2005, the city's general rate of unemployment was 17.8%; however, the rate of unemployment amongst the 'foreign' population was a devastating 43.0%. (Statistisches Landesamt Berlin, 2005, cited in Cohen, 2008, p. 94)

Cohen's analytical overview also noted that Friedrichshain-Kreuzberg had one of the highest rates of ethnic minorities in the city, and this is especially so amongst the younger populations attending school. Correspondingly, it has one of the lowest rates of monthly income (the negative statistics were even higher when Kreuzberg used to be a separate district; likewise the high rate of people 'moving in' to the area is likely to be a phenomenon confined to the up-and-coming Friedrichshain area). Neukölln has the highest rate of social welfare recipients of all our districts and a high number of minority groups, yet the rate of monthly income is slightly above Friedrichshain-Kreuzberg's. The district of Charlottenburg-Wilmersdorf also has a mixed population, but with a generally higher standard of living (partly due to the merging of Charlottenburg with the more affluent Wilmersdorf district).

Table 2.1 Berlin districts 2004: comparison of researched districts

	Friedrichshain-Kreuzberg	Charlottenburg-Wilmersdorf	Neukölln	Reinickendorf	Lichtenberg	Treptow-Köpenick	Berlin
Area (hectares)	2,016	6,472	4,493	8,948	5,229	16,842	89,182
Population (in 1,000s)	258.5	314.7	305.7	245.5	257.5	234.7	3387.8
Foreigners (% of total population)	22.6	16.9	21.8	9	8.1	3.4	13.4
Moving in (per 1,000 population)	52.3	37.6	30	20.3	30.1	23.8	33.9
Moving out (per 1,000 population)	39.9	36.1	30.3	26.5	33.9	27.5	33.4
Foreign school population (% of total school attendees)	32.4	19.2	30.4	11	8.7	3.1	16.4
Social welfare recipients (per 1,000 population)	130	59	143	76	60	43	81
Average net income (d' per month)	1,200	1,625	1,325	1,700	1,475	1,600	1,475

Source: Statistisches Landesamt Berlin, 2005, cited in Cohen, 2008, p. 95.

Meanwhile, the much larger geographic district of Reinickendorf appeared to be well-heeled in comparison to many other western districts. The remaining two districts in the former East Berlin disprove the cliché of poverty-stricken eastern Germany, with Treptow-Köpenick being a large and prosperous district, and Lichtenberg having reasonably low levels of people on social welfare and the employed population earning the average wage for Berlin (1,475 euros per month). The problem both of these eastern districts have is a net outflow of population (whilst the Lichtenberg statistic appears correct, the Treptow-Köpenick statistic is likely to be valid for the more down-at-heel Treptow area rather than prosperous Köpenick).[6]

Additionally Cohen stressed that it was important to note that Berliners 'tend to have a mindset that revolves around their specific locality (known as kiez). This "kiez mentality" becomes even more important to young people in disadvantaged areas who have less access to other parts of the city' (Cohen, 2008, pp. 93–4).

Similarly detailed reports and preliminary mappings were undertaken in all of the areas that we studied, providing valuable background information to contextualise how many community-based organisations were operating in each of our sites, who was attending and what other factors impacted on the perceived success or otherwise of the organisations. In some areas, such as Newcastle in New South Wales, Australia and in the district of Margate and Ramsgate in Kent, UK, the number of active CBOs that focused on youth was minimal. In other sites, such as the city of Berlin, as indicated above and in the previous chapter, the number was overwhelming.

To deepen this knowledge and to understand the on-the-ground significance of these discrepancies, we then drew on the usual anthropological and ethnographic tools of participant observation. These methods included formally approaching the directors of particular CBOs in each site to gain permission to informally 'hang out' and later facilitate and participate in the various leisure or festival activities when invited or when appropriate. We thus not only gained information about the youth who regularly attended but also about the various community, material and cultural resources and processes that supported the official and unofficial youth programs and activities. The information about the cultural resources was complemented by our participating in workshops and attending board and committee meetings, when permitted, and undertaking semi-structured interviews with council workers, managers, directors, ground staff, arts and music practitioners, teachers and youth workers. The aim was thereby to collect an overall multilayered picture of what activities were taking place, under what conditions and through what facilities and facilitators.

Our model was thus deliberately both quantitative and qualitative – indeed, as indicated in the previous chapter, we used a *triple*-layered framework to reveal the interrelationship of people, places and programs/policies.

One way this approach might be best imagined is to compare it with a stack of plastic transparent sheets placed on top of each other; each successive layer combines images, adding a new depth and clarity to that which has gone before. In some cases this seems to create a more complete whole but in other cases the layering can show where certain images are deliberately obscured or highlighted. Or perhaps for some readers a more accessible example might be garnered from the newer technology of GIMP (the GNU Image Manipulation Program: see www.gimp.org), which is a software graphics program or computer tool that enables the easy manipulation and combining of images. The original pictures are not lost but, through the layering of images, the strategy offers new possible interpretations through each combination.

Understood in this way, the familial, social and cultural contexts through which our young participants viewed and negotiated their personal identities through their music activities within their wider cultural milieu become the focus point of the theoretical framework of our study. In other words, it quickly became clear to us that the quality and effectiveness of the young people's confidence, ability and efficacy to investigate, explore and fulfil their potential, especially through their music, heavily depended on the support of their familial and social networks. Many of our young participants were quite explicit about the role that their parents, brothers, uncles, cousins and friends played in teaching them particular skills and mentoring them in performance and style. It is in this context that the young people's ability to engage in 'serious play' makes sense (Turner, 1982; Schechner, 1985, 1993; Handelman, 1990). It is a demonstration of the elaborate and delicate testing out of the boundaries, opportunities and resources, through experimentation, practice, negotiation and risk-taking, that the young people *perceived as possible and appropriate* from within the centre of their social worlds and networks; a stretching of the boundaries just so far but no further. It is also why they undertook to learn particular musical styles and genres in the first place as opposed to other possibilities (Bloustien, 2000, 2003b).

When we added the very specific participatory video methodology, embedding and incorporating the camera within the participant-observation process, this provided access to this central context and, through the resulting footage, demonstrated its significance as the research progressed. The digital video and camera footage of young people's music activities and of their wider social and personal lives was thereby a foreground to a much wider complex background, two interconnected parts of one whole. From out of every experience of the world there emerges a particularly clarifying interpretive perspective, the foreground that rises out of the chaotic background of everyday 'messy' or 'sticky' existence, culture being recreated each time in the process (Wagner, 1975, p. 30). We understood the video and photographic footage as demonstrating the way the young participants placed specific conceptual frames around their own understandings of their own lives. Often it showed a self-conscious reflexivity as they attempted to document, discuss and share representations of their music activities. Significant differences in attitude, behaviour and opportunity were revealed by this interpretive perspective. At the same time the methodology emphasises the dialectic nature of all fieldwork for, as Rabinow has pointed out, 'In the intersubjective world of field work, both the ethnographer and the informants are caught in a web of signification they themselves have spun' (Rabinow, 1977, p. 151). Kirsten Hastrup would appear to agree, for in her own discussion of the intersubjectivity of fieldwork, she argues, 'A reality begins to emerge in the process' (1992, p. 119).

The resultant reality and insights that began to emerge from the use of the cameras, incorporated within the more usual tools of fieldwork, highlighted for us the particular and the local. It also re-emphasised our original perceptions of the inappropriateness of talking about youth culture or even teenage culture as though it were homogeneous and neatly bounded. Our observations echoed Pierre Bourdieu's original observations that to assume homogeneity across what are in fact facets of different social fields was inappropriate and obfuscatory (Bourdieu, 1993, p. 95).

In our process of recruitment we took our lead from the social networks of the young people themselves and in so doing we found that the social groupings could be quite broad, including individuals from a very wide sweep of ages. Fascinatingly, it seemed that the youth were already acknowledging what their formal educators often were not – that someone could have expertise or skills that were not commensurate with their chronological age. When young people were older than we originally had thought to include in our own categories as 'youth' and clearly social catalysts in their groupings, such as some of the young men in Newcastle, DJ Shep in Adelaide or Juri in Boston, we considered them as straddling the gap between participants and mentors.

Another tricky concept for us was to consider what constituted 'risk' or 'disadvantage' in terms of which young people we should focus upon. Some of the adult research team were concerned that individuals in the wider social networks were being included as potential participants and yet were older, more educated or in other ways not as materially disadvantaged as those whom they had originally expected to include in the study. Indeed the term 'at risk' when applied to youth has long been considered a complex and contentious category (at risk from what?), particularly in socio-cultural and educational literature. In our case, the team members constantly reflected upon, discussed and sometimes disputed what 'at risk', 'marginalised' or 'disadvantaged' really meant. For example, on one evening two of the team recorded and reflected on their discussion and 'debrief' after spending some time with one of the young people in our project. The following is a short extract from that discussion:

> BC: I liked him a lot, though he didn't strike me – in the traditional sense – as being 'marginalised'.
> SLB: Well he didn't finish school and... since leaving school he's had a stream of casual work kind of positions, and he's also been sacked before from a number of positions... The job before today that he spoke about was the furniture work... he still said that was kind of casual as well, but I think that was a lot more regular than other stuff he's been doing...
> BC: Yeah, fair enough... the things I noticed of course, not knowing this background, was... the technology and obviously getting out the mobile phone which looked like a very nice, flashy, mobile phone.
> SLB: See, that's the thing with mobile phones – that everybody's got a mobile phone.
> BC: Not everybody's got that one though –
> SLB: Yeah, but a lot of the time, it seems like you have to have the most up-to-date mobile... I'm not sure if that's really any kind of indicator of marginalisation...
> BC: This is why I was also thinking for his DJing that, you know, you have to buy so much stuff to keep up-to-date, but then I was thinking well nowadays that can actually download... burn onto CD and stuff, MP3s... Because I was thinking, otherwise, how does he keep up in his sets.
> SLB: Yeah. But he doesn't seem in any rush to make it...
> BC: It's when he seems to suggest that, like, the difficulties... of breaking in... he still wants to be a DJ, very much... But he didn't realise it would be so hard...

(Recorded discussion, 9 April 2005)

Such shared discussions, which were undertaken throughout our research period, reflected the sensitive and reflective approach by the team members to working their way through complex and often contradictory categories and findings. As with many such defining groupings, the very formation of such a category as 'marginalised' and 'disadvantaged' can be a self-defining and misleading social construction. As Peter Kelly has argued, 'In an age of large-scale and profound social changes, narratives of uncertainty and risk dominate popular, political and theoretical discourses about youth' (Kelly, 2000, p. 263; see also Tait, 1995, 2000).[7]

So overall the team made the decision to make our category very wide in the research study, thereby including any young person for whom a case could be made that the young person is in some way vulnerable, marginalised, disaffected and (perhaps more importantly) considered themselves to be socially disadvantaged or disengaged through their class, ethnicity, economic or social situations. In the most extreme cases they might be young people who were 'lacking self-esteem, aspiration and motivation [so that] they see their futures as pre-destined to be ones of hopelessness, unemployment and even crime' (Youth at Risk, 2010) – and yet through their music practices many felt that they *were* achieving, gaining new levels of recognition and building new opportunities against the odds.

In order to ensure the young people were actively engaged in the research process as participants and not just informants, we invited them to tell their own stories, through camera, videos and the interactive website established for this purpose. Inevitably this meant we too have had to face the thorny questions of agency, distance, objectivity, reflexivity and authenticity – all controversial and interrelated issues in terms of our methodological and analytical frameworks, which we look at more closely in the next section.

Rethinking agency: social and cultural contexts

Alternative and effective models for the study of young people and their worlds are still sadly underutilised (see Hardman, 1973; Suransky, 1982; Caputo, 1995; Wulff, 1995; Bloustien, 2002, 2003b; Bloustien and Peters, 2003) mainly because they require several complex areas to be addressed simultaneously. Firstly, such an approach requires a reminder that 'culture' is far more dynamic and shifting than many research methodologies have allowed for. Inevitably, that means that it is 'messy' and requires a particularly lengthy process to understand and analyse, for the object of study does not stand still. It cannot be contained within a neat theory or formula but changes even as one examines it. Indeed, the 'object' that the researcher examines becomes the meeting point between cultures, a blurring of cultural perspectives as the researcher and researched meet, respond to and impact on each other's vision.

Another way of expressing this is to understand and be aware of the varying degrees to which individuals are and can be 'free acting' agents in their own worlds. On the one hand, in the contexts of youth research this means understanding the 'immediacy' of young people's realities. The 'now' of their world is far more important than the future (Caputo, 1995, p. 290). On the other hand, as indicated above, the free will and agency of young people is limited – it is inscribed and limited by the contexts through which they engage with their worlds.

All young people are of course influenced and framed by their parent cultures and social mores of their own social communities and networks.

That is, the self that we believe ourselves to be and are endlessly 'becoming' (Grosz, 1999), which we 'perform' through self-representational narratives, even to ourselves, is never created or told in a vacuum. Rather it is perhaps best understood as 'creative responses both to individual life experiences and to traditions of narration' (Kaare and Lundby, 2008, p. 105).

Any study, then, of young people and their music-based practices requires that one look closely at the complex relationship between personal agency and social structures, the explicit and implicit social and cultural constraints together with the supporting institutions, strategies and tactics underpinning the young people's perceptions of their own developing sense of personhood. Yet how does one guarantee 'truth' and authenticity? Most qualitative methodological approaches or investigations claim to make every effort to represent the respondents' or participants' views as accurately and ethically as possible. Sometimes part of that responsibility is handed to the participants themselves in order that they might provide their own perspectives via written or visual texts. However, often that can tend to mean that these personal accounts are later interpreted as objectively or 'scientifically' accurate or 'authentic'. In other words, as the fieldwork experience becomes translated into a written textual account, one particular voice or view simplistically becomes portrayed as more 'true' or objective than another's, whether it is the voice of the participant or respondent or the academic/professional investigator.[8] Yet previously, in the *dialogue* of fieldwork 'we talk *across* established difference and create a world of betweenness' (Hastrup, 1992, p. 118; see also Tedlock, 1983, pp. 323–4). That is, it is imperative to understand that the object of our analysis has to remain always the 'intersubjective creation' as well as being the world that we leave behind when we leave the field (Hastrup, 1992, p. 118).

To comprehend this fully means to critique and dispel any beliefs about the 'objective' researcher. This was not an easy task for any member of our multidisciplinary team. Such a concept can challenge long-held beliefs tied to ideologies and disciplinary training. We take up that challenge now.

Up close and personal: translating from fieldwork to textual account

While most researchers would concede that they are historically positioned and that what they observe in the field and what they take note of depends on their own lived experiences, not all fully realise that this also impacts on the methodology they utilise and its 'scientific' validity. For it is quite threatening to accept that all investigators bring cultural baggage to their enquiry that can and will inevitably either help or hinder their understandings. As Judith Okely pointed out:

> The autobiography of the field worker anthropologist is neither in a cultural vacuum, nor confined to the anthropologist's own culture, but is

instead placed in cross cultural encounter. Fieldwork practice is always concerned with relationships. (Okely, 1992, p. 2; see also Adler and Adler, 1987)

Our approach was underpinned by this understanding and was also originally and deliberately designed to challenge the assumption of perceived homogeneity that still underlies the methodologies traditionally used when exploring the world of young people. These assumptions of homogeneity often tend to remain implicit despite the more recent critiques and attempts to enter into a more reciprocal dialogue with those being studied and to make explicit the processes of ethnography in the text. This seems still to be so whether the text is written or visual (Cranpanzano, 1986; Marcus and Fischer, 1986; Rabinow, 1988).

Over the past ten years, work on the implications of the visual in ethnography, including the role of the camera and new digital technologies, has highlighted the complexity and the ethics involved in the process (see Turner, 1991, 1992, 1995; Asch 1992; Banks, 2001; Zeitlyn and Fischer, 2003; Pink, 2007). That is to say, although many researchers are increasingly exploring new visual, ethnographic, participatory and reciprocal methods, they still tend to examine a particular site or group and treat that group as relatively culturally cohesive rather than fluid, dynamic and experiential.[9] There seems to be little understanding of the need to explore the contrasting distinctions between the participants' own perspectives of their worlds against or within another, more structural framework. We would argue in this book that in many studies the paradoxes and contradictions, the gaps between the broader social context and the individual's lived experiences and perceptions, are not sufficiently accommodated in the final analysis.

Sometimes, of course, all of the adult investigators found that we had to confront and learn about fieldwork worlds that we had not encountered before. We knew of course that our primary aim was to understand both the familiar but also the anthropologically 'strange'. So in the main the academic research team all recognised that the type and style of hip hop music, the street art and the breakdancing created and consumed by teenagers in Australia was remarkably similar to that produced by our young co-researchers in the UK, Germany and Boston. However, none of the Australian or British adult researchers had experienced the difficulties of working closely with young people in an American remand centre. This situation required new skills, new sensitivities and other ways of thinking through our approaches, especially in using the visual auto-ethnography and issues of reciprocity.

The use of cameras differed from location to location, partly because of the predilection and varied social situations of the young people themselves, and partly because of the ways the individual academic researchers responsible for that area felt about using the cameras. For these reasons, the use of this methodology was not as consistent or uniform as the authors of this book originally hoped or imagined. However, each locale did produce a large amount of photographic and video camera footage – sometimes taken by the young people in a variety of genres, as detailed below, and sometimes taken by one of the adults with the young people's consent or under their direction or at their request.[10] There were a few exceptions to this such as the participant observation undertaken in Boston at the Brighton Treatment Center, under the direction of the Genuine Voices program (genuinevoices.com) and the guidance and advice of Juri, the founder and director of the music program. The use of digital cameras was not allowed in this facility for obvious reasons but we were permitted to take photographic footage of various workshops from other related but less closed facilities or under strict conditions. Many of the images that we used were taken by Juri, who was also a mentor and worked with us as a co-researcher. Similarly, footage taken by Tuesday to demonstrate the work she was undertaking with youth in after-school care or by DJ Shep in his workshops at an Adelaide youth detention centre had to be censored. As in Juri's footage, the videos and photos in these places had to be carefully framed to show only the hands or bodies of the young people playing their musical instruments but not identifying features such as faces. Despite this, the youth clearly loved the ability to record their sessions and share their music.

> As far as video, the first clip you will see is introduction of the song called 'All My Life' by KC and Jo Jo. It's an old school song these youths parents used to listen. Let's call him Boy E. (17 Years Old). He first asked me if I could transcribe first part of the song from Youtube. When I did he was so excited and wanted to perfect it. Then when I was video taping with my little digital camera (I just used Casio Exilim) he wanted to watch it and wanted to perfect it. I think we tried more than 10 times to perfect it. I really had to go to my next job but he kept saying one more time!! He is very proud. Now we became friends on Facebook and he moved to Connecticut. I was chatting (by Facebook) with him the other day and I sent this link to him (www.genuinevoices.com/audiovideo).
> He was very very excited!!
>
> (Juri, personal correspondence, 13 November 2009)

In each locale, our other prevailing concerns were to ensure that the young people's perspectives were authentically captured. This point takes us back into the controversial realm of representations, ethics, perceived power relations and the issue of voice.

Youth voice? Whose voice?

Quite early in our fieldwork we realised that many of the young people already used some form of camera along with computers and other devices as critical vehicles to reflect upon their own learning pathways. However, despite this insight, not all members of our adult academic research team were comfortable with our proposed approach of incorporating cameras and participatory video into our methodological approaches. This was particularly so for those academics in our team who were not coming from anthropological or immersive ethnographically based disciplinary areas. These researchers felt that the approach was too intrusive and in some ways professionally threatening. So it was necessary for the academic team to have many ongoing discussions about the potentially conflicting issues. These included concerns about the use of real names versus pseudonyms for the young participants, the circulation and potential publication of sensitive material taken from fieldwork notes and particularly the different views about the efficacy and value of using tape recordings with the young people conceived as co-researchers. This last issue was never fully settled. There was finally a compromise that the use of note-takers should be limited but not ruled out altogether. The authors clarified their feelings about this during one of the recorded group discussions about whether the digital note-takers, often used with adult respondents, should be used with individuals from the small group of young co-researchers. They articulated very strongly why they felt this was inappropriate.

> We are asking the young people to be involved very much in trust relationships with us... It is not so much that the people mind being tape recorded and you are absolutely right that the power relationship is always going to be there. It has to be there. It doesn't go away. What we are trying to do, I guess, is alleviate that as much as possible by making all of the process transparent. And if you think about it, the kids are not putting note-takers on us. Remember we are inviting them into the research project. No perhaps they are not going to be worried about being recorded but it is something that we (as adult researchers) would be doing *to* them.
>
> (Academic researchers' group teleconference, 7 December 2004)

The disagreement, based as it was in differences in disciplinary training and ideologies, was never satisfactorily settled even though both sides were equally concerned to ameliorate the inevitable power imbalance between adult and youth as much as possible. Some of the other members of the team articulated their ongoing anxieties and ideological reservations about the methods in the conferences and in their own publications drawn from the Playing for Life project as indicated below:

> Regular semi-structured interviews with music project participants ensured the opinions of young people remained central, and their views on music, creativity, and space are evident in this article. This remains different, of course, to young people's involvement in the initial construction of the project's aims and methodology, which enables youth to 'participate in the research project themselves' (Clark et al., 2001a, p. 2; see also Clark et al., 2001b). Arguably, our very presence alerted the youth involved to the project's preoccupations with music workshop outcomes and their wider relevance to local ambitions in relation to music and cultural policy. This was certainly the case with the adult staff of the community music projects. The proximity of researcher (the Playing for Life team) to the researched (staff, youth who agreed to be case studies, and other young people and youth/cultural administrators encountered at all the sites) 'affects all aspects of the research process from gaining access to analysing and writing up data' (MacRae, 2007, p. 51). Acknowledging this, we have sought the views of the youth case studies and music project staff in the writing-up phase of the project, inviting responses to the team's theories and understandings in early article drafts. This process went some way to filling the various gaps in knowledge that can occur within more straightforward, textual analyses of youth music genres, styles, and attitudes. Crucially, it allowed a postresearch forum for dialogue between researcher and researched that allowed differences in perspectives and motivations to be highlighted, and this is evident to some degree in what follows. Apart from an implicit acknowledgement of their considerable involvement, obtaining the responses of young people and adult staff to our initial findings partially redressed the usual balance of 'professionals who control the interpretation and reporting of the research'. (Clark et al., 2001a, p. 2) (Extract from Baker, Bennett and Homan, 2009, p. 150)

Such discussions and debates are clearly valuable. They are part of the ongoing search for an alternative, reflexive and, as far as possible, reciprocal methodological approach, particularly when researching youth issues. They go to the heart of perceived understandings of distance, 'objectivity', reflexivity, agency, authenticity and power relations. We will return to these debates shortly and in the following chapters. It is worth noting, however, that by the time we entered the field many of these issues were already being aired and several forms of participatory approaches (and critiques) had been developed and deployed in other published literature, at conferences and in other research projects to address the issue of 'ethics' and 'voice' (as in de Laine, 2000; for more recent work see for example Delamont, 2009; Ortbals and Rincker, 2009). First, however, the next section provides a little more detail about the nature of participatory media, its now common use in communities and why we found it such a valuable research tool.

Participatory media in action: a long history!

Certain forms of visual technologies and participatory media have been around since the 1950s, intensified with the introduction of more mobile video technology, such as camcorders, which gained popularity from the 1960s (Willett, 2009b). However, two techniques in particular used participatory visual and other arts-based methodologies as devices both to facilitate research and to increase opportunities for agency, citizen activism and self-awareness. These strategies, particularly video diaries and photo voice (www.photovoice.org), were just starting to become popular when we began this study. They were seen to increase what the researchers saw as the potential democratisation of media access, production and dissemination – or what Schratz and Walker (1995) referred to as 'research as social change'.

The central idea behind the strategy is that creative work by non-professionals can add great value to contemporary culture (Burgess and Hartley, 2005). Not without its problems, difficulties or detractors, the use of visual data in social science research has become increasingly common, particularly for programs that seek a wider dissemination in order to spark reflection on policy and practice issues (Knowles, Cole and Presswood, 2008).

One form of this approach, video diaries, has been around for quite a while but really gained acceptance and popularity in the 1980s when broadcast-quality, lightweight video technology became more affordable and accessible. In fact, the precedents for digital story-making and video diaries were two related but distinct approaches: the first used ordinary people instead of celebrities in front of the camera; the second, often called participatory video (PV), offered ordinary people the opportunity to select and create their own stories for distribution by being the producers not the objects of the narratives.[11] The arrival of computer-based non-linear editing systems for video in 1989 simplified the process of editing and transferring video footage into a usable form and made it economically more feasible and of course therefore more accessible for non-professional use (see Jenkins, 2006b).

Participatory video: the evolution of 'produsers'

The second strategy or technique, participatory video, involves individuals, groups or communities shaping and *creating their own* films, or representational narratives. Archivists reveal that the first experiments in PV were produced by Canadian Don Snowden, who pioneered the idea of enabling grassroots community action through public access to media. In 1967, working with a filmmaker, Colin Low, he developed his ideas as part of the 'Challenge for Change' program on Fogo Island, a small fishing community in Newfoundland. Their strategy was, first, to encourage the residents of the island, who lived in small, scattered groups, to record their own stories and then watch each other's films, thereby coming to see the similarities between their various issues and problems. The second stage was to help the residents work together through these insights to solve their shared difficulties. The films were also used to present evidence of the issues to politicians who had not visited the island in order that policies and decisions could be challenged and changed by dialogue and negotiation with the very residents and stakeholders who should always have been at the core of the decision-making process. Snowden's techniques became known as the 'Fogo process' and were successfully copied in other places around the world (Quarry, 1994; also see the Don Snowden Program for Development Communication).[12]

The Fogo process demonstrates the accessibility and ease with which ordinary citizens can become effective tellers of their own stories and issues when given the means to express themselves creatively. It is frequently seen as a powerful tool for empowering people who are normally disadvantaged, disaffected or otherwise socially marginalised to explore and share issues that concern them and their own communities. It is primarily about process rather than the quality of the product although more recently new strategies have been incorporated to try to scale up the process and produce artefacts and stories of broadcast quality for wider dissemination (see Hartley, 2009).

The process has the potential to enable members of a community to become *subjects* or *speakers* as opposed to *objects* of study, in control of their own situation. More importantly, it can also offer the means of communicating the needs of a particular group to key decision- and policy-makers through dissemination of the stories and perspectives via a public forum.[13] The value of this process became even clearer to us as we learnt more about the ways in which both the youth and their mentors embedded the cameras and internet footage into their music practices, marketing and management strategies.

While there have been many different adaptations of this methodology around the world, the participatory strategy itself became particularly recognisable as a type of 'brand' and acclaimed for its 'democratising' potential through the screening of a BBC television program produced by the Community Programme Unit in 1990. Having established its feasibility and popularity, the idea then really took off when, in 1993, Chris Mohr and Mandy Rose from the BBC2 Community Programme Unit started a new series of programs described as innovative experiments in social anthropology and participatory media, and which they called *Video Nation* (Carpentier, 2003; see also Rose, 2007). The contributors from the general public were given a Hi-8 camera for one year, during which time they filmed their everyday lives. The media responses to the concept commented on the sense of immediacy and authenticity. Over 10,000 videotapes were shot and sent in to the BBC. From these, the producers selected approximately 1,300 shorts to be edited down and screened on television.[14]

So our approach certainly had historical precedent! We also quickly discovered that the practice of recording and disseminating moments from their leisure and music-based activities was common amongst many of our young participants. As illustrated below, in all of the locales in which we researched across the four countries, even before we formally began our study, we found that the majority of the young people had access to mobile phones with in-built cameras. Furthermore, with the obvious exception of the young people in the Brighton Treatment Center and similarly supervised spaces, the youth used the camera phones to capture aspects of their lives as they occurred and to share these moments with others via email or social networking sites.

The controversial and ethical issue is, of course, that it also includes the right to express and disseminate an opinion that is extreme or racist, incites violence or is otherwise excessive, which, as Hartley notes, is an inevitable 'radical utopian-liberal' possible outcome. The challenge inevitably is that: 'In a democracy, everyone has the right to *communicate* a fact or a point of view, however trivial, however hideous' (Hargreaves, 1999, p. 4, cited in Hartley, 2009, p. 148).

We had to negotiate this issue of defining what exactly *is* culturally appropriate material in this and similar projects with young people. We had to recognise that as our young participants told their stories and wanted to share their images and narratives on the project website, it might not be to our liking. Furthermore, different places and different youth cultures in our study had different standards about what was appropriate and acceptable language and content to be recorded and shared. So, for example, in Juri's Genuine Voices workshops in the Boston centre, the youth were not allowed to swear, use racist language or endorse drug use in their rap lyrics. Similarly in the *Youth Revolutions* radio show, the young people were told to select their music carefully for public broadcast as it had to contain no 'profanities' or endorse anti-social behaviour. In the Palais in Newcastle, in the Pie Factory in Kent, UK, Da Klinic in Adelaide and in many of the Berlin workshops, such language was considered part of the local youth culture and argot and so was rarely censored. DJ Roland Samuel's Phatbeats online radio show similarly does not seem to have any type of censorship controlling what he can broadcast.

In terms of this project, we had to tackle the problem of how we as academics and educators were to balance our concern for the young people's 'freedom of speech' with our own disapproval and dislike of racist or sexist material that we might not want to circulate through the project website.

Of course, the freedom to experiment with one's image, self-representation and views can be exhilarating and liberating for, as Bloustien discovered in her earlier work and as she stated previously, 'images could be removed as though they had never been. Old selves could be revisited and scrutinized for their "authenticity" at representing "the real me" or "the me as I am now"' (Bloustien, 2003b, p. 64). In the same way, the young people in our current study not only selected and offered particular images and videos to share on our website[15] but also on their own websites on Facebook, Twitter and MySpace, which sometimes presented ethical dilemmas for the adult researchers.[16]

But non-professionals are often naive or uninformed about the effect of posting or sharing alternative or extreme views in a public forum. For example, although the contributors from the public to the *Video Nation* series had some control over their representations they were not always happy with the ways other viewers responded to these self-portrayals. This is because, although they were assured that nothing would be broadcast without their consent and they had the right of veto over their material, this was not enough to guarantee the long-term good will and trust of the non-professional participant. As we discovered in our own experience and from our own projects, most non-professionals do not understand how the editing process and the deliberate juxtaposition of stories for dramatic effect on television can alter the way their story is interpreted by wider audiences and affect the 'authenticity' of their representations.

Two clear and very public controversial Australian examples of this were the so-called soapumentary, *Silvania Waters* (ABC/BBC 1992),[17] and the later documentary by Dennis O'Rourke on the Aboriginal community in the town of Cunnamulla (*Cunnamulla*, 2001), far-western Queensland, with a population of 1,500 (Beattie, 2004, p. 240). As Simon Royal, journalist for the ABC's *7.30 Report*, explained about the second example:

> It [Cunnamulla] is the town which embodies all of the huge issues which are now the issues of national debate – race...reconciliation...Over two years, film-maker Dennis O'Rourke recorded in great detail the lives of the people of Cunnamulla. Some see the end result as the blunt truth – others say it's a betrayal of trust.[18] ('Facing the Music in Cunnamulla', 2001)

It is a dilemma that only seems to be growing more complex as the use of digital media becomes more widespread and the line between what were previously separated public and private realms becomes more opaque.

Our own approach

In all of these various forms of participatory media, whether video or photography, the aim has been to empower ordinary people by providing access to the media for documentation, creative expression and communication.

To explain and clarify our approach it is important to compare the similarities and differences of these strategies – effective and valuable as they are – with our own. Central to both video diaries and photovoice is the aim to educate and empower. The role of the professional expert or mentor is essential as she or he is the one who provides the skills and training workshops. The mentor enables the participants to learn new technical expertise by demonstrating how to select and narrate their own stories for maximum impact (Pini, 2006; Buckingham, Pini and Willett, 2009; Strangelove, 2010). The participants are offered opportunities to learn professional communication techniques in photography, filmmaking, story-boarding, editing, genre and narrative (see Dowmunt, 1993; Wang, 1997).

We began our research with the premise that in many cases this expertise, in terms of media skills, music, performance and event management, *was already occurring* in the world that we were studying. However, it was not necessarily occurring in ways that had previously been recognised by educational and arts institutions. We were not therefore intending to provide any form of external expertise as an intervention or as part of our research methodology, although we did offer and encourage access to the hardware (cameras) and forum for distribution (website), if our participants wished to do this. Rather, our aim was to focus on what resources the youth were already gaining *by themselves*, through their own communities and social networks. This did not mean they were not selecting and drawing on the skills of mentors and other experts in their immediate worlds. Rather it meant that we wanted to understand who they already regarded as their experts and mentors. What were the impacts and outcomes when the youth were dependent on their own initiative or at least on their own choices about community resources? What worked to help them in their paths towards social inclusion and entrepreneurship and what hindered their journeys? Who or what provided access to these necessary skills? How were they funded? How were they selected? Why were they trusted? What could we learn from this grassroots approach in terms of youth education, social inclusion and innovative approaches to facilitating pathways to future employment?

For these reasons, we felt it was essential in the Playing for Life project that the participants were completely free to 'play' with cameras that we offered for their use. We would offer very basic technical help on how to use the technology, which were very compact Sony digital video cameras and still cameras, if the young people had not used this type of technology before. In 2003 when we first started, as indicated above, it appeared that most of our young participants had little, if any, access to such cameras and video equipment *for their own dedicated use*. While they sometimes had access to cameras and similar equipment available in their homes or in school they were not usually allowed to use them when and how they wished. Such freedom of access and use then was still considered a relatively novel and exciting option for many of the young people, especially when offered in the context of a university-sanctioned and government-funded project. The provision of such access thus also offered an innovative space for us as adult researchers to occupy and an entry to get to know the young people in each locale.

However, as previously stated, since that beginning, mobile or cell phone cameras have proliferated and become extremely accessible and more affordable over the past seven years or so. Therefore, quite quickly over that short period of time of our study, we began to see that many of our young people had become far more comfortable and familiar with the technology. In all cases, though, we made it clear to our young respondents that we were not looking for 'budding film directors' or conventional research subjects. Rather we stressed that we wanted them to be 'co-researchers' or, if you will, auto-ethnographers, reflecting on, recording and demonstrating their usual practice within their everyday social worlds and networks. For this reason, we did not provide studio space, technique workshops, microphones or lights, nor did we give any suggestions about appropriate narratives, format, style or genre. This was not our purpose. Rather, we deliberately encouraged the young people to film as they chose and what they chose.

In summary, what was important to us was to understand how the young people's perceptions and representations of their worlds 'meshed' or contrasted with what we as outsiders observed and understood. Because we got to know the young people in their social and domestic contexts over the long fieldwork period, we were also able to learn what was selected to be filmed and highlighted and what was ignored and left out, what forms of narrative were chosen and why, how the footage was selected to be shared and through what forum – all essential to our understanding of our overall findings. Again, it is important to emphasise that we were not interested in the footage as an artefact, but rather as the *process* of what was selected by the young people for filming in the first place, what was recorded and how, and what was left out of the selection.

The process of selection and negotiation illustrated what we described earlier as 'serious play' and 'fantasy'. In other words, while we were aware even then of debates concerning the issues of scalability and of dissemination from such a method (Hartley, 2009, p. 123), our means of distribution was relatively contained. It was not through broadcasting but through the internet, via our project website. Although this was open to the public for viewing, the interactivity was facilitated and therefore controlled by our own institutionally required gatekeeping processes. While the participants could 'speak' and blog to each other and comment on each other's footage via the website forum, the academic team had to ensure that the youth could only upload their materials via the website manager for reasons of copyright and university liability.

Nevertheless, our plan was that through this forum the young people and their mentors could share their recordings, see each other's music forms and practices and communicate with each other and perhaps thereby assist each other with their mutual problems and issues. So despite our different approach to more conventional types of digital storytelling, we were arguably anticipating the later insights about the uses of digital literacies by John Hartley, in that we intended our approach would 'translate digital storytelling from a phenomenon locked into the "closed expert paradigm" to one active in an "open innovation network"' (2009, p. 123).

So with all of that background in mind, how did the young people make use of the cameras and this opportunity? We turn to a brief snapshot adapted from our field notes, which serves as a springboard to illustrate this process further. This is the first of several vignettes captured below. It occurred when we first began to know Kyle and his world as he perceived it and as he wanted us to know him, through the lens of the camera.

Introduction to Kyle aka DJ D'Andrea

> Kyle, aged 18 (at the start of the study), regularly takes the video camera on a trip to his local shopping centre in Adelaide, South Australia. On one tape, he and his friends were preparing for a rave for the following Saturday night so they videoed themselves purchasing clothes, accessories and especially gas masks as the particular stylistic accoutrement for the evening. That last item, the gas mask [see Photo 2.1, the video still image at the start of this chapter] seemed particularly bizarre, unsettling and anachronistic in our eyes as adult researchers! The camera captures their excitement and their appropriation of public space, including their joyous taking over of the store escalators, as Kyle and his mate, already dressed in sequinned tops and loose trousers, performed for the camera; they broke into exaggerated dance steps every few minutes, even on the escalators, to the squeals of delight of their watching friends and bemusement or annoyance of the older shoppers passing by. In other videos, Kyle documented various parties at which he performed as DJ and in yet another he filmed inside his house as he and his friends prepared for another dance party. The camera recorded the increasingly excited discussions over dress, food and music. Still later, Kyle alone and directly facing the camera, talked about his music tastes and his ambitions as a musician. He begins by demonstrating his mixing skills in his bedroom, before the camera. Then, ending with a flourish, he comes from behind the mixing desk and sits in front of the camera. Here he speaks thoughtfully and seriously, without the excesses of the earlier tapes. (field notes, 2004)

When Kyle faces the camera directly in several parts of his footage, he speaks of his dreams and ambitions as a full-time DJ. He spoke of his mentors and his idols, and his own desire to emulate their high standard.

> As to my aspirations – in the future I would like to work full time as a DJ. I would like to have a permanent gig at clubs or do a few a week, maybe. Then on the weekends, I would like to do raves because I like doing the harder stuff, as well.
>
> (Kyle, direct to camera, 2004)

This brief vignette and description is a good place to start to compare what has been described above, in terms of forms of digital storytelling as interventions, to consider and unpack the differences through what is happening here. In this extract we see different aspects of Kyle's self-representation, when he was alone and when he was with his mates at play – performing, selecting and recording. At different times he would often portray a deliberately flamboyant aspect of himself to camera and then offer a more quiet, reflective persona, all for public viewing. The extract also illustrates our own position as proxy participant observers to Kyle's world thereby providing an entry point to consider some of the very personal and paradoxical ways in which we worked with the youth co-researchers as 'ethnographers at home' in locales of both private and public spaces.

As with almost all of the young people in our study, Kyle was eager to use a camera to document and reflect on his world. He asked to borrow the camera on a regular basis to record his own social activities and his DJ performances at various parties and gigs. We have also seen Kyle change and develop, in his own words to 'become more mature' over the long period of our relationship with him. His musical taste and activities have also altered and Kyle now has a regular MySpace page to advertise his musical expression in the persona of DJ Hi-Brid. Over the seven years of the project, Kyle has remained keen to take the prospective viewers of his footage vicariously both into public places and the more private spaces where normally it would be difficult for us, as adult researchers, to go and be accepted including private parties and inside the homes of his friends.

The adult researchers obviously instigated Kyle's use of a camera, or at least *this* more professional style of camera, but for many other young people the personal use of still and video cameras, both embedded in mobile phones and separately, was becoming an increasingly regular occurrence (Buckingham and Willett, 2009). We found that they used various recording devices in their bedrooms and other domestic spaces as personal teaching tools in order to monitor and reflect on their own music practices or to show others how particular skills could be perfected. They also used cameras as vehicles to publicise their music performances and events. This clearly reflected the way cell-phone cameras and webcams were not only becoming ubiquitous, accessible and affordable but were also more easily linked to blogs and social networking sites. In this way, what we originally conceived as an innovative methodological tool was increasingly shown to be a commonly used cultural and social vehicle for the youth and their networks in all of our research places.

Behind closed doors

Yet many of the young people, like Kyle, had not previously had much opportunity to 'play' freely with a digital video cameras and so these participants expressed excitement at the opportunity to document their activities on camera and to have them taken seriously by the academic research team. The youth were also keen to be involved with something much larger than their own world. For example, Kyle expressed great excitement about the research happening overseas. He was also fascinated at the idea of the project starting in Adelaide and then moving out into 'the rest of the world'. He said he was really keen to be involved with the project and was very chatty about what he had been doing both with music and in general.

As confidence and trust built up in the relationship between the young co-researchers and the adult team, and in the process of borrowing and sharing the cameras, we gradually gained a fuller picture of the young people in their domestic world as well as in the more public spaces. So for example, in our field note observations and reflections we could understand the ways many young people use their bedrooms as a rehearsal space and as a studio for their developing music skills. In the case of Kyle, his mixing and recording equipment took up one corner of his bedroom. We noted that Kyle was already enhancing his cultural capital through his growing knowledge of the equipment: 'I bought my decks through EBay from a seller in WA. This kind are widely used in Europe although not many people in Australia have them' (personal communication, 2004). His music tracks, he told us, were mainly downloaded from the internet and stored on his computer which he used together with his decks and players when he mixed. We learnt too of his peer mentor DJ Ben who was already making a living out of the DJ scene in Adelaide.

Our knowledge and appreciation of the microworlds (Bloustien, 2003b) of many of the young people gradually developed in this way over the three years of the project through our participant observation and developed relationships, complemented by the photographic and video footage.

Bedroom rapping

Kyle was not the only young co-researcher to speak directly and 'confessionally' to the camera in the form of a diary. However, we found that the young people who did this did so very self-consciously, often referring to the behind-the-scenes segments of reality television programs like *Big Brother*, *Australia Idol* or the *X-Factor*. In other words, they were quite explicit about their reflexivity, being well aware of their (imagined) audience whom they hoped would be watching and sharing their own observations on the project website. For this reason, they talked not only about the development of their personal histories and music practices and tastes but also of their personal interests, ambitions and desires in other aspects of their lives. Each speaker too, we noted, carefully 'staged' their diary segments, playing thoughtfully selected background music in their videos as a kind of deliberately evocative, ambient soundtrack and framing their shots to show their homes, their rooms and their personalities through various personal items in their domestic space.[19]

For example, Tuesday, who had been a participant in one of Bloustien's earlier studies,[20] also videoed her diary segment footage several times for this project in her bedroom in London, demonstrated her developing skills as a DJ and as an MC. Her video showed her bed with pink fluffy soft toys from her childhood juxtaposed with her more adult mixing desk and MC equipment. She told the prospective audience for her video that she chose to spend many hours perfecting her skills 'practising and practising and practising' on these mixing decks that her musician uncle bought for her many years ago. Her bedroom was small and crowded within the council flat she shares with her parents and siblings so her music practice has had to be limited by her family's and her neighbour's tolerance of loud sounds into the night.

She also spent some time on her video tapes describing her part-time job in Kentish Town, London working in a private children's after-school care centre where she used her music knowledge to engage the young disaffected children in her care. She had hoped to video some of her own workshops there but, because of the privacy issues this raised, the video footage she took in the centre, as explained above, was only permitted to focus on her own body and her DJing, not the young people's response or their own newly acquired skills.

Vanessa in Adelaide also used the camera in a variety of ways to document her radio show together with her other leisure activities although only once as a video diary. On that occasion setting up the camera in her lounge room, at television height it seemed, she sat before it on the floor with a head and shoulders shot, her dog on her lap, and spoke candidly for an hour. She talked about her music interests, her development of *Youth Revolutions*, the youth radio program that she helped to found on a community radio station (PBA-FM) and her goals for the future.

> Hello! I come from Adelaide and this is my first video for Playing for Life. I've never been in front of a video camera before so it is pretty interesting, It's a bit like making a *Big Brother* movie, isn't it?

(laughs)...you are meant to sit there and put your whole life out there onto video, but it is not exactly like something you can do automatically, is it?

Vanessa, direct to camera 2004

Photo 2.2 'It's a bit like making a *Big Brother* movie!' (video still). © Vanessa Cussack

Initially she introduced herself as one would to a new friend, offering information about her birthplace (Darwin, Australia), about her schooling at a single-sex Catholic school (which she had not enjoyed: 'Don't send your children there!' she warns her audience 'or they may turn out like me') and her unsuccessful search for work. She introduced the viewer to her dog who she feels is like her best friend and she also spoke warmly about her supportive relationship with her family, especially her mother, and her boyfriend (who was also participating in the project).

A type of tongue in cheek intimacy combined with advice about marketing to global confectionary giants (suggesting they might create giant-sized chocolate fun bars because 'That would be *really* fun!') oscillated with more serious explanations, still direct to camera, about the rationale of their music program, *Youth Revolutions* (YR), on a public community radio station. This venture, she told us, was created to give the young people of the 'Peachey Belt'[21] access to and a voice in the media.

> I do radio. I host a radio show called *Youth Revolutions* basically what we do there is we get music and we play lots of it. And we get issues about youth. Anything. Things like from buying your first a car, to youth suicide to self help getting your first job to getting depression to happy stuff like fitness, all sorts of things. We interview bands – all sorts of things.
>
> (Vanessa, direct to camera, 2004)

The serious purpose of their radio program was deliberately structured around their use of popular music. This was for a number of reasons. Firstly, the YR team saw music as essential to entertain and attract their peers to the radio show; like many such radio programs the audience were encouraged to give immediate feedback about the items and the music by ringing the station while the presenters were on air. As these radio programs exist and thrive *because* they are local, the audience and the presenters are usually well known to each other off air; they are part of the same community as we illustrate more fully in Chapter 5.

The music thus served as a way to talk about and help create taste groups or experiential communities around the local musicians and bands in their area. Vanessa explained also that music provided an additional opportunity to discuss some of the more complex, related issues of youth leisure activities, from the problems of accessible spaces for live music to drugs and alcohol and the recurring moral panics around youth gangs, heavy metal, punk or emo genres.

> The way we came about is pretty interesting. The first time we went on air, it (the radio program) was called *Youth R Zone* – how crap is that? We were meant to go on and speak about youth issues and that. But it was so disorganised. The first time I knew about it I didn't want to go on it. I thought it would be really boring. But my mum (she was the one running the program) she pushed me and pushed me. She said we need an emergency person so I went on there. And it worked out and it was fun but the funding ran out. So me and a group of people decided we wanted to take it over and we got funding from the Playford City Council. And now we have *Youth Revolutions!*
>
> (Vanessa, direct to camera 2004)

As the music library at the studio was relatively large but at the same time very limited in relation to their contemporary music taste, the *Youth Revolutions* radio crew would often bring their own CDs to play on air – although this in itself could be the cause of internal conflicts as music tastes were not necessarily shared amongst the team.

The YR crew also carefully researched and discussed the many pressing issues that they felt affected young people in the area which usually did not get aired in the public sphere from the perspective of the young people themselves. As Vanessa explained in her video segments, the list included 'practical help about buying your first car to dealing with depression', to unemployment, low-paid casual work, racism, homophobia, sexism, underage drinking, drug taking, relationships, bullying, domestic violence and school anxieties. Keen to promote local music and industry in their area, the team often invited in and interviewed local bands on air, promoted their gigs and played their music to give them publicity.

Vicci, from the Adelaide Kandinsky Group, also used her direct-to-camera segment at her home mainly to provide a potted history of her own involvement with organising music events. She told the camera about the path which had led her to Carclew and joining the Kandinsky group. She also videoed and directed us to video several of the Kandinsky events that she helped to organise at different venues around the city. Like the few young men that used the camera in this way, such as Will and Shep, she was clear that she was using the camera to reflect on her desired career pathway which she hoped would be in event and music management. It was mainly through her diverse volunteering opportunities that she hoped to enhance her social networking possibilities.

> I started last year with deciding that I had enough of standing in front of the stage just watching bands which I had been doing for the past 4 or 5 years. I decided to see what it took to put on a gig, to learn about the behind the scenes of putting on a gig. I wanted to help out with the April 'Off the Couch' a twice yearly youth music gig event which is run by Carclew, a mainly government run Youth Arts Centre, based in Adelaide. So I contacted them about being a volunteer. I got into the volunteer and I got to work with them through from February to April as one of fifty people. It was the biggest Off the Couch yet or since. There was about 54 bands of varying genres and we put them on at about 6 different venues in 6 hours in one night...
>
> During working on Off the Couch I got to do an Oz Music event management course and that gave me a lot more theory and practice. So I learnt lot more about the dos and don'ts about running a gig and

what you should look out for. But I still wasn't confident enough to go out there and put on a gig on my own. At the end of Off the Couch, it was announced that Carclew was in the middle of getting a grant approved to put on 5 all ages gigs over a 5 or 6 month period. So I put my name down to be a volunteer for that and I got in. Then 2003 became a busy time with one thing after the other snowballing into new opportunities.

End of May 2003, I was selected as one of 12 to work on the 5 gigs that Carclew were putting on. We called the project team [and] entitled the project the Kandinsky Sessions after the Russian painter. We chose this name because we chose 5 different gigs with different themes and genres and we felt that Kandinsky's colours described the music...

As a small team we each got to have a hand in things like production like contracts or agreements that have to happen, the band liaison, venue liaison, marketing budgeting, advertising – the whole works – so it was great to have a good look at what each gig had to offer and what we had to do to make it happen...

Vicci, direct to camera, 11 August 2004

Telling it as it is

Some of the young people made it clear that they did not want to use the camera to record personal aspects of their lives but were happy to have adult members of our research team film their activities, at the workshops, CBOs and at outside venues. The field notes from Newcastle reflected on this:

> I talked with Dave and the use of the videocam on the project, specifically the participants videoing themselves and he's not convinced that they want to do this. We also talked about how time is precious with regard to the use of a space for breaking, i.e., the desire to be training when they have access to the Palais space rather than be doing anything else. Dave adds that he thinks that Jacob does video his own training, however.
>
> While I watch Dave, Jacob and Tom working on a routine, I think over how the videocam was used by the breakers last year and consider how its introduction felt impositional in that I was not convinced that the breakers really wanted to be using it themselves. The only time it didn't appear to be like this was when Pep-c used it functionally for helping

Codo to train (i.e. videoing Codo then showing him the footage in order to help him perfect techniques and moves). (Julie, field notes 9 February 2005)

On the other hand, Julie's notes did show that the camera was often used voluntarily by the young people as a teaching tool.

> Andrew (aka Pep-c) is teaching Codo top rocking. Andrew comes over and introduces himself to me and asks whether he can borrow the videocam. He then uses it to record Codo and Jacob then replays so that they can see their style and perfect their moves. It proves very useful with Codo understanding much more about what Andrew means when he says that Codo is a bit stiff and jerky with his top rocking.
>
> (Julie, 28 July 2004)

And again later that year:

> Jacob is videoing Pep-c doing breaks and Jacob videos him, then they reverse roles. They watch the footage studying their practice, using it to perfect their moves. The videocam is obviously an important learning technology for them.
>
> (Julie, 17 November 2004)

So even when the youth were not happy to video themselves as part of the project it is clear that several of them were already using the cameras as a teaching tool to reflect on their own activities and progress, especially to 'perfect techniques and moves' (Julie, field notes, 9 February 2005).

Mutual respect and trust was brought about by the careful and sensitive approaches by adult team members to the young people's worlds and enabled the collaborative research community to be created. So, for example, it was that ongoing collaboration between the academics, the young people and their mentors that over time allowed the academic team in Newcastle to be invited to attend and record rehearsals and MC performances of Azza and Adam. They were two of the most active members of a hip hop crew called Nameless. In this way we were able to learn more about their ways of learning and opportunities for developing their music skills. The field notes reflect on one of the regular meetings with the two rappers:

> Adam and Azza begin trading rhymes straight away – it is clear that their weekly meetings together at Adam's place have increased each other's confidence, and their respect for each other's styles. They showcase a song they have co-written, Respect. Its key lyrical themes are about multiculturalism and diversity.
>
> I ask if he and Adam would like to video themselves making music. Azza says 'Yeah' and tells me about last week at Adam's house when they were making music and lost track of time forgot when it was three o'clock in the morning and the 'cops came round and asked us to keep it down'.
> (Julie, field notes, 18 October 2004)

In informal discussions, Azza and Adam talked about the ways they usually went about rehearsing for their sessions as Nameless.

> Sometimes we'll write together and sometimes I'll just be sitting at home and I'll write some stuff. We'll ring each other up and say 'Cool. Come down', and we'll figure out a way to write it [organise it?] I might have 4 bars and then the next person might do 4 bars or we might have straight verses on our own. Most of the tracks and the choruses we work on together. Adam will often get some beats down, and ring me and play them over the phone and say, 'What do you think of this?' I'll say, 'I like this', or 'I don't like that' or 'we might change this beat', or whatever...
>
> (Azza, 7 June 2009, personal communication)

Azza told us that he was helping to run a graff (graffiti) workshop at his old school, as part of his new Palais employment. He laughed at the irony of returning to the school where such activities were forbidden, 'My Dad said that if I had done graffiti when I was at school, they would have kicked me out!' (personal communication 2004).

In these ways, as the team members in each locale got to know the young people and their mentors, we learnt not only about processes of shared learning and collaboration, we gained too from the valuable insider knowledge and insights that the older youth workers, musicians and music practitioners were able to offer. For example, to return to the field notes, when one of the youth workers at the Palais was asked whether he agreed with the observer's impression of the growing confidence of one of the quieter young rappers, he confirmed, 'He's much more confident. You move out of the bedroom and take your writing out in the public. Then you perform it. Then you freestyle, then you go on from there' (field notes and personal communication).

Bringing it all together: co-researchers not subjects

In this chapter we have looked at how we, as academic researchers, employed participatory media to encourage the engagement of the young people in our study. The aim was to involve them as co-researchers not subjects but also to tap into how such media were already being perceived and used by them in their everyday music practices. As we shall document further in the following chapters, several of the young people in our project incorporated cameras and other forms of media as tools of surveillance, both of themselves and of others, to monitor and improve on their music skills. Many also used various forms of media as entrepreneurial strategies to promote, develop and disseminate their music for themselves and, even more importantly, for their peers. More than any other individuals these youth showed how such a combining of talent, media and resources, both human and material, can 'make a difference' for their communities.

We indicated above that some of the young participants in our project were already quite sophisticated in using digital media to their advantage – to publicise their own musical talents and to promote the work of others in their community. By the time we heard about them and then met them face-to-face we would be hard-pressed to talk about their situations as disaffected, marginalised or at risk. In fact, however, none of these amazing young people had originally come from advantaged or promising backgrounds. There were about four or five youth in this category over the four countries that we visited who warrant a special mention and the reader will learn even more about them as we talk about their communities and their achievements in the following chapters. They stood out for us early in our fieldwork firstly because they were talented musicians in their own right and were clearly already also strong role models and mentors for others in their communities. Secondly, they knew how to use their social networks and media to achieve for themselves and for others. In a sense they epitomised for us how our own methodologies could and should work effectively but they were doing it powerfully and effectively already and at grassroots level: they were combining people, programs and policies through the media and achieving so much!

We will return to their stories in later chapters but for now it is time to focus on another essential aspect of music, highlighting perhaps its most important quality for youth. That is its very physicality – the way music is created, experienced and performed through embodiment. We argue that all of the musical knowledge, practices and enterprises that the young people envisioned and engaged in, even those based on using new media technologies, were in fact firmly based on their own bodily praxis. That also indicates that we need to see all forms of music as a performance, 'an irreducible social phenomenon, even when only a single individual is involved' (Cook, 2003, p. 206). It is to these two aspects – embodiment and musical performance – that we turn now.

3
'Everyone Wants to be a DJ'

Photo 3.1 Everyone wants to be a DJ! © Kyle D'Andrea

I love (Pink's song) 'God is a DJ'. I think when I DJ it takes me away from the real life and gives me power of the crowd (helping control there emotions @ that time), like god has the power of the universe and it's a fantastic feeling to see what me as an individual can actually create with a few fantastic songs. On the other hand the song is very true, you get what your given and you choose how you use it. I'm a strong believer that Lyrics to songs can help motivate people in ones life and this song is a good motivator in many aspects, DJing, succeeding or just reaching a goal...[1]

Everyone wants to be a DJ. It's DJ mad. Thirteen and fourteen olds at school, which I was, you know, learning how to DJ, and they get jobs, and once all the jobs have gone... you have to volunteer for a night to do it and it'll be like, well we like ya. (Tuesday, personal communication, 30 September 2004)

Learning to play... (seriously!)

Music is ubiquitous; on the radio, iPods, Walkmans, computers, phone ringtones. It marks out our spaces and our sense of who we are. No wonder, then, that many young people aspire to be at the centre of their worlds by creating, managing and controlling the vibe, the mood of the crowd. To be a DJ means having the right networks, to have 'made it' in a way that is recognised as valuable by others, to have gained enough cultural and social capital to be recognised as 'somebody important' in your universe; to have gained enough of both self-respect and the respect of your peers, to be considered 'authentic' and not a 'try hard' or a 'loser'.

But how is this done? How did the youth who participated in this project go about gaining or attempting to gain the skills, techniques and knowledge that led to that respect of 'becoming a DJ', of acquiring that status of being recognised and accepted as a fully paid up member of their particular music scene? What processes of learning did they go through to acquire the perceived, necessary cultural, social and symbolic capital? What skills and techniques and knowledge did they deem necessary to reach their goals and the respect of their peers? In the previous chapters we set the scene by framing the ways the young people in our study had to learn 'the rules of the game' (Bourdieu and Wacquant, 1992), detailing how we observed these processes and how these 'rules' related to 'serious play'. This chapter now moves on to focus on the role of the skilled, controlled body to examine the ways serious play serves as a function of bodily praxis (Moore, 1994) and cultural capital (Bourdieu, 1993). We argue that these processes of learning and acquiring particular skills and knowledge are primarily based on struggling to attain excellence and confidence in bodily control and performance; in other words, they are consciously *embodied* aspects of serious play, from the first experimental steps to more confident, public moves. We note that such a progression is far from easy; it requires dedication, perseverance and appropriate external resources. But it is essential, for on its success depends the constitution and representation of the self.

This is a form of bodily praxis or 'body work' that Shilling described as 'the most immediate and important work of labour that humans engage in' (Shilling, 1993, p. 118). It is also a manifestation of Bourdieu's concept of physical and cultural 'capital' (Bourdieu, 1984; Wacquant and Bourdieu, 1992) used both to affirm social networks and allegiances as well as to differentiate one body from another. Yet, as the examples and vignettes below from our fieldwork illustrate, the 'currency' of this capital is unstable, frequently appearing to vary markedly from individual to individual, from group to group, even sometimes within the same social grouping. That is, for example, while particular hip hop crews might seem to share the same overall music tastes and acquire similar dress codes and performance styles and practices from each other through their global networks, at the same time local distinctions in terms of appropriate clothing, gestures, lyrics, place references, allegiances and language emphasise the significant and valued differences between the groups (Mitchell, 2001; Connell and Gibson, 2003; Rivera, 2003). Such differences indicate necessary symbolic knowledge and hard work, to denote both informed choice and distanciation 'from a vast commercial, retro, second-hand and cross-gender repertoire of possibilities' (Willis, 1998, p. 167). They are choices that mark out 'the structured collectivity of individuals as well as their differences from each other' (Willis, 1990, p. 12; see also Malbon, 1999, pp. 66–9).

Looked at from this perspective, all of the musical activities that the youth and their mentors in the Playing for Life project 'inhabited' (Willis, 1998, p. 164), can arguably be interpreted as being primarily centred on monitoring, managing and 'controlling' their bodies, learning to acquire and perfecting the appropriate musical skills,[2] the most appropriate ways to perform, stand, dress and speak within their particular cultural groupings. While not everyone can attain the status of celebrity as a DJ, this form of surveillance affirms to the self, as well as indicates to others, that the individual in question is an 'authentic' member of that particular grouping; they 'belong'. Through the adoption of particular cultural symbols *together with* a demonstration of competence of specific types of activities, the person signals to all both an individual and group allegiance, identity and 'taste'. Having the right stance and demeanour and adopting the appropriate argot clearly confers symbolic significance on the individuals of any social grouping and institution, acting iconically as direct pointers of social closure (Gerth and Mills, 1974). Clothes particularly can serve to single out 'certain social or physical attributes as the justificatory basis of exclusion' (Parkin, 1979, p. 44). To the initiated, clothes and style indicate whether the wearer has 'got the look' right, really belongs or is simply a 'try hard' (Nilan, 1992), a poor imitation of the real thing, 'a loser', one who attempts to indicate affiliation with a particular group but fails miserably to impress.

To understand this process, we return to our field notes to look more closely at each of these related aspects of bodily praxis in turn; the forms of dress code required in each experiential community; the ways in which particular physical techniques are taught and perfected whether in mixing, rapping, playing a musical instrument, skating or breaking and finally the kinds of language in each grouping to encourage and create insiders and exclude others. First, however, we revisit the concept of the DJ, as the extracts heading this chapter suggest, because it serves as a particularly valuable springboard to think through the complexity of this learning process and has implications and significance far beyond the simple notion of an entertainer. We are not limiting this concept of a DJ's status to hip hop, house, garage or electronica music scenes. Rather, we are applying it more broadly to consider the centrality of particular people in the various local music scenes who through their knowledge, expertise and networking skills are recognised as 'celebrities', 'archivists' as well as 'mentors' for the people within that experiential community and therefore also serve as an ideal or goal to be attained and perfected (Brewster and Broughton, 2000). So in that same category we include equally talented breakdancers, MCs, inline skaters, street artists, singers/musicians and producers in any genre and micro-culture of music practice. In other words, we are taking a creative 'poetic licence' here in appropriating the term 'DJ' to signify anyone who occupies a similar place in the worlds of youth music cultures. We refer primarily to those individuals who have gained significant recognition for their talents, skills and knowledge from their peers in their own music scene, for we believe that they have a similar role. More importantly, the use of the term allows us to focus on the complex processes of acquiring the necessary cultural capital – 'street cred' (credibility) – to gain that status.

Symbolic creativity

The original work of Paul Willis is useful here for he adds weight to our argument that such a role is built on play, on 'symbolic creativity', be it through performance, gesture, dress, adornment, style or demonstrating appropriate musical taste. Like Willis, we argue that such creative expression, which is serious and demanding, is 'not only part of everyday human activity, but also a...part of *necessary* work – that which has to be done every day, that which is not extra but essential to ensure the daily production and reproduction of human existence' (Willis 1990, p. 9, original emphasis).

In his later, more extended version of his earlier ethnographic study on symbolic creativity (1998), Willis argued for several overlapping claims:[3] firstly, that 'symbolic work', such as the *selection* and *management* of provided materials such as collecting and archiving music, clothing and artwork, is deeply embedded in the *reception* of cultural media. Secondly, that the practices of physical, emotional and semiotic *appropriation* of provided or 'found' materials produce new meanings and associations for the individuals often far from the original condition of production and 'social conditions of consumption'.[4] This results in new forms of symbolic and creative work that can be 'articulated, as it were, sideways for lateral and horizontal communication in much wider social relations not only of consumption but also of the connected *production* of meaning' (Willis, 1998, p. 164, all emphases, here and above, in the original).

While Willis was mainly challenging notions of passive media reception in this essay, his ideas also remind us that any such creative engagement with and use of media, music and art by youth is not only hard work and essential, but is also a practice that is fully embodied and, in his words, 'inhabited' (Willis, 1998, p. 164). That is, the world of popular culture in which young people engage is one in which they are both fully immersed (from the outside in) and in which they incorporate in the fullest sense of the word (from the inside out). They also clearly illustrate Bourdieu's insight that the relation between the social agent and the world is one of mutual possession.

This is not to argue, of course, that what is considered fashionable or appropriate for one particular grouping is forever fixed or static. What is fashionable today in clothing, gesture, style of music or language is often described disparagingly or nostalgically as dated or 'old skool' tomorrow. At the lower end of the contemporary fashion market, in strategic contrast to the dateless, classic image, there are a plethora of styles to choose from and a very rapid turnover of what is considered apt for the moment or situation. And yet simultaneously, within each experiential community there is an overall conformity in terms of length of hemlines, shape of tops or trousers, colours and style of outfit; which parts of the anatomy it is considered appropriate to emphasise or expose and which parts should be hidden. As ever, dress and clothing in all its forms frequently highlights experimentation with and displays of sexuality; with each era's and each cultural grouping's fashionable image often reflecting the contemporary mores and interpretation of sexuality and therefore which parts of the body are considered appropriately or excessively sexuality provocative – the waist, the breasts, hair, the legs and so on (see, for example, Tranberg Hansen, 2004a, 2004b). In the twenty-first century, with its emphasis on the rapid turnover of technology, material progress, physical speed and technological advances and convergences of all forms of media, the current fashionable image often seems to emphasise sexual daring, status and knowledge (Gill, 2008). Even in the photographic advertising still, this is portrayed in terms of the frozen moment capturing movement, speed, posture and gesture. Teenage models are pictured actively engaged in a group or as a romantic couple sharing an activity – having fun, eating or drinking, laughing – or they may be shown, with at least one of the group, staring assertively and unsmilingly at the camera. These are people who are 'going places', with confidence and attitude. One of DJ Shep's earliest homemade flyers created to advertise Da Klinic's workshops and retail offerings around Adelaide pictured several of his friends posing in just such a way, as in Photo 3.2.

All of these aspects of embodiment, including the importance of belonging (or being seen to belong) to a group were observed throughout our fieldwork, even if they were manifested in slightly different ways according to the various communities and groupings. In each case 'the body' was perceived as a crucial, malleable symbol that could be, and indeed needed to

Photo 3.2 Da Klinic promotional flyer. © Adrian Shepherd

be, managed and disciplined, in order for it to be acknowledged as a marker of success, through performance, dress, argot, style and posture.

All of this creative process occurs and is experienced, as Greg Corness notes, through 'the senses of the body, regardless of the media used to render it' (2008, p. 21). And yet, again we are reminded that such an interpretation is not trivial for the personal is also always political; such symbolic creativity can often seem to unsettle 'the most fundamental political and social conventions' (McClary, 1994, p. 33; Martin, 1990). McClary's words are echoed in the forceful lyrics of Baby Joker, a young male rapper from the Palais in Newcastle, who asserts through his words the ways in which his music affiliation and developed skills have offered him a new positive identity as 'a hip hop freak and break', one that both challenges and confronts his previous sense of educational and social failure:

> History: born, school fukked me up... and now im a hip hop freak and break. And ppl will be saying is it TRUE, is it YOU? they'll wanna SEE if its ME and every1 will wanna know how they can BE like ME. but they CANT and they RANT and they RAVE and return to their CAVE and every1 will be knowing who i am and where i CAME. (aka Baby Joker. Biographies of the Breakers, previously posted on Newcastle Palais website)[5]

Similar statements of affirmation were given by Codo, another young male breaker from the Palais. He told us that he used to be 'Really shy. You should have seen me at my old school.' But after a 'breaking' event at his new school, he noted that everyone was coming up and saying, 'Hey, you're the breakdancer!' He continued, 'Now everyone knows me!' He was visibly very proud of his breaking achievements and resultant social status. When he was probed further about his new-found confidence to perform in front of so many people (Did he like to do this?) Codo glowed. 'Yes, absolutely,' he affirmed. 'When I windmill [breaking power move] everyone just yells out [cheers]' (personal communication, May 2004).

Written from London, DJ Roland Samuel's Facebook social networking pages inform his friends of his continual battles with work, money and personal relationships alternating with his comments that demonstrate his continuous pride and pleasure, and indeed his sense of 'salvation', through his music-making and online Phatbeats radio show. Despite his constant anxieties and problems, his online profile page asserts

> MUSIC IS MY PASSION!
> I DON'T RISE TO LEVELS – I MAKE THEM!!
> MUSIC IS MY LIFE!!!!! ☺
>
> (DJ Roland Samuel, Facebook Profile circa 14 September 2010)

Across the world, in Boston, Juri's discussions with the young residents of the Brighton Treatment Center give further support to this litany of the positive psychological, phenomenological and physiological impact of music and music practices. Her intervention of bringing music lessons into the facility and to the residents there highlighted the significance not only of the music-making activities and enjoyment but also of the skills acquisition and the cultural capital.

> The music lessons helped me get a sense of how to put it [the music] all together so that when I get home I can show my peers how to put things together properly. I can add my own flavour. I feel I can really do something. I can make something real productive.
>
> (K (aged 17) at Brighton Treatment Center, 2005)

Such comments are particularly poignant when one considers that all of the young residents in such centres previously had only had a continual experience of failure and dissatisfaction in their relatively short lives.

I got very emotional watching C's growing delight in what he could do on the piano. It brought to life all of what we KNOW about the importance of self-affirmation, self-esteem, of learning, creativity and so forth. A textbook exemplar of why we are undertaking the research! M exemplified this too although his session was more low key than C's. M told me he also learnt to play piano with Juri and that his Mum had told him she might buy him a piano when he 'got out'. He was due for release 'any day' and he really wanted to continue his piano and computerised sequencing.

(Margaret, fieldwork personal reflections, 2005. See also Chapter 7)

Any discussion of learning how to be successful, how to acquire and achieve a level of recognised competence or even excellence in particular cultures, then, forcefully brings us back to the relationship between music and embodiment. Achieving cultural and symbolic capital means gaining particular technical and physical skills, manifesting the right level of cultural knowledge through performance and consumption patterns and demonstrating peer recognition and acceptance. As such, clearly, the body is also seen as the 'site of enormous symbolic work and symbolic production' (Turner, 1996, p. 190). A 'work in progress', it is most frequently conceived of as a 'reflexive project' (Giddens, 1991, p. 5; see also Lyons, 1978; Baumeister, 1986; Rainwater, 1989). It is a project that is never complete (Bloustien, 2003b, p. 270) but is seen as endlessly perfectible (Rodin, 1992, p. 58; Dutton, 1995; Jones, 2008).

On the other hand, as our young participants and their mentors continually demonstrated, achieving perfect control of the body was rarely a goal in itself, despite the endless magazine articles and other media programs that regularly seem to promote the way the body can be 'sculpted', 'transformed' and 'rebuilt' (as, for example, Rosenbaum, 2005, amongst many). Rather, for the youth we worked with such control was seen as a sign of the *quality of the effort*, and of the emotional investment. It was the symbol of the required determination, and the disciplined commitment for self-making in late modernity. Monitoring and controlling performance and style thus serves as an essential path to developing symbolic capital and gaining full 'card-holder' group membership, to becoming and appearing 'authentic'. To understand this more fully, we need to revisit the concept of the 'body project' and deconstruct the idea of reflexive embodiment as a mode of knowledge. As we shall see, it is central to performed and visual subjectivity and underpins all other forms of capital, as the next section elucidates further.

Becoming authentic: symbolic capital through embodiment

In more recent years, the concept of bodily praxis, the process by which a theory, lesson or skill is enacted or practised and realised through the body, being the basis of self-knowledge, seems to have shifted and fragmented into new forms of self-identity. New forms of knowledge and cultural capital through the body have taken hold, gaining new vigour (and commercial potential!) as a powerful universalising idea, underpinned in late modernity by the current era's globalising tendencies, its new forms of mediated experiences and its dialectic between the global and the local. For many around the globe, particularly although not exclusively in the West, traditional ways of life have become less compelling and attractive for everyday practice, with the result that self-identity in turn has become increasingly 'a reflexively organized endeavour' (Giddens, 1991, p. 5). Giddens goes on to argue that the body itself has come more into focus, progressively seen and understood as 'a phenomenon of choices and options' (Giddens, 1991, p. 8) – although, as ever, the desire and ability to be able to draw on those potential choices and options is limited by one's education, cultural capital and social positioning.[6]

The changing ways of interpreting embodiment and how it relates to cultural and personal identities has underpinned a great deal of research in cultural studies especially in work that focuses on youth cultures (as in Hebdige, 1979, 1988; Lesko, 1988; Willis et al., 1993; Willis, 1998). This focus on embodiment is clearly central to related ideas in education and educational psychology, and social and cultural anthropology, as for example in the works of Bourdieu (1984, 1990), Turner (1984), Taussig (1987, 1993), Jaggar and Bordo (1989), Featherstone, Hepworth and Turner (1991) and McSharry (2009). It has of course long framed understandings of gender and of the identity construction and self-representation of children and adolescents (Smith, 1988; Ardener, 1993; Bordo, 1993; Moore, 1994; Coleman, 2008; Hickey Moody, 2009). More recently studies in experiences in virtual worlds have only served to reinforce the relationship of our physical selves to online social networking sites (Christie and Bloustien, 2010) and three-dimensional online environments (Bloustien and Wood, forthcoming), even when those Web2 worlds are furnished and inhabited primarily through our imagination. The physical body in these understandings is still the locus and the primary symbol of simultaneously acquiring, articulating and negotiating understandings of the world, reminding us again of Bourdieu's insight that 'bodies take metaphors seriously' (1990, pp. 71–2). Moreover, for youth particularly, as Wexler argued, bodily expression is a highly significant indicator of young people's search for cultural expression: 'The new social movements are movements of identity and not traditional economic and political movements... they are the movements of the body, of personal freedom in daily life' (cited in Lesko, 1988, p. 127; see also Bloustien, 2003b, pp. 67–110).

As we entered and were invited to engage in the worlds of the youth in our project we were immediately reminded of the various ways in which teenagers expressed themselves physically, often quite differently from us adult researchers. Delight in physicality and particularly a lack of inhibition was everywhere, whether we were watching the young people on air at their radio shows, at their planning meetings and at their organised events or gigs, or at hip hop, graffiti art or rock workshops, rehearsals and concerts. Take, for example, our observations at even relatively formal planning meetings such as the one by the *Youth Revolutions* radio show crew, held at Playford Council offices, Adelaide, in the second year of our study (14 January 2004). The members attending on that occasion were three central male members, Bret, Michael and Will (with two members of the academic research team present as contributing participant-observers). Disparate personalities and styles of interaction amongst the small group were immediately obvious: Michael was a very rapid speaker, jumping from one thought to the next and rushing through his verbal interactions in trying to keep up. He was acting as chairperson, and therefore essentially dominated and controlled the meeting. Interjections from others were often overrun as he continued voicing his thoughts but then would come back to what had previously been said, presumably as it filtered past his own internal narrative. He also used his chair as if it were on wheels, despite the lack thereof, which involved lots of shuffling between the whiteboard and table. Bret, in contrast, on this occasion was very laid back, offering ideas and information in a quieter, assured manner – most unusual for him as he tended to be quite ebullient and physically take over physical and sonic space. He and Michael did banter often that day, however, playfully ridiculing or 'paying each other out' at every opportunity, without seeming to take much notice of what was actually being said. Bret's conversation on that occasion flowed and looped indiscriminately between discussion of the radio program details, to how much he missed Vanessa, his girlfriend, who was interstate, to various macho exploits. Will was quieter but not quite diffident, demonstrating a 'backbone of steel', which we were to recognise far more regularly on later occasions. He spoke quietly, but firmly, interjecting his voice into the conversation and would not let the others talk over him. His quiet manner of speaking also allowed him to carry on conversation across the others, even whilst Bret and Michael were bantering.

A central aspect of 'body watching' is the internalisation of surveillance, both of oneself and of others; any changes in appearance through clothes, haircuts or skin were immediately noticed and publicly commented upon in contrast to ways that adults tend to learn to suppress or qualify such comments, unless among family members or very close friends. At this meeting, for example, one of the topics mooted for a future show by Michael was 'self-image'. Bret then elaborated this theme by suggesting the focus be 'fashion disaster'. He recommended that Michael undertake the main research required because 'he is one'! Michael agreeably wrote this up on the whiteboard whilst protesting he had a much better fashion sense than Bret, admonishing 'look at what *you're* wearing!'

This lack of inhibition and freedom from the accepted niceties of (adult) social interaction, as indicated above, still have to be managed or controlled to show affiliation and belonging for particular social groupings, according to the particular codes expected of each grouping or experiential community. Appropriate behaviour, dress and conversation are just as important for demonstrating the correct physical and technical skills for marking out and monitoring symbolic boundaries between one body and the next even within the same social, classed or ethnic grouping. The overall aim is to achieve the right level of discipline of one's body for membership of the desired microculture, aided and monitored by one's peers and other members of one's social networks.

Yet it is important to remember, as indicated above, that even though the rules of behaviour are consciously taught and acquired over time, their contextualising social framing and justifications are often *not* consciously acquired. Rather they are absorbed as embodied facets of one's everyday environment, one's 'habitus', within a particular social field (Bourdieu, 1977, 1993), deeply embedded within the broader context of one's taken-for-granted social and cultural institutions and communities. They are normalised and naturalised – 'the way things are' or 'what one needs to do' – in order to be accepted or at ease in one's selected social grouping. At the same time, the framing context or paradigm that strongly influences exactly *what* one selects, teaches and amends to pass on to the next 'generation' of one's particular social field, as valuable or authentic, 'cool', 'wikkid' or 'deadly' or their opposites, is still determined by social and cultural worlds in which one is immersed. So what we often perceive as the ability to be innovative or creative, or as the freedom to be spontaneous, is still determined by 'the encounter between a socially constituted *habitus* and a particular position that is already instituted or *possible* in the division of labour of cultural production' (Bourdieu, 1993, p. 141, original emphasis).

In this way the particular vocabulary and gestures used to indicate approval, disaffection or opprobrium for cultural objects and behaviours in one's community are the products of one's *habitus*, acquired both by indirect subconscious mimetic posturing and performance and by direct instruction, as we shall see.

'Music through my skin': coolness and belonging

The art of being 'in the know' means having possession of the right knowledge, look, language and posture. Such bodily praxis, because it *is* so deeply entrenched within one's microculture, often appears as innate or 'second nature'. As Dave, a seasoned breaker at the Newcastle Palais, eloquently affirmed, the power and impact of music affiliation often appear to be subconscious, affecting the body's posture, dress, vocabulary and attitude without the individual necessarily being fully aware of its influence (see, for example, the research by Bruner and Gordon, 1990; McNamara and Ballard, 1999; Williams, 2001; Stein, 2004). As with many of the young people in our study, music was perceived as all-encompassing so that its influence became normalised and axiomatic, 'because' as Dave notes 'it just comes through, through my skin'.

> My life is hip hop. From the way I dress, the way I have my hair braided...um...the way I talk to people. And not...purposely, that's because it just comes through, through my skin. Um, I don't sit down and think 'I've gotta talk this way' or 'I've gotta buy these sneakers', just through hip hop, it appeals to me, you know what I mean?
>
> (Dave, Newcastle breaker, personal communication, 2004)

Such intense ways of physically experiencing one's music taste, affiliation, practice and consumption have profound social, cultural and political ramifications (McClary, 1994, p. 33). Bourdieu (1984) reminds us that musical taste or preference should be perceived as far more than conscious and intellectual choice for music is not only 'the most spiritualistic of the arts' (Bourdieu, 1993, p. 103) but also one that transforms immediately into bodily expression.

> It ravishes, moves, stores, carries away: it is not so much beyond words as below them, in movements of the limbs and body, rhythms, excitements and slowings, tensions and releases. The most 'mystical', the most 'spiritual' of the arts is perhaps simply the most corporeal. (Bourdieu, 1993: 105)

Several decades earlier, in his groundbreaking article on the influential impact of music, Roland Barthes too described the powerful corporeal communication between performer and listener, which relies on the 'grain of the voice' (1977, pp. 179–89). He was alluding to the gritty physicality of music that is often overlooked when we consider its aesthetic, intellectual practice. As academic researchers in the field, we were powerfully reminded of Barthes' words ourselves on many occasions. One particularly memorable occasion was on our second visit to Café Lietze in Charlottenburg in 2003.

Photo 3.3 Totally Stressed in performance. © Sandra Wildeboer

There, as part of our investigation of the varied youth centres around Berlin, some of the Playing for Life academic researchers first met the members of Totally Stressed, an all-female acoustic art rock band, which we introduced briefly at the beginning of the book. Even at that first meeting as we watched them in performance, transforming the tiny space of the church-based youth club, we were struck by their raw energy, their determination and their musical skills; through moments of mimetic excess, as illustrated in the image of Tine, Magda and the band taken at Ladyfest 2010 in Berlin on September 17 2010 (Photo 3.3).

We noted how the band members became totally immersed within the sonic experience, a blurring of body, microphone, stage, audience – returning us dramatically to Dave's reference to 'music through the skin'. We were also reminded in watching and listening to this dynamic performance that in all of the research sites we had investigated so far we had talked to relatively few female musicians and certainly no other rock bands consisting solely of female members, except for the youth rehearsing at Tietzia-Madcheneinrichtung, at the time a girls'-only facility in a disadvantaged area in West Berlin.

Some of the reasons for this gender inequity were reflected in the stories later recounted to us by the various members of Totally Stressed. They told of their many difficulties in negotiating and appropriating the necessary space, place and acceptance to realise their determinedly feminist music practices as white, female musicians, particularly when they were performing in the mainly multiracial, mainly hyper-masculinised spaces of East Berlin. It particularly affected their choice of stage clothes.

Markers of distinction

The members of Totally Stressed were not alone in their concerns about their appearance as artists and the effect that their clothes had on their performance. This was so for almost all of the young people who were equally articulate about the need for the right, comfortable clothes for the task of performing. We had noted the mix of skirts, trousers and ties when these girls performed on stage, which, we assumed, was a way of indicating difference and style and challenging limiting gender stereotyping. Magda was far more explicit, however, about the eclectic selection of their stage clothing.

> If you don't feel comfortable, it is hard to loosen up. So I used to think personally about what I should wear so I wouldn't wear things that are so tight. You have to be able to dance and encourage others to dance. So we wear outfits that allow us to move easily on stage.
>
> (Personal correspondence, 2010)

But she also then went on to express the band's perceived need to assert their strong *female* stage presence and persona as well as their technical and musical prowess.

> It's true that we realized very early that we weren't just musicians but female musicians. And being a girl in your teenage years also means that you most likely struggle with body issues, so appearance on stage becomes an important issue – maybe even more than for teenage boys. However, I don't think that it was particularly important for us to be recognized as female musicians because we knew that this always meant that we were different. Today, the aspiration might be different though: Today I believe it's important to be recognized as competent female musician but not because we don't want to be 'just another rock band' but because being on stage as a female represents some sort of role model for other young female musicians. Plus, it also distorts the stereotypical picture that we have of a typical rock musician – a male.
>
> Initially, the more we played the more we got comments about the fact that being an all girls band was strange or different. People would say 'Oh you are an all *girls*' band, that's unusual!' And sound engineers started saying 'Oh an all girls band!' and would start to automatically

show us how where to put the cables. So then we started to notice ourselves that we *were* an all girls' band!

(Personal correspondence, 2010)

Just as Bloustien found in her earlier work (2003b), in this project the authors also noticed the ubiquitous and rigorous (self-)monitoring of clothes and behaviour by young women, in the various rock, techno and rave events we attended in person or vicariously through the camera footage. On stage it was clear that women felt they had to be particularly careful how they portrayed themselves in order to be regarded as serious musicians or artists. In that earlier project several of the very talented female drummers commented that if they wanted to be appreciated as artists they had to wear unisex or masculinised clothes that played down or concealed their femininity.

One example from this project that confirmed this difficulty for young women occurred at The Best Unsigned Music, an important music event hosted by the Tabernacle, Notting Hill. While it appeared imperative there, according to the discussion and comments that circulated in the arena, for all of the young people on stage to feel they were performing and were seen to perform as 'professional musicians', it seemed to be especially so for the young women! This meant indicating the correct knowledge, style and appreciation of the music and dressing in a way that indicated 'musician' rather than 'female'. The event was advertised as 'The best artists from different production companies performing in one night, backed by London's best band Groove Unit.' Hosting the night was a well-known MC named Rahsaan, formerly of the group Damage, and the flyer said he was 'giving his first appearance since leaving the group'. He shared the headline spot with Shola Ama, an established young English singer who had scored her biggest hit in 1997 with a cover of American singer and guitarist Turley Richards' record 'You Might Need Somebody'. A number of record company people were there, and were obviously expected for we noticed in the performance space that the first two rows of seats were reserved for VIPs. Just after 8.30 p.m. the lights dimmed and the show got underway. The majority of the audience were clearly local, and appeared to be of Trinidadian or Caribbean background with only a scattering of Caucasians. This mix was also reflected in the performances where, apart from the two white back-up singers, the only white girl group that performed was Bredfrute. This girl group caused a wave of laughter through the audience as soon as they appeared because of what they were wearing – or not wearing. One of the girls had a sheer rainbow-coloured top on and no bra. With the stage lighting it was completely see through and this was made even more pronounced by the sexy movements that accompanied her singing, including her thrusting her breasts. They did three songs, but it seemed that no one was listening to the music. There was loud chattering and laughter throughout. One young woman called out loudly 'They're not even real', and between the laughter some young men to the left of the stage took out their camera phones to try to take photos of the girl(s). It was a relief when the next female singer took the stage looking very sophisticated and professional. The second-to-last act was singer Tanya Tee with her three accompanying dancers. She not only sang but occasionally joined in the choreographed routine, gaining the respect and attention of the audience. One young man commented loudly and with an expression of appreciative awe, 'she's scary looking!'

For audience members, one's credibility as an authentic member of the experiential community was equally essential. This meant being aware of the appropriateness of one's appearance and clothing on the dance floor or at other events and therefore of how one would be perceived by others. In the initial period of our fieldwork, in 2003, when we attended electronica, rave and garage dance events at all of our sites, our initial, uninformed impressions were that both sexes seemed to wear similar unisex baggy outfits, oversized T-shirts, and wide short cargo pants or long baggy trousers. Fairly quickly, however, we started to notice the explicit, more restricted, gendered dress and behavioural codes for young women. When we looked again, more closely, at the video footage and photographs of the raves, techno, garage and house dance events that we attended in person or vicariously through the footage of the co-researchers, we started to notice the ways that many girls dressed in exaggeratedly feminine styles. Rather than large loose shapeless tops (clearly more comfortable to dance in) these girls would wear short-cropped tops and tight close-fitting pants or short skirts. Often also in strapless or see-through tops, and high stilettos, the girls would reduce their ability to dance freely, limiting their 'dance floor footprint', as it were, restricting their space and their movements. While these clothes were clearly less suitable for dancing, they served a different purpose, marking their wearers out as ultra feminine and therefore more exaggeratedly female.

This seemed in contrast to those young women on stage, as indicated above, where this kind of appearance would tend to invite ridicule rather than admiration. We also noticed in the early days of our fieldwork that several girls at the dance events would take on an infantilised look, possibly deliberately as an ironic or retro appearance. These girls would often arrive with their hair in tiny bunches or little plaits, holding lollipops or large oversized pacifiers, reminiscent of small children. In these clothes they would feel at liberty to take up more space on the dance floor and seemed to be less self-conscious in their dance movements. It was as if this type of costuming became a form of mask that allowed greater freedom and less inhibition.

More recently and in the later periods of our fieldwork, the images and costumes on the dance floor appear to have changed. As with the rapid turnover and fragmentation of technology and media, the dress codes too seem to have altered and become more eclectic. As the numbers of large outdoor or illicit raves everywhere have declined, for pragmatic, political and cultural reasons, smaller house or club parties and outside music festivals have flourished. At these events the participants dress in a much broader range of styles, according to their particular 'neo-tribe' (Maffesolli, 1996; Bennett, 1999), local music scene or community of music. There seems to be far more retro clothing worn, especially from the 1980s. Some of our young co-researchers noted that in the recent decade of the 'noughties' a more generic unisex style was popular, with shorts seeming to be still shorter and tops more revealing whatever the gender of the wearer.

However, our fieldwork showed us other areas where it seems to be still difficult for young women to gain and demonstrate their competences apart from their stage, vocal and instrumental performances. There was of course considerable expertise to be acquired in other fields related to music practices, for example, learning to host a live-to-air broadcast or internet radio program or to organise and coordinate gigs or large-scale music events. Both of these areas required demonstrated confidence, technical, communication, management and organisational skills – as well as cultural knowledge of popular and local music genres and bands.

The radio show *Youth Revolutions* was originally the brainchild of Vanessa, a very competent 15-year-old from the northern suburbs of Adelaide, and it was her determination and drive that kept the program running for as long as it did. All of the young people who were involved in *Youth Revolutions* had to learn particular technical skills to manage the sound equipment and how to host the show smoothly, as does anyone hosting a conventional broadcast media or internet radio program. At this radio station this meant they all had to undergo formal training and gain certificates of competence. In the language of the *Youth Revolutions* radio host organisation (PBA-FM) this task was called learning to 'drive' the show, an expression that initially caused some of the academics on the team some confusion when they heard the youth talk about other adults coming to the radio station as 'drivers'. Until the young people gained their licence or certificate to drive the show, they were considered on probation and an adult technician had to staff the controls for them.

Two of the most competent and responsible members of *Youth Revolutions* were in fact two young women: Vanessa and another teenager called Monique. However, we noticed that despite their obvious abilities both young women tended to be self-deprecating and non-assertive when they negotiated their on-air roles with young men in their team. They often yielded to their male companion's choice of music to be played on air, for example, and Monique particularly would continually refer to her own lack of abilities when she made a mistake or felt she had failed to follow a discussion. Clearly, an intelligent, very attractive young woman with abundant fair hair, in these situations she frequently alluded to her own shortcomings as a result of 'her blondeness'.[7] One of many such occasions was a *Youth Revolutions* radio program in 2004 where the topic chosen for the show was 'divorce'. Monique had brought in considerable printed material to work from, painstakingly collated from a range of sources. This was her usual practice when she was responsible for the background research. On air, Monique drew on her material by reading aloud through a number of lists and documents, including facts about divorce, issues children deal with when their parents are separating, and the benefits of divorce. Although she was always well-prepared with information, her lack of confidence was reflected in the way Monique tended to read from her material as opposed to referring to ideas and speaking more informally. While she read out the information, it was left to the other members of the team to pick up on an issue, expand it and open out the discussion.

During the final track of that program, while the group was off air, Garth and Phillip got into a personal discussion about trading cards, which was clearly nothing to do with their topic that night. Monique looked on in bemusement. When Phillip commented innocently that he was 'a card short of a deck' everyone else laughed, although Monique then admitted that she had not understood the joke. She said she was just laughing because everyone else was. Bret and Vanessa then explained the meaning of the phrase, as being a colloquialism meaning that one is stupid or crazy. Monique asked quite ingenuously, 'but shouldn't it be a deck short of a card?' She then again dismissed her lack of understanding as due to her 'blondeness'. She also frequently referred to herself as blonde on air when she misunderstood a question from one of the others. This was consistent with Bret's teasing, which also made reference to her 'blondeness', implying a woman who is foolish or scatter-brained. When Vanessa or Garth teased Monique they tended to do so without referring disparagingly to her hair colour and thereby linking this to her supposed stupidity (field notes, 2004).

So it seemed to us at all of our sites that it was hard to escape from the restrictions of gender stereotyping either as part of a performance, task or cultural or social grouping. Of course in some genres and music scenes the performers would deliberately and aggressively emphasise their gender and sexuality through appearance, posture and lyrics. Yet we found in our own fieldwork that overall there was a tendency for the young musicians and performers, both men and women, to play down any marked gendering of their appearance, with the aim of taking attention away from their sexualised bodies so that the focus would be more on their music and technical skills and less on the adornment. The only times we saw this challenged was when an outfit was deliberately selected as an ironic statement or retro image, deliberately playing against conventional gendered attributes, or as a way of demonstrating a body toned and controlled with practice and commitment; or when the individual wanted to emphasise a particular body line in a difficult movement such as in breakdancing or inline skating. We will return to this aspect shortly.

Clothing and cultural capital

Clearly one of the most visual ways in which one's body can assert authentic membership 'to keep the vibe good' is how one is dressed. Which clothes and brands are selected, purchased, adorned and how they are worn indicates that one is a bona fide member of the grouping or a loser or try hard and that one's body can be seen with confidence (see Bloustien, 2003b, pp. 82–90). In fact in all of the communities and young people we worked with clothes were clearly central as a manifestation of the self and again a visible sign of one's group allegiance.

Several of the young people made a point of talking about their favourite clothes or proudly displayed their new items to us, commenting on and off camera about the importance of the garments for their self-image. We noted above Kyle's enthusiastic demonstration of his 'rave gear', complete with sparkles, flared pants and elaborate headbands and indeed, quite early in our relationship, he would elaborate on the importance of clothes to indicate belonging and authenticity. For example, in the following exchange Kyle talked about a recent Adelaide music event he had attended and the importance of his outfit to his sense of social belonging and 'authenticity'.

> I really enjoyed the 'Two Tribes' especially the Prodigy set. You know there are three types of people who go to 'commercial' events like 'Two Tribes': an older crowd of 'old school' people; young ravers and 'losers' who are only there because they think it is a cool place to be seen. You know the 'real ravers' because they are the ones that say 'that just looks wikid' [about Kyle's rave outfit] whereas the losers just sneer because they don't understand.
>
> (Kyle, personal conversation, 2005)

Costuming at raves can be very elaborate. The Two Tribes event in Adelaide in 2005 was the first time that Kyle had dressed up for a rave, his outfit including fashion eye contact lenses, which he said he had wanted for a while. He had finally managed to obtain some 'with flames' which would last for about 40 'wears' which for him meant 40 different raves. He had also dyed his hair red, wore a flashing mouth guard and baggy green wave trousers with transparent cargo pockets. He had filled his pockets with glo-sticks and had also wound these glo-sticks through his shoelaces. Other people commented that they thought the glo-sticks looked particularly 'cool' and many immediately emulated his style, winding glo-sticks around their shoelaces too. He had purchased his clothes at a skate store that also sold rave gear and commented that the year before he had seen similar clothes and had thought 'who would wear that shit? – and now I do!'

A few years later, over a quiet coffee and chat, Kyle told us with a rueful grin that he was embarrassed now about the way he had dressed then, captured in his original footage.

> I used to be a raver but now, I am much more into production and being professional. I have to wear different clothing. Look I want to apologise for all the nonsense I put on the camera. I looked right through the video I did and now it seems bizarre. I have changed now. I feel more responsible. I don't party as much.
>
> (Kyle, personal correspondence 2010)

Clothing, appearance, posture and argot can clearly indicate authenticity through allegiance both to social groupings, geographical spaces and places as well as indicating individuality and distinction from others (Malbon, 1999, p. 51). Ben Malbon refers to this as 'the management of cool' (1999, p. 57), inverting Goffman's (1963) thesis on stigma. He argues:

> Goffman looks at those individuals who are in possession of 'attributes which may be deeply discrediting'. I am looking at a situation where individuals may be, or may aspire to be, in possession of attributes that may be socially desirable or attractive. Where Goffman concentrates upon the management of a 'spoiled identity', I am interested instead in the management of what may be the opposite – a 'cool identity'. (Malbon, 1999, p. 58)

As both Ben Malbon (1999) and Tim Wall (2006) have noted, creating a 'cool' persona is articulated through bodily movement, technique, posture and performativity. According to Sarah Thornton (1995), 'coolness' amounts to 'subcultural capital'.

> In addition to the three major types of capital – cultural, economic and social – Bourdieu elaborates many subcategories of capital that

operate within particular fields such as 'linguistic', 'academic', 'intellectual', 'information' and 'artistic capital'. One characteristic that unifies these capitals is that they all play within Bourdieu's own field, within his social world of players with high volumes of institutionalised cultural capital. However, it is possible to observe subspecies of capital operating within other less privileged domains. In thinking through Bourdieu's theories in relation to the terrain of youth culture, I have come to conceive of 'hipness' as a form of subcultural capital. (Thornton, 1995, p. 11)

Although Thornton's reconception of Bourdieu's notions of capital has been extremely influential, we actually prefer to use Bourdieu's original terms, feeling that they already incorporate notions of youth culture and values. In fact, we feel that talking about 'subcultural capital' can obfuscate rather than elucidate the issues of cultural transfer since, as we will argue further in the following chapters, the forms of capital we observed in our fieldwork were closely tied to adult worlds and not separate enclaves or 'terrains' of youth culture. For the time being, it is worth noting that Thornton applied Bourdieu's original notion of cultural capital and distinction to the ways the young people differentiated themselves from each other within the youth cultures she studied in the UK. She argued 'subcultural capital' could be expressed and embodied in 'forms of fashionable haircuts and well assembled record collections... in the form of being "in the know" using (but not overusing) current slang and looking as if you were born to perform the latest dance styles' (Thornton, 1995, pp. 11–12). She also pointed out that the obverse was clearly true, since lapses or failures in such attempts – mismanagement of 'cool' – has the result that one appears to be a 'try hard' or 'a loser'. Rowland, for example, was scathing about the way many of the followers of R&B, garage and hip hop in the UK in the clubs that he was attending seemed far too influenced by American style, including sexist and violent imagery.

> I'm not negative, my mum never brought me up to be that, and when I saw people at clubs or the bigger images I'd see girls with their butts hanging out in lingerie – not meaning I don't like that stuff but there's a time and place and a limit to it. The kids are getting influenced by this stuff, but they're (in) England, its our whole image and identity, but they're dressing and all talking American, they're all walking like it, they're causing all the violence, and I'm like, come on now, give me a break, know what I mean?
>
> (Personal correspondence, 2004)

For all of the music cultures and scenes, clothing was both taken-for-granted by emulation ('that is what you wear') and a self-conscious attempt at self-branding ('this is who I am'). So we became used to seeing the particular markers of 'authentic' hip hop allegiance being the oversized sweatshirts or hoodies, the baggy pants and the baseball caps (previously worn backwards) and the more casual tight-fitting clothes of the techno dancers. Understandings of body image as 'the mental image of one's body as it appears to others' (Featherstone, 2010, p. 194), particularly through consumer culture, are not limited to music cultures, of course. Similarly, Rowland's comments above, about the gap between authenticity and appearing as a 'loser' or a 'try hard', points to something that moves beyond the visual and external. Young people create and affirm their sense of identity through a range of factors, many of them non-visual. Indeed the relationship between desire, image, marketing and identity has become an increasingly complex concept. Or to put it another more colloquial way – it is not just the clothes but the way that you wear them.

Massumi (2002) referred to the concept of the *affective* body image, the notion of the way a body 'experiences or gives off intensities which refuse to cohere into a distinctive image' (Featherstone, 2010, p. 196). Mike Featherstone, for example, explores the role of new technologies and affect arguing that placed alongside 'the conventional sense of body image as something that is fashionable and is actively constructed' (2010, p. 199) is an idea of

> The affective body without image, the more incomplete and open body, which is affected by other people's bodies in a variety of ways, which bypass the alleged 'all seeing eye' and work beneath the level of consciousness and language. (Featherstone, 2010, p. 199)

Increasingly, then, because concepts of authenticity are based on a 'more incomplete and open body' understandings of what constitutes 'the real thing', 'the authentic', the 'hard core' are socially mediated (Gilpin, Palazzolo and Brody 2010), meaning that

> Authority (is) no longer seen as residing within a specific medium or media source: authority is instead earned through a combination of routine practices, meeting audience or reader expectations, and persuasiveness. (Robinson, 2007, cited in Gilpin, Palazzolo and Brody, 2010, p. 262)

Hence the importance of the integrated hip hop workshop and clothing retail outlet Da Klinic, as described in Chapter 1. DJ Shep and his crew explained to us that clothing was the central way in which the business made money and maintained the other aspects of the centre. But it clearly was also a place where people who wanted to 'look' part of the scene could be assured their clothing would be appropriate. This is not simply because of Shep's acknowledged authority on knowing what is fashionable and right for the scene but because of the response from the wider experiential fashion labels indicating affiliation to a particular music genre is still important though. Every week, DJ Shep promotes 'special items of interest' such as particular outfits or accessories on the official Da Klinic's Facebook pages, announcing such promotions as 'Da Klinic The new Boba Feit Star Wars / Adidas ZX Kick's, just in at Da Klinic. Sooooooooo cooooooool' (Da Klinic's Facebook page, 22 August 2010).

Such advertisements immediately lead to dialogic response, queries and discussions from interested purchasers in the experiential community, such as:

J: fuck yes!!!!!!!!
P: how much? ad
J: $960
P: no way.
J: ha-ha calm down i was joking
P: loll thought so·
J: an the real price is something like 200$·
P: ask..(Y)
Da Klinic: $249 - only 1 of each size !
P: loll fake
J: Ha-ha I was so close

(Da Klinic's Facebook posted circa 22 August 2010)

Yet selecting the right look can lead to a paradox for not all the clothes are most appropriate for the task! As the selected outfit had to be comfortable and appropriate for the performing or dancing, this could sometimes lead to a dilemma. For example, in Newcastle DJ Mathmatics's (Dave's) considerable breaking skills could be seriously impeded when he chose style over pragmatics. Julie noted that occasionally when Dave's practised move was less than the perfection he expected of himself, he would look embarrassed and blame his homeboy shorts: 'I can't break in these shorts', he admitted sheepishly (cited in Julie's field notes, 2004).

The clothes also have to be able to enhance or at least not encumber the appearance of the body line as one executes the perfect inline jump, breaker move or dance step. Note the line of the body in the photo of inline skaters, with correct arm and leg extensions (Photo 3.4).

106 *Youth, Music and Creative Cultures*

Photo 3.4   Watch that line! Vaky breakdancing photo. © Adrian Shepherd

Learning to play it cool

The primary markers of symbolic and cultural capital are under constant surveillance and monitoring, ensuring that 'the vibe' is maintained and 'kept good'. As indicated by the examples above, this is first and most overtly denoted through the body's outward appearance and gestures – the total image – which is an attempt to reinforce and reflect the self-contained demeanour. In all of the sites, and in all of our discussions with the youth where we were either participating or overhearing discussions about 'the right vibe', the 'authentic', 'keeping it real' or the idea of 'looking cool', we found that both boys and girls saw a particular type of clothing or look as denoting cultural knowledge and self-possession within their specific social grouping or local music scene. In some cases that meant acquiring and sporting particular fashion labels, brands or designs, either new or second-hand. Or in other groups a more retro look was favoured obtained through op (opportunity) or charity shops. Other groupings particularly inscribed their sense of difference on the skin, through tattoos or piercings; still others by what was ingested and emitted. As should be clear by now, we are arguing that what one does defines who one is. In all cases the portrayal of the body through clothes, style and image was an important aspect of the performed right to authentic membership.

It has long been noted that in all cultures, choices in fashion, style, music taste, slang and in other cultural symbols 'do not necessarily... revolt against normative social frameworks or aim to breach borders of social control and regularity' (Jacobson and Luzzatto, 2004, p. 169; also see Fisher, 2002). Instead they are often used to differentiate oneself from others, either by maintaining relationships and networks considered positive and beneficial or by reinforcing boundaries between the self and others whom one does not like (Cialdini et al., 1976; Bryson, 1996; Jackson et al., 1996). But appearing too similar even to one's friends can also be an issue! As Jacobson and Luzzatto state in their insightful phenomenological study of body adornments such as tattooing and piercing amongst Israeli youth, there is frequently a 'certain tension between the wish to be similar to members of the peer group and the desire to be original and unique' (2004, p. 161). Much of the literature asserts that intergroup differentiation and distinctiveness drives people to attempt differentiation from people who seem too similar to themselves because most people have a strong drive to appear unique (Lynn and Snyder, 2002; Jetten and Spears, 2003). Berger and Heath (2008) have recently argued that people differentiate themselves from others by cultural artefacts and symbols to stress what they call 'identity-signaling' (2008). They do this

> to better understand their place in the social environment or reduce their internal uncertainty about who they are (e.g. Hogg 2000) [and]... to ensure that others understand who they are. In particular people often diverge to avoid sending undesired identity signals to others. (Berger and Heath, 2008, p. 595)

In all cases too the main persona sought is one of individual choice and discernment, the implication being that the clothes and/or physical appearance are making a statement about the wearer's cultural knowledge and status that the individual chooses to emphasise. The central core/leaders in the grouping set the tone of what is supposed to be worn by others if they want to appear knowledgeable and culturally aware. They do this by wearing the clothes, the hairstyles, the tattoos, the piercings and accessories themselves and making derogatory remarks about other styles of clothing or appearance. Again these clothes, styles and demeanours not only suggest group identity but often hint at a wider musical fandom and particular related leisure activities.

'It's a mind thing': the role of the mentor

Interestingly, it was feminist writing long ago that particularly attested to Foucault's original work concerning the significance and goal of the disciplined body (Smith, 1988; Bordo, 1993) and the moral surveillance and responsibility that this entails. More recent studies of the nature of embodiment and the self, particularly from Japanese sociologists, have added to our understanding of self-making through the body, offering alternative ways of considering the body and its relationship to such commitment. These perspectives are particularly useful when considering youth cultures. As Ozawa-De Silva notes, 'while Western thinkers tend to see discipline as subjection and bodily control, which they link to asceticism, Japanese tend to see bodily practice as cultivation, seeking as its end not power, but the recognition of mind-body integration' (Ozawa-De Silva, 2002, p. 36; see also Yuasa, 1987; Deutsch, 1993). The intense commitment to constituting the self as an 'authentic' being, a 'unity' through the body, was expressed by the youth in our fieldwork in the kinds of clothes and purchases they sought out, the endless rehearsals and practices, the training of their voices, the lyric writing skills, and technical prowess on the turntable, guitar or microphone. It was also expressed through repeated attempts to accomplish particular dance movements, gestures and postures at the turntable, on the dance floor or in the street. Such perfecting requires endless practice and determination. Without continual rehearsal underpinning the necessary creativity and seemingly fluid spontaneity, the results can be unsatisfactory and disappointing, as one of the young male musicians from Café Leutze's Rock initiative explained to us.

> We once tried to play 'Smells like teen spirit'. Jeanette knew the song, and we got the lyrics from the web. It's four chords. So we tried to find them on the double bass. The guy who was just standing over there tried to join in on the drums, and some people sang. Sounded absolutely awful – This is how we work. Play a song with whatever is available. *After you've played it five times you get better.*
>
> (Personal communication 2004, emphasis added)

Again and again, in our study, the young participants acknowledged their need for endless practice and emulation of their mentors combined with their determination to refine their skills to achieve their goals and demonstrate a professional attitude. This seemed to be a ubiquitously acknowledged and shared sign of one's commitment to 'body work', recognition of the hard work of play, the need to 'pay one's dues', in old-school rock terminology. Yet it was never expected that one would do this alone. As long as the individual showed real commitment, there would be an army of peers, a dedicated support network, standing in the wings to encourage and offer practical advice. Ali, one of Newcastle Palais' accomplished girl breakers, articulated this as she demonstrated to a newcomer a breakdancing 'power move', a kind of single arm-stand and flip, which is based on bodily strength and mental control. 'It's a mind thing', Ali explained to her 'student'. 'Just think how strong you are. Don't let it beat you' (cited in Julie's field notes, 2004).

Similarly, at a D'Expressions DJ workshop (3 November 2003) held at the Millmead, Holy Trinity Church near Margate and organised through Pie Factory Music, Matt, one of the project leaders for the evening, was explaining the necessary technical skills for mixing and scratching. About an hour into the workshop he called for a volunteer to have a go on the decks. One of the girls was pushed forward by the group to go first and try mixing. Behind the decks she appeared to be very anxious – 'I'm scared I'll break it', she cried as she tried to put the needle in the groove of the vinyl. Holding the headphones over one ear, head tilted slightly, as directed, she alternated between intense looks of concentration as she listened for the beats in the music and outbursts of 'I can't' or 'I don't want to do it.' Under the continual stream of encouragement from Matt, however, she finally gave it a go and looked immensely self-satisfied (and relieved!) when it sounded quite competent. 'If you did that at a party, everyone would be really impressed', smiled Matt, 'they wouldn't notice if it wasn't perfect.'

After this, a couple of other attendees also had a go at mixing and scratching while most of the others disappeared outside for a cigarette. Three boys stayed in the room. One of the lads got some private tuition on the decks from Matt, who again gave continual encouragement: 'You've almost got it' and 'You're that close to nailing it.'

Advice and direction from mentors and trainers, however, are never considered to be enough. It was clear to us from our observations of the workshops and from private discussion with almost all of the mentors that continual practice and determination (outside of the workshop hours) was considered to be essential for any progress to be made. Mentors were tough when it came to berating any of their 'students' who did not show a willing and steadfast dedication and time commitment, and manifest the endurance to succeed. In Newcastle, Dave (DJ Mathematics) stated categorically that he was not going to waste his time on people who just came in for a session or two to pick up 'party tricks'. Ali, his fellow trainer, agreed: just to 'impress their friends at parties' she affirmed, while Dave followed up with an even more explicit comment: just 'to pull chicks!', he stated in disgust. Similarly, DJ Shep expressed his frustration when his students did not practise in between lessons. We observed his taking several workshops. On one occasion, at the beginning period of our fieldwork, Kyle was undertaking his third Da Klinic workshop. It was clear to us as we observed his session that while he was a keen student he was still clearly lacking in confidence. By the end of that particular lesson, we noticed that Shep's style had become less relaxed and less informal and far more directive, as he started to 'play the teacher card' as Kyle expressed it. Indeed Kyle himself noted the change, complaining, 'You've gone all "principal" on me!' Shep justified his more formal approach by retorting 'You need to practise, man! I can only teach you so much. The rest is up to you. You've got to practise.'

The following week, Shep showed Kyle how to scratch to some 'breaks' albums ('the new House', explained Shep) because the faster beats forced faster scratching. Practising to this speed sharpens the skills for the return to the slower beats of hip hop, he explained. Field notes taken at the time note that Shep's demonstration was impressive, due to the apparent ease of his actions and the flow of his movements. He made everything appear effortless, the sign of a skilled practitioner everywhere, we discovered, and it was therefore a pleasure to watch him in action. That particular week Kyle also seemed to have acquired more confidence and therefore demonstrated a greater rhythm and flow. His improvement was undoubtedly due to the extra amount of practice he said he had finally managed to put in at home over the previous week. He told us proudly that he had practised at every given opportunity. 'Until 11 last night and was up again practising at 7:30 this morning.'

Shep then treated his student differently, offering a more sophisticated level of advice on this occasion. He used a particular vinyl record where the beats would disappear leaving a musical opening for improvisation. 'This is the scratcher's space to shine', explained Shep. 'You're the instrument' and then he gave a display of scratching before the beat dropped back in. 'Moments like that can kill[8] ["wow"] a dance floor', he explained.

His instruction on this day centred far more on DJing at parties and how to gain the approval of the 'commercial' crowds. The underlying theme was that even the most simple of scratches could be effective. He told Kyle to go after the class, find and listen to 'classics' such as Herbie Hancock's 'Rocket'. 'It was the theme to Merrick and Rosso's show on Triple J', he explained. 'I think it was Grand Master Flash who originally scratched to it. Notice it is just baby scratches – simple but fantastic.'

These small vignettes of interaction and advice point to another important aspect of the learning process for the young DJs and musicians to which we have already alluded – the particular and complex mentoring role of the DJ as archivist and 'preserver' of the culture. It is to this aspect we turn now.

Mentors as archivists: teachers and (gate)keepers of cultural knowledge

Individual success in whatever music culture we explored depended not only upon peer and mentor encouragement to ensure others were able to learn and achieve the right moves, techniques and skills, but also on acquiring the correct form of the shared cultural knowledge; to disseminate the necessary elements of cultural capital knowledge. As in all cultures, that seemed to be the scene's whole raison d'être. That is, the individual musician, artists, singer and so on sought to become not simply competent in his/her art form but an 'authentic', acknowledged and lauded member of that chosen social and cultural musical grouping or 'neo-tribe' (Maffesolli, 1996). In fact the role of the DJ as teacher, gatekeeper and archivist is paramount, as an almost tacit communal resource; it is this role that gives the legendary DJs their relevance and longevity. This is why they willingly spend so much money on researching and acquiring the right 'rekkids' (i.e. vinyl). This underpins their networking. This is why they do outreach such as DJ Shep's work in Aboriginal remote communities or in the juvenile detention facilities. This is also why and how DJs and other group 'leaders' become social entrepreneurs, which we will explore further in later chapters, creating wealth that then is ploughed back again into the community. And finally, this is also why DJs want to become producers and own their own label, in order to help their own music communities and networks stay dynamic and viable.

Another aspect of the talented DJ is that they can often create what many describe as an almost religious experience (Hutson, 2000; Lynch, 2006), affirmed in song lyrics by the American pop singer Pink that are referenced in Tuesday's words that head this chapter.[9] As the DJ becomes more experienced, recognised and established, as they learn literally to move their audience, they control their followers' bodies, setting feet tapping, heads nodding, then bodies moving and dancing. As the DJ begins to go 'deeper', which means the music seems to call for a more profound psychological level of response, he or she seems to transform the experience of the audience. Observers and audience claim that then the dancers begin a psychic 'journey' (see Laski, 1961, 1980; Malbon, 1999, p. 114). The task of the DJ is therefore not simply to play music and keep people dancing; rather and above all, it is to take the crowd on a journey with the music. This means taking the crowd to higher and lower emotional levels at special intervals so that the crowd gets lost in the music and comes under the DJ's mastery so they will just keep dancing; hence the name 'journey sets' for DJs, which occur between 12 midnight and 6 a.m. The dancers who 'lose themselves in the music' say that they feel a deeper affective and spiritual connection. The religious connotations are obvious and indeed the word most frequently used in this context is 'soul' (Hutson, 2000; Wall, 2006; see also St John, 2009, p. 167). The aim is to achieve a form of trance-like dancing to disengage the conscious mind from the body and connect to something deeper, a meaningful spiritual experience, with or without drugs. Brewster and Broughton effusively describe the role of the DJ as

> understanding the feelings of a group of people and directing them to a better place. In the hands of a master, records become the tools for rituals

of spiritual communion that for many people are the most powerful events in their lives. (2000, p. 5)

Scott Hutson's work on the altered states of consciousness reported at raves similarly cites several ravers who claim to have a spiritual experience through the music and movement but particularly through the skills of the DJ:

With help of the DJ's ecstatic techniques, ravers like Edward Lantz claim to enter 'areas of consciousness not necessarily related to everyday "real" world experiences' (Lantz, n.d.). Though Ecstasy enables altered states of consciousness, drugs are not necessary. (Hutson, 2000, p. 39)

In the eyes of our young participants there was a clear distinction between a 'bedroom DJ' (which in their learning state and process many of them still considered themselves to be) and a 'real' (authentic) DJ, someone who was recognised as talented, someone who had 'made it'. They knew when they were not 'ready yet' and they also knew how to evaluate the best performers and musicians. For example, experienced DJs demonstrate their multitasking ability; they may have one eye on the mixing decks, but their main gaze is on the punters at the bars or on the dance floor – the audience (Photos 3.5 and 3.6). Note too the use of large screens so that the audience in their turn can both appreciate and enjoy the value of the sonic sophistication of the music

Photo 3.5 Mix Master Mike creates a journey. © Alex Parardes

'Everyone Wants to be a DJ' 113

Photo 3.6 Watching the dance floor. © Alex Parardes

and also watch the level of technical expertise that the DJ is demonstrating on the sound mixer and decks. In contrast, inexperienced DJs, if and when they do a public gig, tend to be looking at the decks, not the crowd.

Furthermore, the set of an inexperienced DJ has usually been rehearsed so precisely they cannot improvise or watch the audience's response (DJ NuJeans, personal communication, 8 July 2010). With an experienced and talented DJ, the ideal moment of liminality, where the participants become 'betwixt and between' states of consciousness (Turner, 1969, p. 95), creates a feeling of experiential community. It becomes a oneness, a 'communitas', with fellow ravers where social structure and in many ways a sense of one's individual and individuated physical body and the other disappears or is disregarded (Turner, 1969, pp. 94–7, 125–30; see also Rushkoff, 2004).

While the overall aim might be to merge and lose the individual identity within the anonymous mass, the relationship between the self and the sea of others on the dance floor is complex, as Malbon points out in his vivid account of contemporary clubbing:

> At any one moment, aspects of an individual's identity or aspects of an individual's identification with the crowd will take precedence. One moment a clubber will literally be self-conscious while the next s/he may feel as if they have ceded control of their body and even of their mind to the clubbing crowd, the music and the atmosphere. This fluctuation between self and crowd is a defining feature of the clubbing experience. (Malbon, 1999, p. 187)

In using the Latin term 'comitatus' to express an idea of anti-structure, anthropologist Victor Turner referred to social structure and 'communitas' as 'two major "models" for human interrelatedness'. These models are defined as follows:

> The first is of society as a structured, differentiated, and often hierarchical system of politico-legal-economic positions with many types of evaluation, separating men in terms of 'more' or 'less'. The second, which emerges recognizably in the liminal period, is of society as an unstructured or rudimentarily structured and relatively undifferentiated *comitatus*, community, or even communion of equal individuals who submit together to the general authority of the ritual elders. (1969, p. 96, original emphasis)

In the case of raves or similar events, as Malbon (1999) points out, under the spell of a talented DJ, the audience seems to realise Turner's original model as they appear to blend and become one. James Landau, while conceding that 'the ecstasy of raving is problematic'[10] (2004, p. 107), notes that 'ecstatic raving is an "experience" discursively dominated by recurring motifs of unity, holism and interconnectedness. In the crucible of the rave, barriers are said to disintegrate as once disparate entities overlap and intermingle' (Landau, 2004, p. 107; also see St John, 2004; Pini, 2001 for various critiques and explorations of the concept of 'communitas' and techno and other cultures).

Away from the dance floor itself, the cult of the DJ extends to the ways the commercial music culture products and related artefacts are created and sold. The photos of T-shirts on sale through an online accessories shop illustrate this. Next to the images is the following informative inscription:

> The Flare Scratch was invented by DJ Flare back in 1991 though developed further by DJ Q-Bert. It involves a combo of moving the record around the turntable with your hand with a quick execution of the cross-fader. But you don't need me to explain it to you. Just wear this t-shirt and proceed to read yourself. If you have any trouble reading up side down or in backwards in a mirror, then simply apply a friend who can reveal the instructions to you... all designs are inspired by the beautiful art of DJing. (http://www.everyonedoesit.com, accessed 10 July 2010)

Note the way the DJ's skills and history become part of the symbolic capital attached to the item. Through the image and the text, the mythologising of the DJ and his or her technical expertise is transferred transgenerationally and cross-culturally. Note too that not only is it important for the mentors to provide constant encouragement as they teach the correct moves, style and technique, referred to above, but it is also vital for them to provide the appropriate educational underpinning and historical context which underpins the ongoing mythology of the particular DJ, graff or street artist or musician.

The mythology of the DJ: historical and cultural contexts

At the Millmead workshop, the tutor, Matt, not only offered lessons in mixing technique but also a 'brief history of DJing' including the historical contextualising of the musical genre, noting that this was 'as a precursor to the MCing of today' (field notes, 2003). Historical and cultural contexts were also stressed at the Tabernacle, in Notting Hill. During one visit we were privileged to listen to Director Karin Woodley, a vivacious and talented educator, as she taught the young West Indian youth in her care at a community centre music theory workshop the history and therefore the deeper significance of the Notting Hill carnival. She explained to the workshop attendees, 'One side of carnival is the euphoria, the partying, the celebrating of who you are, but is there another side?' The youth offered back blank looks so Karin tried again. 'What is the political side of carnival?' Alicia, one of the young attendees, answered with hesitation. 'Because of tradition?' she ventured but then added 'but *why* do we have carnival? I've never thought of that.' Jermaine, a fellow participant, then offered, 'It's just a celebration. I thought it was for fun.'

Karin tried to hide her disbelief, and after taking a deep breath started again:

> Right, I'm going to be very Trinidadian...it happens at Lent. Carnival originated because the slaves who had Catholic slave owners weren't allowed to use their culture, dancing, drumming, anything they brought from Africa in their community...so they mimicked their slave owners' religious traditions so their slave owners were led to believe the slaves had taken on their religion...so steel pan was...what materials were available...when the Trinidadians came here...it's one of the Catholic islands...they brought their tradition to the streets of Notting Hill...we go in and politically reclaim the streets because we were brought here to work and then treated like animals...we were brought here but weren't welcome, so carnival tradition is reclaiming the streets...There still is that political reason to get out on the streets and this is our culture and music. We are still highest representation in prisons and of the lowest socio-economic standing...At that time we were living in squalor and race riots were going on. Carnival allows us to use music and culture to come together...there's an element of protest but also the celebratory aspect of it. (Karin Woodley, 27 October 2004, Tabernacle/Mangrove half-term music theory and aural perception course)

Knowledge is power and clearly endows authority! And if there were ever any doubt, we can see the personal become the political through such teaching and contextualising. Plato already knew it well as McClary noted:

> The ability of music to mold physical motion often has ramifications that extend much further. Recall Plato's warning: 'For the modes of music are never disturbed without the unsettling of the most fundamental political and social conventions.' (McClary, 1994, p. 33)

Collectively such knowledge becomes valuable, indeed essential, capital for the creation and ongoing maintenance of each experiential grouping. In each experiential and cultural grouping we saw the same blend of both formal and informal historical contextualising, educational input and practical instruction. This grounding of knowledge together with showing others how to hold, manage and control their bodies for the right effects, demonstrating how to achieve various technical and physical skills whether that were perfecting a power move, scratching and mixing smoothly on the vinyl, accomplishing a complex piece of graffiti or street art or learning to rap or battle through the creation of personal, meaningful lyrics, was essential to acquire the right amount of 'cultural capital' to be an accepted member of one's selected grouping. This was so whether it was hip hop, house or electronic music, rock or acoustic styles or even for the youth who used other people's music – such as those who hosted radio shows such as the *Youth Revolutions* crew in Adelaide, DJ Roland Samuels' regular internet radio program in London or those who managed other people's events and gigs (such as the Kandinsky Group, Patterns in Static or Da Klinic in Adelaide). As we have already seen, the various forms of capital (physical, cultural, social and symbolic) are only valuable and useful in the contexts of these youth cultures when they can be converted and transformed into economic capital and back again. Pierre Bourdieu defined cultural capital as a range of skills, techniques and knowledge that is accrued by an individual, which then needs to be converted into social capital, in order that full acceptance and membership can be gained to the desired grouping. He explained it in this way:

> Social capital is the aggregate of the actual or potential resources which are linked to possession of a durable network of more or less instituted relationships of mutual acquaintance and recognition – or in other words, to membership of a group. (Bourdieu, 1986, p. 249)

So far we have described above how the disciplined body helps to constitute and demonstrate one's hard-earned authenticity and membership and thereby adds to the knowledge base, the value and the symbolic significance of the community as a whole. Achievement is then recognised and applauded. As Saul Standerwick, youth mentor from the Palais, explained to Julie, 'It's like everyone's encouraging each other, so to keep the vibe good' (personal communication, December 2004).[11]

In this discussion we have moved from the analysis of the ideal – the figure of the DJ or her equivalent, one who is a talented performer, a teacher, an archivist (and, as we shall demonstrate further in Chapter 6, an entrepreneur!) – to the other, more rank-and-file members of the grouping: those who also aspire to belong, to be acknowledged and whose identity is intricately tied up in that experiential community. This was confirmed in our research for whatever grouping the individuals belonged to or aspired to, and whatever word they used to express their sense of belonging, to be an accepted, core member of the grouping meant that one had to be seen as self-possessed, confident and competent. How that attribute of 'cool' was manifested and even the words used to describe it, differed between the different groups, but at the same time it relied on a number of broadly accepted givens. Firstly, in each experiential community it connoted an image of superiority, which, although supposedly authentic and innate (some people 'have it' and some don't), was also paradoxically understood to be mainly constituted through style and demeanour, something that could be acquired, worked on and developed. Secondly, the attribute of 'being cool' always retained the characteristics of the adult cultures *from which it emerged*. That is, the concept of 'coolness' was not uniform but heterogeneous. It held a variety of connotations for the youth in our research project who came from different social and cultural backgrounds. So the youth from Kreutzberg in Berlin had a different understanding of what was the favoured 'authentic' look, style and language compared to the young people we met from Charlottenburg and it was different again from the young people in Playford, South Australia, from those in Newcastle, New South Wales and those in North London or Kent. In some groupings alcohol and cigarettes were the social and leisure substance of choice; in others marijuana or harder illegal drugs were far more prevalent. For some groupings body art in the form of elaborate tattoos were worn without comment; this was how things were in this part of the world or within this social grouping. In others the possibility of an individual getting a tattoo was the subject of excited discussion and interest.

This is not to imply that there was no overlap between groupings nor any gender, class and ethnic variations. Of course affiliations or networks within the same music scenes or cultures that emerged within those broad geographical areas also impacted upon group affiliation and cultural identity. In Best and Kellner's words it is also clear that music scenes are very much part of global media culture, where MTV 'has influenced media culture as a whole which absorbs and pastiches anything and everything, turning oppositional cultural forms such as hip-hop and grunge into seductive hooks for fashion and advertising' (2003, p. 84).

At the same time we are not arguing for a deterministic or narrow socio-cultural relationship between the youth, their backgrounds and their leisure activities and choices. Rather, we are reaffirming that what constituted 'real' or 'cool' for each individual in our project was not arbitrary, but instead was negotiated and refracted through the broader socio-cultural and familial networks that the youth inhabited.

Language and cultural capital

While clothing and outer appearance, as we have seen, are a key to this play with cultural image and identity and denote a shorthand way of suggesting knowledge and status, other important, perhaps less obvious, markers exist too. In this final section we want to look briefly at the role of language, communication through the vernacular and in particular the way particular words, 'argot' or 'slang' were used to create and maintain 'authenticity', in groups and out groups across all of the sites in our study. It occurred in two main ways. Firstly, the creation of an argot that was clearly understandable to the group in question and therefore by definition could distance, alienate or just be not understandable to other people who are not in the grouping; this included not simply the type of vocabulary but the context in which it was employed. The second use of language, which was significant, was the way in some contexts particular language usually under some institutional or organisational 'house' rules was taboo. We will look at each in turn.

The semantic shift: the 'Da Klinic' code

Hip hop inherently is a music scene that is about language play so it is hardly surprising that some of the most inventive use of language emerges from this music genre. It is full of self-conscious, reflexive teasing out of alternative meanings whether that is just part of everyday conversations, creating carefully constructed raps or in the expressive graphic art forms and lettering embedded in the street art of graffiti. We had already noticed and noted the reverse language play that particularly occurs in verbal exchanges around MC workshops. For example, as documented earlier, Shep advised Kyle that his innovative use of scratching could 'kill' the dance floor. Despite possible misinterpretations, it was clearly intended as a positive comment, referring to the power of the DJ to ensure that the audience engages and dances. Similarly, when the young people talked about the music being 'bad' or 'wikkid' it was intended to be a compliment.

Most of the words we heard with their reversed or multiple meaning have been collated and listed on The Urban Dictionary online website (http://urbandictionary.com/) with its slogan 'define your world'. Mainly targeting teenagers and youth in their twenties, the site was founded in 1999 by Aaron Peckham while he was a first-year computer science major at

California Polytechnic State University. It started as an online resource with user-defined submissions of new words and new ways of using and changing English language. It now has more than one million definitions for 250,000 words and, according to the online version of the book, more than two million people now visit the site every day. The site describes its purpose as 'a from the streets explanation of contemporary culture, language, available online at www.urbandictionary.com, in the pages of this book or from any teenager' (www.urbandictionary.com, accessed 20 July 2010).

With its content and meanings fuelled and elaborated by global media and popular culture, the dictionary contained many of the words we heard around us (and often had to have translated) as we observed and 'hung out' with teenagers: words such as 'wicked' to mean exciting or excellent; 'sick, man!' (which again means great! wonderful!); 'peeps' to mean people (which tends to mean 'my people' or 'my network') and now many acronyms like LOL (laugh out loud) which found their way into spoken language from online social networking sites or telephone texting. Such language use immediately creates an outsider and an insider, those who understand and those who do not and because so much of it changes rapidly and is inflected by local usage it is the perfect vehicle to ensure that only your particular grouping appropriates certain idioms and phrases your way – and perhaps even create your own. Above all such play with words is fun and self-conscious.

A 2010 radio interview with DJ Shep at the Adelaide radio station NovaFM morning show was videoed and uploaded onto the station's website. In the interview, Shep, who has his own regular Sunday night show, introduced 15-year-old Tyler, a new young talent he had nurtured and promoted through the Da Klinic workshops.[12] In the discussion, two of the hosts, Claire and Jules, and Shep and Tyson laughed between and at themselves as they reflected on their own use of argot to talk about Tyson's opportunities. The language between them was rapid, overlapping and full of puns and insider jokes and gentle teasing, mainly it seemed because Jules pretended to be unfamiliar with the slang being used. It was almost as though he was rolling the words around on his tongue in fun or trying them on for size. The others were laughing at his deliberate self-conscious use of the words and at the same time at their own use of the popular and vernacular abbreviations and idioms. Here is an excerpt:

Jules (clearly impressed after listening to Tyson's competent and talented rap, turns to Shep): Well, Shep. You're a pretty connected man
Shep: Yeah, I know people...
Claire: And your Blackberry... (your mobile phone)

Shep (laughing immediately takes out his phone and starts to text with one hand)
Claire: Can you look under phone (be)cause for us...
Jules: ...You are one of the most connected people in Adelaide
Shep: Yeah, yeah I know people
Jules: Could you hook up Tyson? Could you hook him up with one of the Hip Hop...
Claire: He (Tyson) mentioned Trials (as one of his heroes and influences)
Shep: I think we could easily get Trials involved. Yes easily (texting on his phone as he speaks). Look, Trials is always up. He's a crazy guy. He's always up for stuff and he loves working with local artists.
Claire: When you say he's *up*, can we get him up before 9 am?
Shep (laughing): Yeah that will be the hard bit. (but) he has a manager now so I am going to speak to his manager and you know, get those wheels in motion...
Jules: How would you feel about doing it ? Will it be *collab*? Is that what you are saying? How would you feel about doing it *collab*? Or could you *hook up*?...
Claire (in mock admiration): You are so *street* (*wise*?) now, Jules!
Jules: Or you could *hook up*. Is that what you say? *Hook up*? you could hook up with... How do we *hook* you *up*, Tyson?
Claire: Jules, why don't you say to Shep, 'Shep, can you hook a *brother* up and *collab* with...'
Jules (repeating, as though from a lesson): Yeah! Shep, can you *hook* a *brother up* and *collab* with Trials?
Shep: Most definitely, T! (laughing and gesturing to Tyson and saying the next sentence with beat of a rap). I'll get big T to hook up with little T and we'll make some beautiful music...

Note the ways that Jules, in pretence of mocking the particular language that the others are using automatically as part of their own membership of the hip hop scene, takes up Claire's joke concerning Trials' ability to be 'up' for anything (including being able to rise early in the mornings!) to create a humorous reflexive exchange where the others deliberately highlighted and played with the words they would normally take for granted: 'collab' (collaborate); 'hook up' (make connections with/network with); 'brother' or 'bro' (a 'wigger' word? The term here means fellow rapper but it was a term that previously we had only heard used unselfconsciously by the African-American and West Indian youth in the US and the UK, such as the youth at the Boston Centre and Rowland, respectively). The program banter continued along that vein and then it was arranged that the next day Tyler would rap on air for the program's audience with the established hip hop celebrity Trials from The Funkoars. This they did and again the video was uploaded onto the radio station website and both interviews were uploaded onto Facebook, via Shep's Da Klinic link.

Taboo: voice, swearing and silences

This chapter has examined how the youth learned their skills through bodily praxis, what skills they had to acquire and what resources helped them to do this and especially what role and particular supports they gained from their mentors, such as DJ Shep above. This last section concerns the use of voice and silences. We look at situations where youth musical expression may seem to be restricted by limitations placed on it by the institutions and organisations that seek to help them. We already saw a little of this in the *Youth Revolutions* radio show. Although the team were allowed to tackle any controversial topic they wished as the theme of the show, which they did to their considerable credit, they were not permitted to play any music they wished or to use profanities on air. The rules of the funding and the use of the station meant that no swearing was permitted. Sometimes this was challenging for them as they had to censor exactly which tracks of which artists they could choose and how the music might be interpreted by the authority figures.

We found similar discussions about use of swearing and racist, sexist or otherwise concerning subject matter in the youth's lyrics occurring at several of the CBOs we visited. Most of the organisations did not censor the language beyond mild suggestions about what was considered appropriate in public forums as they argued that the young people would normally be using these worlds as part of their everyday experiences. Sometimes, as we have noted elsewhere in this narrative, the team felt that the result could be confronting and potentially created an exclusory sonic space where young women or particular ethnic groups were made to feel unwelcome. However, one place where this tactic did seem to work effectively was in Juri's sessions for Genuine Voices.

As described above, Juri worked with very troubled incarcerated young people, usually young men who had a history of violence, and substance and personal abuse. The language they brought into her music lessons was the angry, sexist and racist language of the street. However, she brought her own rules that restricted their use of such expression and insisted that the lyrics they chose were to move beyond this experience. They were, she stressed, to try and express their anger or vent their frustrations using the power of their music to develop new coping strategies and new ways of negotiating their world. Most of them managed to do this although their struggles to do so often became the source of interesting discussions between the members of the research team and with Juri herself.

Clearly, though, for most people feeling that one has the 'permission' to create and express oneself through music is not automatic; the places and spaces have to enable and facilitate such creativity and opportunities. It is this aspect of youth and music we explore next – how the 'spaces of cool', spaces for serious play, were carved out and facilitated in the lives of our young participants, sometimes despite many hurdles and difficulties en route.

4
Creating Spaces

Photo 4.1 Tuesday's practice space (video still). © Tuesday Benfield

It's all about ownership. One guy's bedroom had a lock on the door – but his room was a temple... Their rooms show what they can control. 'Out there' they can't control, so they can sing, make a CD, play a sport well, then it's theirs; no one can take that from them. (Interview with William Stewart, Probation Officer, Boston, MA, Board of Directors of Genuine Voices, 3 September 2004)

A sense of one's place as the sense of what one can or cannot 'allow oneself' implies a tacit acceptance of one's position, a sense of limits ('that's not meant for us') or – what amounts to the same thing – a sense of distances, to be marked and maintained, respected and expected of others. (Bourdieu, 1991, p. 235)

Knowing your place

In the previous chapter we explored the ways in which the young people in our study learned to acquire and perfect their musical skills and to accumulate their cultural and social capital through careful control and surveillance of their own and other people's bodies. We argued that learning how to gain the requisite knowledge, techniques and confidence to present oneself and perform correctly requires committed serious play; it takes dedication, commitment, time and hard work. Yet such a task was necessary in order to establish and maintain authentic membership of one's chosen experiential community. But gaining knowledge through bodily praxis is only part of the story for serious play can only take place within spaces that are comfortable, accessible and encouraging. That is, the ability to experiment *and* to negotiate spaces to do this – often described as 'private spaces' – is encouraged or hindered by the symbolic boundaries of that microworld. Far more powerful than any physical containment of space, the self-perception and self-surveillance of what is or is not considered appropriate and acceptable, what was or was not questioned and questionable in their worlds, limited and constrained the form of and predisposition of 'play'. Bodily praxis (Bourdieu, 1990, 1998; Moore, 1994) does not occur separately from its physical contexts, as both Pierre Bourdieu and William Stewart indicate in their respective comments above.

It is significant that the processes of learning that we described earlier for each young person in Adelaide, Newcastle, Berlin, London and so on occurred in the particular places and spaces that they did – whether in the overcrowded bedrooms of Kyle, Tuesday, Will, Adam or Dave or in the studio of the PBA-FM radio station for crew of *Youth Revolutions*; the draughty workshop spaces of the Palais, Da Klinic, the various Berlin youth centres or the Tabernacle in Notting Hill for keen, developing rock bands, DJs, breakers or MCs; the common outside area in an outback Aboriginal community; in the confined area of the Brighton Treatment Center or in the particular neighbourhoods or 'hoods' that are described and recognised in the raps of particular hip hop groups. For example, the Hill Top Hoods, now an internationally famous hip hop group that we first got to know about through Da Klinic, formed in 1987 when MC Suffa and MC Pressure met at their local high school. Although their main influences include American hip hop artists such as Notorious B.I.G., KRS-One, Gang Starr, Wu-Tang Clan and Public Enemy, their name came from a suburb in south-eastern Adelaide known by the local youth as the Hilltop, where Flak, Suffa and Pressure grew up (see http://www.hilltophoods.info; also McCabe, 2007). Similarly, several people at the workshops at the Palais proudly interwove information about their local area in Newcastle into their 'beats and rimes'. Azza was particularly concerned about emphasising the local in his music. There would be frequent neighborhood, community and topical references in his lyrics with allusions such as: Miss Universe 2004 (who hails from Holmesville); 'goin' as fast as BHP', referring to the Broken Hill Pty Ltd (BHP) steelworks closure of 1999; the Brewery (a hotel on the harbour foreshore) and lines that are replete with maritime metaphors, referring to the dominance of the sea and shore in the Newcastle landscape. Another participant in one of the workshops at the Palais who recorded his verse using a Jamaican or West Indian accent and rhymed about 'wiggers'[1] also made local (Novocastrian) references to 'Newie beats and rhymes', 'the castle' and 'coal'. In his lyrics Psych made reference to the earthquake that hit Newcastle in 1989. It was important to express everyone's different take on the subject of Newcastle 'from all angles', explained Adam.

Particular geographical places including the local neighbourhood or 'hood' have long been linked to particular musical behaviour and taste (see Cohen, 2008, p. 92). As Bennett observed:

> One of the ways in which individuals make such simultaneous realisations of society and space is through the act of musical consumption. Indeed musical consumption has proved to be both a particularly distinctive and enduring medium for collective reconstruction of public space. To map the public space of any industrial or post-industrial conurbation in terms of the patterns of musical consumption which exist there is to discover a series of shifting and overlapping territories. (2000, p. 64, also cited in Cohen, 2008, p. 92)

These geographical and discursive maps of the city are also personally, professionally and politically highly significant for the local creators of music of all genres and has been recognised as such by many scholars of youth cultures and youth cultural expression (see Cohen, 1994; Stokes, 1994; Mitchell, 2001; Connell and Gibson, 2003; Dunbar-Hall and Gibson, 2004; Hudson, 2006; Bennett, 2008; Cohen, 2008). Such associations of place with particular music sounds or scenes are often superimposed from outside of the locales, as a form of narrative 'fictional gloss' (Bennett, 2008, p. 71), a result of global media flows, producing what Keith Kahn-Harris describes effectively as 'a hybrid and flexible concatenation of the discursive and the real' (Kahn-Harris, 2006, p. 133).

Again to cite Bennett:

> Part of the process of associating music with place involves a desire to make the music 'real', to give it roots and an everyday 'lived' context in which to explore its meaning and significance, lyrically, musically and culturally. Even if the reality of contemporary popular music is that it holds little relationship to place in any concrete sense, audiences like to believe that it does. (2008, p. 72)

So particular places can metaphorically signify a place of belonging and identity for particular groupings, including youth cultures, but equally can indicate a place of exclusion. One of the youth workers in Berlin felt this very strongly as he explained to Bruce Cohen, one of our research team members, that 'Berlin is very divided... There is the hip-hop track, people who are only into hip-hop, who don't look left or right, only hip-hop, only drum and base' (cited in Cohen, 2008, p. 91).

Musical expression signifies place and in each particular place the creativity, composition and experience of the music occurs because the place in question facilitates play in some significant ways for the individuals involved. That is, there is a crucial nexus there between the specific geographical place, the times when the explorations and creativity take place and the young people's perceptions of that place. The relationship between place, time and subjectivity highlights the importance of what is usually described as 'private space', a space where one feels one can engage in 'serious play', a space to feel safe, experiment, risk-take, test out the boundaries (see Bloustien, 2003b, 2004a, 2004b). Ben Malbon, in his earlier study specifically referring to dancing, raves and clubbing, also describes the complex processes of 'play' and how these can be facilitated by emotional responses to particular places and spaces, arguing:

> Time may take on a different quality and feeling during the practices of play – 'time flies when you're having fun' – and the spaces and contexts of play might be perceived as different or special, and endowed with a powerful significance or even totemic quality. (1999, p. 138)

However, we would argue that the relationship Malbon describes has to be turned on its head! Play is only possible in the first place because the arena selected for such activity has been perceived by the 'players' as open for such exploration and opportunity, open for the kinds of 'self-making' that we described earlier. To understand this complexity it is valuable to revisit the concept of body-space (Csordas, 1994; Duncan, 1996; Lewis, 1996; Mahmood, 2001; Low and Lawrence-Zúñiga, 2002; Low, 2003). In other words, we need to explore how 'space' to play is created, hindered, negotiated and facilitated through bodily praxis and to understand the relationship between particular places and our embodied selves more fully. To do this we need to adjust our analytic lens again to focus on how the young people in our study acquired the perceptions of who they believed they were and who they imagined they could be through their knowledge and understandings of particular geographical places. We argue that these perceptions of their neighbourhoods and domestic locales occurred not only through their physiological experience of being but through the interrelated and integrated aspects of bodily praxis – in other words, in the nexus between space, place and play. Here we discover that the concept of private space becomes crucial to the rhetoric of 'self-making', demonstrated both in the video and camera footage and in the informal discussions between the young and adult participants of the project. Within the home, bedroom spaces become particularly significant, as one might expect, to explore body-space, since most young people indicated that these rooms signalled an area of potential creativity and reflexivity, where one can 'really be oneself'. William Stewart, whose words head this chapter, expressed this succinctly when he affirmed that the bedroom space of even the most disaffected and disadvantaged youth, even when they are shared and used for a range of purposes, can become 'a temple...Their rooms show what they can control.' In other words controlling space means controlling your body, controlling your sense of self, controlling your sense of identity. That means the concept of space is actually about power relations.

Spaces of power relations: gender, ethnicity and class

We have already seen that to be embodied means that one is always moving or being moved through different geographical and physical environments. Perhaps even more importantly, as noted above, some places seem to allow more freedom of movement than others even though at the same time we may be aware that such perception of permission and freedom is arbitrary. After all, Azza, Asher, Saul, Dave, Ali and Codo all displayed varying degrees of confidence to perform publicly in very similar spaces even when they might, to an outsider (or to the uninitiated), have shown similar aptitudes in their particular DJ, MC or breaking skills.

Another related aspect and one explanation for the differences between the perceptions different individuals have of the same area or place is that ultimately every geographical *place* is actually experienced as a *space* of power relations and therefore for individuals not every arena is deemed equal. As Nancy Duncan has argued, 'social relations, including importantly gender relations, are constructed and negotiated spatially and are embedded in the social organisations of places' (1996, p. 4). Bourdieu understood this too, noting that space was more than simply a material or physical boundary, realities that could be 'touched with the finger' (Bourdieu and Wacquant, 1992, p. 228). Rather, he argued, places needed to be appreciated and deconstructed as 'a space of relations', an arena of continual and shifting struggle for 'symbolic power' (Bourdieu, 1991). This means of course that space is never neutral; it is inevitably always gendered, classed, and perceived as inclusive for some and exclusive for others. Space is therefore also frequently contradictory (Gregory and Urry, 1985; Soja, 1989; LeFebvre, 1991; Massey, 1994). Places and the way we conceive of them as spaces are both the *setting* for social interaction and perhaps, more importantly, they are the *medium* for social processes (Gregory, 1986, p. 451). As Shirley Ardener affirmed, 'behaviour and space are mutually dependent' (1993, p. 2) and this can have far-reaching consequences for how specific individuals experience and negotiate their environment.

Researchers often conceive of this kind of experience of space as deterministic, in terms, for example, of how particular ethnic or gendered groups might collectively or hegemonically negotiate particular spaces. This frequently leads to resulting observations being often far too simplistic and obfuscatory rather than illuminating. For example Doreen Massey has noted that

> The limitations of women's mobility in terms of both identity and space has been in some cultural contexts a crucial means of subordination. Moreover, the two things – limitations on mobility on space, the attempted consignment/confinement to particular spaces on the one hand and the limitation on identity on the other – have been crucially related. (1994, p. 179)

Massey is right of course. In fact, concerns about the difficulty of girls being able to gain equal access to facilities at the many youth CBOs were clearly expressed by all of the educators, youth workers and mentors wherever the location of the club or youth centre. This was partly due to the girls who were restrained from using the centres for social and religious reasons by family or community expectations or demands. This in turn often became a vicious circle: smaller numbers of girls used the space so therefore there was less justification for providing the single-sex spaces that were then needed in order that more girls might be attracted or allowed to use the facility! Some clubs did manage to create spaces for the girls, despite the difficulties. In Berlin, a city transformed and fragmented since the reunification of Germany in 1990 (Häußermann, 1997; Häußermann and Kapphan, 2001), we visited Wutzkyallee, which is a multifunctional centre in the Gropiusstadt neighbourhood, an area full of high-rise public housing and subsidised housing. The centre is basically open for all ages, works closely with neighbouring schools and communities, and offers a very wide variety of activities for every kind of local resident or general visitors (from mothers to elderly people to small children and teenagers). It is mainly young people between 12 and 20 who use the diverse rooms and facilities for the music-related activities with 70 per cent of them being boys. It is worthy of note that the youth workers described the majority of general visitors to us as 'non-German', in other words, the 'visitors' were seen as ethnically distinct and mainly of Arabic, Turkish, Polish and Russian, but also Bosnian or Serbian, origin.[2] Possibly because of this cultural mix and therefore religious concerns, the club does offer a small girls-only space for rehearsal and practice.

Tietzia-Mädcheneinrichtung, in Reinickendorf, north-west Berlin, is even more gender conscious. The director, Karin Marker, told us how the centre was once for boys and girls but in 2001 the local government decided it would become a girls-only facility and until recently it was still the only gender-specific centre in the district. However, the centre has more recently experienced some imposed changes; they have now been forced by their main funding body, Bezirksamt Reinickendorf, to re-open the club for boys as well as girls and to offer more mixed-gender events and courses. This ruling has been applied more generally for all social and educational interventions and programs across Germany – the interests of boys are back on the main stage. We were told by our respondents that the new concern is that boys 'need special support and opportunities', hence the more recent political focus on boys' education, which affects the social work undertaken as well. However, as indicated above, Tietzia has been one of Berlin's most important and most central girls' social work institutions for the northern areas during the past twenty years and it still tries hard to argue for girls-only spaces and the importance of social programs dedicated to girls. But as our respondent told us recently it has become increasingly difficult to convince the sponsors and politicians of the significance of their 'girl-focused' work.

The centre shares the building with three other groups – a kindergarten, a mother–baby group, and a musical education program for under 8s. However, each of these groups has their specific room. The centre has an area with a pool table where discos are held each month for 10–14-year-olds – the only time boys may attend the centre. There is also a large concert space, and a counselling room where the staff can speak privately with girls who come to them to discuss problems. They are also working on a peer-mediation program. While the centre can be used on a drop-in basis, it is mostly used by girls under the age of 27 who come for specific projects. The main workshop program we saw at the centre was for drumming, which clearly is an unusual activity for girls[3] and there are also street-dance classes at the centre.

On the other hand, good intentions and even good policies may not be enough to rectify the gender imbalance of facilities. Wolfgang Fischer, former Director of Statthaus Böcklerpark, Berlin, pointed out that they always tried to instigate activities exclusively for young women because the educators at the club felt it was important to provide girls with their own space. However, implementing this was quite another problem, he felt. The girls want to meet boys, to spend time with them and also to have spaces for themselves:

> So the girls say 'oh we want to dance together'. Okay so I open a room and let them dance but I know it doesn't need more than half an hour before the room is full of boys and *they* want it. So I don't know, I think our problem is we have no female colleague who wants to work with the youngsters and to make female work. We haven't. So what shall I do? (Personal communication, 2010)

Sometimes the reasons against providing girls-only space or activities came down to a mild form of institutionalised and unrecognised sexism. The mentors and trainers felt that they did not intentionally set out to exclude the girls from the shared spaces but their belief that the girls are not able to perform at the same level as the boys often had this effect. Michael, one of the talented members from the hip hop breakers crew Flying Steps at Haus der Jugend, openly affirmed this view

> I think break dance is hard to learn. It is hard physical work. Maybe you have noticed how acrobatic it is? It's not just a little turning. It's jumping and big movements that are physically challenging. I think that is why less girls are into it, they don't manage to do it physically. Also I think it's weird if one or two girls come into a room full of boys. I think that's problematic for girls. I think that few girls do come into training once in a while, but not many. Some of them give up because it is too hard, or maybe because they are not actually all that interested. But I think that the main problem is that there are too many boys. I also noticed that many of the boys ignore the girls. They are not open to say 'Hey, come on, let me show you some steps', instead they go 'Man, they're not going to make it anyway.' I think this is the main problem. (Personal communication, 10 February 2004)

Yet, at the same time we need to consider other factors behind the reasons *why* particular people feel that they can or cannot appropriate particular space. As Doreen Massey's argument indicates, the ways in which people can create, negotiate and reclaim their right to space is complex, creative and paradoxical despite perceived or actual restrictions arising from gender, sexual orientation or ethnicity. Personal experience and ethnographic examples remind us constantly that there is frequently a far less deterministic relationship between 'limitation on mobility' and 'subjugation' than might appear at first sight. For example, as Bloustien noted in her earlier work, 'such references to women's experiences blur over aspects of class, race, and age' (2003b, p. 114). That is, not all women are equally subject to particular limitations of mobility, as Henrietta Moore (1994) and bell hooks (1991) remind us. In Bloustien's previous study, she found that one of the most disadvantaged groups she worked with, teenage Aboriginal girls, had a very different perspective of the city and other public institutions to that of their more privileged non-Aboriginal peers. While their ethnicity might mean an increased likelihood of being hassled by the police or other authority figures, it also could mean more licence. These girls often expressed the view through passing comments or disparaging remarks that for the police they represented Aboriginal *youth* rather than (Aboriginal) teenage *girls*. This was a fascinating observation by the girls, whether it is supported by material circumstances or not, since within their own communities their gendered status was paramount. Any deviance from what was considered appropriate behaviour or attitudes for women was strictly monitored within their own social circles. Being categorised by police and other authority figures as *youth* rather than *female* seemed to give the girls permission to behave in more aggressive and assertive ways in public. Perhaps this was why it seemed that some of these same groups of girls had appropriated similar ways to their brothers of taking over city space and seemed to be far more confident than many of their non-Aboriginal peers in accessing more 'public' locales. From within their own social groupings of Aboriginal *youth*, however, they considered themselves to be, and were considered by their peers as, less powerful and more vulnerable because they were *female*.[4]

Similarly, what we, as outside observers, might believe to be a form of constraint and limitation due to class, lifestyle or other form of affiliation, may not be understood in the same way by the individuals in that situation. So for example, Tayfun Atay (2010) in his study of a Turkish-speaking immigrant community in London not only observed how the three subgroups – the Turks, the Kurds from Turkey and Turkish Cypriots – coexist and cooperate with each other but also how these groups simultaneously expressed frictions and conflicts over ethnic, political and ideological issues. This resulted, he argued, in an uneasy situation where these various groups who are identified or who identify themselves as Turkish have to exist together yet do not understand themselves as a unified group. 'The Turkish-speaking community in London appears, at first glance, to be relatively homogenous; that is, they are all Muslims. However, there are inner-divisions making this picture more complex' (2010, p. 126). See also Gardner and Shukur (1994), Hannerz (1996), Kusow (2001), Fangen (2007) and Hopkins (2007) for other examples of the complexity of ethnicity, identity work and space.

We observed a similar paradox in Berlin. According to Wolfgang Fisher, the local Turkish youth we observed at Statthaus Böcklerpark in the neighbourhood of Kreutzberg would fight amongst themselves as well as with other youth groups because they felt undervalued and disadvantaged within the broader German community. Yet whenever they felt particularly disadvantaged or excluded in mainstream German society, they would cooperate with other groups, feeling a sense of wider belonging that often linked into a pan-Islamic, religious extremism. 'Allah becomes very, very important in that moment', explained Wolfgang. So the battle over the physical and sonic space of the club house would be acted out over choice and style of religious music and dancing and the appropriateness of the girls' attendances, not only between the Turkish and non-Turkish attendees but within the different factions of the Turkish-speaking communities in the area. Hence, Wolfgang explained further the significance of memorialising the death of Kreutzberg rapper 'Maxim' on 13 June 2003. We were told several times (indeed, at each visit) of the significance of the large mural painted on the entrance wall of the main clubroom. The image commemorated the death and celebrated the life of Turkish Kreutzberg rapper 'Maxim'.

When we visited in April 2004, the centre was about to hold a memorial event to mark the first anniversary of Maxim's death and we discovered that his celebrity status went beyond the immediate vicinity of the centre.

> Maxim was Turkish, but I'm not sure, I think he's not born in Berlin, I'm not sure, but everybody says he was the founder of the hip hop activities here in Kreutzberg to open hip hop to the Muslim company. They were a bit locked [out] to these subcultural activities coming from the USA, coming from the Christian world. I think it's a sign of both where they stand and of their ethnic backgrounds – and philosophical backgrounds probably. I think the Muslim world teaches more about living together, living in society, helping each other, it's not so individual socialisation as we have here [in Germany]. They have to train themselves to learn and they want to be strong, to be successful. The Turkish youth have fathers who are not successful any more so they miss this part; they lose respect and lose themselves somewhere...
>
> Maxim was killed by a 70 or 65 year old man – it is a ridiculous story in fact because it wasn't necessary but it happens. Maxim and the old man were just talking but the old man got afraid, became panicked and used his knife. It was a bad situation but it was good luck for us... because people came together who haven't been talking for years because they had the same roots. They said okay this is such a mess but we want to make something to help the family and to help the son and they made this benefit, arranged this benefit event and they wanted to do it here because they say Maxim's roots are here in this house. I don't know if it's right but I don't have nothing against it because it's positive. Yeah it may give us the chance to involve and to be seen in this hip hop scene because the hip hop scene is very, very far from rules of society, rules of the nation, of the state, rules of pedagogical intervention. I hope we can take this idea, the philosophical thinking behind the activities of the hip hop of Maxim of coming together, finding your own centre of yourself, being strong because whether you're surviving and not depends on you're having a job or doing things like that. I hope we can take that and I want to start something like open mike.
>
> (Wolfgang Fischer, personal communication, May 2005)[5]

The rapper's death and the circumstances of this death had apparently improved relations between young men in the centre because it had given them a common cause and reason to bond. After our visit that day and on the U-Bahn as we travelled on to our next meeting, Sarah noticed a wall backing onto the track with graffiti saying 'Maxim RIP', suggesting not only a statement of personal loss but also significance for the youth of the wider Turkish community in the area beyond the club house.

Despite the untimely death of the young man, the eventual outcome was seen by many in the area as positive 'because people came together who haven't been talking for years. They had the same roots but they went different ways and couldn't look at each other', Wolfgang explained. It appeared that after the death, all members of the various factions between and within the Turkish community united and came together with others in the local area to help the family and together they arranged the benefit event, 'THE MAXIM-RIP Memorial Jam', the hip hop event held in the grounds of the club. The event took place without the usual cultural divisions and conflict and the club itself became important as a focal point for unity 'because they say Maxim's roots are here in this house. I don't know if it's right but I don't have nothing against it because it's positive' (Wolfgang, personal communication).

It seems that this event and the decision to hold the 'Memorial Jam' allowed many of the young people who normally felt excluded or uncomfortable at the youth club to feel a new sense of belonging. This example highlights again the link between bodily praxis and physical spaces in that the more constrained the actual or *perceived* frameworks for material existence, the more internalised and appropriated become the constraints and the more controlled and limited the ability to *imagine* possible alternatives. In other words, we argue here, as in previous work, that there is a direct correlation between perceived restriction and the ability to 'play' freely. This is not to suggest that all victims of oppressive regimes passively accept their lot or that there is no struggle to negotiate perceived constraints. Rather we argue that a far more complex phenomenon applies. Limitation of movement does not only apply to those with a physical or material boundary to freedom (such as those young people in the Brighton Treatment Center enrolled in Juri's Genuine Voices program) or to those with a restriction of access to certain locales or resources, imposed on the youth or other marginalised groups by powerful or authoritative 'gatekeepers'. We are also suggesting that such constraints become naturalised so that effective boundaries are erected and internalised.

Goffman referred to a similar concept in his notion of perceived symbolic 'frames' that modify behaviour in different social contexts. Play is essential for the testing and pushing out of symbolic boundaries, and play itself has to be understood to be socially permitted within a particular cultural context (Goffman, 1956; Bateson, 1982). This understanding is very different from the more conventional notion of 'play as resistance', for we are arguing, as we have elsewhere, that play is more about accommodation, an embodied evaluation of where the individuals feel that they can comfortably negotiate the 'rules of the game' rather than 'subverting the ground rules'. Implicit in this understanding is getting a 'feel for the game' – a tacit recognition and acknowledgement of the symbolic boundaries – which as we outlined in the previous chapter include, in the musical cultures we observed, what to wear, how to move, what to say and how to say it! This link between play, space and place in this framework is the perceived prerequisite of '*space to play*' (Bateson, 1982; Handelman, 1990). Actual or perceived limitations on mobility (Massey, 1994) and the constraints on (self-)identity, including the perception of freedom to move or even to be in certain spaces, are directly related to the perceived ability to explore other possible ways of being – 'permission', as it were, to play. Many forms of play are mimetic and, as Bourdieu also reminds us, mimesis includes both an active and a cognitive component – how we act and how we believe we can and should behave.

An essential aspect of that embodied experience, then, is that each individual's interpretation of that material world is based on her actual and perceived gendered and socio-economic positioning within that culture. Each person experiences and creates manifestations of power and distinction through her everyday negotiation of social relations and the dominant cultural discourses. This interpretation of play and space and the role of mimetic activity returns us to the notion of bodily praxis as a mode of knowledge. While play may seem to occur anywhere and at any time, its emergence and its political and strategic power and efficacy are directly related to where and when the activity is interpreted as being allowed to take place. So, far from being trivial, play is powerful precisely because it can enable the redefining of places. As Rubin argued, 'The power to define is the power to control' and it is play and fantasy that allow us to 'create reality wherever we go by living our fantasies' (1970, pp. 142–3). Hence the power of music and related embodied practices undertaken by our young participants, for like the serious play from which it evolves such activity 'challenges official culture's claims to authority, stability, sobriety, immutability and immortality' (Schechner, 1993, p. 46).

But as we indicated above, not everyone is equally able to 'define' or to 'control'. Not everyone sees the necessity of challenging 'official culture's claims to authority'. As we have already described, the individuals in our study experienced their worlds and negotiated their spaces differently. Individuals even from the same geographical areas, neighbourhoods and similar social backgrounds could have quite different understandings of their need or ability to play in this way and to explore other alternatives. They may have different understandings of what is meant by 'personal', 'private' or 'public' space.

Different individuals have a range of micro-cultural values, and so their particular 'habitus' has been acquired and accumulated over a lifetime in their homes and in their particular familial communities. As this notion of 'habitus' has significant implications for our findings in this study it clearly deserves further, more detailed consideration. To do this we turn again to our field notes and consider how the different young people in our research sites negotiated and contested the spaces around them *from the perspectives of their own micro-cultures and belief systems*. Not everyone, as indicated above, has the same understanding of what spaces were actually open and welcoming to them both in the public and the private spheres of their worlds. Not all of them shared the same desire to engage in 'serious play' and to extend their music potential fully in the same spaces. As a way into untangling some of the complexities of such conceptions of space, we will use some examples of how a number of the young people used the spaces that *were* available to them for experimental play. For some, the first area that offered this freedom to explore appeared to be their domestic spaces, which often meant their bedrooms.

Bedroom spaces: consuming and creating

Bedrooms were certainly serious *work* spaces for many of the young people with whom we worked – in other words these were areas where they consciously decided that their music activities could be practised, rehearsed and improved. Obviously within the home conceptions and material realisations of private space were not uniform. Teenagers and youth from less affluent families often had less physical domestic space at their disposal than youth from homes that were materially more privileged. Teenagers from separated homes or blended families, where they might occupy two or more dwelling places, thought of their bedroom spaces in different ways from young people who had only one such space to call their own. Some teenagers shared their rooms with other members of their family or were expected to give up their rooms regularly for a visiting relative or family friend. So ideas of what constitutes private space even within the domestic realm are far from straightforward.

Those young people in our present study who were lucky enough to have the area solely or mainly to themselves and not shared with a sibling or other relative tended to turn their bedroom into a pseudo-recording (or sometimes a genuinely sophisticated!) studio, writing and performing space for lyric writing, rapping, mixing and other skills in DJing. Often the noise levels were reported to us as a recurring issue for the family and for neighbours, obviously then impeding the creative process! As Azza explained, he and Adam often worked together at Adam's house making music. Once or twice they lost track of time only to find it was three o'clock in the morning 'and the cops came round and asked us to keep it down' (personal communication, June 2009). Other problems could occur too in using a variety of 'mobile' rehearsal spaces in that the equipment itself might not be uniform or consistent. At one of the Beats and Rimes workshops, Azza complained to some of the others that the height of the turntables at 'Scoob's place' made his own practice difficult. 'It's so high. I'm used to this one here. There [where it's higher], I'm like this [here Azza mimes scratching at shoulder level] and I can't get my crabs and flares happenin'.[6]

Will in Adelaide used his bedroom as his office. His central aim was to perfect his nascent IT business, Zahra Interactive, through which he intended to channel the networks and publicity he gained through *Youth Revolutions*. We visited Will at home to learn more about his work on the *YR* publicity. He greeted us at the door of his parent's home in Greenwith, a newly established housing development in a northern suburb of Adelaide with a solemn 'welcome to my world'.

Will's parents were professionals. His father was a psychologist with his practice, Access Psychology, held in an office in the family home. Consequently, Will too arranged for his bedroom to be the locus of his developing computer consultancy business. The room had a single bed with an old 'Transformers'[7] quilt cover, a desk with computer books and computer and two cupboards (one he described as his stationery cupboard and it was immaculately organised; he showed us how he has all the different *Youth Revolutions* stickers neatly arranged in bags on the inside of one door). There were three computer chairs in the room for this was where he also received his clients for his business. His computer audio system was also set up for music, having six speakers for surround sound – three along the wall above his head, one under his desk and the others on each side of the computer. Will used this setting to create a direct to camera formal account of his role in *Youth Revolutions*. He entitled this segment of his promotional DVD for *Youth Revolutions* as 'backranch' and used it to contextualise and accompany audio highlights from previous programs of the show. His aim was to attract new sponsors.

> Hi. My name is Will. I do the administration and marketing here for *Youth Revolutions*. I will show you some of the work that has been produced here as well as some projects that are currently underway. Starting with promotional pack. This is what it looks like (holds it up to the camera). It was created to assist us in sponsorship and attracting new crew. It contains a CD, a business card and Messenger newspaper article that was written about us last year, late 2003.
>
> (Will, direct to camera, January 2004)

Photo 4.2   On the air at *Youth Revolutions*. © The City of Salisbury, South Australia

In contrast, Kyle's approach was far less formalised and business-like but still aimed for professionalism. We noted above our early visit to see the rehearsal space in Kyle's parents' home in Adelaide, where he kept his mixing and recording equipment. However, Kyle also used his bedroom for the setting of much of his own camera footage. He set the camera up to show his mixing decks which took up one corner of his bedroom before demonstrating his developing skills and talking about his aspirations direct to camera. Kyle's room was dominated by his double bed, which took up almost the entirety of the long narrow space. One wall alongside the bed was lined with shelving, covered in books, magazines and other paraphernalia. At the end of this, and taking over one corner of his bedroom, were his computer and mixing decks. Behind it was a small window overlooking the yard. We noticed in 2003 that he did not have many CDs or vinyl records sitting around but he did mention that he had a lot of MP3s and so stored a lot of his DJing tracks on his computer.

i wouldn't call what I do now at home is 'practicing' as such. I don't DJ as much as i used to at home, I'm spending a little more time 'producing' these days.

The main difference between DJ'ing mixing and producing is that, mixing is the art of seamlessly combining different songs into a musical 'set' or 'performance', and even combining songs to create a whole new one. But mixing generally is done live, via turntables, cd players or even digitally via digital dj software.

Producing is actually 'producing' a song. Or making it from scratch if you will. Most dance producers create their music for dj's to mix. I'm getting more heavily into producing these days, it's far more involved and definitely more difficult and challenging. But it appeals to my creative side a little more. :)

The main difference with practicing mixing/production in my own space (out of parental home) is freedom. While I'm quite respectful of my neighbours and the hours that i make noise, if i really want to... i can blast music throughout the day's i have off work without disrupting my family. I have more opportunities to mix with friends, because I'm not stuck in a little bedroom. In saying that, my parents were quite supportive of my interesting musical tastes while i was still at home. But the last thing they needed to hear was banging hard dance at 10pm on a monday night.

(Kyle's reflections, personal correspondence in May 2010, language as in original)

Tuesday in London has also been using her bedroom in the small family council flat as a rehearsal, practice and workshop space for the past seven years – although often also being curtailed by complaints about noise. She lives with 'my Mum, my three brothers, my step-dad, my dog, and anyone else who moves in and out the house'. She took several video tapes during the time of our fieldwork demonstrating her personal work space, her decks, her mixer and her music collection and self-recording her developing skills. The later tapes include a voice-over commentary about her changing music tastes and ambitions to be a professional MC, DJ and also an event organiser. Her footage was extremely subjectively shot, the camera swaying rhythmically from side to side to the beat of the music as she filmed and talked in voice-over, demonstrating each piece of equipment and each DJ move with her free hand as held the swaying camera with the other – she clearly found it impossible to remain still and listen to the beats. She also took footage of other bedroom rehearsal rooms where DJ friends of hers, such as Mario, had similarly created and produced albums and helped her to learn and improve her own techniques. That is how 'bedroom DJs' learn – through practising on the equipment at their own or their friends' homes, by watching others and also by performing at what ever gigs they can. Edward Soja claims that all such spaces should be 'seen as filled with the products of the imagination, with political projects and utopian dreams, with both sensory and symbolic realities' (Soja, 1996, p. 62). He describes such places as simultaneously 'real and imagined spaces'; both a place of liminal mimetic blurring (the imagined, the not real) and yet one also carefully marked out as a separate, discrete territory (the geographically 'real' – that which *can* be touched with the finger!). In their very creation, indeed, such spaces seem to demand a redefining of space and thus an unsettling of some of the usual, simplistic ways in which space is categorised into private and public arenas.

Carving privacy in public spaces

The terms 'private' and 'public', like the concept of space itself, although freely used in popular discourse are never unproblematic or uncontested. Firstly, like the concept of ownership and management of the body, privacy also involves the ability and the affectivity of the agent to be in control. Yet of course not everyone experiences the same right or means to control. Similarly not everyone shares the same perceived concept of privacy. Secondly, as suggested above, geographic places alone do not automatically prescribe which activities take place within particular physical boundaries. There is no such thing as space that can be definitively used for public or private activity. Privacy can be enforced and indicated by a material boundary such as a padlocked door or gate or a sign that indicates 'keep out' or 'private property', or a state of mind. One can be engaged in 'private', such as exclusive conversations or secret business deals or even daydreaming in a very public environment, for example in a street, a cinema or a shopping centre. One can immediately be excluded from a group in a space where one felt included and belonging by a sudden move by some of the members physically turning away and holding whispered or separate conversations. We noticed this occurring even in the confined spaces of the radio station at PBA-FM amongst the *Youth Revolutions* crew especially as their group became more divided and their internal tensions began to surface more clearly.

Privacy can have several other contradictory connotations too. It can indicate constraint (for one can be either inside or outside the symbolic or material boundary) but it can also simultaneously imply protection and shelter from realities that may be perceived as dangerous or corrupting. Furthermore, clearly spaces that are understood as private such as the home are not necessarily safe for all the people within their walls, as in cases of physical or sexual abuse. Several of the youth in our project indicated that their sense of safety in the home was not assured, including of course quite a few of the young residents of the Brighton Treatment Center, Boston.

From his earliest structuralist account and insights of gender relations drawn from his participant observations of a Kabyle house (Bourdieu, 1977, p. 191) through to his later sophisticated applications of symbolic power in contemporary global societies (Bourdieu, 1990, 1993, 1998, 1999; Bourdieu and Wacquant, 1992), Bourdieu has demonstrated that power, privilege and privacy are both formalised and internalised in the day-to-day negotiations of family and community members. He highlights, for example, the ways in which the meanings of particular spaces never exist a priori so that particular bedroom spaces are not equally private for all members of a household. Clearly for the young men in the Brighton Treatment Center this is particularly apparent and acute but it is also so for many of the youth we worked with across the four countries. Furthermore, it is also clear that even the concept of private space is not a universally understood notion amongst all cultures or even within one culture. An individual's social positioning within her wider culture affects her understanding of access and use of space. For some the notion of personal or individual 'private space' is a right; for others it is an anathema. As Lidia Sciama points out in her anthropological study of the meanings of privacy amongst Greek and British communities 'the concept of privacy has no precise and uniform content'. In fact the concept for some just doesn't exist (1993, p. 87). Nancy Duncan agrees. She argues that the distinction between private and public spaces, and the relation of this distinction to private and public arenas, while 'encoded in law and deeply rooted in North American and British cultures is nevertheless unstable and problematically conflated with related distinctions such as that between domestic or familial autonomy and public spheres' (1996, p. 127).

On the other hand, spaces that are often considered to be public and therefore assumed to be *inclusive* such as shopping centres or city malls are frequently *exclusive* for marginalised others – the young, the less affluent, the homeless, the unemployed in the community – who primarily want to congregate and socialise but do not have the monetary means to purchase and therefore do not have the 'right' to linger. Other public places such as bars and dance clubs can permit some very private behaviour to take place simply because in the large crowds one can be anonymous and often invisible to those in authority. Indeed, in all places, relative anonymity can encourage some very exclusive activities. Conversely, places usually designed for private activity such as bedrooms, especially for teenagers and young adults seeking places to entertain their friends or to engage in serious play, as we have described above, can sometimes be used for very public activities. Kyle and Tuesday's respective video footage included parties of friends held within their and other people's houses, including the bedroom areas. What emerges from all of these contradictions is that the shared perception of privacy being a physical and a symbolic state is closely aligned to cultural understandings of power and, as such, is also directly related to bodily praxis.

If serious play is contained by symbolic boundaries *inside* the home, we are left with the question of what experimenting and playful activity could occur in other kinds of spaces, such as the youth clubs, the street, the shopping mall and other more formalised and constraining institutions. How was privacy conceived of *outside* of the home? How might serious play and self-making be encouraged and enabled in the spaces we instinctively might consider to be more public? In these (apparently) more inclusive places, the activities of self-making could paradoxically be sometimes more dramatic, more daring, more experimental – paradoxically because such areas considered more 'public' can often offer greater anonymity. They can enable and offer more 'private' space to play. Before we look more closely at examples of this, we need to revisit the recurring myth of public space and its assumed greater accessibility to all.

The myth of public space

It is perhaps ironic that there are more possibilities for young people to explore and play within areas understood to be public than in the more constraining domestic realms. We use the word 'ironic' advisedly because one usually speaks of people feeling more 'themselves' and more able to relax their more formal codes of behaviour within the home space as opposed to more public spheres. We argue that it is the relative anonymity of the 'street' away from the domestic sphere that allows young people to 'step into the subjunctive' as it were, to experiment and explore other possibilities of 'self-making' including those that rely on developing their musical and their shared cultural identities. Yet of course we are not suggesting that any public space, including concepts of 'the street', has intrinsic meaning separate from the social and cultural meanings that emerge from bodily praxis. It is important to recall that youth as a generic grouping, because of their age and relatively low social status (and therefore low spending power), only appropriate *any* private space with great difficulty. The ability to redefine and negotiate personal space and spatial relationships is directly linked to conventional divisions of power and social hierarchies, such as class, gender and ethnicity.

At first sight, the concept of public space seems far more straightforward than the notion of the private. Certain geographical locales such as parks, shopping malls, city streets and public gardens are considered to be accessible to everyone. Many areas that appear to be open and accessible to all are in fact simultaneously understood by many to be symbolically bounded and 'off limits'. Categories of social ordering and related status, such as age and gender, impose further symbolic boundaries on who is and feels welcome in particular spaces and who does not.

We noted above, for example, the ways in which girls might officially be considered able to access youth centres and workshops in Newcastle and Berlin and yet in fact felt unwelcome and unable to participate due to the extreme masculine atmosphere and discourses that were dominating the space. Frequently a number of these symbolic categories apply simultaneously, adding further complexities to the boundaries. For example, several of the youth workers in the Berlin CBOs told us that different types of music were used by the participants to create both a material and simultaneously a sonic space of both belonging for one group and exclusion for another. So some young people would demand the right to play Turkish or Arabic music, carving out a separate space through music and language that the non-Turkish speakers at the club felt they could not enjoy or understand. At the same time, groups who only wanted to play heavy metal or hip hop would be excluding the young people from the Turkish-speaking or some of the other Muslim communities.

At all of the sites that we worked in, youth presence in community public spaces outside of the CBO was perceived to be a problem. In every country the media discuss the issue of 'youth crime' and 'youth gangs' on a regular basis. While more academic articles tend to be more sympathetic to the complex issues of 'policing' competing public spaces (as in Werbner, 1996; Malone, 2002; Valentine, 2004; Walsh, 2008; Crawford and Flint, 2009), the articles in the tabloid press or popular media tend to be negative or eager to examine the latest solutions to perceived youth street crime or nuisance (Jones and Yamagata, 2000; Juszkiewicz, 2000; Riley, 2007). However, not all popular media articles are unperceptive. The following is a short extract from a recent article in the popular (and politically aware) German art and culture magazine *Zitty*, which seemed to discuss the issue of young people in the centre of Berlin empathically.

> When the sun goes down and the TV tower's silver ball is sparkling, they show up: hundreds of youth, weekend for weekend, every Friday and Saturday. Some day someone must have been the first one who had the idea of making Alexanderplatz the meeting place. There are the gothics, who gather in the shadow of the few trees with their black leather coats and black fingernails. There are the punks with their dogs and their loudly coloured irokese haircut, who drink bottled beer on the park benches. There are the ravers with their ghetto blaster and backpacks filled with red-bull cans. There are the hip hoppers with their XXI clothes. There are the emos with their fringe hairstyles and drainpipe jeans. There are the skaters who dash against the kerbstone with bloody knees. And there are some that just come to Alexanderplatz because there's always something happening and meeting friends is easy there. They chat, some get drunk, and some are kissing each other. Hanging out. Sometimes ravers have a row with the hip hoppers, because the ravers are annoyed by the jumping of the hip hoppers and the hip hoppers can't stand their techno beats. But most often they get along. They know each other. They greet each other – 'hey dude!' With well-practised handshakes. Micky's there,

Borste is coming soon. 'What about Kitty? Haven't seen her for a long time.' Almost everybody has a nickname.

Lots of neighbours had high hopes with the alcohol ban that the youth would look for another meeting place. But the youth stayed. They don't accept regulations where to meet and where not. They like Alexanderplatz. Some of them stroll down Alexa [big shopping centre] in search of a bargain at H&M in the afternoons. Some buy cheap liqueur at Plus [supermarket] in the Rathauspassage. There you can get the stuff for 2.99 Euro. To avoid getting caught drinking alcohol, they hide in the bushes.

Alex and the youth – they belong together. A place, an unfinished mix of modern Berlin and GDR scenery. Shopping centres, high-rise socialist buildings, red city hall, Neptune fountain, cinema. Next to the River Spree, Karl Marx is sitting next to Friedrich Engels, both of them larger than life size moulded into bronze. The youth on their search for identity and boundaries. They know Marx and Engels just from history lessons, and from the Berlin Wall they only know the piece at the East-Side Gallery. Christiane F.'s 'We Children from Bahnhof Zoo' (a famous book about drug abuse at Bahnhof Zoo in the 1970s/80s) was also only read at school. Some of them have a life like Christiane F. – day and night on the streets without a permanent place of residence. Others grow up in broken families. Some drink themselves into a coma, others do not. Some just dream to get discovered by a TV show, others want to come with the territory. The differences between the different biographies of the children at Alex couldn't be more blatant. (Koppelstädter, 2010)[8]

Wilson, Rose and Colvin recently reported on their study of surveillance cameras and youth in an Australian academic publication, similarly stressing the 'problem' of young people hanging out in commercial centres – youth with nowhere to go and nothing to do – who increasingly come under the surveillance of police and security guards.

> Studies of the operation of CCTV surveillance would suggest however, that young people, particularly those perceived to be 'troublesome' do receive disproportionate attention from surveillance operators. This is intertwined with the wider politics of public space in which marginalized young people are perceived as 'flawed consumers' (Bauman, 1998) and frequently find themselves at the sharp end of processes of exclusion which seek to remove those perceived as threats to order from public spaces which are increasingly exclusively configured as spaces of consumption. (Wilson et al., 2009)

Their article included comments reiterating the same issues from the perspective of the young people themselves such as Jayden, who complained that surveillance and security existed because 'Just want us away from their areas because apparently we make their business look bad or whatever like. But that's not the case; it's just that we don't have our own place to XXXX chill' (quoted in Wilson et al., 2009).

The authors of the article also note that these experiences of constantly being on the receiving end of such close monitoring sometimes lead the young people to 'play with surveillance' with 'little acts of resistance', arguing that 'such play served to enhance their visibility in a society in which they are often ignored and excluded' (Wilson et al., 2009).

As we have seen above, girls from all backgrounds tended to be granted less access to public spaces of status, knowledge and power than their male counterparts (Spain, 1992; Ardener, 1993; Massey, 1994). In many societies and eras, the exclusion of women from what have been designated 'male spaces' is effected through a number of social practices and discourses that contribute to women's restriction of movement or sense of belonging. At the same time, it is clear that for all of the youth in our study, even those girls who felt at ease in public spaces, as well as their teenage male relatives and other boys in their familial and social circles, home was no longer a satisfying place to be. Even in quite straightforward physical terms, an adolescent body takes up far more room, makes more noise and requires more area than does a small child. In addition, lack of physical space, lack of privacy and the obvious connection with childhood and protection render the domestic sphere far from being a place where the young people could easily experiment with 'alternative selves'. Yet their relatively young age and their mainly unemployed or low paid status meant that they were without independent financial means and therefore had few places where they could go and congregate with friends outside of the home. In this context and in terms of 'private space' meaning 'negotiating space to play' many of the young people we met during our fieldwork certainly affirmed that they had 'no space of their own' (White, 1990; Willis, 1990). Hence the importance of the CBOs and the youth spaces for the young people we worked with at all of our sites, as we detail further in the next section.

CBOs, youth spaces and a space of their own

As indicated earlier, since 2003 we have been engaged with twenty field sites or CBOs across the four countries. Some were far more active than others and some far more directive. For the reasons outlined in Chapter 1, we found we were unable to undertake intensive participant observation and get to know the youth involved to the same extent in each place. Similarly the young co-researchers and their mentors themselves, that is our 'key' respondents/youth and non-university research partners, were drawn from only seven out of the potential twenty sites as for various reasons we could not attract or maintain the interest or engagement of the youth in our project from the others over the long period of time. The ones who did engage have continued to contact us and provide us with information about their current musical activities and ambitions. In the case of the Brighton Treatment Center, we were unable to follow the young people's musical career paths beyond the institution for practical and ethical reasons. On the other hand, we were able to observe at *all* of the sites to see what activities were offered, how the youth engaged and how their youth workers, mentors and educators went about making the centre a welcoming, creative space of belonging – a space for serious play. Because there were a range of approaches and ideologies underlying the different CBOs which in turn varied in their efficacy for their young clientele, we will draw the examples in our next section from what we saw as two different categories: places primarily designed to enhance socialisation and cultural cohesion with minimal teaching programs and instruction in music, and places primarily focused on the role of the arts to enhance cultural capital and increase cultural cohesion where teaching and mentoring programs and instruction in music-related activities were central and tended to have more pedagogical structure. However, it is also important to stress that, firstly, *all* of the institutionalised CBOs' programs were at least partly designed and funded to solve the perceived local problem of youth anti-social behaviour, disaffection, marginalisation and disengagement.[9] They all attempted in some way to prove a safe and inclusive space for the youth to be and to belong; to reduce the local community concerns about youth violence, alcohol and drug abuse, illegal drug-related crime and gang warfare; and to provide pathways for increased opportunities for employment and greater social cohesion and inclusivity. Secondly, the physical atmosphere created by the CBO – in its building, décor, ambience and access (including public transport infrastructure) – contributed to the success or otherwise of the programs offered within.

We also selected each of the sites studied in the Playing for Life project because that particular locale had been previously identified and categorised by educational, social and political policy-makers as a 'problem' area with the majority of young people there regarded as being disaffected, disadvantaged and 'at risk'. Overall, then, there was a central aim to get young people, especially groups of young people, off the streets and into some safe area for socialisation where behaviour could be monitored and positively directed. To that end the places had to be welcoming and voluntary and, secondly, offer activities that would interest or could be positively channelled or redirected to enhance the learning and life skills of the youth. This means that three aspects were central to the success of the task. Firstly, the spaces had to feel welcoming, attractive and appropriate to the age, ethnicity and gender of the groups involved. This in itself is often difficult if not impossible to achieve, of course, as many centres were located in multiethnic and multicultural areas, they catered for a range of ages and purposes from quite young children through to older teenagers, including allowing for both girls' and boys' attendance and sometimes the spaces were also used for programs for elderly clientele in the community.

The second related aspect was that the staff or the mentors themselves had to be approachable and, depending on the particular aim of the centre, had to be trained and experienced enough to offer both counselling and psychological support (youth workers) *and* be able to teach technical skills that the youth sought in music or other specific aspects of youth cultures to illustrate the different areas and impact of the new technology, media, music genres or related fields (educationally trained arts workers/mentors). Usually that required two different sets of expertise and so two different sets of people. However, ever-tighter budget restrictions often led to a lack of such specialists being available or else they could only be contracted into the centres for very short times. This in turn meant that only one of these requirements could be met. The centres themselves were subjected to increased evaluation and accountability – not a bad thing in itself perhaps except that all of the staff's energy and time would be spent seeking additional funding for creative short-term programs and attempting to meet the required key performance indicators (KPIs) (see Chapter 5 for more information on this dilemma and its consequences).

The third related aspect was that the programs and activities offered at the centre had to be meaningful for the youth involved so that they could recognise that the centre offered genuine pathways to authentic and transferable life skills. That also meant that resources had to be available and accessible to all. The three aspects of course are intertwined at each successful venue or clearly missing when CBOs seemed to be less effective or successful. At the centre of this conundrum is the materiality of the space itself, as explored further in the next section.

The role of heritage buildings

Almost all of the centres and CBOs in our study did attempt to make the buildings and the spaces within them inviting, friendly and flexible. To that end their internal design attempted to be the antithesis of more structured and formal educational institutions such as schools. At the same time, several of the CBOs such as Carclew in Adelaide, the Palais in Newcastle, Australia, and the Tabernacle and WAC in London were housed (albeit sometimes temporarily) in heritage, often Victorian buildings or architecturally significant buildings, which in their previous life had been private stately homes, theatres, cinemas, ballrooms or places of worship. Their exterior façade was still imposing and dramatic, representing that country's colonial past. The reason such buildings were often used for youth centres and venues is because they were often owned by councils, almost as 'white elephants'. The local authorities did not know quite what to do with them: they were often too large to be used for anything other than an event venue, in too much of a state of disrepair to be restored/renovated for residential properties, and often the council was bound by heritage regulations so that they could not completely restructure or change the outside of the building too drastically. This meant they were handed over to youth arts/youth services departments to use as workshop spaces, concert venues (where still possible) and offices.

Fascinatingly, empty heritage buildings are often appropriated illegally by various groups, often by young people in Europe, to create community or social centres. These buildings can then be used for a range of disparate, not-for-profit, activities. Because the buildings tend to have large open spaces they are ideal as organisational hubs for local activities, providing material and social support networks for minority groups. The size and openness of the buildings also mean that they can be used to host activist meetings, concerts, bookshops, dance performances and art exhibitions. The reclaiming of such a building for a completely different purpose and clientele from that which was intended adds another dimension to the youth's sense of empowerment in that the building itself seems to provide an exciting sense of 'trespass' and incongruity; clearly, the activities currently being undertaken in the buildings were not what the original architects or owners had in mind. Furthermore, the participants in these new activities were from a grouping that previously would not have been admitted or welcomed into that space, except as servants or slaves.[10] Perhaps that is one of the reasons Karin Woodley was so keen to talk to her students about the slave origins of

Photo 4.3   Carclew. © Jaclyn Bloustien

148 *Youth, Music and Creative Cultures*

Photo 4.4   Interchange Studios and Weekend Arts College. © Jaclyn Bloustien

Photo 4.5   The Tabernacle. © Jaclyn Bloustien

the Notting Hill carnival and contemporary gospel music, as they sat within the workshops at the Tabernacle.

The symbolic division of public arenas into either legitimate spaces for occupation or places of trespass by the young people reflects their incorporation of the time-honoured cultural divisions of status and conventional

Photo 4.6 The Palais Royale. © Jaclyn Bloustien

social hierarchies. In their extreme manifestations, such divisions signify the places where high culture is 'legitimated', 'protected by their legitimacy against the scientific gaze and against desacralisation that is presupposed by the scientific study of sacred objects' (Bourdieu, 1993, p. 132). Anyone entering such a 'sacred' space usually assumes appropriate stance, behaviour and appearance and possesses the necessary cultural capital to appreciate such knowledge and artefacts. When individuals or groups of people behave in ways that differ from this traditional, usually implicit code, their actions are immediately read as inappropriate or deliberately subversive.

When the appropriation of such space *does* occur, it is where 'subversive', 'incongruous' or 'illegitimate' activity is understood to be *possible* – even if it is purely through imaginative play. This echoes Bourdieu's concept of 'counter-legitimacy':

> spaces that belong to the dominated classes, haunts or refuges for excluded individuals, from which the dominant individuals are in fact excluded, *at least symbolically*, and for the accredited holders of the social and linguistic competence which is recognized on these markets. (Bourdieu, 1991, p. 98, emphasis added)

So 'private space' in this conception becomes arenas where those who feel they usually cannot, do. It appears in the gaps between official and legitimate cultural discourses, even, it would seem, in the most 'inappropriate' of locales.

> If there is a tradition (and not only in the West) of constructing grand monuments specifically to present performances – arenas, stadiums and theatres – so there is a long history of unofficial performances 'taking place' in (seizing as well as using) locales not architecturally imagined as theatres. (Schechner, 1993, pp. 48–9)

Schechner here is mainly thinking about the streets as spaces of improvised or non-commercial performance and we might also consider in this context shopping malls, car parks, public squares for dances and raves, inline skating and skateboards; corporate and city walls for illegitimate street art and graffiti; the imposing front of the Palais Royale, Newcastle and the highly decorated graffitied walls on the side and back! Such play allows the voicing of those usual *silences* of dominant cultural understandings – even if sometimes that voicing occurs just above a whisper or has to take place in the form of distancing humour. When the CBOs we visited were housed in one of these once-splendid colonial buildings, they also seemed to evoke this atmosphere of 'mimetic excess' – a transformation of space for the serious but almost 'disrespectful' play of youth, through the incongruity of twenty-first-century popular (loud) music, street art and the noisy cacophony of creativity.

Our first impression of the Palais, for example, was of almost a cathedral-like arena, with a central open area, a massively high ceiling and on each side separate areas, some on raised platforms but few with doors, where a variety of activities could take place simultaneously. The building, which still had its art deco façade when we first saw it, was shabby but colourful, reminding us of a colonial lady in faded clothes trying (and somehow managing) to maintain some of her former glory and hold on to her dignity, despite the walls around the building being used as graffiti projects for the young people. Sometimes we could pick out particular tags and signatures on the graffiti, including the name 'Azza' – someone we were to get to know well as one of our co-researchers! The Palais was on a main street near the sea front, which at the time of our first visit was in the process of being regenerated. The railway, which runs directly behind the building, was going to be (controversially) cut back from the sea front and this area to allow further development to happen. Some buildings on the other side of the railway line had already been turned into business or residential properties. The notorious 'Duck's Nuts' Hotel lies opposite the Palais. Together with the local McDonald's located a further street back from the main street, these places were seen as giving the area a seedy and criminal reputation where young people were prone to hang around. This was something that the council wanted to change with the development of this area for their older constituency, thus the move of the Palais to the Loft, its new premises.

Beyond the large entrance to the Palais lay the main concert hall, including a large stage at the far end, a lengthy bar to one side and capacity for up to 1,000 people. There were also a number of small rooms off to either side of the hall – one part of a side room held about five or six PC stations which could be used by any young person, another part was office space for the youth workers (six or so desks). Outside, towards the back of the venue was a small skate park – occupied at that time by about ten young boys, either hanging around watching or performing moves with their skateboards (not always successfully). This was regarded as a 'skate clinic' session although there was no youth worker there to assist or help the young people with their skate moves.

The walls outside the back of the building were also used for graffiti training – a concept in itself difficult for some councils and educators to understand. The people on the trains often look out the windows with astonishment at these young people doing graffiti on the back walls! The other side of the main concert hall contained a pair of decks and music software – this is where the hip hop lyrics and freestyle workshop took place. There was also an upstairs part to the Palais, containing another concert and bar area.

We felt that the whole open area therefore allowed for freedom of movement, a sense that while dedicated workshops were the main 'business' of the CBO there was also opportunity to 'hang out' and licence to move from space to space. Not everyone involved in the Palais felt so positively about the space, however. The director of the Palais, Barney Langford's insights are provided in the text box below.

Prior to my appointment as Coordinator I had only had a fleeting association with the Palais. The Palais had occupied a kind of geographical landmark in my life. It was here when I first came to Newcastle in 1970 and its location in Hunter St Newcastle West was like a kind of emblematic gateway to the CBD. It had been in its more than 100 year history an ice skating rink, a dance hall, a rock venue and a nightclub.

I think I had been there once during its heyday when it hosted Barnesy and Cold Chisel and AC DC et al (popular Australian Rock Bands). My most constant association was being mates with the guy who did the sound and lighting there during the 80s. He referred to it as the 'Palais de Troc' (short for Trocadero). At this late stage the Palais had degenerated into a kind of seedy nightspot frequented by desperate and lonely souls on the cusp of middle age. Shortly afterwards it closed all together as an entertainment venue and re-opened as an even more seedy pool hall. Then it closed completely.

Two years later it re-opened as the Palais Royale Youth Venue. The Palais may have been a great nite spot. But as a youth venue it left a lot to be desired. It was great when we had a large gig where its barn-like interior could accommodate the 1000+ people who might attend. But for most of our activities, its cavernous interior was not conducive to the small-scale workshop activities which were the bread and butter of the youth venue's workshop program. Its run-down condition and its location in the seedier west end of Newcastle did little to encourage parents to entrust their children to attend activities there.

Its decrepitude after 100 years was well and truly on display. As an example, one afternoon I was approached by a number of young people complaining that they found it difficult to hear each other over the noise made by the termites chomping away in the walls of the computer room.

Despite this the Palais was loved by the young people who attended activities and events there. For new and emerging bands the mystique of playing on the same stage alongside the ghosts of the greats of Australian rock was a real plus. Its outdoor area allowed us to incorporate a skate ramp as an additional resource for young people. I guess for them the history dripped (sometimes literally) from the walls and ceiling. And there was something quite imposing about the sheer scale of the interior.

When we moved to our new premises the young people decided that they would like to somehow take a little bit of the Palais with them. They decided to name our new home THE LOFT as a remembrance of the upstairs area of the Palais. A stained glass door with the name Loft encased has also made its way to a new home. And two of the scores of plaster casts of a dancing lady which adorned the ceiling at the Palais now hold pride of place at our new home. They remind us that the purpose-renovated home we now have would not have materialised had it not been for our original site. And they are a tiny reminder of the Palais which was razed to the ground 3 years ago and of the more than 100 years of history which the Palais represented in the social and cultural life of Newcastle.

(Barney Langford, personal correspondence, 2010)

Barney summarises perfectly the ambivalent attitude that both youth and their mentors feel towards particular venues; there is the excitement and romantic nostalgia of gaining access to that enormous, historical space together with the sense of being part of an ongoing history, with 'the mystique of playing on the same stage alongside the ghosts of the greats of Australian rock'. We, as new visitors to the venue, also felt that 'there was something quite imposing about the sheer scale of the interior'. Yet, at the same time, Barney reminds us of the other side of being part of the living history – that the Palais' severely 'rundown condition' (where you could hear the termites munch!) and 'its location in the seedier west end of Newcastle' detracted from its past glory and made it really difficult to utilise in the present.

Although quite a number of the CBOs we visited and worked in were housed in older buildings for the reasons given above, few were fortunate enough to take full advantage of the potential of the building, even if they wanted to, because they were usually funded insufficiently to use the open spaces as they might have wished. Over the period of our fieldwork, many of the research sites we visited had to limit their activities to tightly scheduled workshops or close up altogether. We will return to some of these programs and related issues in the following chapters. We just note here perhaps the obvious point that the kind of space available and accessible to the young people affects and frames the activities offered in that space.

Barney points to a related significant aspect of particular places for youth as a venue just to 'be', to 'hang out', and thereby to explore 'serious play' fully. That is, the attachment to a city, a neighbourhood and a particular venue, even if it is dangerous, unsuitable or sometimes unwelcoming, is still valued as a place of belonging. We noticed in the 'beats and rimes' lyrics of Azza and Adam that they would jump to the defence of Newcastle when they were in competition and others were disparaging about their home town even though they might be critical themselves in their own verses. Indeed it was observed by several of the research team that there could be a fine line between 'we like putting shit on Newcastle but we're still very proud of Newcastle' and 'no one else is allowed to put shit on Newcastle, but we are', concluding 'if some else does, then we get stuck into them'. Or to put it another way: 'we know it's a shithole, but it's our shithole' (personal communications, 2004).

This tension or ambivalence towards a place of belonging becomes particularly acute when that place is under threat of being taken away completely. One such example that aroused community debate and action also involved Newcastle. The successor of the Palais in 2009 as a youth venue was the Loft, as Barney indicates above, but that too came under threat of closure. The local youth organisations and committed individuals expressed their concerns in an advertisement and poster campaign, through the social

154 Youth, Music and Creative Cultures

Photo 4.7 Save our Loft! Campaign poster. © Julie Pavlou-Kirri

networking sites of MySpace and Facebook and also, as in the extract below, through the Indent[11] website:

> The Newcastle City Council's Sustainability Review has recommended to close The Loft Youth Venue, sell the building and all the assets. For years The Loft has been the centre of Newcastle's all-ages music scene: playing host to many bands, Indent workshops, allowing young people to get into a recording studio and providing many other positive art-based opportunities for young people in the area. If it closes there will be no more all ages gig space, no more arts programs, no more radio program, no more recording studio, no more aerosol art workshops, no more beats and rhymes workshops, no more free art activities, no more inzine, no more youth art exhibition space, no more school holiday activities, no more computer space for young people to use, no more youth

venue…For many years The Loft Youth Music Team has been an active Indent team, gaining funding from us and staging countless gigs in the venue. Many young bands have cut their teeth in that room, playing largely to audiences of their friends. Indent has run countless workshops, brought performers to the venue and professional producers to the studio and through this has gained an understanding of just how integral The Loft is to the continued vibrancy of the Newcastle all-ages scene.

The decision to close The Loft will be made at a Newcastle City Council meeting in June. If you do not want this to happen then get involved to Save the Loft! It is your venue, you shouldn't have to fight to keep it open, but you're going to have to. So let's step it up so we can make a change, and who knows…we could even make history. If you have something to say about saving The Loft, leave a comment! (www.indent.net. au 2010)

The local city media, including free and community, independent or alternative street papers and popular social networking sites also ran regular comments and fed aggressively into the campaign about the impending closure of the Loft and the perceived social dangers this might bring (see Adoranti, 2009; Harris, 2009; O'Brien, 2009; Williams, 2009). As twenty-year-old Nicole Molyneux, creator of the 'Save the Loft' MySpace and Facebook webpages, explained, she had been going to the Loft since she was 16 years old. She argued that many young people participated in the Loft's activities and went to gigs held there: 'There are so many activities young people can do at the Loft. There would definitely be an increase in boredom if the Loft shuts down and that might lead to social problems' (quoted in Adoranti, 2009).

Nicole Molyneux claimed that the venue was a place for young people to go and feel safe, 'a way for kids to express themselves. If it is shut down, the young people, who attend the Loft, will lose their link to the community' (quoted in Adoranti, 2009). The campaign so far has been relatively successful in at least gaining a reprieve of two years. The 'Save the Loft' MySpace website, however, indicates that the youth feel the fight is far from over:

Last year, it was recommended to Newcastle City Council, through the Sustainability Review report, to sell and close down its only Youth Venue as a way of saving the city money. But when the young people of Newcastle found out about this they decided to fight this recommendation. So we created the 'Save The Loft' MySpace and Facebook network and we advocated to keep The Loft open.

After lots of lobbying and campaigning to the Council and the community, Council decided on June 25 to keep The Loft open for at least another 2 years in order to create a 'Youth Strategy' to promote and improve the services of the Youth Venue. So…we played a huge part in saving The Loft! I would like to thank every one who has been involved so far! But our fight is not over yet. Get ready for 'Save The Loft 3' between now and 2011. (http://www.myspace.com/savethelofttakeii, accessed July 2010)

Undoubtedly, the concern of the youth of Newcastle would be that this would be the second time their venue was under threat. As Barney Langford pointed out, the Loft itself carried with it memories and sentimental attachments from the old venue, the Palais. The closure of the Loft would intensify the sense of loss and the sense of youth issues being completely undervalued in Newcastle.

Outside spaces

As indicated above, a successful youth venue is valued for the additional areas it offers beyond the building itself. Outside spaces attached to youth centres were less common in Berlin. Many of the CBO buildings there, which clearly had been purpose-built between the 1960s and 1980s, were quite characterless cement or brick low-rise buildings offering some space within but little relief from the urban concrete environment outside. On the other hand, a few did have useful outside spaces. Alleins e.V. was one – a self-financing, non-profit-making private youth work company in south-eastern Berlin in the district of Köpenick. The old youth centre was located in a site that was recently purchased by an international investor who plans to build condominiums and lofts there. So the venue has had to move to Mellowpark (also financed by Alleins e.V.), a major (internationally known) skate and BMX park with a huge variety of sports and event locations. Only the youth club and the office have remained at the old address but the club is happy with the move as now they have more space and are more directly linked with Mellowpark.

Another venue, Statthaus Böcklerpark in Kreuzberg, also had a thoughtfully planned outside area for different age groups and purposes but has had a less happy outcome. It was considered one of Berlin's most well-known social institutions for open 'low-intensity' youth work, particularly with male ethnic minority youngsters. It was located in the middle of Böckler Park, close to the canal with a little zoo and a variety of street ball, basketball, soccer, table tennis and skate facilities and surrounded by public housing estates. With the exception of the public housing buildings, the entire neighbourhood has undergone a gentrification process, whereby all single households comprise white middle-class people, while the family households in the area are almost 100 per cent ethnic minority members. Hence, the visitors of Statthaus previously were nearly 100 per cent ethnic minority groups, mainly of Arabic or Turkish descent. The director told us that he had once undertaken an informal survey that asked people to identify their ethnic origin. He said he found that more than fifty ethnic groups from over sixty countries were represented at the centre.

In July 2010 the centre was suddenly and summarily closed by the local council and all the staff were relocated or fired. The local council's aim, we were told by the former director, was to open a new centre with different objectives. But Wolfgang Fischer was very concerned. Particularly under the new school system, he said, schools were set up with a completely new and highly regulated schedule and framework. This was exactly the kind of setting in which most of his former clientele would fail because they need a more open and creative space that accepts unconventional, even what Wolfgang Fischer described as 'deviant', behaviour (see the following chapter and Chapter 7 for more information and the significance of this development).

Another Berlin CBO was SPIK e.V., located in Hohenschönhausen, in outer east Berlin. It was surrounded by high-rise buildings from the 1970s and 1980s. It had no outside space but its inside areas were very large, mainly because the building also hosted several other organisations that all dealt with social work, open youth work and music pedagogy. A similar situation existed for Wutzkyallee, a multifunctional centre in the Gropiusstadt neighbourhood. It was located in a mixed socio-demographic area, one containing both high-rise public housing and subsidised housing, and also lower middle-class people. Located next to an all-track school complex, the centre found that a reduction in funding over the last two years has required a corresponding increase in cooperation with that adjacent school and many others from all over Neukölln. A new program is the 'Bildungsmeile Wutzkyallee' (education mile), where they work closely with the teachers, school social workers and pupils of different ages, but they also offer new family days, senior days and so on in order to get as many locals involved as possible.

In both parts of the postwar, pre-unified Berlin attempts were made to 'raise all young people as citizens of the state' (Youth Law of the GDR 1974, para 1.1, cited and translated in Smith, 1998, p. 289), even though their methods and rationale were slightly different. In the German Democratic Republic (GDR) the aim was to educate the young people in Marxism-Leninism and to protect them from Western influences by controlling the spaces they could occupy (Mahrad, 1977; Freiberg and Mahrad, 1982; Frisby, 1989; Waterkamp, 1989; Pilkington, 1994; Smith, 1998). A parallel aim in West Germany was to educate the youth to reject all forms of fascism but also communism! Fiona Smith argues that, while political rhetoric dominated youth movements, the young people themselves used particular places in the city as 'sites of resistance' against this rhetoric before and after reunification. Before 1990 the GDR state attempted to control young people's spaces through the rigidly formalised and unified education system and through the only officially authorised youth movement, Free German Youth (FDR). Smith argues that even before reunification East German youth sought to utilise space and place as sites of resistance, often finding other spaces, using the margins of or subverting the use and significance of official spaces. This covered a range of scales and sites... [including] state defined youth spaces such as clubs or work; new places in neglected spaces of old buildings and neighbourhoods; private spaces in homes and among friends; state controlled public spaces and the free spaces offered by GDR churches. (Smith, 1998, p. 291)

Smith goes on to explain that perhaps ironically, the only state-sanctioned 'freespace' (*Freiraum*) in the GDR was in fact in buildings that belonged or were connected to the churches. The churches offered spaces for rock and other popular music concerts, and for free discussions – 'a space to meet that was unstructured by the state and the FDJ' (Smith, 1998, p. 296). In our own work, we also found church-owned spaces were very popular with the youth. Café Leitz in Berlin, for example, was still important for young people seeking a place to meet, explore and perform their music. (Chapter 5 explores this further.)

Across the sea in Ramsgate, UK, another youth centre, Pie Factory Music (PFM), has made use of a church space. The Pie Factory, which was located in Margate when we first visited, has since moved to Ramsgate. There, in a disused church, the youth centre finally has found a larger space where it can expand and undertake the kinds of activities it wants to – although it is already outgrowing this space too. Our first visit to the youth centre was in 2003, a year after it became the charity Pie Factory Music. The director and his team had intended to be situated in the former Pie Factory building in Margate but by the time the feasibility study had been completed, in 2004, the local council decided such a move would not be cost effective based on the finding of the feasibility study from the Future Building Fund paid for by the council. The name stayed, however, as apparently, as part of the long-term regeneration plans for the city, all of the organisations were naming their companies after where they were going to end up in the old town. Even though they did not end up at the Pie Factory, the name had been attached to the centre for at least two and a half years and it felt catchy and attractive to their clientele!

The youth centre continued to be housed in the Community Pharmacy Gallery, a section of the Margate Council Chambers, although it was unheated and far too small for their needs. The move finally occurred when one of the other organisations they had been dealing with, and which had been located in an old disused chapel in Ramsgate, decided to move on. Brian Spencer-Smith bought the building as an investment but with the underlying aim of enabling PFM to move and expand. Although he is effectively their landlord, so that they pay a nominal rent, he allows 'free run of the building, as long as we don't wreck the place' (Mike Fagg, personal communication, October, 2010). They have renovated internally so that they now have an upstairs office, workshop space and a main open area for about thirty people. The old kitchen is now a recording studio and they also built on a 'live' room, toilets, a little kitchenette and a front room. Downstairs new offices have had to be constructed as there are now seven people employed there full-time. Yet already, said Mike Fagg, they have outgrown this building and they have applied unsuccessfully for several opportunities for funding. Interestingly, the reasons for their lack of success in the funding bid were again due to problems with space and design. A new government initiative called 'myplace' has been introduced in Britain, with the aim of investing in young people's buildings and services. The government intends to build about 25 state-of-the-art multi-million-pound buildings and they invite funding applications for constructing or renovating buildings of up to £5 million. The initiative thus offers communities the chance to bid for an exciting purpose-built youth centre or to restructure and refurnish older buildings, on the condition that the youth are completely consulted and engaged in the process of designing the building. Open youth venue, in Norwich, was the first building to be created in this way – completely refashioning a magnificent former Barclay's Bank building. The following is an extract from *The Guardian* newspaper's very positive assessment of the scheme:

> Apart from the school and the home, most of our built environment ignores young people unless they have money to spend, which they usually haven't. We always seem to look for ways to 'keep them off the streets', but where else can they go? This is especially true in Norwich, where the town centre can get pretty rowdy at the weekend; binge-drinking and teenage pregnancy rates are higher than average, not to mention the usual teen pitfalls of drugs, crime and antisocial behaviour. Boredom is part of the problem, the common complaint being: 'We had nothing else to do'.
>
> The *Open* youth centre in Norwich is the first of what is hoped will be a new generation of 21st-century youth venues. Since it opened late last year, it's been attracting growing numbers of 12- to 25-year-olds, and hosting sell-out events – not just gigs like Basshunter's, but regular under-18s club nights and events with local bands. And it's not just the young who are flocking there: architects, politicians and community groups from across the country have been descending on the centre to see if what's been done here can work elsewhere.
>
> *Open* was part-financed by the government's 'myplace' initiative (small letters and joined up, for extra youth-friendliness), which is being billed as the largest ever government investment in youth facilities. Myplace is putting £270m into creating (or improving) youth venues around Britain, with some 60 projects under way... Most of the myplace schemes are being designed with a high degree of input from young people

themselves. In many instances, following a precedent established by *Open*, local youth forums have been established to work with the architects. And these 'client groups' have been pushing their designers to go further... Open's youth forum, consisting of about 40 people between the ages of 12 and 18, had a say in everything from what activities should go on inside to the graphics, signage and furniture. They even selected the designers: Hudson Architects. Their key demands, says architect Anthony Hudson, were bright colours, decor that spoke to their demographic, plus music and media facilities, a climbing wall, and (high up the list) good toilets. These demands have been met, without going overboard. Outside, *Open* is a stern, Edwardian-looking building; inside it's bursting with playfulness. Funky furniture abounds; on the walls there is bespoke graffiti and Shepard Fairey's Obey artwork. The signage is big and bright. It's not a circus – it feels quite calm – but neither does it conform to sober, grown-up expectations. (Rose, 2010)

Photo 4.8   Open youth venue, Norwich. © Jaclyn Bloustien

Several conditions set out by the forty-plus young people involved in the myplace youth forum before Open was built at Norwich echo what we have indicated above: that the youth centre should include a live music venue ('Because you can't really go to see gigs if you're under 18, or afford them': David and Tris from the forum, quoted in Burt, 2009, p. 7); that the furniture and the décor should be hardy but also cool to look at; and that the centre should be open and free to allow the youth just to 'hang out'. As one young woman confirmed, 'We don't have to sit on wet grass in parks shivering all evening, or hurry to finish drinks before being kicked out of coffee shops' (Faye Tattam, quoted in Burt, 2009, p. 8).

Unfortunately, we were told that the bid by PFM was unsuccessful because the council had offered PFM a new warehouse that they could use the grant money to convert and refurbish. However, one of the main criteria of the myspace initiative, as illustrated above, was that the youth had to be integrally part of the design process, both inside and out. As Mike Fagg explained, 'We couldn't do anything about the outside as it had been built to particular specifications for the area' (personal communication, 20 August 2010).

Their original funding has steadily declined but they are now receiving multiple sources of funding, which target different groups of young people. They continue to receive funding from Youth Music but this is about 40 per cent less than it was for the first few years. Although their clientele are from the local area (we noted during the time of our regular visits that, as in Playford and Newcastle, the youth tended to stay within their home neighbourhoods rather than venture further afield for activities) PFM has attempted to alleviate this somewhat by their outreach program. With a grant they have purchased a new minibus which they converted into a mobile recording studio. That way, 'rather than wait for the young people to travel from Margate to Ramsgate or vice versa, we drive the music to them, wherever they are hanging out. Then they get on the bus, six or seven at a time and make their tracks and then we bluetooth it to their phones or give them a CD' (Mike Fagg, personal communication, 20 August 2010).

This discussion with Mike Fagg from PFM highlights and echoes the arguments we set out earlier. Firstly, providing geographical and material places and appropriate décor matter to facilitate and encourage young people's personal identity exploration and self-making, because the amount of 'free space' and 'private spaces' within both public and domestic places – spaces for serious play – are often limited. Hakim Bey (1991) referred to such ideal spaces as 'T.A.Z.' or 'Temporary Autonomous Zones' – liminal spaces for experimentation. As we have already suggested and as articulated clearly in the *Guardian* article by Steve Rose cited above, the inside of the venues – the furnishings, furniture, colours, internal structures and flexibility of space – can affect the way the young people creatively engage and negotiate their worlds.

As we indicated above, the area has to be not only open and available but also psychologically welcoming and accessible and that too can depend on the structure of the spaces and the décor within. While relatively few venues can offer the ideal opportunities of the new buildings like the Open youth centre in Norwich, many of the CBOs in our study still managed to make their spaces accessible and open so that young people wanted to be there. For example, Da Klinic, which is described in more detail in the following chapters and which offered fairly structured workshops in the different elements of hip hop, still offered a place where young people could come and be welcome. Even before it became the sophisticated retail and training venue it is now, it provided a space for less affluent young people to 'hang out', watch others and network. Similarly, while the *Youth Revolutions* crew were creating their on-air radio programs, several of their friends would also come the studio, sit, support and 'just be'. Not part of the official team – and sometimes not even wanted – they nevertheless still felt able to take part in the activity, to participate as part of the wider social network.

Closed spaces: youth and juvenile detention centres

One CBO that we visited was of course unlike any of the others and in some ways was not a material CBO at all but rather a peripatetic program offered in a number of places. We speak of course of Genuine Voices, the charity in Boston set up by Juri Panda Jones to provide free music lessons to young people at risk. On the invitation of Juri, four members of the Playing for Life team visited Brighton Treatment Center, a young offender institution in the New England region of the USA, during April/May 2004, August/September 2004 and April 2005. We observed and to some degree participated in the music workshops offered by the young director of Genuine Voices and her music student volunteers to the young people at the facility. Although Juri took Genuine Voices to a number of facilities, some of which we also visited,[12] it was in this institution that we mainly saw her at work and also where we noted the huge disparity between the emotional and psychological 'space' that the program of the music lessons intended to offer the young people in detention and the material place of their confinement. The Brighton Treatment Center has been closed down since our visits and has been relocated at the Eliot Short Term Treatment Center for committed males under the age of 21. Most of the residents were from the Boston area, although many were from outside the Boston CBD, at least two hours away. This meant that few of them had any visitors for three months and many were not allowed phone calls as a punishment. The length of time in the centre depended on the individual cases but could vary from a few days to nine months. The average, we learnt, was ninety days. The youth we met were male, mainly youth of colour and around the age of 16 (youth detainees were aged from 12 to 18 years), detained for a range of offences to do with substance addiction and abuse, anger management and, in extreme cases, robbery, assault and violence, which were often linked to substance abuse problems.

The building itself was a large brick Victorian building – grim, oppressive and colourless on the outside with barred windows and a large cement forecourt. It reminded several of the researchers of how a similar institution, the boys' juvenile detention centre in Magill, Adelaide, used to look in the 1960s and 1970s. DJ Shep and the tutors from Da Klinic still provide outreach music programs there in a similar way to Genuine Voices. Inside, the rooms used for the music sessions seem to be in keeping with the rest of the building. It felt hot and claustrophobic, with a bunker feel to the whole building. The reception area was bare apart from a few old chairs and couches, with yellowing walls and no artwork, just lists of instructions pinned up at regular intervals. The staff themselves though did not seem to wear a set uniform – most of them wore very casual clothes of loose trousers and jumpers or sweatshirts. All the staff carried huge bunches of keys, which were certainly a reminder that this was a lock-down institution!

The youth came upstairs from their residential quarters in the basement of the building – so there was both a general literal and metaphorical sense of the young men 'coming up for air' when they came to the rooms for their workshops. The youth often expressed a sense of relief about being able to come upstairs for a short time; it was almost a palpable sense of cognitive and spatial freedom from their other activities, and possibly even the boredom of their 'free time'.

One clinician described the centre to the Playing for Life researchers as being very militaristic in style, with its early mornings, responsibilities, chores and strong sense of discipline, and added that most youth found the program very difficult to adjust to at first, although they were provided with support in the form of youth workers and clinicians to help them cope. In the youth centre, 'clinician' meant someone who was part therapist, who ran individual and group therapy, and who also organised medication, where necessary. They took on the role of the young person's personal 'trainer' and advocate – although budget cuts often meant that there were not enough clinicians to go round. The clinicians did not have to have any medical or legal background.

One of the staff told us that when the youth came into Juri's class they felt they could be 'at peace'. Downstairs they have to 'keep their eyes open' she explained, indicating that violence was a regular occurrence amongst the residents. Downstairs too they are given responsibilities and chores. They struggle with all the discipline, she said, when they first arrive there. They could earn privileges though good behaviour but they could have their time in detention extended if they were seen to be disobeying the rules. The ages, we were told, were from 12 to 18. The youngest person this staff member had ever worked with was aged 11. From 18 they were sent to the next level of severity of incarceration, a place where Genuine Voices also attempted to run a program for a time.

The Genuine Voices' volunteer tutors ran piano, guitar, rap and sequencing lessons twice weekly for interested youth at the centre. Only those who had earned privileges through good behaviour within the centre were invited to participate. While the lessons were conducted with individuals, small groups of young people tended to 'come up' to the workshops at a time. Juri stressed that it was preferable to her to work with detainees who were there for extended periods. This enabled tutors to 'slowly work at each student's individual level and therefore obtain the best results over a longer period of time', she argued (personal communication, March 2005). We will discuss the structure of the program and style of the mentoring in the next chapter in more detail but for now it is just worth noting that, instead of being formally structured, the Genuine Voices lessons were deliberately designed to be casual and relaxed. In opposition to the rigidity and distancing of their normal existence in the centre, the staff member told us, in the music classes the residents 'feel a lot of love'. Some young people always want to participate – they start getting ready hours before Juri comes.

While other similar institutions also ran music classes, we were told they were far more formal and structured. Juri deliberately kept hers casual and one on one. The tutors felt it was essential to provide individual attention for each youth participant. For many of the residents, the sense of (brief) liberation from the cognitive and spatial constraints of daily life in the centre was clearly evident. At that time, the instruments, like the students, were 'unlocked'[13] and allowed to show their potential. While for some youths, as the clinicians observed, the program offered an acceptable alternative to the more regimented structure of daily life, many of the youth clearly gained from the opportunity to learn new skills and express themselves in new ways. As one of the volunteers asserted, the youth were not just starved of music but of 'attention and respect'. 'Their past experiences "bring out their darkness", he explained. "You bring out a kid's light"' (cited in Dreilinger, 2010, n.p.).

It was fascinating to see how often spatial metaphors were used by the youth themselves in lyrics but also in the ways their carers and tutors spoke of their music and achievements. We will take this up again in the following chapters but for now we will reflect on the words of Jessica Perlman, the clinical director of Eliot Short Term Treatment Center, where Juri now runs her program. 'I can't speak highly enough of how great it's been. It's a safe place for them to be and express themselves' (as cited by Juri, October 2010).

We will return to Genuine Voices and other programs in the following chapters where we consider funding issues and the ways in which places and spaces are influenced by the types of program held within them and vice versa. As we look at the other contexts in which the youth create, develop and explore their music practices, we will move on to consider what other types of locales they negotiated to do this – both real and imagined spaces. This includes virtual spaces, which are ephemeral and can disappear and change before our eyes. But first we return to the more mundane but essential questions – How are these spaces funded? What sort of financial and policy issues have to be in place and locked in before such 'risky business' as youth creativity can be realised? It is to this aspect of music and self-making, of 'serious play', that we turn now.

5
Money Matters: Government Policy, Funding and Youth Music

Photo 5.1 Remains of The Disco space at Statthaus Bocklerpark. © Anna Steigemann

> How do you take the anecdotal evidence of effectiveness of the funded projects to show governments that this is working, important...? (Sally, UK Youth Music program, interview, 13 January 2005)

> We want them to participate, to have responsibility in order to help them grow up. That's a big part of it. (Youth worker, Haus der Jugend, Berlin, interview, 16 April 2004)

> The trick for you [funded youth programs] is to justify the programs through hard and fast numbers. I know I am doing a good job, but I don't know how I am doing it. (Youth worker, Boston, USA, interview, 9 September 2004)

All things to everyone

Community-based organisations (CBOs) are conceived of as much more than designated creative and cultural 'safe spaces' for youth. They are increasingly viewed by policy-makers, and very often by marginalised youth and their youth workers, as pathways to employment. CBOs are increasingly becoming strategically governmentally positioned as significant nodes within a broad socio-cultural, economic and political web of reflexive networks (Hartley, 2005). As outlined in Chapter 1, the CBOs in our project are defined as alternative learning sites that are used by youth voluntarily to meet a range of skills-based needs. They encompass youth clubs and special programs for youth within performing arts, community, detention and church centres.

In this chapter we explore the implications of policy and funding on youth music programs at both macro and micro levels. We analyse the tensions we found that were raised when organisers and participants in youth music programs were increasingly placed at the heart of a global governmental push for a 'creative economy' and community-based organisations were projected as 'organisations of the future' as Estelle Morris, the 2004 Minister for the Arts in the Department of Culture, Media and Sport (UK) designated them (Morris, 2004). Ms Morris' portfolio was responsible for creative industries and gender within the Department of Culture, Media and Sport and her government provided £40 million in Creative Partnership funding to 'deprived' areas such as the Thanet region where our research site, Pie Factory Music, was located. The Arts Council of England also provided £10 million annually through its Youth Music arm in designated Youth Action Zones. Youth Music was a lottery-funded organisation that aimed to promote and develop music-making opportunities for young people in England, up to the age of 18.[1] (See Chapter 7 for further discussion of Youth Music.) Since its establishment in 1999, the organisation has involved over 880,000 children and young people with its confirmed expenditure on supporting projects for the period 1999 to 2006 being £10 million per year. Estelle Morris kept in close contact with Youth Music and in particular their *Endangered and Protected Species* project. Launched in 2003, this provided £1 million per year of grants for the Local Education Authority (LEA) Music Services to tackle the problem of falling numbers of young people playing specific instruments, for example, the bassoon and the tuba. Ms Morris was often quoted in the press as stating that the government was re-gearing itself to recognise creativity as the heart of the economy: 'the creative revolution that is with us at the moment' (Morris, 2004, p. 3).

Across all four countries in which our research took place, we found an increasing governmental push to develop a youth 'enterprise culture'. Funding to CBOs, as discussed in depth later in this chapter, was frequently allocated to youth projects as a way of keeping marginalised youth off the streets. Particular governmental anxieties existed around race and ethnicity, and putting money into youth programs in areas of designated 'disadvantage' was viewed by governments, and particularly local councils, as a way of engaging marginalised youth through their interests. At the time of our research, anxiety about youth 'ethnic' gangs seemed endemic to all governments across all of our sites, no doubt fanned by real anxieties, perceived threats and populist media comments within each country. *The Sunday Observer* carried the dire headline 'British hostility to Muslims "could trigger riots"', warning that: 'Hostility towards Islam permeates every part of British society and will spark race riots unless urgent action is taken to integrate Muslim youths into society' (Doward and Hinsliff, 2004).

Doward and Hinsliff were reporting on a recent report by the Commission on British Muslims and Islamophobia, which was chaired by a key government adviser to the Stephen Lawrence inquiry. The report noted that as Muslims felt increasingly excluded from society the 'simmering tensions, especially in northern English towns' were in danger of 'boiling over' (Doward and Hinsliff, 2004). Similarly, see Cohen's observation that the support of youth clubs in Berlin was clearly divided along race and ethnic lines as well as along former East–West Berlin geographic divisions (Cohen, 2008).

In 2009, the recent words of an Australian journalist from a 'quality' Australian newspaper, *The Sydney Morning Herald*, still echo the same theme:

> **Manly 'morons' rampage was racist: academic**
> Manly Council and local police have their 'heads in the sand' if they believe racism had nothing to do with angry scenes in the northern beaches suburb yesterday, an academic says.
>
> Mayor Jean Hay and police commander Dave Darcy were today hosing down accusations that a group of about 80 drunk teenagers who ran chanting and yelling through the town centre wrapped in flags were targeting ethnic Australians. (Robinson, 2009)

While the ethnicity of the youth in question changes from year to year according to who are the latest migrants to come to the country or who has been affected by the latest immigration policy changes, disaffected young people always seem to be a constant concern for those in charge of governance, policing and education. So, for example, in Berlin anxiety about Turkish youth changed in 2009 to worries over 'Arab' young people; in Australia, in many cities, the current concerns are with Sudanese youth (see, for example, Robertson, 2009).

In such climates, CBOs were and still are being framed as 'urban sites of possibility' (Fine and Weiss, 2000) where youth can safely develop their own sense of creativity and cultural meaning (Bloustien, 2008; Cohen, 2008;

Peters, 2008). The concept of an 'enterprise culture' is frequently understood then as 'a set of attitudes, values and beliefs operating within a particular community or environment that lead to both "enterprising behaviour" and aspiration towards self employment' (White and Kenyon, 2000, p. 18).

CBOs throughout the period of our research were becoming much more than designated creative and cultural 'safe spaces' for youth. Policy and funding arrangements were coupling most of the projects to employment goals. Explicit in funding arrangements for many CBOs was a set of guiding principles that spoke to developing youth initiative, improvement in risk management, and developing a commercial orientation and equity. This is evident at both the macro and micro levels, which we discuss later in this chapter. In the UK this is evident in programs such as those run through the Prince's Trust; the British Council for Livin' It; AKarts/Equator Media; Jump Start; Youth Music; Midi Music; the Tabernacle; and the Children's Fund which also supports Pie Factory Music. This does not mean, of course, that all CBOs are pleased with such developments. For some the 'push' for programs linked to creative industries and enterprise means many young people miss out – or that the policy misses the point.

Alexis Johnson's involvement as a co-director, later sole director, of AKarts, which for a time was also known as Equator Media, was focused on developing youth arts media enterprises as well as running workshops to introduce marginalised groups to new media technologies. Alexis was also a campaign committee member of Venus Rising, a group of twelve female practitioners working in fine art, design, new media and technology. As Peters (2008) has written earlier, Venus Rising was an initiative of Cybersalon (www.cybersalon.org.uk), which aimed to examine technology, arts, science and business issues from a feminist paradigm by bringing these issues into the public domain via workshops, debate, research, artists in residence, creative labs and so forth.

Funding was, of course, a crucial issue underpinning all Alexis' ventures. As well as being part of the Prince's Trust Business Start-Up Programs (this is further delineated in this chapter, below, and at www.princes-trust.org.uk), Alexis also applied for British Council funding through Enterprise Insight on a project called 'Make it Happen: Music', which aims to show young people how to make the most of entrepreneurial opportunities in the music industry. Both the Prince's Trust Business Start-Up Program (henceforth Prince's Trust) and Enterprise Insight are UK-wide. As with many members of the creative industries, Alexis worked part-time to support her work on AKarts projects. Gaining funding is always precarious, as Alexis frequently outlined to us. Alexis was acutely aware of the various UK government initiatives, such as Skill Set and Modern Apprenticeships, but was most focused on gaining funding that had a mentoring relationship inbuilt – 'not one that blurred into the role of counsellor' (Alexis, personal communication, April 2004).

She highlighted that many of the young people she mentored through the Prince's Trust program ended up asking her to help them start their own business. DJ Roland was a recipient of her one-on-one mentoring of entrepreneurial and behavioural skills. For example, mentoring support of Rowland included weekly meetings with him to guide the preparation of the business plan that Rowland submitted to the Prince's Trust (entitled 'Soulful House and Garage'), using a template that Alexis had used herself when she applied to set up the 'Creative Learning Labs' at Westminster Kingsway College. She also helped him prepare a CV and other funding applications, such as a successful grant from Community Champions, and various job applications in the music industry.

Mentoring roles, such as Alexis', play a critical part in building confidence, self-esteem and awareness of the political context surrounding grant applications and funding bodies' expectations of recipients, in addition to developing specific entrepreneurial business skills. Mentoring, and being mentored, is intensive and emotionally demanding. Building Rowland's confidence in applying for a Prince's Trust grant was fraught:

> I went there [Prince's Trust] last year, or was it early this year [2004], something like that, anyway, and the guy just gave me so much negative vibes. I was just like 'oh man', you know, [he said] 'you've got to get a loan, you've got a lot of people doing the same thing as you, you've got to be different', and I was like, 'oh forget this, you're supposed to be helping us'. All they're doing is creating more negative vibes which we already know already, you know. That's not helping, that's just like being, that's just putting folks down, man, putting people's feelings down, man. [That] man's in a secure job and all of that, just sitting [on] his arse there telling people that...that there's going to be a lot of people wanting to do the same thing. That's not being "thing" [Rowland's emphasis]. You got to be positive about it, be realistic but positive, man...People just want to dash your hopes like that. That's not right man, that's wrong.
>
> (Rowland, personal communication, March 2004)

The success of the subsequent application was in no small part due to Alexis' patient and persistent mentoring in helping to build Rowland's entrepreneurial, communication and social skills, helping him understand and deal with risk management, and giving him informed business advice based on her own successful entrepreneurial activities.

Risk management was very much an ongoing challenge for all our organisations, particularly Pie Factory Music, our other UK research site. Although they received direct funding from the Thanet Region to incubate music programs amongst disadvantaged youth in the region, the organisation was obviously less entrepreneurial than the much larger Prince's Trust scheme that Alexis and Rowland were involved with and was not designed to focus on business start-up programs. Despite the much vaunted publicity by Estelle Morris, the then 2004 UK Minister for Arts, positioning organisations such as Pie Factory Music as being at the heart of a governmental push for a creative community and being an organisation of the future, this did not readily translate into Pie Factory Music being a sustainable organisation. So it was fascinating that our initial concerns that Pie Factory Music would undergo 'hard financial times' and maybe disappear have not yet been borne out.

To understand why, despite a 2008 global financial downturn, Pie Factory Music continues to exist, we asked Alexis Johnson from AKarts to discuss the organisation's continuing survival with its Program Manager, Steve Kreeger. As Alexis' notes from her interview with Steve reveal, the organisation is not 'out of the woods' yet but is surviving, albeit on little more than passionate goodwill and threadbare funding.

> When I met Steve he described Pie Factory Music studios as a 'Tardis', since a great deal of equipment and resources have been merrily shoehorned into a very small village hall. I think this is a very good metaphor for the organisation as a whole; it services a huge volume of beneficiaries across two boroughs on a very tight turnover. And the organisation has grown disproportionately if you consider nine staff (mainly part-time) now deliver provisions to 2,500 young people per annum. Passion is clearly the driving force, but this feat has also been made possible by an entrepreneurial spirit from the directors; and on a practical level a huge bank of industry talent (70) referred to as 'Music Leaders' who deliver programmes, and who have a strong partnership working and an extensive outreach programme. Building a business on a flexible workforce is risky, but Pie Factory Music also has a nifty way of ensuring loyalty, hard work and commitment from their freelancers. They (the organisation) invest in them, and undertake workforce development.
>
> Pie Factory Music is an organisation that is very much established; its reputation has grown and continues to stimulate its growth. Organisations even partner with Pie Factory Music to use its name to advertise events.

Programmes have matured and are now part of the fabric of the region; used by local schools and youth clubs. And the organisation is now a registered OCN awarding centre for the region. Its early cohorts of young people have also matured, and in some cases have returned as Music Leaders for the next generation to be inspired.

This is an organisation that knows what it delivers best and that's exactly what it is doing. But the storm clouds are brewing; our new government cuts in public expenditure will have a potentially devastating effect on Pie Factory Music. Despite their entrepreneurial approach they are still reliant on 95% revenue funding from the public purse. (Mike Fagg notes that earned income from other sources is about 20% of our turnover but the profit from that converts into 10% of PFM budgets.) They are now waiting to see how great the cuts will be; at best three of their staff will be made redundant, at worst the directors may have to resign. Despite the uncertain future, Pie Factory Music is still laying down future plans, it has considered investment (which would fund the much hoped for move to bigger premises) and the directors are now looking to benefactor funding as a potential solution.

(Alexis, personal correspondence, October 2010).

Photo 5.2 Entrance to the Pie Factory. © Alexis Johnson

Photo 5.3 Pie Factory music room, whole room. © Alexis Johnson

Our UK organisations highlighted the crucial interplay between entrepreneurialism and successful youth arts music initiatives. In Adelaide, South Australia, the Playford City Council youth development initiatives such as *Youth Revolutions*, the Kandinsky Sessions program at Carclew, and Da Klinic echoed and exemplified, at varying levels, this UK move to marry youth creativity with youth entrepreneurial development. In Newcastle, New South Wales, the Newcastle City Council initiatives for youth such as the Palais Royale youth venue and Newcastle Arts Centre, in the USA the not-for-profit Genuine Voices program in the Brighton Treatment Center and in Providence, Rhode Island the AS220 and the Broad Street Studios programs are similarly all examples of pathway to employment initiatives.

We began our research at a time when global economies were beginning to focus increasingly on risk management. Funding youth-run and supported programs for 'youth at risk' was gaining political and economic credence as a way to support such youth as managers of their own risk. Linking education and employment policies was at the heart of the establishment in 1999 of a UK National Advisory Committee on Creative and Cultural Education (NACCCE). As early as 1999, the then British Prime Minister Tony Blair described this coordinated policy aim as developing 'a nation where creative talents of all people are used to build a true enterprise economy for the 21st century – where we compete on brains, not brawn' (NACCCE, 1999, p. iv).

In 2004, governmental expectations were high regarding the concept of entrepreneurship as a way of managing risk, particularly for marginalised disaffected youth. This notion of risk management was discursively synchronised with the need for all new economy workers to learn and adapt to changing technologies, evolving markets and evolving policies (Peters, 2008). At the time of our research, funding youth music and arts-related programs was viewed as 'up-skilling' youth, which ultimately would assist nations to be effective and successful in the highly competitive knowledge-based economy. The concept of 'sustainability' was also emerging globally at this time so it became important for both macro and micro enterprise programs to seek multiple funding sources to ensure their sustainability. This led to a rapid increase in the number of stakeholders in youth enterprises, as we highlight in some of the examples discussed in this chapter. This range encompasses government sector, private sector, donor agencies, internal investments and a myriad of local fundraising activities. An expected outcome of this plethora of funding sources was an expectation by governments that they would not be the main source of youth 'training' and other services to community-based organisations. Youth enterprises were to be suitably addressed at a local level, engendering sustainability.

Galligan (2001) had earlier encapsulated this need for sustainability as one where individual creativity could only be fostered in a supportive environment that was structurally embedded (e.g. funding support), which allowed creative processes to become a reality. National economic and social goals were becoming inextricably linked with CBOs' goals of developing and sustaining youth music and arts-related programs. CBOs' complex outreach of networks, sponsors, mentors, advisers, trainers, peers and participants could be utilised not only to build relationships at the micro level (developing increased self-esteem through 'identity work', see Wexler, 1992 and 'self-making' as in Battaglia, 1995) but also to build relationships between youth, adults and the broader community. With its coupling to/with micro-enterprises, a solution could begin to be found for the growing problem of youth unemployment in industrial and OECD countries.

Social cohesion in increasingly risky economic times is critically important in developed and developing countries alike and CBOs have been increasingly positioned as sites within which marginalised youth can gain a sense of belonging and meaning and a chance to improve their economic livelihood. The challenge for the CBOs we researched was not so much the creating of meaningful opportunities for youth to develop their music-related skills, but for CBOs to gain sustainable funding that supported and promoted youth entrepreneurship, provided access to business development services, built individual youth capacity, and also provided both CBOs and youth with a voice at national/governmental policy and funding levels.

Policy versus practice

We spent considerable time researching the national youth-related policies of all four countries in relation to CBOs and youth music and arts-related programs. This macro view was complex and frequently discursively contradictory (Peters, 2008). For example, Germany, the UK and the USA have school-based entrepreneurship schemes that provide pathways into similar schemes run by CBOs. In Australia this concept, at school level, has arrived very late on the scene and is still being developed. This has frequently resulted in an even greater sense of disengagement for marginalised youth, who often leave school prematurely. Policy and funding issues play a major part in underwriting this sense of disengagement when so little financial support is allocated to youth at risk. In Australia, for example, there are three tiers of government – federal, state and local – and rarely do they work in concert with each other in relation to youth programs.

As indicated in our introductory chapter, we had deliberately chosen to work at CBOs and extra-mural facilities rather than schools and formal educational institutions because we were working with young people who had either rejected formal schooling or who had been unsuccessful in this kind of environment. Yet although most of the successful CBOs did seem to offer quite flexible programs and youth-centred, problem-based, experiential teaching methods, over the year, others became increasingly dependent on developing structures and educationally accredited programs in order to be able to work closely with schools and other institutions. This was in order to encourage a wider range of people and groupings to attend their sessions and thereby gain greater opportunities for funding. The youth centres in Berlin illustrate this situation well and deserve a little more space to explain their unique situation. In Germany, youth clubs were enshrined in national policy as part of postwar reconstruction. In the former West Germany, and particularly in West Berlin, youth clubs were a strategic plank in the civic education and care of young people. However, in reunited Berlin, the Berlin Senate was and still is in considerable financial debt, which has resulted in fragmented funding to youth clubs as some parts of Berlin have economically transformed at the expense of other parts. The nine youth clubs/centres we focused upon were spread across reunited Berlin, with six centres in the western part and three in the eastern part. During the time of our research in Berlin, neighbouring Poland joined the European Union (in 2004), escalating further tension around 'foreigners' taking jobs away from locals and potentially increasing the unemployment rate.

The fragility of funding to youth clubs in Berlin has become even more acute since we began our research. In Berlin, the links between schools and youth centres have increased as part of a pragmatic strategy which occurred when a controversial state law was passed during 2005/6 regarding full day attendance at school. The pivotal argument and debate concerning the new ruling regarding full day school attendance had emerged from a crisis situation arising in the Rütlischule in Neukölln, which had a 90 per cent migrant and socio-economically disadvantaged population. The teachers from the school wrote to the Senate, saying that a dramatic solution was needed. However, all-day schooling had been discussed since the early 1970s and the more socialist states within Germany had started to implement the new system earlier than the more conservative areas. As the educational system is federally governed, schools in Berlin have suffered from financial cutbacks and most teachers were and still are not trained sufficiently for the new all-day offers. The Rütlischule revealed that most parents in Neukölln did not have the resources to take care of their children adequately, and in the former system the teachers could not either. Hence the teachers demanded a completely new reform for such students and the all-day school law was one of the answers.

This 'strategy' increased by law the school day from a half day to a full day. Before this, very few schools had offered whole-day schooling. This new law was instigated by the social democrat and left political parties in the Senate who became increasingly concerned about language and literacy levels in the German language and overall competency and knowledge. In Berlin particular concerns were raised by the Senate as to the poor educational performance of children from immigrant and low socio-economic areas. The reform of the school day was also partly due to increased agitation on the part of working women who were demanding more opportunities to work full time. Increased free 'childcare' or structured programs for school-aged children became a rallying cry.

The outcome to date is that not every school in Berlin in 2010 offers full-day programs but most of them offer a program until either 4 p.m. or 6 p.m., with many still requiring a small fee. The current Berlin social and youth work system, which includes the youth clubs that we observed in 2003–5, is still not designed to fully complement the new school schedules. This has severely affected many of the youth clubs as most cannot get enough youth attending due to the numbers still at school in the afternoons. Poor coordination still exists between the different stakeholders regarding integration of the various social institutions and youth centres with school programs. All of the youth club directors and staff we spoke to in 2010 highlighted this problem. The school settings were seen by the youth club directors to be very tightly focused, often conservative and highly structured and therefore not the appropriate setting for the diverse range of youth, particularly marginalised youth, who used to engage in the youth club programs such as the ones we had observed during our fieldwork.

A further issue which has affected the financing of youth clubs is that school zoning has meant that wealthier parents have removed their children from schools in areas where zoning has concentrated large groups of immigrants and economically disadvantaged children and parents. This presents particular challenges for youth clubs in attracting and finding financial resources to support their youth activities. As Cohen (2008) has pointed out, Turkish and other former Eastern bloc residents, along with new arrivals from the Middle East and the Mediterranean, make up over 40 per cent of the unemployment rate of around 18 per cent. Sustainability of funding as a pathway to social cohesion among Berlin's youth is obviously of critical import. In an increasingly fragmented Berlin with escalating racial and ethnic unrest, developing and sustaining a sense of local identity for young people and the opportunity to practise, produce and consume their own music-related activities within relatively safe social spaces becomes increasingly important. It was not surprising then that many of the local music-related practices of the centres reflected the racial and ethnic identity of the participants. For example, the predominantly Turkish/Muslim hip hop identity at Böcklerpark has seen, according to the breakdancing facilitators at the centre, a gradual change to a more inclusive culture, where breakdancing has come to be understood as a multicultural activity, not just the preserve of a particular ethnic identity, producing a greater sense of social cohesion amongst and between ethnic minorities in the Zillestrasse area (Wolfgang Fischer, personal communication, 2004).

Not all organisations we researched in Berlin were totally state funded. Café Lietz, in Charlottenburg, where we met Magda and her all-girl band (refer to Chapter 3), is mainly funded by the 'Landeskirche', the Berlin-Country Evangelical Church, whose local congregation pays for the rooms at Café Lietz and for the staff. Café Lietz is in the cellar of the church hall adjacent to the church itself. Some state provision exists in that Café Lietze can also be funded by the Office for Youth Work in case they need additional staff, and if they need additional equipment they can also ask for support from the national public youth department. But according to the director, Michael Buschbeck, such additional payments were small and infrequent, and were decreasing over time.

The money Café Lietz receives from the church pays for a 1.5 position which is divided into three employees operating on a division of 6 hours per week, 28 hours per week, and 10 hours per week, with Michael Buschbeck, the director, working the 28 hours per week. We first met Michael when we attended gigs run at Café Lietz. Michael spent time showing us over not only the performance and technical/music spaces but through the adjacent evangelical church. Michael is a member of the congregation and spoke about the opportunities that attendees at gigs could have to become members of the church, particularly through the confirmation programs run by the church for 12–16-year-olds. Café Lietz ran church-funded annual music camps to Ireland and other parts of Europe which Michael described as also being a mechanism for bringing the youth taking part in the camps into the potential orbit of the church (Michael Buschbeck, personal communication, 2004).

When we spent time at Café Lietz in 2004 and 2005, the youth attendees were mainly between 16 and 21 years old, but the centre was and still is open to everyone between the ages of 14 and 27. While there was a strong desire to attract females, particularly through the presence of female social workers, mostly young males participated. When Anna, our research assistant in Germany, followed up on Café Lietz in 2010 young males were still the dominant participants but the outreach aspects of church-funded music camps to various countries had diminished noticeably. Michael informed Anna that the last (2010) very big music event, involving teenage musicians as well as technicians, was a church day in Munich, to which they drove in a big team with several buses and played a lot of concerts there.

As we outlined above, what has changed during our research period is that Café Lietz, along with all the other youth centres in Berlin, has experienced a radical change due to the 2006 introduction of a new law that mandated full-day schooling, with the result being less free or leisure time for school-aged children. This has affected the afternoon youth music offerings by Café Lietz, such as sessions to build technical music skills. Falling attendances were further caught up in diminishing funds received from the church as the global financial crisis of 2008 hit. For example, guitar lessons were gradually removed from offer and other cuts were made. These financial cuts happened across all the church-supported venues and consequently the number of institutions financially supported by churches shrank. There were twelve evangelical youth centres in western Berlin twenty years ago; in 2010 there were only four evangelical institutions. However, this has had an upside in that these four centres have become prominent and they work together to plan and offer much bigger joint events, sharing their equipment and supporting each other as a way of managing further risk.

In 2010, Café Lietz offered few major trips to bigger events and they were mainly church-related. Local effort is put into supporting gigs on three Fridays a month where there is the 'Live Café', a jam stage, where different styles are performed, such as heavy metal, hard rock, folk pop and singer-songwriter. Plus, there is the Folk Café one Thursday a month, where the organisation's social worker, together with the youth participants, use many different types of instruments ranging from banjos, wooden drums, didgeridoos and guitars, to developing their own folk songs. The didgeridoo is a particular favourite of Michael's who had learnt to play it in Australia in the 1980s while backpacking on an extended holiday. (During our visits in 2004 and 2005 we were variously entertained by Michael's playing of this favourite instrument.)

While many of the musical instruments remain unchanged from our research period, the main styles that dominated our follow-up in 2010 were folk, rock, blues, singer-songwriter and 'Liedermacher', the German school of indie-German-pop, which Michael described as 'sometimes political

178 Youth, Music and Creative Cultures

Photo 5.4   Michael and his self-made didgeridoos. © Anna Steigemann

and sometimes not!' (Michael, personal communication, 2010). The Café's biggest established band is called 'Adam Fuge'.

Despite straitened financial circumstances, Café Lietz holds around twenty concerts a year, one large-scale music camp, and two or three open-air festivals. Straitened financial circumstances have also meant that rather than large-scale trips to other countries Café Lietz organises various music programs with local schools, and band workshops are frequently organised by additional volunteers from the Youth Social Service.

It is interesting that attracting female youth to such centres in Berlin was not just a problem for Café Lietz but a noticeable feature in most of the organisations we researched. There were deliberate state-run initiatives to support girls in claiming spaces and activities that would otherwise be dominated by young males. For example, we participated in a live-in, girls-only weekend at Alleins e.V., a club in Friedrichshagenerstrasse kiez in the lovely old former East Berlin city of Köpenick. This involved almost two hundred girls coming from as far away as Poland and Russia as well as across Germany to experience the club's large indoor and outdoor spaces, to experiment with hip hop, graffiti art workshops, and an open mic rap night on the Saturday evening. It was noticeable, however, on the weekend we attended that there were very few Turkish girls taking part. It was difficult to discern whether this was a one-off or whether, being held in the former East Berlin, the place was not attractive to Turkish girls from the former West Berlin or whether parental permission was not forthcoming. When this question was raised with the facilitators of this particular weekend program, the response was that all girls are welcome to attend as funding is provided. Funding for these events comes from the state and Berlin is one of five German cities that offer this weekend once per year. Information was not available to the researchers as to the ethnic breakdown of attendees at any of these live-in girls-only weekends held throughout Germany. Overall, annually, the program is offered eight times a year, with funding reviewed by the state authorities.

Discussing ethnic identities was not a difficulty for the researchers at Wutzkyallee, a centre frequented by white German youths from the surrounding district. Talking to some of the youth at the centre we were frequently told there were 'too many Turkish troublemakers' and that 'this centre [Wutzkyallee] was not a place that welcomed Turks' (Unnamed youth, personal communication, April 2004). Funding for this centre was from the government, supplemented by fee-paying events such as the heavy metal concert we attended. As well as providing a place for youth to engage in rock and heavy metal music gigs and practices, it was also a site where a particular form of local identity could be proclaimed and reaffirmed. During our period of research Berlin youth clubs were much more focused on articulating forms of identity and social cohesion through specific music- and arts-related practices rather than as pathways to economic employment.

In the USA, we found that CBOs were inextricably interwoven with issues of identity, social cohesion and micro-entrepreneurial practices. Funding was critical to the sustainability of the three organisations we studied there: AS220 and Broad Street Studios in Providence, Rhode Island, and Genuine Voices, a not-for-profit organisation running a music-related program at the Brighton Treatment Center, Boston. We also found that the UK was similarly deeply involved in such policy and funding imperatives.

The impetus of government-based youth funding, or the lack of it, varied from country to country. An all too familiar theme in all four countries was the espousal of government youth policies but a dearth of funding to support community-based programs. In the case of Genuine Voices, a USA-based program for incarcerated youth at the Brighton Treatment Center in Boston, which we have discussed in earlier chapters, finding sufficient money from any willing non-government source to keep the youth music program going was always an uphill battle. Juri had to work part-time to support herself and her program. In Juri's case her part-time work was casual employment at Starbucks as well as engagement as a music tutor and accompanying pianist at Boston's Berklee School of Music, from which she graduated in 2002. This institution continually offered Juri strong professional as well as material support, providing musical instruments and a source of volunteering Masters students as instrument tutors. The Berklee College of Music, according to Curtis Warner, the community relations director, decided to get involved in supporting Genuine Voices because the philosophy underpinning Juri's program at the treatment centre accorded with their own community values. Berklee's own music program, Berklee City Music, provided an opportunity for a no-cost music education to students from disadvantaged backgrounds, but had not included youth in detention facilities. So Berklee saw an opportunity to expand their current community programs by supporting Juri in her venture. Berklee Music School was always ahead of its time, according to Curtis. It had been established as a jazz institution when 'it was the hip hop of the day. You can imagine now trying to establish something on the basis of hip hop, that's how extreme Berklee was when it was founded' (Juri, personal communication, May 2004).

But it was not only funding that was challenging; it was finding supporters in the governance of the juvenile justice system in Boston in the first place who would allow Juri access to the Brighton Treatment Center. William Stewart, Probation Officer on the Board of Directors of Genuine Voices, recollects it this way:

> Twenty-eight years ago, if this young lady [Juri] had walked into my office, I wouldn't have time for her, I wouldn't have talked to her... When she first came here, do you remember the old Mickey Rooney/Judy Garland movies of the 40s, where they'd say, 'I have an idea, let's put on a show'? Well, it's 'I have an idea, let's put on a program'. This side of the table, the system side, can now say 'go ahead'. Everybody sitting on the other side of the table [the system side] that sits in that chair has failed. So if a resource comes in and wants to try something... we say 'let's see how you do'. She started off with 4 kids...
>
> (William Stewart, May 2004)

Juri had 80 youth in her program at the time this discussion, above, took place (Juri, personal communication, May 2004). The youth Juri worked with at the Brighton Treatment Center had a variety of backgrounds and problems: parental abuse, drug abuse, crime, poverty and lack of formal schooling.

An Australian music student at Berklee, Clare McLeod, had been a volunteer tutor at Genuine Voices and had this to say about the challenges she faced in this role: 'The most striking thing about teaching [at the centre] was thinking, with some of these kids, this is the only time of the week where they get the full attention of someone for half an hour to an hour each week.' Clare also spoke about her initial shock of teaching youth with marks of violence on their face, such as black eyes, and obvious signs of being tired, hungry and distracted (Clare, personal communication, May 2004). Juri has provided in her own words many stories to illustrate the successful outcomes of her program. As in all of the stories concerning Juri's work and her incarcerated clients, the names have been changed for reasons of confidentiality under the rules of the Department of Youth Services (DYS).

When I met M (17 years old African-American) for the first time he was shy, and I was not sure if I would ever be able to break through to his heart. I asked what he liked, and he told me that he liked cooking. Immediately after I heard this, I mentioned the similarities between cooking and music. A spark lit in his eyes as he asked 'How so?'

I went on to explain how music and cooking are organic. How the creation of both food and music require one's senses in order to be made right; right being defined by your intuition, and judged by the taste, the sounds, the heart. He was so intrigued that he engaged in extended, direct eye contact with me.

We had many great conversations until the day he was discharged, which was April 2010. He called me after being released and I took him to a job interview. Later, I asked him to perform at our fundraiser, which was held in the John Hancock Center in Boston. I paid him $75 to perform his song and speak about his experience participating in Genuine Voices programs while incarcerated.

When I met him after the performance, he ran to me and gave me a huge smile and hug!! I kept telling him he is so intelligent and he should surround himself with intelligent and accomplished people. Since that time, he has agreed to perform in two more events that will take place in September 2010.

Many of these boys think they can't do anything good due to a lack of parenting and very low self-esteem. I know however, from experience, if you can make one connection with someone, then they will open up. If you can make them feel confident, then they can gain a different perspective in life. If you can touch one's heart, he or she will touch yours in the future.

Just recently, he texted me out of the blue, and simply asked 'How are you Juri??' That meant the world to me and gave me so much confidence in the hard work of Genuine Voices, as we reach out to those who have experienced so much trauma in their lives and are feeling like a failure, dwelling into the unfairness of their lives. We don't judge them because of how many charges they have. We judge them as a person and give them the opportunity to have a voice through music. M now feels he has a voice that is genuine and a safe way of expressing all that he has been through.

(Juri, personal correspondence, October 2010)

Juri's experiences and her approach particularly and dramatically highlight the ways music is integrated into the lives of so many young people and how it can provide pathways for them to acquire new knowledge and new levels of cultural and social capital. Sometimes this can be with quite startling results. If learning to play it 'cool' through music can mean, as we have argued, learning new levels of self respect and self-possession and also learning to become a responsible member of one's community then music is a very powerful tool indeed.

The biggest challenge for Juri and the graduates of the program at the detention centre was that no follow-up music program existed for them on their release. The graduates either went back to their old youth gangs, and frequently criminal activity, which saw many being sentenced to an adult prison, or sometimes a few joined the military and were shipped out to Iraq. Juri knew of very few who were able to re-enter their community with enhanced skills and opportunities. This was where AS220 in Providence, Rhode Island, provided a very different set of pathways with some spectacular individual and group successes.

CBOs as places to grow micro-entrepreneurs: an exemplary example

In terms of community-based youth-organising activities, one of the most interesting spaces and places we visited in the USA was Broad Street Studios, 790 Broad Street, Providence, Rhode Island, an offshoot of its founding organisation, Arts Space 220, known as AS220. While it did not become part of our project as a detailed case study, due to time constraints, it indelibly informed our sense of what can be achieved when youth and the community work towards social, cultural and economic sustainability within the creative industries.

Broad Street Studios was listed in Future 500, a list of youth organising and activism in the United States, with the following minimalist entry:

> A local arts, culture and politics incubator. Young artists produce a bi-monthly youth magazine, have access to a recording studio and artist studios to create, market and produce their own small business in the arts. Many of the youth come from under-resourced communities and work closely with youth at local juvenile prisons. They orchestrate monthly youth open mic performances and host monthly dinners dubbed Food for Thought. (Kim et al., 2002, p. 131)

To breathe life into the description above, we can add the impressions of two of the adult researchers of Playing for Life who were researching the CBO in Boston. They travelled by train to Providence to spend the day both at Broad Street Studios and at its headquarters AS220 – Arts Space, at 220 Empire Street, Rhode Island. We initially heard about the organisation from Professor Shirley Brice Heath, a member of the project's reference group, who had Masters students at Brown University, Providence. The students were volunteering in projects at the Broad Street Studios. The two-hour train trip eventually took three-and-a-half hours due to a loss of power part way through our journey; not an auspicious beginning. There we were greeted by John, one of Professor Heath's current Masters students, who became our initial guide and who invaluably introduced us to key organisers and youth participants.

Before we describe our participation and observations in more detail, it is important to understand the policy and funding context that supported the organisation from the beginning. Broad Street Studios exists because of community 'partnering', a concept clearly understood in Australia but not always so clearly articulated. In the USA there is a body known as the Corporation for National and Community Service. It is a network of national service programs encompassing education, public safety, health and the environment. It has the concept of sustainable communities as its rationale. In 2004 this body had partnerships with 2,100 non-profit groups, public agencies and faith-based organisations.

Members of the networks tutor and mentor youth, build affordable housing, teach computer skills, clean parks and rivers, run after-school programs, and help communities respond to disasters. The National and Community Service (N&CS) was created in 1993. More than two million Americans of all ages are engaged in projects in a given year. A specific arm of the N&CS is called American Vista. One of its specific planks is to alleviate poverty by strengthening the capacity of agencies who serve low-income communities. American Vista is a network of funded partnerships with local communities. The partners must provide 33 per cent of program costs and 15 per cent of members' living allowances (Kim et al., 2002).

In 1997, in Providence, AS220 was formed. The AS stands for 'arts space', and it began life as a gallery space in Empire Street, in the central business district (CBD). According to Sam Seidel, the coordinator of Broad Street Studios, AS220 was formed as a non-profit organisation as part of the Community Partnerships arm of American Vista, under the umbrella of the Corporation for National and Community Service (personal communication, 2004). AS220 uses a combination of its own resources and Vista's to promote paid youth volunteers. In 2004 it supported twenty Vista positions and ten projects in Providence.

In discussions with the founder of AS220, Umberto Crenca, we learnt that AS220 began life from his passionate belief that everyone should have an opportunity to develop their creative voice and present it to the world. A Vietnam veteran who had experienced more than his share of violence and dislocation, Crenca turned a disused warehouse in a run-down part of the city into a free space for the public. AS220's mission statement positions the organisation as a local forum for the arts through the maintenance of residential and work studios, galleries and performance spaces. It is 'unjuried' in being open to the public with a particular emphasis on showing artists who cannot afford to exhibit elsewhere. The gallery space is used for exhibitions and performances and has a darkroom, silkscreen area and print shop. During our visit it was being used to house an art exhibition as well as having several youth and adults using the darkroom and print shop. At the main street entrance it also has a thriving café, which operates as a meeting place for AS220 participants and the general public (Mr Crenca was pleased to show us the Australian wine on offer in the café).

At the time of our visit, May 2004, Providence had been hard hit economically by the downturn in the timber industry and unemployment was high. The city had statistically high numbers of African-Americans amongst whom unemployment was rife. Drug sales and substance abuse had emerged as chronic community problems. Youth detention, particularly amongst young male African-Americans, was also statistically high. Umberto Crenca told us that in 2001 he had been involved in running weekly youth arts programs and writing workshops for young males in custody in the Rhode Island Training School (RTS) – a detention centre – and for youth under the supervision of the Department of Children, Youth and Families. The sessions had been running successfully but Crenca noted that many of the youth continued to offend after their release. He leased a warehouse in Providence's economically depressed South Side, about 5 kilometres from the CBD, so that workshops and programs for these youth could continue on their release.

Broad Street Studios began in 2001 from $4,000 funding, gained through the Lila Wallage Readers Digest Fund. In 2004, at the time of our visit, AS220 had successfully grown to have an annual budget of $300,000 of which Broad Street Studios' programs contributed approximately 40 per cent of income received. Sam Seidel, the Director of Youth Services at BSS, showed us over the centre. It was vast and had areas set up for a range of creative arts activities, as described in more detail below. Sam explained that eleven adults and twenty paid young people were on the staff. A particular feature of the young people on staff was that nearly all of them had either been in the Rhode Island Training School (detention centre) or had been at some stage under departmental supervision orders.

Sam stressed that payment of staff and the young people was critical to the success of the studio. It was employment. It was concrete economic support, which made it possible for young people to survive without resorting to crime: 'They can still make more money selling crack, but this gives them an alternative and some status' (personal communication, May 2004). This also explained the importance of the mission statement of Broad Street Studios: 'Fostering young people's creative development and incubating arts-based businesses' (www.as220.org/broadsheet).

The warehouse was not only a space where young people could practise music and arts-related activities but also focused on fostering their entrepreneurial skills. Sam explained that there were six businesses based around six projects currently running at BSS. Each project had a business manager and part-time staff who ran them. Each business followed a business plan drafted by the youth with the assistance of volunteers from Bryant College, a Providence business college, and a local accountant. The studio also had a Product Development Team, which was a program that taught youth how to turn their art into marketable merchandise. We saw examples of commissioned logos for local companies, logos for city events, designs printed on T-shirts featuring Providence-related activities, and other visual material. This employed a full-time graphic designer/co-coordinator, a volunteer who taught students about concept designs and how to leverage branded images that represented the values of social responsibility and environmental concerns that were upheld by Broad Street Studios.

The six businesses encompassed:

1. Broad Street Orchestra, which involved young musicians composing and performing music based on Caribbean and African drumming traditions. They performed at paid gigs in Providence. It is important to note that the instruments were the same brands as those supplied to and used in the Rhode Island Training School so that continuity of performance skills could ensue for those youth who moved on to the Broad Street programs.
2. Broad Street Press, which allowed young people to be taught the craft of publishing their work, with a focus on creating literature that was relevant to youth. Young people's books were published along with two bi-monthly publications: *Muzine*, emphasised as 'an open forum for the uncensored voice of Rhode Island youth', and *Hidden T.R.E.W.T.H.* (Tabloid Realism Enlightening Worldz Troubled Humanity), a literary journal from the Rhode Island Training Scheme.

    A rap that featured on the cover of *Hidden T.R.E.W.T.H.* captured the stated intent of Broad Street Press to 'help young people learn the craft of publishing their printable expressions, while simultaneously developing a nationwide network of young people and organizations devoted to amplifying these voices' (www.as220.org/broadsheet).The rap stated: 'If time was reversed, we'd be able to see our problems before they happen, but you can't see the future from now, that's why we gotta pay attention to the traps around.' Expression, communication, awareness and responsibility were encouraged in the magazine rather than 'silence, censorship and denial of complex issues' (www.as220.org/broadsheet).
3. Broad Street Sisters, which was formed to redress the imbalance of males to females in the Broad Street community. Young women participants, largely African-Americans from the local community, were given the

opportunity in the Sisters program to share and create an all-female space where older women artists from a diverse range of the creative arts in Providence mentored and shared their skills with the participants in the Broad Street Sisters program and supported them to find external opportunities to showcase their art.
4. Hip Hop 220 was a youth-led performance group, with their own label, who learned the skills of 'entrepreneurial realism' (www.as220.org/broadsheet) as they developed their identity as performers and hip hop artists. They performed an annual 'Rhode Show' which focused on positive messages – such as anti-tobacco corporation messages, anti-drugs and environmental sustainability – which they showcased throughout Rhode Island. The group learned and performed DJing, beatboxing, rapping, breakdancing and graffiti art.
5. Photographic Memory, which provided opportunities to shoot and develop black and white photographs of iconic Rhode Island sites. Learning traditional portrait photography provided a pathway to employment as Photographic Memory staff were frequently hired to produce corporate photographs. A set of seven photographs has been developed into postcards, which are sold in museums across the USA.
6. Broad Street Visuals is a young group of artists who were commissioned by non-profit organisations (and others) in Providence to design and produce murals, flyers and logos. Their work can be seen throughout Providence and has adorned buses as well as buildings and billboards.

An emergent element is that Broad Street Studios attracted neighbourhood youth as well as those from the state's juvenile detention facility and those under the guardianship of the Department of Children, Youth and Families. Between AS220 and BSS, a high recognition factor has been achieved across the state and nationally. Its programming stretched far beyond its original target group; and all this on a start-up of $4,000.

An example of the extent of its growing networks is a partnership with Brown University, Providence, where students undertaking a Masters degree in education were involved with the BSS from the beginning. Research placements at the BSS are part of a formal Masters program, with initial mentoring provided by Professor Shirley Brice Heath from Brown and Stanford universities. This has formed ongoing synergies as many of the graduates of this program teach in local Providence schools and continue their connections and those of their students to the BSS programs. Such connections can be seen in the production of the bi-monthly magazine, *Muzine*, which features writing from young people across all high schools in Providence. Competitions are held that encourage story writing, and poetry raps are also a central part of both the magazine production and performance events.

BSS musical events attract young people from across Providence and beyond. The 'success' of this widespread youth engagement in music and arts activities emanating from the BSS has been influential in the decision by the University of Rhode Island to develop a community school for young people transitioning from the Rhode Island Training School.

These and many other examples highlight the powerful effect AS220 and the BSS have had (and are having) on their community. From the founding vision, a community-based team of mentors, tutors and volunteers have worked to build relational power within a community so that as an organisational network they can sustain not only personal transformations but come together around the transformations of their community. What other policy-makers need to learn from this is that *appropriate funding* and other support underpinned these initiatives and outcomes.

During our time at the BSS we talked to several of the members of the BSS Orchestra who had turned up to practise, several youth putting down tracks, and staff and tutors. Curiosity about why Australian researchers would be interested in what they were doing was overlaid with an even greater curiosity about what other youth-based community organisations were doing around the world. They were impressed that other organisations would be interested in their programs; it validated in a very strong way their commitment to and belief in their community.

The conversations that we had with several of the youth present and their mentors at the BSS lent support to the sentiments expressed in the AS220 mission statement. One part of the mission statement says:

> The pride we have in who we are as individuals and a collective is manifested in our hard work, the loving way we treat each other, and the positive representation we uphold of ourselves and our community by way of the truest art we can create. Through youth empowerment and strong relationships, we build skills in life, art, critical thinking, and shared responsibility. We maintain an open, safe space for all young people to convene and share in a common dedication to creation. (www.AS220.org/Muzine)

We caught the train back to Boston late at night (without a power failure) and felt even more depressed about the Brighton Treatment Center which, despite Juri's innovative program, had no equivalent of a BSS to allow the creative work to continue, let alone provide a space to develop youth-centric arts businesses.

Please sir! Can I have some more (funding)?

Most of our CBOs needed more of everything: volunteers, mentors and support from the government and private sectors. The most successful national program we researched, after AS220 and the BSS, was in the UK: the Prince's Trust Business Start-Up Programs (www.princes-trust.org.uk). As we stated at the outset of this chapter, Alexis, the director of AKarts, and DJ Roland were involved in this scheme. We have previously written about the funding arrangements at some length (Peters, 2008) but it is important to note that this is a charity founded in 1976 by His Royal Highness, the Prince of Wales as a way to support young people to reach their potential. The Prince's Trust is the UK's leading youth charity focused on 18–30-year-olds.

The Prince's Trust supports micro-entrepreneurial initiatives. Its 'recipients' are unemployed or underemployed youth who are unable to gain support from the finance sector. As well as financial assistance, mentoring and training is a critical component of the scheme. This allows young people like Rowland to set up their own business with the support of volunteer business mentors, such as Alexis. The critical component, along with the financial support, is that the mentors develop close relationships with their mentees and they do not just help them to start up a business but also offer advice, support, training, mentoring and personal development opportunities. The Prince's Trust business start-up support involves counselling, help with the preparation of business plans and business training. Rowland had to pitch his idea for his own DJ business to a panel of local business people who select the candidates. As well as having a sound business idea, Rowland had to have experience as a DJ and his 'personality' was also evaluated. The grant awarded was £3,000.

How does the Prince's Trust fund this scheme? We were astonished (as this has no equivalent in Australia) that more than 50 per cent of the annual funding comes from donations. The rest comes from a range of sources: the trust's own funds, grants from the UK Employment Department, and funds from the European Regional Development Bank. The UK government's very partial support of the trust is its only support of a national youth entrepreneurship program, despite the (then) Blair Labour government's rhetoric about creative industries, creative hubs and a 'third way'. What we also found fascinating about the Prince's Trust was that it had a skeletal paid staff. During the time of our research the trust had more than 600 unpaid volunteer advisers and more than 600 unpaid volunteer board members (Prince's Trust, 2003). Like Alexis, these advisers were experienced in running their own businesses and very keen to pass on their skills and knowledge to youth potentially to help the youth to change their lives. Also important to the advisers' success with their mentees is that they lived and worked in their local areas. Advisers came from across the sectors – public, private and not-for-profit – and worked with a mentee for the first three years, although, as we found with Alexis and Rowland, the supportive relationship often went well beyond these initial three years.

We were also impressed that by 2005 this scheme had supported more than 50,000 young people to start their own business with 60 per cent being reported in annual OECD reports as still operating in their third year. In our discussions with Rowland about his experiences of the trust and the support he received from Alexis, it is apparent that he continued to value both his personal and business relationship with Alexis. Particularly after the death of Rowland's mother in 2003, Alexis became an even stronger career mentor and guide. Rowland was very devoted to his mother, who had come to England to provide a better life for him and his siblings. Our discussions with both Rowland and Alexis clearly revealed that despite, or perhaps because of, the closeness of their relationship neither of them viewed the Prince's Trust as operating as a social or welfare service. The take-up rates by youth of these micro-entrepreneurial start-up programs are a salutary reminder to governments that there is an urgent need to design national youth policies that provide such support.

Government funding for youth centres in the UK varies markedly and is inherently precarious. Another of the community-based centres in our research project was the Tabernacle Centre for Arts and Learning in the Royal Borough of Kensington and Chelsea. In 2004, Karin Woodley, at that time the director, informed us that the Tabernacle received £160,000 from the Royal Borough of Kensington and Chelsea, £85,000 from Bloomberg – a private sponsor – £100,000 from hiring the building to the community, and £40–50,000 from the Arts Council England.

As well as the major sponsors listed above, a series of other sponsors were involved for varied amounts of money. They included Flash Photographic, The Angels, Virgin Media Group, the Stone Ashdown Trust, Notting Hill Housing Trust, Nu Lines, Mario's Locksmiths, John Lyons Charity, and the Robert Gavron Charitable Trust. According to Karin, several individual donors support the Tabernacle but on the basis of anonymity. In 2004 when we were involved in the Tabernacle, the borough, its major sponsor, began to shift its interest from the development of arts/education programs to 'regeneration' through arts and education programs. This resulted in less designated funding for youth group activities to a broader community focus and in turn this led Karin to tender her resignation.

The subsequent advertisement for a director offering a salary of £38,000, placed in *The Guardian* 'Jobs and Money' section on page 33 on Sunday, 30 October 2004, highlighted:

> Are you looking for a unique opportunity to champion diversity? Do you have the passion to lead community regeneration, arts and education centre in one of London's most culturally diverse boroughs?...We challenge cultural stereotypes and ghettos; give voice to Kensington & Chelsea's many diverse communities, and engage new audiences and learners of all ages.

It seemed that youth voices now were only one of the many competing sets of voices to be 'heard' at the Tabernacle.

Who listens to youth in Australia?

In 2000, the year after the Broken Hill Propriety (BHP) steelworks closure, Newcastle City Council resolved to foster the building of new tertiary economic sector drivers to replace Newcastle's reliance on its traditional industrial base (i.e. primary and secondary economic sectors) and to contribute to the reinvention of the city by consciously disarticulating its imaging from its industrial heritage. A key plank in this rejuvenation was a strategic commitment to youth by the council (Newcastle City Council, 2000a). In this key position paper, Newcastle City Council (NCC) acknowledged that young people are a heterogeneous group and an integral part of the community, and stated its aims to encourage inclusion in all facets of community life, promote recognition of achievements and ensure that the well-being and diverse needs of young people are incorporated into all council activities.

This 'commitment' comprised thirteen actions of which the following were the most relevant to our research project:

- Establish a youth venue (implemented and venue leased 2000). The council's intention was to 'facilitate the establishment of an appropriate centralised facility with the potential to offer a wide range of activities suitable for both males and females and catering for the diverse needs and interests of young people'.
- Facilitate young people's access to public areas and acknowledgement of their use of these areas by consultation with owners and developers and businesses. These conversations determined how the needs of young people could be reflected in the design and management of privately owned public space, and promoted increased understanding between the police and youth in the use of public space.
- Employ a Youth Program Coordinator.
- Develop the youth venue 'to promote a shared use of public spaces throughout the city and ensure that the needs of young people are addressed in new release areas'. This was implemented in 1998–9.
- Promote and allocate resources to the Youth Council as a Youth Advisory Body and sponsor an annual Youth Forum in Youth Week.
- Provide information technology in libraries, available to youth.
- Encourage participation of young people and diverse cultural groups in city activities including representation on fora and committees; NCC's education program to include secondary school students.
- Increase critical understanding of media representation of young people and promote their positive contributions (for example, NCC Media Officer to report on youth activities).
- Promote activities for 12–14-year-olds through programs at the youth venue, and develop youth services through liaison with funding bodies and government departments.

- Address interests and issues for young people in council planning.
- Promote cultural activities.

The council stated its intention to recognise and encourage diverse youth cultural expressions as a cornerstone of the council's policy development through the support of various activities including 'socially responsible aerosol/graffiti art' and the provision of 'legal mural space(s)'. Interrelated with this commitment was the identification of new and existing 'youth employment opportunities' as part of the council's Economic Development Strategy (NCC, 2000a).

The major interest for our research in Newcastle was this dedicated commitment to access to public space, the provision of affordable recreation activities, access to employment/educational opportunities, and a commitment to overturning a 'negative' public image of Newcastle youth. Our research in Newcastle particularly focused on several specific NCC strategies:

- the development of events/social activities that encourage people of different ages to interact positively;
- ongoing monitoring and support for the youth venue and its activities;
- implementation of the Skateboard Improvement Program; and
- the encouragement of the development of programs that facilitate intergenerational learning.

According to the key document, referenced above, relevant significant strategies included targeting specific businesses and sectors. These businesses and industries included the arts, entertainment and education sectors in which a central activity area was seen to be assisting and facilitating study into 'the establishment of performing arts and visual arts incubators to provide artists with the skills necessary to market and export their work' (NCC, 2000, p. 4).

The Palais Royale

We began our research project at the Palais because it seemed to hold out the promise of achieving many of the key goals identified in the earlier 1999 NCC policy document. According to its 2003 statement of aims and objectives, the Palais Royale Youth Venue is a 'youth cultural development project' established and sponsored by the council since 2000. The Palais was then one of Newcastle's largest all-age venues which offered a range of creative activities for young people aged from 12 to 25. It supported activities such as 'all-ages gigs, electronic music, comics, aerosol arts, visual arts and crafts, creative writing, zines, breakdancing, fire twirling, web design, theatre and performing arts' (Palais Royale, 2003).

Of particular interest for our study was that the Palais also intended to support the development of youth cultural businesses through a youth business incubator and resources. It also supported youth cultural events such as the Noise Festival, National Young Writers' Festival, Electrofringe and radio Triple J's show[2] *The Unearthing of Newcastle* (Palais Royale, 2003). *Unearthed*[3] was a particularly significant forum for young Newcastle musicians to gain recognition and opportunities:

> Here at Triple J, we've been unearthing new Australian music since July '95. So far we've received over 4300 entries and we've unearthed over 70 bands and visited over 40 regions all over Australia!
>
> *Unearthed* provides young bands and musicians living in the regional and city areas of Australia with a means to have their talents professionally recorded and played on national radio.
>
> It's a great way for young people across Australia to hear what other young people are into. (Triple J, 3 May 2004)

The title of the youth venue was taken from the name of the leased premises from which it operated, which was a building with a continuous history in excess of 150 years. The Palais had been a popular dance and concert venue on the main street of western Newcastle city, Hunter Street. Sadly, during our research period the building was sold to developers as part of the re-gentrification push that saw apartments spring up in its wake.

The aims and objectives of the Palais as a youth venue were particularly interesting to our research project and were informed by several council reports and policies, especially their report *Commitment to Young People*. They included the following:

- to promote a positive image of young people as active members of the community;
- to establish the venue as a key youth cultural development facility that provides equitable and affordable opportunities and resources for all young people;
- to encourage the participation of a diverse range of young people in all aspects of running the venue;
- to promote youth participation as the organisers and managers of their arts and cultural activities and events;
- to provide an environment that encourages skill sharing and provides training for young people, thus promoting their self-reliance;
- to create partnerships with other youth and cultural organisations;
- to provide a self-funding council service that operates as a best practice and environmentally aware establishment (Palais Royale, 2003).

When we made our first visit to Newcastle and the Palais in 2003, two new full-time staff positions had been created, that of Youth Venue Coordinator and Youth Venue Administrative Officer, in addition to the Youth

Program Coordinator, the Youth Venue Activities Officer and the Youth Venue Volunteers Coordinator. The venue also employed casual staff on an as-needs basis for activities and events such as gigs, 'special projects' and aerosol art. In addition, the Palais had 70 youth venue volunteers who organised and managed a range of venue activities and events. While the Palais building and its surrounds had certainly seen better days, the organisation of the venue's programs and activities was undertaken by enthusiastic staff, volunteers and youth participants. Our conversations with those staff present in August 2003 revealed that there was much cause for optimism among the paid staff. This sense of optimism was not to last.

> From my interviews and discussions with Palais staff it is clear that 2003 was a year of change in both management structure and culture for both staff and members of the Palais with the introduction of the Youth Venue Coordinator and Youth Venue Administrative Officer's positions bringing a more direct relationship with council to the venue. Previously the council's Youth Policy Officer divided her time between council building-based policy development duties and overseeing the youth venue in what could be described as an 'arm's length' capacity, whereas now both the Venue Coordinator and Venue Administrative Officer are now on-site at the venue bringing a stronger 'part-of-council' identity to the Palais that is reflected in the lesser involvement of Palais' youth volunteers in the venue's administration.
>
> (Julie, personal communication, 2004)

In this reading of the policy as discourse, Julie reflected that this more direct relationship and identification with the council was 'also evident in the form of discourse used in the above-mentioned aims and objectives created in 2003', especially with regard to the description of the venue as 'a self-funding council service' and a 'key youth cultural development facility'. Julie's 2004 discussions with staff, and her own and their speculation as to what future changes might bring in relation to a foreshadowed service and cultural policy shift from youth arts activities to youth cultural development, interestingly did not see the expected swing away from youth 'dropping into' activities or attending organised gigs at the Palais. The key performance indicators for the Palais did not manifestly change, including attendance numbers at gigs and workshops.

The conflict or confusion between stated council 'youth arts' and 'youth cultural development' policies and actual funded key performance indicators for community-based organisations is evident not just at the Palais but at most of the community-based organisations we researched, particularly in the Playford City Council's (South Australia) support for the *Youth Revolutions* program (Peters, 2008).

In Newcastle, the shifting of the Palais' activities to the Loft in the Hunter Street Mall, in the heart of the CBD, after the lease on the Palais building expired in August 2004, was further expected to support the council's integration of the operations of the project into the council's cultural policies and plans. Instead, for many youth participants the demolition of the Palais building meant that the youth lost their 'own space' and many did not relocate to the busy inner city location. Stated intentions in a policy, even when some dedicated funds are attached, are never enough by themselves.

Youth Revolutions: a youth-led community radio program

Youth Revolutions in Adelaide's northern suburbs began as an initiative of the Playford City Council's Community Cultural Development (CCD) focus (see Peters, 2008, for a detailed overview). In 2002 the council employed a CCD Officer, Don Chapman, whose position was funded by an Arts SA grant. Don established the Playford Arts Community Team, which brought together stakeholders to work as a reference group in developing a community audit and strategy for Playford. Stakeholders included Anglicare, Northern Adelaide Community Youth Services and the Elizabeth Arts Society.

Don Chapman was also employed as a project officer for the Northern Sound System, which was in its initial stage of development when the Playing for Life researchers began interviews in the region in 2003. The Northern Sound System project was funded by the federal Sustainable Regions Program and aimed to provide a region-based youth community music centre with a focus on creating a cultural industries hub. As noted in earlier chapters, the centre offered a range of facilities including performance, training, rehearsal and recording facilities (City of Playford, 2002). As in other cities in our research project, the researchers could begin to map the link between youth arts practices and the idea of sustainable youth entrepreneurship. It became clear that networks of agencies and stakeholders predominated in the northern Adelaide suburbs, although it was not always evident at the outset as to how this worked in practice nor how closely the council's and youth workers' stated aims resonated with the youth participants.

The Playford Youth Network was comprised of the various youth agencies and services in the council area. Their bi-monthly meetings were directed at sharing information and establishing networks to facilitate the further development of services for young people and instil coordination and cooperation among the various agencies. In 2003 the network was working on establishing a youth website, which Playford Council funded, including employing a school-based apprentice to develop and maintain the site.

Lilly Buvka, the Youth Development Officer (YDO) employed by the Playford City Council (see Peters, 2008), was also involved with the Regional

Youth Services planning committee, which covered the northern region and included people from Gawler, Tea Tree Gully and Salisbury, as well as Playford.

This group was essentially a youth services planning group, which focused particularly on the health of young people. It encompassed groups covering mental health, sexual health, homelessness, drug and alcohol use, and early school leaving. The broader planning committee included a subset of youth development officers from across the northern region, who focused on networking, information sharing and collaboration. In 2003 they were working on producing a comprehensive list of youth services in the north.

A Playford Youth Services pamphlet was produced which detailed the various agencies and services for young people in the area. It was aimed at youth workers, rather than young people themselves, as a quick reference guide. Lilly explained that it was designed to assist new workers in the area by providing a brief description of each service agency, their location and a contact number:

> It's really good for in terms of professional development and keeping my sanity... We all might do different things but they all deal with madness as well and they all have huge workloads as well... I don't know whether it's just their nature... [that] we tend to do... heaps of stuff – can't say 'no' – or we just have heaps of work. Or you're making up for all those years of nothing happening and you really need to get stuff happening. (Lilly, personal communication, 2003)

Making marginalised youth a priority highlighted the significance of youth workers and youth services in the northern suburbs but it often did so contradictorily. As we have discussed in earlier chapters, 'space' and 'place' are contested 'territories'. Alienated youth did not always respond to the funded opportunities Playford City Council provided in ways that were aligned with the official rhetoric. This became obvious over time in relation to the concept of a youth-led 'guerrilla' radio program which became known, with irony intended, as *Youth Revolutions* (see Edwards, 2003). The signature rhyme, created by the *Youth Revolutions* radio 'crew' themselves to introduce the radio program, highlighted some of these tensions:

> In a time of revolution, gotta step back and listen
> In the midst of confusion, find a voice in the system
> While we'll offer up a dose of social comment and wisdom,
> We're giving you the most because we're a youth on a mission...
> We got the music that you like, all the reviews which you need.
> With Playford Council helping keep us all up to speed.
> Because we're from the North, we like to say what we mean,

> We question all the reasons why we're stuck in our scene...
> (Will, personal communication, November 2003)

With *Youth Revolutions*, the space was a community radio site, PBA-FM, at the back of a local secondary school in Salisbury. The weekly 30-minute evening program was sandwiched between a Greek community music program and a hard rock program. This was not quite the creative youth hub envisaged in the council documents. The site was difficult to get to by public transport, so the opportunity provided was tempered by the financial constraints of getting there.

The Playford City Council paid the radio station directly for the *Youth Revolutions* show, drawing up a funding agreement with conditions such as the council having access to records, Lilly Bukva, the YDO, being on the steering committee, and set guidelines about any language that could generate possible complaints from the radio station, participants or the community (Peters, 2008). The extensive youth networking in the region meant that several of the key youth in *Youth Revolutions* were already involved with each other in youth activities in the cities of Salisbury and Playford. *Youth Revolutions* was developed to 'celebrate the creativity and skills of Northern suburbs youth' (Peters, 2008, p.182) with a focus on enhancing agency, self-esteem and social inclusion by giving people a voice in their own community.

That voice was meant to be self-supporting eventually in terms of funding. As part of the South Australian government's youth enterprise model, the youth accepted responsibility for developing, mentoring and delivering the radio program. After the initial eighteen-month start-up funding, the youth were to find their own sponsors to keep the radio program going. Many of the young participants supplied their own tapes to keep costs down and provide variety and there was the further constraint of having enough of the youth available to script and run the show. Planning meetings also became a challenge in terms of attendance. Emails were a key part of organising the format for the shows.

Will, Kristin, Vanessa, Bret and Michael were the original members, joined later by Garth and Monique. Michael described the original crew's roles as Vanessa as the overseer; Bret, the music manager; Kristin, in charge of events; Will, the administrator; and himself as 'the all round gopher, but that was a good thing 'cause I could stick my hands in everything' (Michael, personal communication, May 2005). It was interesting that Will saw himself not as an administrator but as a 'researcher of stories'. This included undertaking pre-recorded interviews. He also spoke of fruitlessly trying to bring more structure into the crew but felt that each time he tried to introduce more effective policies he was blocked by some of the team for 'only Michael supported me' (Will, personal communication, May 2005). In 2004 Bret, Vanessa and Monique were already discussing with Playing For Life researchers the problems they were having with Will's ambitions to professionalise the show. Vanessa stated: 'That's not what it's about. It's supposed to be fun.' All three complained about Will's production of a document that listed the mission statement for *Youth Revolutions* and an organisational chart. Bret commented, 'Does he really think we have the time to read this stuff?' and Monique disclaimed: 'It's full of rules.' Vanessa recognised that a mission statement was necessary for 'corporate stuff' but they all felt he was missing the point of the program. Will did not see 'having fun' and being 'entrepreneurial' as an 'either-or' proposition (Will, personal communication, 2005).

> WHO
> Micheal
> Monique
> Vanessa
> Bret (maybe)
>
> WHAT
> Song Analysis
> (micheal i present you with a challenge!!!!!! Either do this on a song requested or on a song i know you don't like...i wanna really test your song analysis skills in seeing a message that wasn't obvious to us in the first place lol [laugh out loud] im sure you will do a great job and hope you accept the challenge...put it this way the way we learn is through dong new things sometimes and i wanna see how you do lol even if its stupid and you don't have to agree with the message. if you don't agree with the message then you can voice this on radio too, it makes it interesting)
>
> (Vanessa, email to crew, 4 March 2004, original spelling and format)

Over time the enthusiasm of the youth volunteers to run a cutting edge radio program was eroded by escalating financial and interpersonal constraints. As Lilly Bukva explained:

> *Youth Revolutions* was not part of a council 'enterprise development program', we simply provided funding/sponsorship to *Youth Revolutions* as their previous funding arrangement [from Northern Area Community and Youth Services (NACYS) http://www.nacys.asn.au/] had ended...From a youth development perspective, I wanted to see *Youth Revolutions* be successful in what they were doing to provide support where I could, outside of any formal, policy or program framework. (Lilly Bukva, cited in Peters, 2008, p. 180)

Under the youth enterprise model, which forms part of the South Australian government's policy on youth development strategy and which local councils can access, the council paid the radio station directly to allow the group to broadcast their program which meant that, according to Lilly, the council believed that 'it was ultimately responsible to PBA-FM Radio and liable for the *Youth Revolutions* show' (Lilly Bukva, cited in Peters, 2008). Lilly was therefore on the steering committee, the council had access to all records and produced guidelines about the use of language and restrictions on the playlist.

It is important to understand that Lilly's role as a youth development officer was very different to that of a youth worker. Her role was to chair the steering committee for *Youth Revolutions*, not to be actively working with them on the project itself. Despite Lilly's strenuous efforts to support (and voluntarily mentor) the group, the passionate commitment and extraordinary input from this small group eventually dissipated and imploded. Tensions between group members increased, often around the perception of unequal input, the 'revolutionary' aspect of youth voices as part of the informational base of the programming dwindled to mainly playing music tracks, 'no shows' from presenters became prevalent and external funding never materialised.

In a conversation with Lilly about *Youth Revolutions* and its eventual folding, she stressed that the key factor that the Community Development Unit of Playford City Council had learnt from *Youth Revolutions* was the importance of having an adult paid role in supporting and mentoring such initiatives. Despite Lilly's suggestions for new avenues of funding and sponsorship, the radio crew had not acted on them. The suggestion from Lilly was that a paid adult support/mentor could have been instrumental in seeking financial viability as well as ameliorating interpersonal tensions between the crew (Lilly, personal communication, 2005).

Yet Lilly also was clear that the terms of the funding agreement between the council and the radio station made *Youth Revolutions* the responsibility of the youth. If the council, as Lilly explained, had taken responsibility for the project it would have made them liable for transport for the crew to and from the radio station, and to have a staff member present at the station during broadcasts. As it was, *Youth Revolutions* was youth run and their responsibility, from planning to production. The development of entrepreneurial skills and behaviours was somehow assumed, if actually factored in at all.

Kandinsky Sessions at Carclew

The Kandinsky planning sessions were held face-to-face at Carclew and differed markedly from *Youth Revolutions*' email planning sessions and infrequent steering group meetings. The Kandinsky planning group met fortnightly in the loft of an old stone outbuilding in the grounds of the once gracious mansion of Carclew, described in Chapter 4.

At our initial meeting with the group in May 2003 the participants took turns talking about the purpose of Kandinsky Sessions. They said it had emerged from the Off the Couch project, which was a highly significant youth arts venture sponsored by Carclew. Potential involvement in Off the Couch (OTC) was advertised at the annual Big Day Out Concert in Adelaide, a one day in January mecca for youth and for all styles of Australian and overseas bands. Off the Couch was usually restricted to about 20 youth who were then divided into subgroups of about 6–8 members to handle production, publicity, staging etc. of the youth arts/music event (see Vicci's personal account, direct to camera, in Chapter 2).

Organising Off the Couch had led to recognition of the shortage of all-ages gigs for young people in Adelaide to go to: 'apart from punk gigs [there is] hardly anything for all ages in Adelaide' (Mike, Kandinsky member, personal communication, 2005). So Kandinsky was born with an original team of twelve youth volunteer organisers, including some members of the organising committee from Off the Couch keen to extend their event management skills, and a mentor, Nev de Boer, from AusMusic, who was funded by Carclew to mentor the group. While four of the original youth had dropped out by the time we began our involvement with the Kandinsky Sessions, the founding group in their first year of operation had organised gigs at the Enigma Bar, Mojo West and Rhino Room (all well-known 'alternative' live music venues in Adelaide). Ben, one of the original group members, had been involved in Nev's funded research project at AusMusic involving youth performers. Original members Mike and Alicia were both in an indie guitar band and performed at the local well-known Adelaide city music venue/hotel, the Grace Emily. Clare was a founding team member of both Off the Couch and Kandinsky Sessions. Vicci also had been volunteering with Nev when undertaking an events management course through AusMusic. As well as being musicians, the first members of Kandinsky were hungry to develop their skills at 'putting on gigs'. According to members of this first organising group, the initial gigs Kandinsky Sessions organised were very successful in terms of attendance and proved to be excellent incubators, particularly for those who had not been involved in organising events for Off the Couch, to acquire basic marketing, public relations, financial and industry sponsorship skills.

At our initial meeting, the group talked about how the gigs they organised 'were done not for profit, and had free entry'. They mentioned that the Rhino Room had cost them $250 to hire, and that they were able to cover this cost 'by making money from the bar [drinks]' until they had raised this amount. Not all of their gigs, since their first year, had been successful. Although they had identified a gap in the market for 'all-ages gigs' (in other words, events that would allow attendance by minors), this was proving to be a two-edged sword. In discussing this further, Ben said that their 'electronica gig... wasn't exactly a roaring success'. This statement was greeted by much laughter from everyone present. As well as selecting a genre and type of music according to what would be well attended, it was also apparently proving difficult to identify how to manage the issue of under eighteen-year-old participants at the venues; members of the group discussed the problem of the prevalence of fake identity cards and the fact that many underage youth wore the wrist bands that enabled them to purchase alcohol. Policing this was clearly going to be difficult and there was long debate over the efficacy of doing so.

The first year had provided many opportunities to learn what worked (and what did not) and in which space; the venue was critical for gaining support for particular types of bands. Rhino Room, which was an intimate space, worked better for acoustic gigs while indie gigs worked better at the larger venue Jive. It was also a case of which type of band and fan community already attended these venues! This attitude of 'learn as we do' could be nurtured and supported because some of the financial pressure was relieved though a base of funding from Carclew of AUS $2,000–3,000 per year. This allowed the group, according to Ben, to have 'money in the kitty' for the production of flyers and promotional material for the gigs. Additional advertising was then organised by the group through local Adelaide street magazines such as *dB* and *Rip It Up*, both of which have a strong youth readership.

The Kandinsky group was learning to become promoters of youth music as well as event organisers. They had to take full responsibility for hiring the groups, selection of the venues, providing security, promoting the events and gaining financial sponsorship for the events. The Kandinsky meetings were the vehicle for exploring a wide range of operational matters and issues. This analysis of organisational minutiae drilled down to matters such as what would be happening with the bands on the night and whether the Kandinsky members should be providing the musicians free drinks on the night.

This last was an issue discussed while we were in attendance at one of the planning meetings. Apparently the group had previously given free drinks to the bands at their gigs – a usual form of 'honorarium' when any artist performs which they termed a 'rider' – e.g. the free provision of jugs of beer, amongst other small inducements. Ben was unsure as to whether or not the bands needed to organise this for themselves, or whether the venue would take care of it. Nev advised Ben that they would need to do it themselves. This led to a lengthy discussion of how they would arrange this. Michelle, one of the group members, suggested that they could use a ticket system where bands would be given tickets to take to the bar to get drinks. The Kandinsky group would presumably either pay for this in advance or pick up the bill afterwards.

This vignette highlights the nascent development of entrepreneurship skills at the grassroots level. In these ways the Kandinsky group was learning new business skills through tasks involving event management, team management, marketing, distribution, publicity and problem solving. At each meeting we attended, the serious work of networking, collaborating, achieving and creative problem solving was always on display. For example, the meeting of 17 September 2003 was devoted to discussing the challenges involved in promotional work. Ben began the meeting by discussing the advertising and promotion they had been doing for the gigs. He said that they had tried to do a feature in the last *Rip It Up* magazine, a free street magazine devoted to music, but that there had been a mix up, and that their article had not made it in. Apparently they were running an advertisement in the same edition, which would provide some coverage for the upcoming gigs. This led to focused and, at times, strong discussion by members on the need to avoid such 'stuff ups' by being organised well ahead of time.

Later on in the evening, comments were made about the advertising they were doing for the final two gigs (one mid-October, a hip hop gig, and another on Halloween, a punk/hardcore gig at the Enigma Bar). Mike said that they should run a full-page advertisement in *Rip It Up* magazine, which apparently would cost $700 and referred back to the budget still remaining that Carclew had given them, which he suggested was about $3,000. Ben said that they had not paid *Rip It Up* yet for the adverts they had run, and he showed the group an invoice that the magazine had sent them. They then needed to pass the invoice on to Carclew who would pay the magazine. There seemed to be some confusion about exactly how much money was remaining in their budget. Mike gave an estimate of $3,000, but nobody knew exactly how much was left. Nev, their mentor, then guided them through a series of actions they needed to take regarding their financial position and the importance of having this information 'at their fingertips'.

Risk management is an ever-present part of youth entrepreneurial ventures and one aspect that has given rise to many detractors of the 'new creative economy' who see such activities as masking youth unemployment (McRobbie, 2002b). In the case of Kandinsky, Nev played a critical mentoring role in helping the inexperienced group understand, manage and minimise the financial risk inherent in running their gigs. His guidance and informal support also helped the group develop a set of attitudes, values and beliefs that enhanced their enterprising behaviour and skills.

It was interesting then that the group, as it evolved and its membership changed, decided in early 2004 that they did not need a paid mentor; they wanted all their money allowance from Carclew. In 2005, founding member Clare stated it was a question of 'do you want to advertise your gig or have Nev?' Instead, the group, according to Clare, 'applied for extra money for the mentor model but this wasn't successful'. Clare reflected that 'the program with all its ideas still hasn't the right funding' (Clare, personal communication, 2005).

After Nev's employment ceased, a series of unpaid coordinators worked with Kandinsky members. This has highlighted the very big difference between the role of a coordinator and the role of a mentor. Coordinators help get the gigs organised but do not necessarily develop the business skills of the members. Mentors, as we have witnessed first-hand in this research project, play an integral role in the development of entrepreneurial behaviour and skills. The group's members, along with the unpaid coordinator, continued to 'audition' prospective musicians for the (usually) five gigs per year through a request for an audio track and then one member of Kandinsky usually attending a live performance of those groups who were shortlisted.

This eventually led to tensions between some group members who felt they were doing more work than others in setting up the gigs. As some members got paid work, and as some 'lost the love', as Sam put it (Sam, personal communication, 2005), the original group dwindled to four core members by 2005. The selection of Kandinsky members was monitored by the various unpaid coordinators but without a mentor the new members' development as event managers and entrepreneurs was somewhat haphazard. An unforeseen problem also arose with the increasing popularity of the gigs. It became increasingly difficult to book some performers, particularly hip hop groups, as according to Vicci they 'were suspicious they would be dobbed into Centrelink', the Australian government unemployment agency, for not declaring income earned (Vicci, personal communication, 2005). This became a point of ongoing tension between the dreams and the reality of the gigs providing the opportunity to break into the paid music scene and make a living.

Da Klinic

As outlined in earlier chapters, Da Klinic emerged from an initial small business start-up funding model which allowed two former school friends, Adrian Shepherd – DJ Shep – and his business partner, Jeff, to sustain their vision financially. Through this funding and also by keeping on their part-time jobs in other spheres, they were able to realise a space and place where young people could learn a variety of skills from skating to hip hop, turntabling, breakdancing, and DJing.

As described earlier, Da Klinic had a street-level entry to a retail outlet that sold clothes, inline skates and Australian hip hop music. The basement was a fascinating mix of spaces marked out for an indoor skate ramp, two dance floors, a space where turntabling was taught, and in the furthest recess an office. This fascinating mix reflected DJ Shep's constant emphasis on providing youth with 'education and opportunity'. In the provision of skills, Da Klinic provided a very different model of funding to most of our other CBOs and centres. DJ Shep had a distrust of politicians and other funders who dismissed turntabling and hip hop as 'not real music'. In a personal anecdote, Shep related attending a state government enquiry into youth arts and music funding in Adelaide in 2002. After he had talked to the group about Da Klinic and what it offered youth, a senior politician said to him: 'But you can't really be serious that the community would want us to fund kids to play records [turntabling] when we could fund kids to play real music in youth orchestras' (Shep, personal communication, 2005).

Shaped by such attitudes to funding, DJ Shep and his partner Jeff ploughed whatever they earned from elsewhere and from Da Klinic back into the business; the sales from merchandise also went back into the business and the money from workshops went directly to the instructors for the workshops. Da Klinic also handled sales of tickets to many gigs. While most of the time Da Klinic did not gain any money from the sales of tickets unless they had event-managed a large interstate gig, the events did bring prospective customers for their merchandise into the shop.

At the beginning of our project, Da Klinic was largely a word-of-mouth venue, gaining recognition through recommendation by people who came into the shop or booked for workshops. This was viral marketing in action! This network was also extended by the many people who saw DJ Shep perform at public events and would speak to him after his gigs. From such networking, entrepreneurial activities grow as described in more detail in Chapter 6.

Conclusion

So what have we learned about supporting youth-based arts/music community programs and entrepreneurial activities? In all the programs and activities we were involved in during our research, common threads were found across all four countries. No matter which country or what the policy was surrounding youth music arts programs, if youth were not at the centre of the policy, if their voices were not heard, then sustainability of the program was a high risk. As Shirley Brice Heath has highlighted, such community-based arts/music programs are 'generally left unattended, minimally supported, and almost completely unexamined' (2001, p. 10).

What is sharply in the eyes of policy-makers is accelerating youth unemployment rates at a time of the increased impact of globalisation on economic change. Thus there is a tension between implementing creative arts policies for youth as 'pathways to employment' and policies that support, sustain and develop entrepreneurial skills and behaviours amongst our youth. If such programs are developed solely 'from the top down' rather than from young people themselves, this is not a strong long-term option for all concerned.

All of the CBOs and centres we worked with had similar goals that highlighted some, but not all, of a range of desired organisational outcomes such as skills building, business development services, entrepreneurship promotion, capacity building and advocacy. As we discovered, there was not always a clear set of objectives in the youth activities organised. While there was frequently a strong commitment from councils and organising bodies to supporting youth arts/music programs, the mix of social and economic goals was frequently blurred and youth themselves were often not part of the initial conceptualisation of the program.

Funding was and is a critical element. Even Da Klinic, which has not relied on government funding, managed to gain an initial government start-up grant. But for many youth entrepreneurial activities, such as *Youth Revolutions*, often the expectation to gain self-sufficiency had too short a timeline or did not have a mentor with business expertise attached. The need for informal mentoring and access to adult advisers, especially for the very people who have not had a history of success and opportunity, is a critical finding in our research. Not only does this provide support for inexperienced (and often disadvantaged) youth in managing risk but it helps develop confidence and entrepreneurial behaviour. Rowland would not have returned to the Prince's Trust and been successful in gaining a grant if he had not had Alexis to guide him through the intricacies of writing an application that needed a strong business plan and a workable budget – all in the language required by such grants.

The applicants for youth arts music funding also need funding bodies to articulate clearly that their programs have a commercial focus. This was an issue for Juri's Genuine Voices work with the Brighton Treatment Center. It was so much harder to find multiple funding partners when, unlike AS220 and Broad Street programs, there were no follow-up programs for the youth to become a part of when they left the detention centre. Without a commercial focus, youth participants can easily become 'beneficiaries' rather than active and responsible 'clients'.

A critical element for sustaining successful programs is access to highly skilled adults, whether as specific music/arts skills developers or as entrepreneurs themselves with considerable business expertise. Training is a very important part of skills building, ranging from helping to put together a résumé, applying for grants or jobs, putting on gigs, developing web pages, and so forth.

Where ongoing funding can be the difference between sustaining and ending a program, the selection of which youth to be involved in the programs is critical. While choice should be underpinned by equitable and ethical principles, it is important to recognise the passionate commitment from youth who self-select to be involved in CBO activities. Where a team or crew is involved, mentoring can help diffuse interpersonal tensions.

We found that youth will usually prefer to be in programs where there is a network of local people who have experiences and skills that can be provided informally to them. This worked well at the Tabernacle, at Da Klinic, in Genuine Voices, at the Palais, and at the Kandinsky Sessions in its earlier days. Where this was noticeably successful was at Broad Street Studios where most of the tutors and mentors were former 'graduates' of the state's juvenile detention centre. Another positive aspect of having mentors and tutors who had experienced first-hand the juvenile detention centre and, for many, adult prisons, was that developing community values and community capacity building took on particular 'real world' urgency. An important part of paying tutors and mentors at Broad Street Studios, even when the sum of money involved was very small, was that it also enhanced the self-esteem of the mentors and trainers, even if, as we were reminded, they 'could make more money selling crack'.

It was also pointed out to us by adults involved in running youth arts/music programs that sustaining government funding or another agency's funding was dependent on formal program evaluations. Empirical data impressed and could be validated, where self-reporting could not. Otherwise, funding could be, and frequently was, reallocated to other areas designated as priorities. Many of the adult participants in our Playing for Life project saw their involvement in our study as a way of gaining wider recognition for the essential but often unacknowledged work that they do. There was a constant interplay and tension between the human, social and economic needs of youth participants in entrepreneurial and other music and arts-related activities. Policies need to be cognizant of those tensions and needs and the best way to begin to do that is to listen to youth and their mentors and trainers. Our next chapter takes a much closer look at the development of grassroots entrepreneurial skills and the creative uses of new technologies that support the crafting and growing of these skills.

6
Becoming Phat: Youth, Music and Micro-Enterprise

Photo 6.1 Katie Williams in performance. © Davi Matheson

You move out of the bedroom and take your writing out in the public. Then you perform it. Then you freestyle, then you go on from there. (Saul, Palais, personal communication, June 2010)

The most politically relevant point is surely that music today is also a place of employment, livelihoods and labour markets. This fact is obscured because being creative remains in our collective imaginations as a sort of dream world or utopia, far apart from the real world of making a living. (McRobbie, 1999, p. 134)

Introduction

As we demonstrated earlier, so many young people are working hard on developing and perfecting their musical skills and networks in difficult, often seemingly uncompromising, circumstances. But some do seem to 'make it'. They not only achieve recognition or are awarded some degree of celebrity status from and beyond their peers and local communities, but they also reach a level of 'excellence' or in the current youth vernacular become seriously 'cool' or 'phat'. Possibly even more importantly, they have started to make some sort of viable living from their art and passion, gaining self-funding through sustainable entrepreneurial activity. This chapter focuses on the meaning of this form of micro-enterprise for some of the young participants in our study, their mentors and the community-based organisations that support them, not only as a manifestation of the new economy 'on the ground' but also for its vitally important function of enabling a stronger sense of social identity, social cohesion and self-making within the contemporary world of blended work and leisure. That is, we are looking at what it means to 'become phat', to 'make it' in the difficult world of the music and related industries. This does not mean that these young people necessarily desire to follow the conventional professional pathway such as a 'sign up' with a commercial rather than an independent record label, for this is not always perceived as the most sought-after pathway for many young musicians today. Rather it is the point when the music activity can start to become one's 'day job' or, as Shep once told us, it has become the way 'to make money from what we love' without government assistance.

This is not a contradiction, however, despite the persistence of romantic discourses about music and art; as Angela McRobbie points out in the quotation above, art and enterprise have never been distant bedfellows even though we often imagine that 'being creative' is 'far apart from the real world of making a living'. Possibly though, because of such circulating discourses, such achievements through micro-enterprise or grassroots entrepreneurship are often manifested as 'in your face' brash confidence, almost as a gesture of defiance. The youth in our project who had started to become successful seemed to metaphorically shout their achievements from the rooftops in their promotional posters, photos and websites. For example, Katie Williams promotes her popular covers band, Regulator, on Facebook as 'The best covers band in London...Not my words, but the words of TOP GEAR MAGAZINE !!!' Rowland's recent Facebook profile similarly publicises his Phatbeats UK Garage Show (http://www.phatbeats.co.uk/garage_studio/) declaring 'Failure is not an option!'

Of course, in reality, failure *is* an option; many new forms of independent youth enterprise are certainly still risky and potentially exploitative, but they also often bring to the fore new forms of agency, networking, collaboration and trust. These are aspects that make the challenge worthwhile. They add greater substance to the ephemeral representation of the self in a shifting world, perhaps making it seem more manageable and solid than it really is. It is for these reasons we now look closely at this element of youth music practice, firstly through some of the more successful initiatives of the youth themselves. To begin the discussion, we take another vignette from our recent field notes, which describe the mood and atmosphere created by Katie and her band of young musicians at a central London venue.

We learnt about Regulator, Katie Williams' energetic four-piece covers band only recently even though the band members have been playing together under a different band name since 2002 with both female and male lead vocals. Katie Williams is now their main front vocalist with Charley, on drums, also singing on occasions. Guitarist Alvin and bassist Juan both draw on their professional musical backgrounds: each is trained to a high standard and has considerable experience in the music industry. Between the four of them, the band members have played in a broad range of well-known London venues including the Jazz Café, Islington Academy, Shepherd's Bush Empire, ULU and Underworld. They have also worked with and supported some very big names in the music industry including Mark Richardson (Feeder/Skunk Annansie), Eric Bobo (Cypress Hill), Chad Smith (Red Hot Chilli Peppers), Stef Carpenter (Deftones) and have recorded in studios such as Abbey Road, Air and Metropolis. Regulator plays a very eclectic set covering all styles from the 1960s right through to the most up-to-date pop and rock hits. Based in North London, the band have already made a name for themselves for being very popular on the live scene and play regularly at various large venues in and around the M25 area and very often further afield. On their website they emphasise that they 'are happy to travel, and are always wanting to entertain! Nothing is impossible!!!!!' (http://www.myspace.com/regulatormusic00).

One of their regular venues and events is now the Rockaoke[1] sessions at the Roadhouse nightclub. This live music venue (a place loved by some as a great social meeting space but hated and described by others as a noisy 'meat market'!) is part of Jubilee Hall complex, at one end of the Covent Garden Piazza in the fashionable centre of tourist London. During the day, the venue merges into the bustling commercial market, sitting close to the icon of sophisticated high art – the Covent Garden Opera House. At night, however, a different form of tourism competes for sonic and physical space, dominated by an alternative clientele with quite different music tastes; the younger generation of 'party goers'! As we approached the outside of the club on one particular Monday evening, the first thing we noticed was the long queue to get in and the large number of male security guards. All men were 'frisked' before entry (their clothes, shoes and bags were searched for unspecified illicit items, perhaps pre-purchased alcohol, drugs or weapons) but the women were waved inside with a smile. When we asked why this discrepancy existed we were simply told that the male security guards were not allowed to 'search the women'.

Inside, the décor and iconography were a mixture of 1980s disco and the 1950s, with atmospheric low lighting interrupted by spinning spotlights and laser effects. The neon signs and posters together with the red leather upholstered dining booths nostalgically recreated the *mise-en-scène* of an American 1950s diner. Around the walls were diverse photos and artefacts of 1950s and 1960s American teenage cinematic culture, particularly highlighting the themes of excitement, escape and adventure; film posters, parts of cars, motorbikes, number plates and oversized neon signs hung from the ceiling, including one stating boldly in massive scarlet lettering 'DRUGS'. The food menu was advertised as quintessentially 'American', offering burgers, nachos, chips and steak. Cocktails were relatively cheap in this night venue, which was particularly famous for its wide range of exotic alcoholic mixtures and the spectacular juggling and multi-tasking skills of the cocktail waiters. There was little waiting time for drinks so there was constant movement to and from the bar. Many of the girls were holding glasses with quite unusual-looking coloured drinks but there were also more obvious beer and spirits in evidence. The non-stop music which was already deafeningly loud outside of the venue was described in one online review as offering 'a mix of seventies Carwash funk and soul right through to classic rock' (www.lemonrock.com/roadhouse, October 2010). It assaulted the auditory sense even more as we moved deeper into the underground rooms. Verbal communication was reduced to screaming or simply became signs and gesturing as ordinary speech without a microphone was inaudible.

We arrived just before 10.30 p.m. since, as was the case with most clubs, the 'action' doesn't really begin until after 10 p.m. The atmosphere was already noisy, boisterous and crowded; we found this a little surprising as this was early in the working week and after the long days and heat of summer. Only taped music was playing when we entered the area but the majority of the audience was still dancing exuberently on the dance floor, particularly in the confined space immediately in front of the stage, between the scattered drinks tables. This was despite the presence of other couples and groups and staff pushing to and from the bar in a steady stream with drinks and plates of food balanced precariously in their hands. The elaborate bar was centrally located on a raised platform with bar stools postioned around it and a large motorbike hanging (also precariously) from the ceiling above. Customers approached the oval bar from all sides but seemed to be served speedily (as the web advertisements promised) and then having obtained their drinks moved out again to the dance floor or to the tables at the side of the room.

To the right of the stage were more impressively muscular and imposing security men in uniform and with headsets and walkie talkies. Several of these security staff were dotted around the room, usually standing on slightly raised platformed areas so that they could continually survey the crowd. We were not sure what they were looking for as the crowd seemed affable enough and in fact indifferent to their presence, but obviously there was a great deal of drinking and possibly other kinds of social drug taking occuring that was less obvious to our eyes. One broad security man was particularly prominent, clearly there to prevent any unauthorised person from walking across the stage or to ensure that no member of the audience overdid their three minutes of celebrity as a performer at the Rockaoke. The careful frisk search of the male entrants at the door also returned to mind, which made us wonder if the venue had had a few violent or difficult incidents in the past. One regular patron offered this positive online review of the venue for fellow customers.

> Bouncers are friendly but yes, they will throw anyone out who is drunk. I've hardly ever seen any fights in there and never any drugs. A lot of off duty policemen go there for a drink so maybe that's why. There's live bands every night except Sun and they are good crowd pleaser tunes to sing along to. It can be a bit of a meat market at the weekend but generally people are down to earth and friendly. You can wear what you want – jeans and a hoodie or a cocktail dress or fancy dress – they don't mind. (http://www.beerintheevening.com/pubs/comments.shtml/3481/, 8 November 2010)

The dress code in fact was quite eclectic and casual – both baggy and skimpy tops for the girls over tight leggings or jeans. Men were equally casually dressed although we also saw a few older men in suits.

We spotted Katie amongst the throng almost immediately as she was one of the few people in the room to walk purposefully through the milling crowd towards the stage and the sound technicians; she seemed to be a woman on a mission that night! Like the rest of the crowd, she was dressed very casually in jeans. On this evening she wore an oversized red and black check lumber shirt with sleeves rolled up, and a matching red flower in her hair. At about 10.30 the rest of the four Regulator band members, Charley Taverner (vocals/drums), Alvin Ho (guitar/BV) and Juan Rodriguez (bass/BV) took to the stage and without much in the way of a formal introduction or announcement, they quickly started their performance of a few popular songs, raising the riotous mood and anticipation of the crowd even further. As the band sang the chorus lines, the audience screamed back well-known lyrics and gestured in unison. The atmosphere was already electric and primed for the main entertainment of the night, the Rockaoke. The audience singers on the list were then invited to step up onto the stage one by one, relishing their few moments of celebrity in the spotlight. Katie now took on a new role; she was no longer just the lead vocalist for Regulator but the MC for the night. She introduced each contestant in turn by name, encouraged their effort, reminded the audience to applaud and join in the chorus lines and vocally filled the gaps when the contestant forgot the words or lost their place. The songs selected by the contestants from a long possible list of titles were as eclectic as the dress and the décor of the venue. We heard ebullient renditions of pop and rock songs from the 1960s to the present day including the most popular hits of the Beatles, Madonna, Credence Clearwater Revival, Lady Gaga, the Monkees, Wilson Pickett and other 1980s and 1990s popular artists. Behind the scenes and prior to the peformances, the Rockaoke website advises the contestants to select their songs carefully.

- Sign up starts at 9pm and the competition gets under way after 10.00pm! Make sure you come down early as the list fills up incredibly quickly and entry is operated on a strictly first come, first sing basis.
- A Few Tips to Help Make Your Performance a Success
    - Pick a song that you are already familiar with.
    - If you are an inexperienced singer don't choose a song with a wide vocal range.
    - Try and learn the lyrics if you can (lyrics will however be provided on the night).
    - Arrive early and soak up the atmosphere. A few drinks beforehand always helps with the nerves.
    - Bring your friends down for support.
    (http://www.roadhouse.co.uk/rockaoke.php)

By midnight, the Rockaoke performances were over but the crowd was still buzzing with excitement. It was then Katie's task to bring them down gently, ensuring they still enjoyed the night (while still drinking), to choose with her band that night's winner and announce the name of the lucky contestant. Regulator completed the night's entertainment with another music set of their own as the audience drank and danced on. Katie usually followed up with her own assessement of the evening on the band's Facebook fan page.

What a great turnout down at the Roadhouse last night for Rockaoke. Some wicked performances but a massive 'well done' to Kerry who was the runner-up and Dean, who came in first. Don't forget, Rockaoke EVERY Monday and Wednesday night. We'll be back next Monday night !!

Up the down staircase

This account of the Rockaoke night at the Roadhouse nightclub serves as a valuable springboard to discuss what it takes to become successful or 'phat', to be a significant player in the contemporary global music and related arts industries, even on a local or minor scale. There are several aspects to achieving this level of recognition. Firstly, a particular standard of professionalism and musical expertise has to be reached and maintained. Katie has performed in a range of public venues and organised various cover bands for the ten years that we have known her but during that time we have seen her develop and become increasingly confident and professional. This chosen career path has never been lucrative enough to be her sole job – she works as a retail sales assistant at a large clothing store during the week. This gives her enough money to live on (living at home with her parents) and the freedom to focus on her music several nights a week and on the weekends. Her new band Regulator, only in existance for a year so far, is demonstrably popular and successful. In fact, the band also performs at different venues under the name Toucan–Chu with a separate fan page and a managing agent. Their popularity and success in both bands are due, firstly, to their versatility, expertise and professionalism together as performers – the professional training of at least two of the musicans in the band is in evidence in their ease on stage and the high standard of their performance. Katie, who has also gained training in music, stagecraft, related business and management skills and invaluable contacts through the courses at Weekend Arts College, has improved her own vocal range and her confidence on stage over the years, and is now demonstrating an ease and relaxed, seemingly effortless engagement with her audience.

Secondly, to be successful in today's multifaceted world, one has to be flexible, adaptable and capable of multi-tasking; not just appearing as a performer but simultaneously as a (self) promoter, a technician, a lyricist, an event manager. One has to be a team player – someone who is knowledgeable and competent in all aspects of the contemporary music industry even though the combination and complementarity of various skills is required within the musical group. This was true of all the achieving young people in our project; where they did not possess all the skills necessary they learned to work symbiotically and cooperatively with their network of friends, expertise and knowledge being shared amongst the group. The word 'crew', as in the film industry, is commonly used for a group of musicians, dancers and techicians who work collectively for a particular band. The concept of 'the crews' as applied to the arts originally emerged from friendship groups and from shared neighbourhoods but they now also form for a variety of other reasons such as theme (JabbaWockeeZ), gender (Beat Freaks), ethnicity (Kaba Modern) and dance style (Krump Kings). They are not exclusive to one band though. It is common for performers to be involved in more than one crew, especially if one particular group is style specific and the individual wants to perform in a variety of genres or styles. It is important to note that although it is more common to talk about (dance) crews within the hip hop context where they are more prevalent, many crews now perform in house, dance and other contemporary forms of music. Such dance crews include Culture Shock (USA), Lux Aeterna (USA), Boy Blue Entertainment (UK), Bounce Streetdance Company (Sweden), 2Faced Dance (UK), Funkbrella Dance Company (USA), Blaze Streetdance Company (Neth) and Zoo Nation (UK).[2]

Even when the individual works mainly as a lone performer, he or she still needs and draws on others to provide or enhance the publicity, and technical and moral support necessary to improve. So, as noted above, for example, DJ Roland Samuel regularly hosts a UK garage radio show, Phatbeats, over the internet where he mixes, plays requests and discusses the music interactively though Facebook with a small group of local fans. For the past year he has teamed up with another DJ, Alex, aka DJ HOD, so that in the studio they can alternate roles between DJ, MC and sound engineer, bouncing off and complementing each other in approach and banter. The studio

Photo 6.2   Row and HOD at Phatbeats studio. © Geraldine Bloustien

has a web camera and a computer with an online connection so that during their on-air performance the musicians can also respond immediately to live comments by their regular fans received via the internet. HOD and Row acknowledge and reply to these comments and repartee by calling out the names of individual fans as in 'Shout to...(Alex, Jo, Claire and so on)', laughing at the in-jokes and noting their fans' requests or critiques. The webcam, noted above, records the program in real time so that each week the fans can observe what occurs in the studio as it happens (see http://www.phatbeats.co.uk/dance_studio, 10 September 2010?).

When we were in the studio, watching the perfomance, it was easy to forget about the camera until Rowland and HOD reminded us of its presence. 'Smile and wave to the camera, guys', they told us. 'They want to see your faces!'

Facebook and other social networking sites also allow a direct and intimate communication to occur with the fan base so that the communication is able to swap continually between addressing the wider group and answering individual comments and queries. So a recent communication thread appeared like this:

> Rowland
> I want to hear any ideas on how to improve my Sunday Phatbeats radio show guys as i know there's room for improvement. Constructive views please :)
> J.
> Get me on doing a guest mix ;)
> Rowland
> if you can get your ass to Enfield then..... IT'S ON!!!! :D)
>
> (Rowland's Facebook wall, circa 4 November 2010)

Sometimes links are deliberately made to other shows, stations and other media to ensure that the 'vibe' continues:

> IF YOUR LONGING FOR YOUR WEEKLY FIX OF MY KEEP IT MOVING SHOW IN THE MIX (AS IT WON'T BE ON THIS SUNDAY DUE TO MY WORK COMMITMENTS).
>   THEN CATCH MY OLD SKOOL HOUSE GUEST MIX ON DJ PUGWASH'S [Neil Pugwash Maclean] SHOW RIGHT NOW TILL 10PM

ON www.pressureradio.com AND THAT WILL CURE YOUR CRAVING TILL I'M BACK NEXT SUNDAY ON PHATBEATS :)

(Rowland, Facebook communication to his fans, circa 6 November 2010. Style and spelling as in original)

Also in London, over the past year Tuesday has teamed up with a promotion company called God Made Me Funky and she is now regularly performing as a DJ and helping to promote other local acts. Her Facebook page serves as her community billboard as well as reflecting her increasingly developed confidence, skills and ambitions:

Looking for some Club Classic DJs, 80s soul and commercial to play at events over the next couple of months. Also need to find some Indie/Rock Bands who have time to travel. Please send me a message if you are interested pref a link with your music.

(Tuesday, Facebook communication, 12 October 2010)

As with Rowland, Katie and Tuesday's Facebook announcements serve additionally as effective promotional tools for forthcoming events:

2night 2night – The Big 1, Benny Majors Bday PARTTTYY!!! at Fulham's Sugarhut. The God Made funky team, Myself Tuesday Benfield, Crazy Cousins and much more. £5.00 tickets (not many left) More on the door. For info please call 07814228472 or inbox me. All drinks £2.50 b4 11pm. You will be crazy 2 miss this one.

(Tuesday, Facebook, 7 October 2010)

In all cases, it is clear that the internet has become an essential tool to disseminate and to promote the music, events and related artefacts that the youth produce. It enables the young musicians to perform to a wider, potentially global network of fans; it allows them to share CDs and videos of their work, which can be downloaded and therefore easily disseminated, often in real time through webcam and YouTube; it allows fan networks to form and grow, techniques to be taught and shared and rapid communication to take place between friends and experiential communities.

Katie and her band, Tuesday and Rowland and his 'crew' are just a few of a new breed of micro-entrepreneurs: young, creative, prepared to take risks and eager to exploit their own skills, opportunities, networks and enthusiasm for activities that they love, creating 'new ways of earning a living in the cultural field' (McRobbie, 2002a, p. 521; also see Leadbeater, 1999, 2002; Leadbeater and Oakley, 1999). Twenty-seven-year-old DJ Shep whom we met earlier is another. He is also, it needs to be said, one of the more successful of all the young people we met for such initatives are not without difficulty, problems and paradox. The issues were particularly highlighted for us when we saw for ourselves how dramatically Shep had struggled and how much he was able to achieve. For example, by the second year of the project we were startled and impressed by the kinds of initiatives Shep and his team had been able to accomplish. He gave us regular updates and often invited us to see how his new premises and programs were developing. Gerry Bloustien's notes at the time capture our fascination at Shep's skills and success.

> Shep greeted me in his usual frenetic style at the door of his new premises, eager to show me around. His hip hop retail/workshop outlet had just moved to space above the original basement shop in the heart of Adelaide. The effect was not only a doubling of floor space but also a new level of sophistication and professionalism. While the graffiti art, skateboarding, breakdancing and rap workshop studios still existed in the basement below our feet, the retail shop above ground was newly refurbished. It was now light, modern and open, stocked with a wide range of hip hop clothes, music and accessories for breakdancing, skating and graffiti art. As we chatted, a diverse group of customers wandered in, some very young and some clearly way past their teenage years – some to browse, some to accompany children and teenagers, some purposefully to obtain the latest coloured spray cans for graf art or to pick up clothes especially ordered in their size. 'Now', said Shep with satisfaction, 'the parents feel cool about coming in and shopping too.' He showed me his new flyer advertising the business. Although designed on his computer, it looked professional and slick. The triple folded A-4 sheet advertised specials on local and overseas products such as Adidas (limited edition) sneakers, Poynter and iPath shoes, Stussy t-shirts and bags and Tribal Jeans, and featured several of his friends modelling the clothes and accessories with attitude. Things had clearly changed since my very first visit to Da Klinic two years earlier! I looked up. 'Don't you ever get accused of somehow "selling out", becoming too corporate?' I asked tentatively. Shep became even more animated. 'No one does their job for free! Everyone wants to get paid for what they do', he exclaimed, 'and so do we!

When people say that to me, I tell 'em – watch out! I'll get a BMW before you do!' (Gerry, field notes, May 2004)

Shep's description of his endeavour inadvertently yet articulately echoes McRobbie's words cited at the start of this chapter. Both comments highlight the tension between the dreams and the reality of achieving success in the new creative knowledge economy and, as such, serve as a particularly poignant springboard to discuss the subject of youth enterprise with all of its attendant themes of desire, ambition and risk.

Self-making in the new creative knowledge economy

The stories of youth enterprise that we draw on in this chapter highlight the ways many young people produce and consume music and popular culture as tools of committed personal expression and identity-making while strategically enlisting commercial enterprise techniques to fulfil their dreams and ambitions. This is not unthinking or even uncritical engagement with globalised corporate capitalism. It is 'not an abandonment of critique but its implementation' (Hartley, 2005, p. 13), an implementation that is frequently passionate but still realistic.

Observations of the ways in which popular music frequently blends the discourses of art and commerce are not new. Following the early critiques of the ideas that emerged from the work of the Centre for Contemporary Cultural Studies, later studies also interpreted youth street cultures as 'radical only through their entrepreneurialism' (Gelder, 2005, p. 145). Sarah Thornton's work on dance cultures noted the ways in which raves offered experience and training in entrepreneurial activity, developing social networks 'crucial to the definition and distribution of cultural knowledge' (Thornton, 1995, p. 14). Similarly Rietveld (1993), McRobbie (1999, 2002a) and Luckman (2008) note how contemporary enterprise is encouraged, facilitated and made possible through young people's effective integration of their creative leisure activities with wider commercial interests. The youth use their social skills, including their networking, their grassroots-acquired business strategies and a wide variety of media forms to accomplish their goals.

At the same time, the efficacy and politics of the concepts of creative industries and the new forms of youth enterprise have been rendered problematic, often by some of their staunchest advocates. Leadbeater, for example, notes that the new knowledge economy does not benefit everyone and that 'advances in knowledge improve our lives but only at the cost of creating uncertainties, risks and dilemmas' (1999, p. 123; see also Luckman, 2008). Similarly, the structural limitations of race, class, ethnicity and gender mean that some young people are able to develop their dreams and ambitions far more than others; invisible boundaries prevent many from being able to formulate such dreams in the first place (Fornäs, 1992; Bloustien, 2003b, 2008; Grossberg, 2005). Other critiques of the knowledge economy (Leadbeater and Oakley, 1999; McRobbie, 1999, 2002a, 2002b; Miller, 2009) focus on its tendency to replace one form of marginalisation with another, making the individual who 'opted for this kind of unstable career choice' (McRobbie, 2002a, p. 521) more vulnerable and open to exploitation for 'maybe there can be no workplace politics when there is no workplace, i.e. where work is multi-sited' (2002a, p. 522).

Recent scholarship has demonstrated that music skills and knowledge are often acquired through immersion in the everyday music and musical practices of one's own social context (DeNora, 2000; Green, 2001), often rendering the lines between music production and music consumption increasingly indistinct. The stories and narratives we have delineated throughout this book build on these understandings, highlighting the very serious and difficult work that young people bring to their everyday tasks of music activities. Beyond the hard work of play such activities reveal that entrepreneurship and micro-enterprise are taken very seriously at the 'grassroots', effectively blurring the lines between the public and private self. Conflicting benchmarks of success become insignificant as 'self-making' here incorporates both the possibility of financial wealth and power *and* self-fulfilment. This is a fascinating demonstration of young people networking, collaborating and achieving – hard at work 'travelling up the down staircase' – with many of the young people expressing an overwhelming sense of optimism despite the inevitable setbacks and failures. In 1999 and 2002 Charles Leadbeater described attempts to counter the pervasively pessimistic sense of gloom and cynicism resulting from the rapid economic, political, technological, social and environmental changes of the twenty-first century as being like travelling up a down escalator: slow progress and hard work. Our use here of the related metaphor of a staircase is deliberate, emphasising the treading of an even slower, more difficult and arduous path than Leadbeater perhaps imagined, because of the youth, naivety and overall inexperience of those at the centre of such creative enterprise.

Social capital, skills in new media technology, social networking, creative problem-solving and performance underpin a newly empowered, confident and creative sense of self which, in turn, often leads to new livelihoods, employment, funding and career opportunities. As we have illustrated, many youth seek out appropriate mentors, new networks and creative pathways through established government and non-government organisations with the deliberate aim of developing and fine-tuning the skills to develop this capital further. Financial reward, although desirable, is not considered the main motive, however, for many of the young entrepreneurs still hold on to the romantic and paradoxical distinction between art and commerce, preferring to see themselves as skilled artisans who one day may gain secure relevant employment through their craft. As DJ Shep explained, that would mean they do 'not just do what we love but actually get paid to do what we love, because we still both work night jobs just to run this place'.[3] Or as Tuesday more recently proclaimed on Facebook, 'Music is my life and 1 day my life will lead!'

When we look again at many of the young people in our study we find that their narratives highlight the same tensions and desires. Apart from their own music performances, we see that they have all extended their music interests into forms of micro-enterprise. One example is that of Alicia in Adelaide who with her friend Michelle created a music event management business and independent music label some years ago called Patterns in Static. Another, as indicated above, is in the UK where Tuesday as DJ LadyLick and Rowland as DJ Roland Samuel have also been working on their own respective, as yet fledgling, event management businesses. Thirdly, from Boston, USA we return to the story of Juri who not only performs and produces her own CDs, but also has created a not-for-profit enterprise Genuine Voices to teach contemporary music skills 'to youths in juvenile detention centers and other educational and institutional settings across the United States and Worldwide' (www.genuinevoices.org, accessed 16 December 2005). In fact, that last point concerning the *social* arm of entrepreneurship is important to emphasise, for we found that a common thread running through all of these youth-based enterprising projects was the social and community benefit itself; in other words the youth entrepreneurship was underlaid by a genuine altruistic concern for their local communities. This unique and idealistic element underpinned all of the ambition and determination of these young micro-entrepreneurs. We will return to this shortly, but firstly we will look closely at the variety and scale of the youth entrepreneurship that emerged in our fieldwork. This task involves looking at all three components of successful creative enterprise: performance, production and integrated marketing.

Even a cursory glance at any of the websites of the young people mentioned above shows that the three categories are very much interrelated. Furthermore, while clearly drawn from the rhetoric of business, in the world of the young entrepreneur they apply equally to the invaluable process of self-performance and self-making, as we shall see from a closer examination of each category.

Performance

The creative knowledge economy relies on artistic performance: the production of something that can be created and performed to others. A major difference between the young entrepreneurs and their older counterparts is the way in which the catalyst for the enterprise is their own engagement and expertise as artists rather than consumers or producers. In the case of the young people described here, it is their personal embedding in music performative activities. So for example Alicia, co-founder of the event management organisation Patterns in Static (http://www.patternsinstatic.com) was previously a bass guitar player in what was a successful local band, Paper Tiger, and now plays acoustic guitar, keyboard and bass in her more recent band Aviator Lane (http://www.aviatorlane.com.au). DJ Shep is a keen inline skater as well as a rap artist and turntablist, active in the local hip hop scene. Tuesday is an accomplished rapper, and while she also DJs in a range of genre she prefers to play R&B both in live gigs and on her internet radio show on Radio 2MO. Her new, privately produced CD (using a friend's home studio) is about to be released within her local networks. Rowland is becoming an accomplished UK garage turntablist. He performs locally in London, also has his own internet radio show as we have seen and has performed on invitation in Germany. Juri is a classically trained pianist but also a pop singer with several privately produced CDs in circulation. While still in Japan, she performed with various artists including B. B. Mo-Franck, a King Records recording artist. At the age of eighteen, Juri auditioned and was awarded a scholarship to study at the Berklee College of Music in Boston, MA.[4]

Apart from their own music performances, all of the enterprises created by Shep, Alicia, Rowland, Tuesday and Juri also aim to facilitate the performance of others in their social networks. So for example, in the case of Da Klinic the performative element consists of workshops and events that demonstrate and teach the skills behind all the elements of hip hop culture: breakdancing, turntabling, inline skating, rapping and aerosol art. Each of the photo and video links to the workshops on the Da Klinic website show the organisation's crew and associates in action, demonstrating the excitement and the exuberance of their performances at concerts, events and workshops. The 'Playing for Life' website (www.playingforlife.org.au), which was a direct outcome of our research and was active between 2003 and 2008, contained other clips that young people in four countries have contributed to show their skills in action. Although the website is no longer active, several of the photos in this book have been taken from the original videos and photos submitted by the young people and their mentors and were originally posted and shared online.

As discussed earlier, elements of performance automatically highlight the importance of the body in action, for the body is central to all of these enterprises, whatever the skill. Most of these young entrepreneurs had had little opportunity or success in formal educational settings before finding their successful pathways through music. Yet once they realised their own delight and competency in music and related activities, they voluntarily worked tirelessly to fine-tune their cognitive and physical skills – putting in the extra practice hours that would have delighted any formal educator. Wexler's comments, written over two decades ago and cited above in Chapter 3, noted the relationship between the body, 'new social movements' and 'personal freedom in daily life' (1983, cited in Lesko, 1988, p. 127). He could just as easily have been referring to the recent manifestation of youth enterprise especially where it relates to music practice. Through its fluidity and abstract qualities, music potentially allows a greater playing with image and identity than any other art form. As Simon Frith noted, it 'gives us a way of being in the world...music doesn't represent values but lives them' (1996, p. 272). As each new technology develops, new ways of creating, consuming and marketing music produce marked effects on the cultural meanings emanating from all of its forms, including the perceived authenticity of the performer and consumer of particular music genres.

For these reasons, getting performance 'right' becomes essential to the art of self-making and the creation of authenticity. Contemporary practices of engaging with music, particularly through what Taussig described as the ever-evolving 'mimetic machinery' (1993, p. 20), and also through recording and duplicating digital technologies, repeatedly blur the lines of time and space. The music may be someone else's original composition or lyrics, but when it is performed anew by someone else, as in sampling, the emotions and meanings are transferred, reshaped and resignified. Music indeed becomes a powerful vehicle of mimesis, a connection that Raymond Williams (1980) noted in advertising through what he termed 'sympathetic magic'. No wonder music is so integral to the advertising industry.

Extending the self: production and beyond

Tuesday aka DJ Lady Lick provides us with other insights regarding the nature of youth enterprise and creative practice. Under the pseudonym of DJ Lady Lick, Tuesday has been performing in various bars and clubs since she was fifteen and has already produced two CDs on independent labels through friends. In her small bedroom in the family council flat, she practises her mixing and turntabling skills for at least two to three hours every night. Now at 26 she is also teaching others the skills necessary for DJ performance. Her part-time job in an after-school care centre allows her to teach these skills to young people in her neighbourhood, developing their confidence and expertise. At least once a month she now also stages gigs at local pubs, under the name of her event organisation 'Emotion', to offer other local DJs the opportunity to practise and perform and to raise money for various charities.

Her uncle, a well-established musician ('He used to play with Sting',[5] Tuesday told us proudly on several occasions), originally used to accompany her to the gigs to help with technical aspects. He would speedily mend broken cables and wires where necessary and protect her from unwanted attention from clientele. One north London pub was particularly rough although, as Tuesday explained stoically, 'At least it ain't violent because most of the [clientele] are too stoned.'

Tuesday invited us into her home to observe her music practice. She practised her DJ skills, while carefully explaining the intricacies of turntabling and mixing. To reach her goals, she has had to be focused and determined:

'If it takes me three hours or three days I still practise and practise until I get that mix perfect.'[6]

The account above is drawn from various field notes, observations and personal discussions with Tuesday between 2003 and 2006. In 2010 she was still working hard to polish her skills and realise her dreams as we can see from a recent personal message through Facebook from her.

> I am DJing nearly every weekend or finding gigs for others to do and taking a cut out of their wages, like a small DJ agency. I am working for a promotional firm called God Made Me Funky and it seems that they are doing really well, so it's nice to be involved with them. As my everyday work is manic I am finding it hard to juggle music and life, so my heart is not in what I love doing most of all and that is MUSIC!!! I have been offered a show on a pirate radio station and that means that I get to play in big, well known clubs on a regular basis but the manager has asked me for consistency and that is something I can't give at present. To be honest, I am strongly thinking to give up my day job and become a full time DJ and Promoter, I'm just waiting for the right opportunity to open up and I know this will happen!!!
>
> Music is my life and one day life will lead xx
>
> (Tuesday, personal correspondence, 14 October 2010)[7]

Such activities themselves stay 'backstage' (Goffman, 1956), of course, only becoming entrepreneurial in the new 'knowledge economy' (Kenway et al., 2004) when they become public, involving the production of an artefact. Creativity thus is expressed and made public in a range of forms that both underpin, support and disseminate the original performance – through live music events; service and outreach workshops and programs; the creation of CDs, DVDs and videos; graffiti/aerosol artwork; clothing; equipment (e.g. skateboards); IT and website design, creation and maintenance. Again, a quick glance at the websites referenced above reveals a broad range of products created by the young entrepreneurs described here. Alicia and Michelle, for example, not only produce and manage live music gigs under the umbrella of Patterns in Static, but also act as an independent record label, producing albums for local and interstate musicians, and creating fan merchandise to promote particular musicians and artists.

Large badges, enabling the fans to show allegiance to their band, sometimes several bands, and to their particular music scene, had been popular for a while but small ones, about three centimetres in diameter, had not been seen before in the Adelaide music scene. The girls created, marketed and

Youth, Music and Micro-Enterprise

Photo 6.3 Patterns in Static: integrated marketing. © Alicia Woodrow

then sold the small badges, mainly through their website. Although widely accessible interstate and internationally through their website, the produce is deliberately displayed and promoted through quite intimate language – the direct address together with the use of the inclusive first person 'we'.

> We love button badges, so it was no surprise when we decided to import a 1 inch badge machine so we could make our own. Worn on shirts, bags, hats and guitar straps, they're often a topic of conversation and a great way to promote your band, event or organisation. Or if you're an individual who has a few ideas for badges of your own, we can make those too. (www.patternsinstatic.com, accessed 12 December 2004)

Integrated marketing: publicity, markets and distribution

The use of direct and personal forms of address is integral to enterprise in the new creative knowledge economy. We have already noted that every aspect of such youth enterprise is not just about the product but by extension about the artist and therefore very much centred on the self. Every aspect of the promotion and marketing scene is integrated, demonstrating the variety but interrelationship of their wares across a range of media. So for example, as can be seen in Photo 6.3 a range of goods and activities displayed on the website is simultaneously linked to other goods or activities in the business. The young entrepreneurs tend to know their target audiences and markets

224 *Youth, Music and Creative Cultures*

Photo 6.4 Buttons for Patterns in Static. © Alicia Woodrow

because they are themselves embedded in the same geographical or experiential community. As noted above, when Alicia and Michelle developed the concept of small promotional badges to be worn at music gigs the badges were very specifically created for the niche market of the local youth culture. The concept works both inclusively and exclusively, for the promotion relies on the potential customer who is part of the same music scene recognising the names of the various Indie bands listed here:

> We've made badges for Deloris, Remake Remodel, Aviator Lane, Popboomerang Records, Midwest Trader, City City City, Bit By Bats, The New Pollutants, I Killed the Prom Queen, Last Years Hero, Paper Tiger, Heligoland, Pharaohs, Chapel Gesture, Kulkie, Stolen Skateboards, FTM and Para//elo, amongst others. (www.patternsinstatic.com, accessed 12 December 2004)

There are no further links to tell potential customers about the bands. If the consumer does not know the bands, they are not part of the fan circle. However, there is more information to promote the albums themselves on the website and to link the CDs with the live performances and the tours, also arranged by the youth organisation.

The websites not only promote the products and the businesses but also promote the individual creator. They use the language and format of web logs (blogs) rather than traditional marketing discourse, offering very personal insights into (auto) biography as well as information about events and products. So one of Rowland's, 'It's a Naturel Thing' (IANT) previous websites created at WAC announced:

> Yes it is me – owner of this site putting his profile up for all to see!! Read on and find out more... I got into DJing by listening to my older brother's rap and soul record collection (as he used to DJ as well in the late 80's/early 90's) and by watching music shows on T.V. during the late 80's/early 90's (e.g. Westwood – Night Network, Behind The Beat, Dance Energy, TOTPS, YO MTV RAPS etc... Since 96 i have steadily improved and now i am really confident that i can play at any rave anywhere the world! I haven't done anything big yet – just house parties and some low key raves. The biggest thing i did was to do a set in Germany last September (for the Payin' Clients Cru) and it was probably the best thing that happened to me so far when it comes to DJing. (http://www.wac.co.uk/mediaplayer/media/web/sun2002/rowland/index.html)[8]

What young entrepreneurs lack in sophistication, they tend to make up for in originality of marketing and distribution methods and approach. Their products are often promoted scattergun style – through their websites, word of mouth and through online lists, group emails, SMS messages and letterbox flyers. It can be a very effective method. It is through this approach that Rowland received invitations to perform in Germany, Tuesday was offered the opportunity to perform in Spain and Shep increasingly gains many of his educational and corporate clients. Far from seeing such marketing tactics as amateurish, many of his corporate clients who subcontract Da Klinic to undertake workshops for schools, clubs, regional or remote communities and youth (detention) centres, recognise the fresh appeal of the more youthful language and discourse, such as:

> DJ LESSONS WITH DJ STAEN 1 are every SAT, call da klinic to make a booking with the current 3 times AUSTRALIAN CHAMP!................... BREAKIN CLASSES MON, WED, FRI & SAT..................... HIP HOP DANCE THURS & FRI................. peace............... sHEp. ('latest news 11.3.06', daklinic.com)[9]

Risk and counter-risk: trust, networks and mentors

It is important to keep in mind that the production and marketing of these events and artefacts are inherently risky and of course this is one of the main criticisms that has been levelled against the new creative economy, which devolves responsibility and liability on to the young individual, masking rising levels of unemployment, creating new levels of insecurity for those who do have jobs and increasing the casualisation of the workforce (see again Bourdieu, 1998; McRobbie, 2002a). Because most artefacts in the new creative knowledge economy tend to be ephemeral, any organisation involved has to 'deal with the risks that accompany products with a truncated life cycle' (Rifkin, 2000, p. 24). Young entrepreneurs tend to be inexperienced and untrained in terms of conventional marketing philosophies and practice and they are also dealing with a transient customer/fan base and selling products that have a short shelf life. However, they are also necessarily thinking outside conventional business models to take those risks. Sometimes the risks require a relatively small investment of capital, such as Alicia's imported one-inch badge machine, but at other times the risks are bigger. Shep and his business partner Jeff recently decided to invest all of their assets to enable Da Klinic to co-fund a South Australian DJ championship show starring Mix Master Mike, 'the Turntablist for the Beastie Boys, 3 time world DMC champion and global hip hop legend' in August 2005. It was 'a massive gamble', Shep admitted:

> We did all the publicity and promotion, used our contacts, printed the forms, got the front cover of *Onion* magazine, designed and distributed flyers. We could have lost the lot but we had about 900 people attend. The proceeds paid for our new shop. (Personal communication, April 2006)

Young entrepreneurs attempt to counter the very real risk factors involved in their businesses through three main methods: collaboration, networking and mentorship. For example, in the case of Da Klinic, the business team, now larger than the original two founding members, refer to themselves as the 'Da Klinic (Hip Hop) Crew', complementing each other's skills by applying the usual way of working together in a music performance to the world of business. As Shep explained with wry humour:

> I realised early on that I was the visionary – the ideas man – and Jeff has the business skills that I don't have [laughs] like he can spell and add up. He is also the realist when I get too excited: 'No Shep we can't buy a Ferrari and put the Da Klinic logo all over it!' (Personal communication, April 2006)

Another friend, Simon, designs the flyers and the website, and the business subcontracts other well-known DJs and other music and aerosol artists from the local hip hop scene as tutors. This means they can competitively tender to run events and large workshops in Adelaide and interstate for both government and private organisations, sell and promote locally made hip hop clothes, videos, CDs and other accessories as well as import prestigious items that 'are only issued to few outlets, old school stuff. The hard-to-get stuff that kids on e-bay will pay a fortune for' (Shep, personal communication, April 2006).

To maintain its autonomy, Da Klinic has followed an independent business model (Moe and Wilkie, 1997; Shuman, 1998), deliberately choosing not to apply for non-profit status and thereby inevitably making themselves ineligible for government arts funding. This is also a reflection of their collective disenchantment with governmental and educational bodies after several initial unsuccessful requests for financial support or attempts at more systemic collaboration. 'I gave up on the government long ago', mused Shep, explaining to us how, despite their clear progress and success, all the staff have to hold down day and night jobs to survive.

Shep had originally sought help from established arts organisations to get his project off the ground. As in all of the projects described here, the young people used their social networks to obtain some financial (seeding funding or grants) or in-kind resources and mentorship from adults and established figures in their communities when first launching their projects. For some, the original connections came through outreach educational programs and community-based organisations such as WAC and later AKarts in London for Rowland and Tuesday. For Alicia, Michelle and Shep in Australia it had been through the Adelaide youth arts organisation Carclew. A different model has been adopted by Juri in Boston. While also holding down several part-time jobs, her main enterprise is Genuine Voices, noted above. Its slogan 'We can touch lives, we can make a change through music' reflects the philosophy of the Music Therapy Department, Berklee College of Music through which she originally gained support in the form of mentoring, grants and financial aid. Juri's project offers an appropriate segue into the final section of this chapter, on social entrepreneurship – the desire by young people to move beyond the commercial venture to aid the wider community.

Social entrepreneurship: still 'mixing pop and politics'

All of the youth entrepreneurs outlined in this chapter seek to engage with and improve their own communities through their music and art. This aim stems from the participants' personal belief and experience in the role and power of music to provide pathways to greater self-esteem and a sense of agency. Apart from the work mentioned above, Da Klinic is also now frequently subcontracted by other organisations and communities to provide regular hip hop workshops for young people in juvenile detention centres and in remote communities. The fees are minimal, only covering their travel expenses and the cost of hiring individual artists as tutors. Tuesday and Rowland voluntarily tutor other disadvantaged young people in their community in music and new media skills. Juri runs several other programs that have evolved from her original vision for Genuine Voices, including the one at Boston Metro Youth Service Detention Center, which serves young offenders who have been committed to the centre while they await their court date or further placement in the justice system. As noted earlier, her tutors are mainly music students who are also volunteers. The young offenders range in age from 11 to 20 years old and can be at the centre for up to one year.

This is 'grassroots politics' but wider political and social issues do not go unnoticed or unspoken. Using their music lyrics, their event publicity and their website forums as vehicles of protest, the young entrepreneurs often raise social issues including racism, poverty, corporate greed, homelessness and ecology. Alicia's latest struggle is against 'the incorporation by the professional music industry', which she battles under the umbrella of an organisation called 'Really good in theory'. The 'homemade' press release is headed:

> ADELAIDE MUSIC UNITED AGAINST PROFESSIONALISM
> What's really good in theory? – a chance to celebrate and unite Adelaide's rock'n'roll cottage industrialists... What's really good in theory is a corner shop for the local music neighbourhood, where everyone knows everyone, you look after each other's kids, and nah, we can't sell you the ice-cream scoop, but you can borrow it for the weekend. It's that kind of spirit – spiked with the necessary rock'n'roll bravado & art school affectation. That's really good in theory.[10]

Sometimes the political awareness occurs unexpectedly, as seen in a weblog posted on Da Klinic's website a few years ago. Under the heading 'M1 Protest: Police, Protesters, a Camera and Me!' Shep wrote:

> It was the morning after the finals of the Australian titles street comp [in Melbourne] and we had spent the night celebrating the fact that we like to skate. Myself [Shep], Dj David L and Pimp master AGE stepped out of our hotel room and were confronted with over 30 police just chilling there... we realized that we had been lucky enough to stumble across the Melbourne leg of the M1 PROTEST. Oh what a feeling I felt, knowing that for the rest of the day I would join thousands of other fellow run-a-mucks and cause destruction against global corporations. There were people of all walks of life there to show there concern for the cause. People where dressed in costumes and there was even a DJ on the back of a truck pumping out phat beats turning the streets into a dance party at like 11 in the morning. So have a look through the pic's and have a watch of the movies and make sure if you ever get a chance to participate in a M1 PROTEST do so for it is great for the SOUL! (Da Klinic archive, accessed 20 December 2005, spelling original)

Yes, there are very real concerns about exploitation and high risk, the depoliticisation of the workplace and inequality in the new creative economy. And yet, we would argue, it is also necessary to recognise that there is still a great deal to be celebrated in the ways young people are using the new creative knowledge economy to their own advantage – particularly for those who would have great difficulty achieving traditional roles in the workforce. They are travelling up the down the staircase, often slowly and painfully, but gaining new forms of access, opportunities and agency along the way. One of the most common forms of opportunity came through access to unofficial forms of radio, as explained below.

The role of pirate radio stations

We indicated above that 'backstage' practice is essential to performance. Lift the lid off any of these youth enterprises and you will see the role of rehearsal, studio space, workshop and mentor – all leading to the perfecting of the skills to construct the ultimate 'authentic' performance. One of the ways in which the youth get their backstage practice is through the many pirate radio stations that exist, particularly in the UK. A brief account of pirate radio follows here, but a comprehensive account is beyond the scope of this book and can be found appropriately enough online at such creative commons internet sites as Wikipedia (http://en.wikipedia.org/wiki/Pirate_radio), as well as through more academic references (e.g. Mason, 2008; Kemppainen, 2009; Marks, 2009; Levin, 2010).

The term 'pirate radio', sometimes known as bootleg stations, clandestine stations or free radio stations, is used to refer to illegal or unregulated radio transmission. Although the origin of the term stems from the fact that the transmission is unlicensed, the name also comes from the way sea vessels positioned offshore have been occasionally though conspicuously used as broadcasting bases. Commonly used to describe illegal broadcasting for entertainment or political purposes (Chapman, 1990), the word also describes illegal two-way radio operation often used in the cause of activism on all sides of the political spectrum (Ke, 2000; Abdelhadi, 2004; Balint, 2010). Different countries vary in their regulations and tolerance of illegal radio transmission. In the USA and many European countries, as many types of radio licences exist, the term pirate radio generally refers to the unlicensed broadcasting of FM radio, AM radio, or short wave signals over a wide range. Usually the notion of illegality is applied to the source of transmission, but in some countries it is also illegal to receive the transmission, particularly when the signals cross a national boundary. Other stations can be deemed 'pirate' if their content is considered to flout the decency or political regulations of the transmitting country or if the format of its transmission is not carried out according to required regulations. Occasionally a station can be considered 'pirate' even if the transmission is via a web cast, as this is technically illegal if its transmission power (wattage) does not meet the relevant regulations.

Until the public airwaves began to be formally regulated in the United States, radio piracy clearly did not exist. Before 1926 there was no formal regulation of the airways and initially radio or wireless activity was seen as open to playful experimentation by hobbyists and amateur inventors. However, radio's more official use by the United States Navy was taking place as early as the late 1890s so it was not long before the US Navy formally complained that such amateur transmissions were interfering with their own more serious purposes and so indeed the illicit nature of pirate radio parallels the maritime beginnings of wireless. Some of the earliest broadcast regulations occurred at the London Radiotelegraph Convention in 1912, the reason stated being the supposed interference with ship-to-shore transmissions. In a now famous *New York Herald* article, entitled 'President Moves to Stop Mob Rule of Wireless' (17 April 1912), President William Howard Taft declared an initiative to regulate the public airwaves. The Act to Regulate Radio Communication was passed on 13 August 1912. It assigned a certain frequency spectrum to amateurs and experimenters and introduced licensing and call-signs, and thereby the legal space for illicit broadcasts was created. In 1927 the Federal Radio Commission (FRC) was established, succeeded by the Federal Communications Commission (FCC) in 1934. These agencies went on to enforce regulations concerning call-signs, assigned frequencies, licensing and acceptable content for broadcast.

The use of pirate or free radio is on the rise throughout the world, and it is used by a range of communities for educational, political, training and entertainment purposes. As Jeff Ferrell points out:

> many countries have been creating new cultural spaces, new arrangements of public meaning...Like hip hop graffiti artists, micro radio operators and sonic hackers construct alternative channels of communication, create alternative cultural space for themselves and others, out of little more than their own illicit knowledge and righteous defiance. Like graffiti writers, they transmit unregulated images and signs into public spaces, inscribing a sort of sonic graffiti on airwaves otherwise bought, sold and regulated. (2001, p. 10)

The youth in our study also attempted to gain access to as wide a variety of public fora as they could, as we have seen. They used community and pirate radio stations to gain confidence, become known in the wider community and to reach a wider audience – and often created their own form of 'sonic graffiti'. Inevitably, as is the nature of all such experiences, this access and practice is never completely without risk or difficulty, as Tuesday explains:

> I used to MC on a pirate radio station that actually got cut off because of a big pirate and a year later it opened but it was so far away from

where I was and it was like graveyard shifts and 12–2 in the morning and I was like, oh no, I can't travel all the way down there. And you have to pay them to go on the stations. There is stations around here looking for DJs, but they are only looking for DJs who know the DJs already on the station. It's all about keeping secrets with the pirates because if the – the people who shut them down, if they find out then the station's gone, and if they're earning a tenner off every person who walks in the door and they are having fun, they've all got names, everyone on that station, and their names have been built, they've got a high profile you know so if you don't know the actual people, one of the people, and you've got to know them as well, you can't – and that's the hardest thing about getting on the station. I don't blame them... If the police get in there, everything is going to be broke, you know. I've been there when there's been a raid and it's like record decks damaged, 3000 pounds of equipment gone, the windows smashed, and sometimes its in people's houses as well. They smash everything up. It's very underground you know. There's [still] loads [of pirate radio stations in London]. Two or three years ago there were pirates, garage radio stations everywhere, it was massive, but now its a little bit of R & B, but the majority of it is funky house stations now.

(Tuesday, personal communication, 30 September 2004)

Despite the risks, because of the dearth of alternative opportunities, pirate and other illegal outlets are clearly important personally, professionally and politically for these nascent musicians and artists. Rowland explained this further, articulating with his usual insight just why the 'underground' is still so important:

People are rebelling, and they [regulatory authorities] don't seem to get that which is why they're upset about Napster and all those internet things and all of them. You know, the underground always, if you don't talk to the streets, if you don't talk to the streets, you're finished. That's the problem, no-one talks to the streets. No-one actually talks to hard-core Britain and goes 'Yeah, what do you want? What do you want?' Yeah, they just give it on a plate to them. Look at the radio stations. They think that's what Britain wants. They don't go to the things. That's why they don't like pirates because pirates give the people what they want. They give them what they want. The streets are restless. The streets will rebel. And this is it, the streets are rebelling. The streets need to rebel, you know.

(Rowland, personal communication, 2010)

So the pirate radio stations often provide a valuable forum to enable young people to gain experience, confidence, performance and management skills. This, combined with the resources and training of youth arts organisations, can provide the necessary pathways for the young musicians to gain confidence and, for some, potential careers. However, as we saw in Chapter 5, the youth are not the only people who have had to learn to develop and fine-tune their micro-entrepreneurial skills.

A slice of the bigger pie: CBOs and micro-enterprise

The CBOs that have offered youth resources, training and support have also had to learn to be less dependent on government funding and become more conscious of how to market themselves differently to ensure ongoing financial viability. The balance of meeting the demands of the marketplace while maintaining their original creative and educational vision has not been easy to achieve. The final chapter then brings us back full circle to consider the larger implications of how best to fund and resource such creative potential that we have examined above. What are the long-term implications and challenges to provide quality youth arts education and development in the current, highly competitive global financial marketplace? What can we do to ensure that our young people can continue to 'play for life' – develop their talents and their musical skills and fulfil their creative ambitions, whatever their social and cultural background? It is to this quandary we turn now.

7
Taking Flight: Creative Cultures and Beyond

Photo 7.1 Taking flight. © Adrian Shepherd

> There are times when I wish
> I could turn back the glass
> Take me back to the old times
> Things happen so fast...
> Life's full of memories
> Dreams are my enemies. (Extract from 'Smooth', rap by Genuine Voices student)

It was August 2010 when I met him, and he was dealing with 2 huge open cases as a very heavy hitter in a gang (Blood). He'd been shot at, stabbed, and was coming to realize the unfairness of life, an issue he would later address in his rap.[1] ...I once asked his caseworker if he had changed [after taking the Genuine Voices music program]. She said 'Yes, big time! He's no longer afraid to confront new challenges and is willing to try things outside of his comfort zone!' (Juri, personal correspondence, 1 September 2010)

The extracts and image that head this chapter underpin our central arguments about how performative creativity and experimentation occurs through music cultures as 'serious play', as we have discussed and illustrated throughout this book. Photo 7.2 of a mural at the Pie Factory, deliberately juxtaposing the creative space of the music studio with a more mechanistic factory assembly line, draws our attention to the use of self-reflexive irony, humour and fun, typifying the ways young people approach their self-making through music.

Unintentionally, perhaps, through the deliberate, humorous juxtaposition of the world of the factory (assembly line) and the open-ended connotation of a creative music studio, the mural also evokes the notion of 'serious play' as hard work; of potential challenge, of creative possibilities, a 'stepping into the subjunctive', the world of 'what if' actions described in Deleuze

Photo 7.2 Mural, Pie Factory music room. © Alexis Johnson

and Guattari's (2004) work as a 'line of flight' working within and through constraining frameworks. For, as Deleuze and Guattari remind us,

> The line of flight marks: the reality of a finite number of dimensions that the multiplicity effectively fills; the impossibility of a supplementary dimension, unless the multiplicity is transformed by the line of flight; the possibility and necessity of flattening all of the multiplicities on a single plane of consistency or exteriority, regardless of their number of dimensions. (2004, p. 10)

Deleuze and Guattari's conception of the possibilities of becomings, nomadic lines of flights or rhizomatic multiplicities, can best be understood as radical types of thought and action that are constantly changing. Our application of the term 'lines of flight' here is tempered by the notion that any music culture, practice or activity is not completely in 'free fall' but is always affected by 'a form of cultural politics' (Hutnyk and Sharma, 2000, p. 56). That is, because the meanings of those music cultures are embedded in their particular social histories, 'they operate on an ideological field of conflicting interests, institutions and memories' (Walser, 1993, p. xiii, cited in Hutnyk and Sharma, 2000, p. 56). Elizabeth Gould also employs the metaphors of Deleuze and Guattari to consider the notion of productive desire and performative literacy, especially in the ways that music education can be imagined and understood. Adapting the notion of 'becoming animal' from the work of Elizabeth Grosz (1995, p. 18), Gould offers the following insight. She considers that the idea of 'becoming musician'

> is thus no longer simply a question of being [musician] but rather, what kinds of [musician] connections, what kinds of [musician]-machine, we invest our time, energy, bodies...? What is it that together, in parts and bits, and interconnections, we can make that is new, exploratory, opens up further spaces, induces further intensities, speeds up, enervates, and proliferates production (production of the body, production of the world)? (2009, p. 50, adapting Grosz, 1995, p. 18)

Thus 'becoming musician' is always shaped, enabled and hindered by particular social and cultural forces. This is exactly what we observed in the many activities, performances and forms of serious play of the youth in our study. In other words, as we have argued throughout this book, the continuous 'lines of flight' by the youth were only possible through the people, the spaces and the programs that were made available to them along their journey.

The extracts that head this chapter help to illuminate this. In the first, we hear Mike,[2] a 17-year-old African-American resident of Brighton Treatment

Center reflecting through his rap about his life and dreams, longing for something better. In the second extract, Juri tells us a little more about him, highlighting why he found the Genuine Voices music program so important in his life. The music came to him despite the locked doors and the confined space of the detention centre. He told her that it brought an understanding, a promise that through this opportunity and his mentors he would be seen not as a 'little bastard', 'a criminal', a description that several of the residents gave of themselves, but as a human being who could be creative, had something important to say and could learn the ways to say it. Music became the vehicle for his sense of freedom and his reassessment of himself.

These stories lie at the extreme end of our spectrum of personal narratives about youth and music, in that the youth were incarcerated for drug abuse or violence and so the changes that the music made in their lives were particularly remarkable. Yet the stories point to the most important aspects of our findings, which apply to the experience of *all* of our co-researchers, which is that 'serious play' – what we have argued is the central vehicle for creative thought and freedom to experiment – can only be fully realised through personal relationships that enable a sense of an open, accessible space to 'play'. We found the primary motivating factors and resources in all of the young people's lives to be the individuals with whom the youth connected along their musical career path. These were the people whom the youth saw as knowledgeable, accessible, positive and 'open-minded' and whom we identified as mentors in our study. They offered expert advice and often provided meaningful links to real career paths. Another student from Genuine Voices expresses this poignantly.

> I feel it's not about the instruments or the technology or any of that. It's about the open-mindedness and the kind hearted people who put this whole DYS [Department of Youth Services], who put this whole music thing together because they could have said 'to hell with them. They are just a bunch of little bastards, criminals' but instead they came in and saw stuff for what it was. They weren't so close-minded.
>
> ('Clive', personal communication with Heather Slater, Program Director, Genuine Voices)

The second factor that underpins these quotations is the creation of a space for this to happen. As described in Chapter 4, for creativity to take place the venue has to be perceived as flexible, open to imagination and serious play, and where the young people feel welcome and have some level of ownership. This is the creation of a space of possibility, a place where they feel risk and experimentation can safely occur. No matter if that place usually has a different function, such as the confined and closely supervised rooms of a detention centre. What matters is that, through the relationship of youth and mentor and through their shared engagement with music, the venue can take on a new meaning. It can become a liminal space, a 'temporary autonomous zone' (Bey, 1991), a space for testing out boundaries of what is possible, a 'third space' (Soja, 1996), a space that is both real and imagined.

This final chapter comes full circle to consider the ways these two interrelated factors, the people and the places, combine with the third element – the programs themselves – to ensure the success of any creative endeavour. The twelve young people whose stories are documented throughout this volume have already demonstrated their passion, their ongoing engagement and their remarkable persistence, often despite hurdles and disappointments, to continue to develop and hone their musical skills. We would argue that their successes and self-fulfilment are due to the ways the three elements – people, place and programs – were able to cohere, the whole being far greater than the individual parts.

As we outlined at the beginning of this book, the focus of our investigation lies at the intersection of these three overlapping spheres (see Figure 1.1). The top sphere represents the individuals who were either the young emerging musicians or their mentors. Sometimes, as in the case of Shep and Juri, they are in both categories. The second sphere represents the programs such as the structured and unstructured workshops and training opportunities that the youth are offered by their mentors, such as Beats and Rimes at the Palais, DJ workshops at Da Klinic, the Pie Factory and the Hip Hop Mobile in Berlin. These were where the youth were able to practise, network, gain and share knowledge and fine-tune their skills. Other programs that we observed offered more formal learning opportunities such as the kind of instrumental or advanced music appreciation lessons that were offered at the Tabernacle or Genuine Voices. Into this category of 'program' we also include the kinds of music event management opportunities such as those offered to the Kandinsky group from Carclew or radio training, such as that offered to the *Youth Revolutions* crew. The third sphere represents the places where these programs or training workshops took place. This means the organisations, and particularly the community-based organisations, that provided spaces and resources for these valuable opportunities to happen. All venues, of course, are also affected by the physical, geographical and social-economic context in which they are embedded. The recurring thread in our narrative has been the power of music itself as the central vehicle for self-realisation and as a pathway, for many, for a meaningful livelihood.

While the number of young people and their social networks with whom we engaged and followed closely for seven years is admittedly small, we believe that many more young people around the world share similar experiences and frustrations. That is, the potential of so many young people is under-realised because these spheres of opportunity for some reason are not available to them; their creative abilities remain hidden, unexplored or translated into angry, anti-social behaviour. So we are left with the question of whether our findings from close-on-the-ground observation and discussions with the youth themselves could inform other educators, youth workers and policy-makers about the possibility of enhancing opportunities for 'play'. Is what we have discovered about the ways particular young people learn music applicable to other contexts? What do our findings suggest about the kinds of resources that need to be accessible and open for organisational programs to be effective?

Our observations echo many of the recent debates circulating in the academic literature and popular media concerning specialised music education curricula in schools and colleges. These timely debates are concerned with the value of the arts in general and music education in particular as funding is further reduced by global financial instability.

Music education for all: current debates

> Young people are the lifeblood of creativity in the UK. We produce some of the greatest musical talent in the world but there is so much more that can be done to harness the passion and enthusiasm that children have for music. (Ed Vaizey, UK Minister for the Creative Industries, quoted in Department for Education, 2010)

On 24 September 2010 in the UK, Michael Gove, the Secretary of State for Education, supported by the Minister for Culture, Communications and Creative Industries announced that there is to be an independent review of music education in British public schools. The aim of the review is to see how the funding available for music education might more effectively be used to secure the best music education for all children and young people.

Chaired by Darren Henley, Managing Director of Classic FM,[3] the review articulated eleven key underlying assumptions that it felt were essential to realise enhanced musical creativity, learning and development for all, including:

- Government priorities recognise music as an enriching and valuable academic subject with important areas of knowledge that need be learnt, including how to play an instrument and to sing.
- Secondary benefits of a quality music education are increased self-esteem and aspirations; improved behaviour and social skills; and improved academic attainment in areas such as numeracy, literacy and language. There is evidence that music and cultural activity can further not only

the education and cultural agendas but also the aspirations for the Big Society.[4]
- Public funding should be used primarily to meet the government priorities of every child having the opportunity to learn a musical instrument and to sing.
- This review should focus initially on securing the best music education for all children and young people (aged 5–19) but should also take account of and make recommendations as to how cultural education could be delivered, based on the proposed models for music.
- The focus should be on delivery models which meet the needs of the child or young person as defined by parents and schools rather than being supplier led.
- There should be a clearly defined journey of progression, including the opportunities afforded by the current Music and Dance Scheme and the publicly funded national youth music ensembles.
- Recommendations should include thoughts on initial training and continuing professional development to improve the skills and confidence of classroom teachers to teach music (tackling the main Ofsted criticism of music teaching)[5] as well as specialist teachers and professional musicians going in to schools.
- Ways of including high quality performance opportunities for children and young people should be put forward.
- The review should take account of music experience for children and young people both in and out of school.
- Recommendations should include thoughts on whether, and if so how, the pupil premium could be used to fund an approach that uses music to drive improvements across a school and wider into the community.

In order to evaluate what 'best practice' and what 'best music education' might mean the review refers back to the *Making More of Music* report by Ofsted (2009). This earlier report had already highlighted a number of challenges facing the music education sector as well as emphasising and making explicit what has been understood for a long time by many parents, educators and youth workers at the coal face, as it were: that engaging with music and particularly perhaps music making for young people provided many positive social effects both in school as well as out of school.

On the whole, most government and non-government arts education sectors in Britain received the Ofsted report optimistically. This was reflected in the response from the very influential National Foundation for Youth Music (Youth Music) who noted that it 'is a very positive time for music education' and the 'recognition of need [for music provision] is well founded' (Youth Music, 2009).

However, as their website also notes, Youth Music's experience showed that such desirable social outcomes were not automatic but depended upon the provision of a consistently high quality music instruction. This view had been confirmed in the Ofsted report:

> The schools where the provision was outstanding showed how music education could contribute very successfully to pupils' personal as well as musical development. In these schools, every pupil benefited from music. There was a clear sense of why music was important and the schools made considerable efforts to ensure all were involved. As a result, the whole school benefited from the way in which music could both engage and re-engage pupils, increasing their self-esteem and maximising their progress across all their learning and not just in music. However, not all the schools were realising the potential of music. (Ofsted, 2009, p. 5)

Ofsted found that the patchy quality of music provision was partly due to schools and local councils taking a scattergun approach, when the opportunity of music experience was being offered in the same ways to all children with little note taken of the existing levels of competence and interest of the students. It was a one-size-fits-all approach. A related issue was that the programs offered also seem to have overlooked the need to provide sufficient additional professional training and support for teachers. Few of the staff who were expected to implement music instruction or appreciation had received professional training and this resulted in a lack of effective dialogue between music specialists and classroom teachers with 'too much activity...developed in isolation' and insufficient use of technology (Youth Music, 2009).[6]

This finding was echoed in our own observations: in learning situations outside of formal schooling we found that the young people flourished in their music engagement when they were taught by people who had both the necessary professional skills and possessed the essential 'street cred'. That is, these mentors were already tightly networked into the particular music scene, experiential community and/or the wider music industry (see Westerlund, 2006 for a supporting argument). And because these teachers or trainers were usually practising musicians or artists themselves they understood about the need to be open, flexible and responsive in their approach. The youth in our study did not see their music practice purely as entertainment or as an activity for relaxation. They saw it as 'serious play', a strategic pathway to achieve their life goals as young adults and therefore required that their teachers or mentors possessed the necessary level of expertise and knowledge and responded to them as one (emerging) artist to another. One of the students, 17-year-old 'Jake' from the Brighton Treatment Center, articulated this clearly to Juri.

> They should get more money on original beats so we can rap over it. And they should get more instruments. Like, I wanna play drums like

rock stars, you know like Green Day[7] and all that, and they should have more people who know how to do more stuff come around and show us how to do that. (Interview on Genuine Voices website, http://www.genuinevoices.com/audiovideo, accessed 23 November 2010)

Youth Music's website also articulated that 'partnership working' is the most effective way to provide quality music engagement for young people. By this term, Youth Music meant the importance of developing and utilising key networks. Because the organisation primarily works with children and youth *outside* of schools, they have learnt from their own long experience that partnerships and networking are the most effective means of meeting the needs of local communities. They do this by approaching their program content from the bottom up. They consult with young people themselves and adapt their genre and creative methods to suit the local context. This means increasingly using the latest digital technologies to engage and sustain young people's interests.

The effectiveness of this approach was confirmed in our own study where we saw for ourselves the ways in which many of the organisations, including Pie Factory Music in Kent, effectively adapted and expanded their programs to meet the needs of the youth they were working with. This involved developing far more entrepreneurial approaches over the past decade to ensure their offerings aligned with the ambitions and the needs of their local community (see Chapter 5). One of PFM's initiatives was to set up the Music Business School in September 2006 to provide their tutors with professional teacher training and to give their young participants the opportunity to extend the musical skills they had gained from the workshops into a nationally recognised qualification.

> The Music Business School is set up as a business to create affordable opportunities for young people and adults, from 16 years and above, to train in all aspects of the music industry. That includes publishing, copyright, record labels, promotion, radio, marketing, internet music, digital rights management, live gigs, PA & lighting, distribution, CD production, audio engineering and a variety of software training, with a view to run accredited certified training in well-known audio software. Many of our units are accredited through the National Open College Network (NOCN) through Pie Factory Music so we can offer full qualifications with the right mix of modules from levels 1–3.
>
> (Mike Fagg and Steve, personal communication, 5 August 2010. Additional information also available on the PFM website)

Such an approach not only ensures that the emerging musicians are in contact with professionals in the industry but it can also provide them with life experience and the possibilities of pathways into potential careers. Notice that, as Mike Fagg explains above, the particular experience in the music industry offered here is not limited to one genre, instrument or even one career path. Rather the young people are helped to understand the connection between and interrelatedness of all aspects of the industry and offered expert mentorship in each one.

Alexis Johnson, founder of AKarts, also understands the importance of this broader aspect of music education. She has worked for many years chiefly across visual arts, creative writing and digital media including graphics, web design and film, but frequently integrates dance and music into her projects. As outlined earlier, she mentored Rowland and Tuesday to help them make connections between their own music development and experts in their field. This included, as described in Chapter 5, assisting Rowland to gain funding through the prestigious Prince's Trust scheme. Alexis has an extensive background working in informal education and youth and community development in both the private and public sector.

Her personal experience and expertise are awe-inspiring: AKarts now delivers arts education consultancy, brokering and project management to London School of Commerce (LSC) Central, Film London, thirteen London borough councils and seven central Further Education Colleges. She is a trustee of DreamArt, a youth performance charity, and undertakes extensive mentoring work with young people from disadvantaged backgrounds.

> Mentoring is crucial in the personal development of young people from disadvantaged backgrounds. It acts as a substitute to absent parenting and opens a gate toward ambition and a future beyond the cycle of their parents. AKarts found that Mentoring through Production (making a creative product) the most effective and worthwhile methodology. But important questions came up, such as when do you stop mentoring an individual? Can mentoring become too much of a crutch, slowing down young people's necessity to stand on their own two feet? To what extent does environment (housing estates), and disadvantaged young people's sense of belonging in a community shape who they are and therefore their sense of ambition and self-belief?
>
> To tackle these questions I shifted my mentoring focus into Social Mentoring. This coincided with a commission from the City of Westminster's regeneration agency South Westminster Renewal Partnership (part of Westminster Council). Here through AKarts

I investigated young people's attitudes to where they live and found a huge prejudice between the young and elderly residents was causing the vast majority of the issues that Active Mentoring was trying to treat. Elderly residents are scared and threatened by young people hanging out in groups on the estates. Young people feel safe within groups and feel angry that elderly residents view them with such disdain.

With the view that prevention is better than cure I went about designing intergenerational participatory arts models to explore how communities can be brought together. And in so doing find ways that elderly residents can mentor their young neighbours. We came across a few surprises along the way of successes we hadn't anticipated, especially when we found we were no longer simply dealing with the young and the elderly, but all adults from disadvantaged backgrounds especially those on long-term incapacity benefit and some with mental health issues. These people have a great deal to offer and even more to gain around this model of Social Mentoring.

(Alexis, personal communication, November 2010)

Photo 7.3 Alexis on her boat. © Geraldine Bloustien

Alexis understands the importance of developing personal relationships and collaboration within all forms of mentoring to ensure that young people can use networks within their own communities for support and to take advantage of the often hidden expertise that is there.

In her projects Alexis rarely views music in isolation from the ways the community at large engages with music to make its own meaning and identity. Her best-known work is 'Passport 2 Pimlico' (2009/10), reimagining the 1949 Ealing film by 850 Pimlico residents, broadcast on television and exhibited at Tate Britain. Such projects connect her to some of the most disadvantaged communities in London. Through this type of activity unique relationships are brokered, social issues of understanding and cohesion tackled and skills shared in a 'live' learning environment.[8]

> 'Passport 2 Pimlico' was the first of these projects (using social mentoring), delivered across seven housing estates in Pimlico. Designed in response to South Westminster Renewal Partnership (SWRP) 2007 report identifying prejudice between young and old in SW1 regeneration areas, it's about bringing the Pimlico community together, young and old, to do something extraordinary. They have performed scenes live in local estates, streets and public spaces across Pimlico. And this has been filmed so that we can document the coming together of the community.
>
> The project has been designed in consultation with the community, local council and housing services to address the community cohesion needs of those who live, study and work in South Westminster. It aims to build active community and large-scale inter-generational community cohesion across Pimlico and within its seven estates. Darren Levy, Director of Customer Services at CityWest Homes, who manage the Churchill Gardens youth club said: 'This project is a great way to encourage young people to communicate with older people living in the area. It is important that young people have an understanding of history and projects like this help to create a greater understanding by bringing history to life' (personal communication).
>
> The project has captured the imagination of residents. What started as an AKarts short project in October 2008, supported by Groundwork North London, SWRP and L&Q Housing, has snowballed with 489 locals taking part to date in the short film and 1450 residents asking to get involved in future activity.
>
> But AKarts continues to explore and refine these models to identify self-sustainable models with mothers, children and young people in Haringey; and communities in Camden, Kentish Town and Newham.

The biggest supporters have been local councils, who have backed and supported these initiatives by facilitating local partnerships and sometimes funding the initiatives. The biggest obstacles have been the funding models of small short-term grants that work against communities' need for long-term sustainability and security. These grants are a lottery, and take a long time to write. With a small staff it takes time away from delivery.

(Alexis, personal communication, November 2010)

Photo 7.4   On the street set of Passport 2 Pimlico. © Alexis Johnson

In these ways, Alexis develops meaningful relationships with all of her clients and extends her connections to enhance each individual's potential creativity. She helps them to explore and enhance their abilities and through the programs she gives them a genuine voice in decision-making, thereby facilitating their personal and professional development. Over the long period we have known her we have come to see that she is committed to supporting other people and especially vulnerable young adults to realise their full potential. As our previous chapters have demonstrated, she promotes agency by providing them with the opportunity to learn by doing, to experience belonging and seize ownership of whatever project they are undertaking together.

As Alexis knows all too well, innovation in youth music programs depends increasingly on adequate funding but also on thinking outside of the conventional square. In Britain the myplace initiative enabled the exciting purpose-built and designed youth centre in Norwich, which was officially launched in 2009 (see Chapter 4). The original impetus for the youth centre stemmed from an earlier city initiative called the SOS Bus, a project designed to respond to alarming and growing rates of youth alcoholism and drug abuse in the city.[9] While this reacted to the obvious and serious problem of youth at risk, the project leaders felt that a more proactive, positive approach was required; action rather than reaction! In 2002 local entrepreneur Graham Dacre established the Open Youth Trust as a charity to tackle youth needs from a new angle. With part funding made available through the myplace government initiative the trust bought and completely renovated a 50,000 square foot heritage building. Myplace has been promoted as the largest ever government investment in youth facilities, providing £270m for creating (or improving) youth facilities around Britain. Currently sixty venues are in the planning stage or development.

As in the best youth arts programs that we observed in our study, the myplace initiative puts the youth at the centre of the decision-making process. For example, in the case of the Open Youth Venue, a youth forum was set up 'to ensure the centre would be relevant to the generation that were to use it, not the one that was funding it' (Sparks, 2010, p. 14). This youth forum, which became the centre's steering committee, was integral to all decisions, from layout, facilities and furniture to which activities and events would occur and what types of professional expertise the staff needed to possess. Dedicated social networking sites such as Facebook and MySpace enable wider consultation to continue.[10]

The Open Youth Trust website, which shows the venue and details the programs and activities, also contains a number of videos to explain the history and purpose of the initiative. Russ Dacre, the Project Manager of Open Youth Venue and son of the founder of the Open Youth Trust, explains the journey and what they learnt, including the importance of collaboration: 'It wasn't that the [existing youth] services weren't of a good quality but there could be major benefits from their coming together in one space and people knew that they could access them in a comfortable environment' (Dacre, 2010).

The successful strategies employed by the Open Youth Venue in Norwich to re-engage disaffected young people through the arts parallels what we saw as best practice, including the importance of dedicating flexible space where the young people have had very real input in terms of design function and management. Underpinned by collaboration, networking and professional mentoring, creativity and a real sense of accomplishment can flourish in this type of setting.

A recent edition of *UNESCO Today* (vol. 1, 2010) focused on the nature and development of arts education in Germany today, outlining the major changes in pedagogical approaches to explore the most significant contemporary developments. Earlier approaches had emphasised a socio-cultural education, focusing on the development of creativity in all areas of the arts. More recently, this style of pedagogy has been taken further with even more emphasis on personal development.

> The process of modernization increases the demand for culture and education (general education as defined by Humboldt [Institute]) and the development of subjectivity. Concurrently the need for cultivating everyday life has grown, too. Therefore it has become a widely shared view that it is necessary to develop experiences that nurture such competencies. Not only creativity, which too often is regarded as a 'cure-all', but also the highly developed arts are especially relevant in this respect. Institutions of culture and education must offer opportunities of learning and personal development for all young people. In modern times one learns the best for life through the arts. (Liebau, 2010, p. 13)

This was an approach that all of the youth centres we visited in Berlin seemed to understand. For the most part their approach had been youth-focused and ground-up, responding to the kinds of music genres in which the youth in their local community expressed interest and then using a variety of music activities to attract and engage a range of young people. While all of the youth workers at the centres were professional social workers many were also trained teachers, musicians and artists. Their successful pedagogical approaches seemed to draw on what Lauri Väkevä has described as a 'garage band' model. This she describes as

> A model to encompass various modes of digital artistry wherever this artistry takes place. This might include: in face-to-face pedagogical situations, in other contexts of informal learning, and in such open-networked learning environments as remix sites and musical online communities. (2010, p. 63)

The central role played by new communication technologies and particularly social networking platforms (SNP) in these informal learning situations has been highlighted by Finnish social media researcher Miika Salavuo. He particularly emphasises how the internet has changed the ways in which 'people listen, create and practice music and how musicians collaborate'. It is, he says, 'a change that has been as much cultural as technological' (2006, p. 121; also see Draper, 2007). In line with our own findings, his observations show that social media services (networking platforms), such as Facebook, MySpace and YouTube, have created opportunities for people to share expertise, learn from one another and collaborate. In these ways then, informal learning becomes 'on demand learning' which has long been common in other settings such as in the creation and development of garage bands (Green, 2001; Westerlund, 2006; Väkevä, 2010) and hip hop crews. Formal institutional sites for music education such as schools and colleges of higher education seem to underestimate the importance of this insight. 'The idea of the collaborative processing of knowledge, alongside the culture of contributing one's own creative work and ideas, are contradictory to traditional practices of education and are often alien to the existing learning culture' (Salavuo, 2008, pp. 122–3).

Much of the current literature and policy reports on music education in schools continue to focus on the notion of 'progression' rather than the more informal and collaborative approaches to learning that we have outlined above. Progression in the context of the curriculum refers to two related ideas. Firstly, that acquisition of knowledge or skills is, or should be, sequential. This is often underpinned and limited by ideas of cognitive and age-based development and locates the source of knowledge and power in the teacher. Stephane Pitts' (2001) preliminary study analysis, for example, argued that it would be far more effective if all of the stakeholders involved in music education could arrive at a mutual definition of what it actually means (also see Finney, 2003). Ruth Wright's study (2003–4) with 13- and 14-year-old students in a Welsh school noted the tensions that arose between teacher and pupils over the teacher's control over what aspects of the course were taught and the methodologies chosen to teach them. She considers the solution might be in the kinds of 'informal' pedagogy that locates 'the production and development of musical knowledge with the pupils themselves' (Wright, 2008, p. 389; see Green, 2001, 2006, 2008a, 2008b),[11] even though she saw this as potentially problematic.

> If such pedagogy is to become more widespread there are big questions to be asked about the type of person suited to becoming a music teacher and the sort of music education and initial teacher education and training they require. (Wright, 2008, p. 389)

This 'solution', however, overlooks the fact that in the elective music-making in which so many young people engage out of school, as members of popular music scenes such as hip hop crews or rock bands, the pedagogies involved are far from 'informal'. As we have described in several chapters above, the youth select their mentors from people whom they recognise as having the requisite knowledge, skills and street credibility. There is little patience even by the peer mentors for any imprecise movements, vocals and performance of their 'students'. Rather expectations are high. For example, we recall here both Shep's (Da Klinic) and Dave's (Palais) insistence that the attendees of their respective workshops have to practise endlessly in between the sessions. We are also reminded of the endless practice sessions and the resulting excellent performances we attended, watching Tuesday, Rowland, Katie, Magda and the numerous bands at the Kandinsky gigs. Even Juri, who was working with the most disadvantaged youth in a detention centre, used quite formal approaches to teach her young charges.

> As someone who completed all the seven grades to complete the Australian Music Association (AMusA) piano theory and performance qualification, I couldn't believe what I was seeing. Many of these young people were barely literate and most had never had the opportunity or inclination to use a music instrument, especially not keyboards and guitars. Yet Juri began from the premise that none of this was important. She believed that no-one should leave even from their first 'lesson' with her or her carefully selected tutors without having experienced actually playing a piece of music that they already knew and loved. She began with the expectation that they would learn to use both hands simultaneously and have the correct hand positions on the keyboard. She created exercises around learning major and minor scales as part of their learning to hear the different sounds on the piano. Many young people then asked to be taught the correct music notations so that they could create their own simple music compositions.
>
> (Margaret, personal reflection, November 2010)

The youth themselves were often their own hardest judges. Each performance, whether live on stage, at a breaking or beats battle or performed via broadcast or the internet, was reflected on, evaluated and critiqued in order to improve their next performance. For example, as described earlier, each week following DJ Roland's Phatbeats show he receives both positive and negative responses from his fans on his Facebook page.

The second use of the word 'progression', in relation to music and arts education, tends to refer to the viability of career pathways and lifelong learning. This aspect of progression already underpins the fundamental passion that drives young people to create and engage in music in their own time. While they recognise that the road to professional success in the music industry is limited, they also see that music offers them a pathway to a stronger self and cultural identity. It also ties them more closely into their broader social and cultural networks and gives them an opportunity to express their views and their understandings of their worlds (see Westerlund, 2006; Meyers, 2008).

Youth, music and creative cultures

Our journey has given us many insights about many disadvantaged youth and their music practices. We learnt about what they did, how they did it and why. Firstly, then, we have learnt a great deal about the range of music cultures the young people engage in. Although we were to observe many different kinds of music cultures, music practices and activities related to music, we focused mainly on what the key players in our narrative, the young people we invited into the study as co-researchers, were engaged in through their particular passions, ambitions and networks. That also meant that, unlike many similar studies of youth music cultures, we did not just focus on one genre or scene such as hip hop or even one location but rather explored, on the one hand, a broad range of genres while, on the other, we delved into the depths of what each particular grouping and music culture meant to the youth participants themselves within their particular experiential and social networks.

Across the four countries of our study, we did notice some important constants. The first was that whatever the genre or music scene that the young people were involved in, their engagement with music was not separate from their engagement with the experiential community. That is, the music enabled the individual to feel part of a social and cultural support network. Secondly, if the individual was passionate about creating music or music events for themselves, they sought mentorship from experts around them. While some of these mentors were around the same age, that was not the key factor. It was the expertise of the mentor that was essential and so many intergenerational collaborations and serious partnerships occur within the scenes. Thirdly, engagement with music was seen as a collaborative venture; it was expected that the other people in the scene would support and freely share their expertise, their knowledge and their time. The fourth important finding was the extent to which all of the participants and co-researchers used social media and especially audio and video files on networking sites to share their knowledge and information, to arrange, plan and promote particular events, to seek help and advice, to find archival footage, music or information, and to disseminate copies of their music and performance videos.

Although we participated in many different youth music cultures during the life of this project, hip hop proved to be the most popular music genre with the youth we worked with. It is of course traditionally known for its four distinct though interrelated elements – rap, breakdancing, graffiti or street art and turntabling – and perhaps it was because of this variety that it was so popular. It is also the music genre that was still seen as being able to provide an effective vehicle for a political voice. Since all of the youth in our project had been identified as being materially or socially disadvantaged or disaffected, it is probably not surprising that one of the few places that they found they could effectively voice their anger or personal concerns was through this music culture (see Chapters 3 and 4 for more examples of their musical expression). Hip hop culture was also the most publicly performed of all the genres we explored. We were frequently invited to and attended many local music beats and breaking 'battles', turntabling contests, inline skating events, and broader music festivals that often incorporated art, music, skating and dancing all in one venue. One such festival was the This Is Not Art (TINA) Festival 2005 in Newcastle, New South Wales, which brought together youth from all over Australia. In the particular year that we visited the festival included a new item, 'The Strike Project', described in the program as 'a new addition' that

> brings together aerosol and visual artists from across Australia to create a new work during the festival... The TINA artists will work in teams of two or three representing the state that they currently reside or originate from. Each represented state will be allocated a 12m × 3m space to paint that will then be incorporated into the collaborative mural with illustrations by visual artists Josh, Phibs and Store.[12]

In 2005, the Newcastle City Council had authorised the huge mural measuring forty metres by seven metres on the side of the former Water Board and temporary Trades Hall building, prominently located next to the Newcastle Panthers Club in Bull Street, Cooks Hill. Saul from the Palais was listed as a featured NSW artist and many of the youth we knew from Newcastle attended and performed.

Of all the music scenes, hip hop also seemed to have the highest public profile and, because so much of hip hop is now regarded as mainstream, many of the young people in our research were performing in commercial venues. Many South Australian hip hop events were regularly listed on Da Klinic's Facebook page where Shep would post their proudest achievements. One recent initiative (2010) has included Da Klinic's home-made but very sophisticated advertisement now appearing on commercial television as well as on YouTube. Da Klinic also proudly posted an image of their inclusion in the City of Adelaide's Christmas pageant 2010, an achievement for the second year running. Cleverly entitled 'Christmas (W)Rapping' their mobile float consisted of a large skate ramp mounted on a truck. A Da Klinic DJ and a rapper performed at the front of the float. Behind them several active inline skaters performed tricky manoeuvres as the float travelled in the procession along the street.

Many of our other co-researchers were involved in a range of other electronic and digitally based music genres such as garage and R&B. In Britain, variations of UK garage were the genre that we heard the most frequently,

Photo 7.5 Christmas (W)Rapping Float. © Adrian Shepherd

with both Tuesday, Rowland and their friends performing in live venues and at community (and pirate) radio stations. However, as we documented in the earlier chapters, we were also extremely aware of the endless workshops, practice and rehearsals that were behind those polished performances at all of the sites. These practices were observed by us and documented on cameras by many of the youth themselves for reflexive learning purposes, the footage often being then shared and disseminated through their networks via the internet. The perfecting and sharing of technique was clearly an embedded cultural practice; it was taken for granted that anyone who was serious about their vocals, art form, dancing or turntabling skills would seek a mentor and peer critique.

Relatively few of the youth co-researchers in our study chose acoustic or rock music as their music-making genre of choice although many still enjoyed listening to this style of music or reinterpreting it in new ways through DJ mixing of old vinyl records. It did seem to be the young people who had been professionally trained to any degree using music notation who preferred to perform on stage as a rock band rather than focus on the more electronically based music. In Germany, Magda's band Totally Stressed continue to perform and describe themselves as an acoustic folk rock band. This band too continues to compose, experiment and perform their own music at both local venues and now further afield. Their Facebook page shows their latest success of being headlined at LADIY, the Berlin Feminist

D.I.Y. music festival in Berlin. On the other hand, Katie, lead vocalist of two bands in London, prefers with her bands to focus on interpreting and playing covers. This way, she says wryly, she and her bands can still get to perform and make money but do not have the pressure of knowing that they have to be unique and perfect to make it in the industry.

We documented above that not all of the youth engagement with music activities that we studied involved stage performance. *Youth Revolutions*, of course, came together to host a community radio show. Their aim was to use a major cultural vehicle to attract and engage their listeners but then use the platform to air and discuss political and social concerns of interest to youth. Apart from the lively discussions and debates that occurred on- and off-air about the relative merits of different bands and styles of music, the show also provided a valuable forum to showcase local bands whose music was then played and the bands interviewed. Being involved in the radio show as on-air hosts further provided valuable research, social and technical skills that could be transferred to other jobs in the music and media industries. Will, as we previously noted, already understood this and worked on the marketing and promotional strategy for *Youth Revolutions* as a learning opportunity to develop his emerging IT and public relations business. His confidence and his abilities have gone from strength to strength. He recently noted on his Facebook page:

> I just started working with a couple of web developers as part of my new team for making websites – one's in the US and the other is in NZ. I've also outsourced most of my administration to India and the Philippines and I'm in the process of setting up a print communications team in Australia (Qld and Vic). Never a dull moment!
>
> (Will, Facebook wall communication, 18 November 2010)

Several other young people in our study, such as the Kandinsky Sessions Group, Da Klinic, Kyle and Tuesday have also turned their attention to production and event management, even if they are also still involved in performing music or other music-related activities themselves. We suspect this was because it allows them to gain more control and to feel they could be far more influential in their local music industry. For example, Alicia now rarely performs with her band, Aviator Lane ('I needed a break': personal communication, 29 October 2010), but she still enjoys her challenging work of managing local music events, sourcing bands from interstate and helping emerging musicians to create and distribute their CDs through her record label and business, Patterns in Static.

The role of the CBOs

The notion of 'creative spaces', 'cultural precincts', 'cultural hubs' and so forth dominates national youth agendas but the literature usually provides a top-down view only. What we have focused on in our study is how the youth, despite the many constraints placed in their way, continue to invest in their own creative music-making activities. The local community-based centres and settings are crucial for so many of the youth, providing not just space and place but critical resources in terms of equipment and networks of culturally diverse interrelationships with local mentors, trainers and tutors.

Against the backdrop of rising youth unemployment across all of our research sites, we have seen youth music-making activities suffer as a result of funding cuts to many of the community-based centres and organisations. In Berlin, for example, we have witnessed the sacking of many youth workers and the closure of some centres. This circumstance has arisen not just from economic downturn but a major change in schooling hours; full-day schooling has directly impacted on attendances at centres that had formerly provided a place for youth to go when school hours were much shorter. Yet we have also seen that some centres, such as Café Lietz, have regrouped, survived and joined with other funded evangelical centres to continue to provide mentoring and training for youth music-making activities – albeit on a smaller scale.

In Newcastle, New South Wales, we witnessed the closing of the Palais site due to the increasing gentrification and redevelopment of Newcastle. The relocation of the former Palais youth centre from its space along the Hunter riverfront to the Loft in the Hunter Street Mall in the central business district of Newcastle was initially very unpopular with youth who had been strongly attached to 'their place' at the Palais, but it continues to attract youth to the array of music-making activities on offer – despite the longer distances to travel to the Loft from the outer reaches of Newcastle where the majority of the youth live. Part of the efforts of the youth to reclaim this new space in a busy city mall, where the visibility of unemployed youth 'congregating' had been a source of concern to the new apartment dwellers and business owners and operators, was boosted when the local council and staff from the Loft negotiated an aerosol art agreement for the youth to design murals on a freeform wall in the South Newcastle Beach area. Youth were invited into a reference group that has responsibility for designing and managing community murals. The Loft is now 'owned' as 'their place' by a new generation of youth, including the recent arrival of Sudanese refugees, passionate about their music-making activities, and this has occurred despite ongoing tensions and contradictions around the local council's understanding of 'youth-designated' space and place. But the precariousness of funding is ongoing for the Loft, evidenced by the council's unwillingness to approve a lease beyond a two-year time frame at any given stage.

Youth-designated spaces have to be fought for by the youth who use the facilities, the staff and volunteers at the centres, *and* the community within which the centres are located. The staff and youth attending the Pie Factory in the Thanet region in the UK know this all too well as we demonstrated in earlier chapters. In spite of relocation and major funding cuts, Pie Factory Music continues to resonate with youth in the area through their provision of music-making projects and activities and the network of adults who work with them. When any one of the 'partners' in the network of youth-centred community-based relationships – be it the council, the government, the regional authorities, the staff, the youth or their mentors – flags in their joint commitment to youth music-making activities, youth lose out. We saw this in the demise of the *Youth Revolutions* radio program in the Playford City Council region in the northern suburbs of Adelaide, South Australia.

Youth and creative industries

Despite the many detractors of the concept of 'creative industries' a decade or so ago, such as Hudson (1995) and O'Connor (1998), our research points to many successful micro individual and collective outcomes where the agenda is not just about a crude governance mechanism for youth containment or a fantasised pathway to employment. However, we remain mindful of Chris Gibson's comment, specifically on musicians, that 'intermittent examples of success merely entrenched constructions of "work" that were dependent on participants' willingness to remain unpaid for current activities, traded against promised future gains' (2001, p. 208). Leadbeater and Oakley in their 1999 report *The Independents: Britain's New Cultural Entrepreneurs* had been very careful not to overstate employment opportunities in the 'emergent' creative industries: 'many cultural entrepreneurs run fragile, low-growth companies in industries that have low barriers to entry and a high turnover of talent and ideas' (1999, p. 19).

Young people in our study know this only too well. They know the risks and the potential to be exploited. But they still engage in grassroots music-based activities because they need to, they love what they do, and they are passionate about developing their skills, knowledge and self-worth, despite economic fragility and the risks associated with such a choice. We heard from former youth detention inmates in Rhode Island that they chose, for a very small payment, to tutor and mentor youth at risk in their own community, so as to provide opportunities for others to avoid following in their footsteps. Instead, many of the tutors could be making vast sums of money selling drugs on the street. Working with youth at risk is a very different form of 'freedom' and self-realisation. AS220 Broad Street, beginning in 2001, gives a different slant to those who question the long-term sustainability of youth-centred music-based activities. Ten years on they have grown six successful business models drawing on a range of community support, from local businesses, volunteers, schools and universities across Rhode Island.

Still, many will say that for every successful sustainable youth music project, a lot of others will fail. We do not deny that. What our research highlights are the key elements that contribute to growing community-based micro-entrepreneurial youth music activities: the youth, community support and funding, and a network of local adult mentors, tutors, volunteers and youth workers.

We have spent much time in our earlier chapters highlighting the importance of targeted funding for sustainability, from an array of sources, yet have also become acutely aware that funding is a critical but not the only element underpinning youth music-based activities. We have learnt that youth also need to be encouraged to find local mentors, undertake a form of internship or learning journey, spend time with other youth and begin dialogues with diverse organisations or community-based centres who can help them to learn new strategies, gain new skills, share victories and challenges, and find a role model and be a role model.

The biggest challenge for all of the young people, the mentors and the CBOs that support them seems to be the plans by governments everywhere to privatise the usual providers of support, such as local councils, greatly reduce or eliminate funding, and make partnership support so much harder to find. While many of our organisations have been innovative and resilient, looking at commercial models and new forms of entrepreneurship to enable their activities to continue, it is continually an uphill battle. The UK's Big Society is just one example of new moves to justify the reduction of funds and the replacement of the activity of the public voluntary sector and local councils.

AKarts is one among many of our CBOs to express concern that, despite their best attempts over many years to help communities to help themselves and to build up their capacity to do this, this greater reduction of financial support will hit hard. As we have shown throughout the narratives in this book, youth, their mentors, the supporting community organisations and their communities themselves all still need leadership, structure and direction to continue the kind of valuable and exciting initiatives that have been detailed here. Without this kind of long-term support, few of the young creative people in our communities will be able to see their music practices as something they can continue to play for life.

Appendix: Our CBOs at a Glance

Australia

Da Klinic, Adelaide, South Australia

Adrian Shepherd, aka DJ Shep, and his friend Jeff Ottaway set up Da Klinic in 2002 in an underground basement space in the centre of Adelaide with a mini skate ramp, break room, DJs, skating and scratching workshops and skater gear with just $5,000. They invited friends with a skater gear label to display their stock rent free, adding a clothing element to the Da Klinic experience. Developed largely by word of mouth, they have now built it into one of Australia's leading hip hop/skate shops, running major hip hop and skating activities for youth as well as providing tuition in the full range of hip hop activities. As well as staging hip hop events for local councils, Da Klinic works with many marginalised youth including young male juvenile offenders and remote Aboriginal communities (www.daklinic.com).

Kandinsky Sessions, Carclew Youth Arts Centre, Adelaide, South Australia

Carclew Youth Arts Centre is South Australia's only multi-art form and cultural organisation dedicated to artistic outcomes by and for people aged 26 and under. It provides young people with opportunities to try different art forms, supports emerging artists to develop their craft and advocates for youth arts practice. Carclew's programs consist of workshops, events, arts projects, funding programs and skill development opportunities, one of which is the Kandinsky Sessions. Youth-run, with minimal guidance from a paid youth arts mentor, the Kandinsky Sessions team are taught all aspects of running and promoting a variety of music gigs (www.carclew.com.au).

Youth Revolutions, Playford City Council, Elizabeth, South Australia

The City of Playford is a diverse urban and rural community, located on the outer northern edge of Adelaide's metropolitan area, 20 to 35 kilometres from the CBD. Its youth unemployment is the highest in the state of South

Australia outside of some rural Indigenous reserves. Within Playford lies the suburb of Davoren Park, which in 2009 had increased its reputation for violence and dysfunction to the point where it had become 'a place where emergency crews fear to go'. Otherwise known as the Peachey Belt, Peachey Road runs through the centre of the suburb. In 2003, Playford provided the initial funding for a youth-run half-hour radio program, as part of an initiative for the youth of the Peachey Belt. The vibrant radio program *Youth Revolutions* sadly ended in 2006, as a result of under-resourcing and the shifting passions of the youth presenters (www.imaginepeachey.org.au).

Palais Royale and The Loft, Newcastle, New South Wales

In 2000, Newcastle, a regional city in the state of New South Wales, established a youth service at the Palais Royale youth venue, the region's first multi-arts and youth cultural facility for young people aged 12–25. It offered a number of arts activities in the areas of music, visual arts and performance in response to the needs of young people including being a safe drop-in space. In September 2004, Palais Royale was sold and demolished, causing the relocation of the youth venue to its current site in the Newcastle Mall. In 2006 this site was relaunched as The Loft Youth Arts and Cultural Centre where it continues (precariously) to serve as an incubator for young artists, musicians, promoters and performers while providing a safe space for social engagement and recreation (www.newcastle.nsw.gov.au/my_community/youth_venues).

Berlin, Germany

Spik e.V., Hellersdorf

In the north-eastern outskirts of Berlin, Spik e.V. developed out of the local Protestant congregation's youth work in 1991. The artistically graffiti-painted youth centre is surrounded by typical GDR high-rise buildings, housing a comparatively high number of socially disadvantaged families. The ethnically diverse local residents, who struggle with poverty, unemployment, emotional stress and psychological problems, are mainly of Russian-German, Kosovo-Albanian/ex-Yugoslavian and Vietnamese descent. The youth centre's clientele are mainly from German and Russian-German backgrounds (www.spikev.de).

Tietzia e.V., Reinickendorf

Tietzia e.V. is a central institution for girls, women and young families in the northern part of Berlin. It offers an open youth work area, an internet café, events and a range of programs and workshops for schools. Originally, the institution successfully focused on programs for girls only, but more recently the district authority of Reinickendorf required them to offer broader programs in response to cutbacks in other local social institutions. Visitors come from all over northern Berlin; however, less than 10 per cent of the visitors are from an immigrant background (www.tietzia-berlin.de).

Wutzkyallee, Neukölln

Wutzkyallee is a multifunctional social centre in the south-eastern Berlin neighbourhood of Gropiusstadt that is famous for its high numbers of high-rise public housing and subsidised housing estates. Wutzkyallee is open to all ages with a very wide variety of activities including music-related activities for youth (70% of whom are boys) who use the diverse rehearsal, concert and recording facilities. The majority of general visitors are non-German, mainly of Arabic, Turkish, Polish and Russian, but also Bosnian or Serbian origin (www.wutzkyallee.de).

Statthaus Böcklerpark, Kreuzberg

Statthaus Böcklerpark is one of Berlin's most famous social institutions for open low-threshold youth work, particularly with male migrant juveniles (mainly of Arabic and Turkish origin). It is located in the middle of Kreuzberg and surrounded by its little zoo and street ball, basketball, soccer, table tennis, skate and other sports facilities. Some of Kreuzberg's major public housing estates are very high rise and are located on the outskirts of Kreuzberg. Almost 100 per cent of the occupants of these public housing estates are from ethnic minorities, while the centre of Kreuzberg is adjacent to some of Berlin's most gentrified streets. Visitors to Statthaus Böcklerpark are aged 10–25 years and come from all over central Berlin, with the majority from the adjacent public housing estates. With the recent privatisation of social centres in Berlin which used to be funded by the respective district authorities, Statthaus Böcklerpark was closed in 2009. In 2010 it reopened under the guidance of a new private sponsor and with new employees (www.statthausboecklerpark.de).

Café Lietze, Charlottenburg

Café Lietze, financed by the Protestant congregation of Berlin, is located in an affluent nineteenth-century neighbourhood in the west of Berlin. In the cellar of the neighbourhood congregation's centre, the three paid employees offer a wide variety of instruments and music lessons to the neighbourhood's youth and also to visitors from other Berlin neighbourhoods. The users, mainly aged between 16 and 21 years old, tend to be well educated. Most of the youth are male but recently there has been an attempt to attract more girls to the centre (www.Cafe-lietze.de).

Haus der Jugend, Charlottenburg

Haus der Jugend is located in the less affluent northern parts of Charlottenburg-Wilmersdorf, a comparatively wealthy district in the west of Berlin. The centre is funded by the district authority of Charlottenburg and some additional projects are paid for by the neighbouring youth club cooperative. As with most of Berlin's social institutions, the funding has decreased over the last few years. The staff situation is tough, but Haus der Jugend still manages to offer the same activities for their core target group of 8 to 17-year-olds as they have previously done. Depending on the specific music or youth work programs, 70–80 per cent of the users are boys. The majority of the local attendees are male, mainly of Turkish and Arabic backgrounds although youth from immigrant Russian, Polish, Serbian, and Croatian ethnicities also use the centre (www.jugendclubring-berlin.de).

Hip-Hop/Rock-Mobil, Treptow and all over Berlin

The sponsor of Rock and Hip-Hop-Mobil is Wetek e.V., a non-profit private provider that focuses on media and music offers for young people from all over Berlin. Together with other youth centres, schools and other providers of youth support, and also together with the different Senate departments, they provide a huge variety of projects dealing with media work, cultural work and training measures. Funding comes from different EU and German institutions; the music projects Hip-Hop-Mobil, Rock-Mobil, musikfabrik and the so-called feedback recording studio are mainly sponsored by the Berlin Senate Department for Education and Sciences and the Senate Chancellery for Culture as well as by the European Social Fund. The staff consists of professional musicians, many of whom are famous hip hop artists. The mobiles' target groups are teenagers aged between 10 and 20 years. The social, gender and ethnic backgrounds of the participants depend on the respective youth centres, neighborhoods and school with which the mobiles and the musicians work (www.hiphopmobil.de; www.berliner-rockmobil.de).

Alleins e.V., Köpenick

Alleins e.V. is a non-profit private youth work organisation in the verdant south-eastern district of Köpenick. When the old youth centre (located next to its current location) was bought by an international investor recently, the centre had to move permanently to Mellowpark, an internationally known skate and BMX park with a huge variety of sports, concerts and other event locations. In addition to its eight full-time employees, Alleins employs several voluntary co-workers, depending on the season and the demand. The local bands and music-interested visitors that use the Alleins facilities are primarily boys (80 per cent). The centre holds girl-only live-in weekends to encourage young women to use the range of music, arts and sports-related facilities. The majority of centre users come from the eastern and southern neighbourhoods of Berlin, but Mellowpark and Alleins also attract youth from all parts of Germany for the bigger concerts, contests and events (www.alleins.de).

UK

AKarts, London

Created in 2002 by artist Alexis Johnson and filmmaker James Johnson, AKarts works across visual arts, creative writing and digital media including graphics, web design and film, integrating dance and music. Based in Pimlico and formed as a not-for-profit organisation in 2003, AKarts specialises in combined media arts projects, developed on a bespoke basis, that explore issues relevant to youth culture and society. Experienced facilitators, mentors, artists and creative industry experts are brought in to deliver the projects. Through AKarts, Alexis undertakes extensive mentoring work with young people from disadvantaged backgrounds (www.passport2pimlico.co.uk).

The Tabernacle, Notting Hill

The Tabernacle, in West London, ran a broad range of youth arts and music related activities which catered predominantly for the African-Caribbean local youth but also for the local community as a drop-in centre. With a mixture of government and private funding it became a central hub for calypso music, steel bands, as well as activities ranging from dance and ballet classes to techno music classes. Following the change of director and diminution of funds, the Tabernacle has moved away from its youth arts and music focus to become an entertainment venue that offers a range of theatre, comedy, live music, dance, film and poetry events. In becoming an entertainment centre it is no longer home to the many youth who cannot afford to book its studios or take its high-cost dance classes (www.tabernaclelive.co.uk).

Pie Factory Music, Ramsgate

Based in an old chapel at 67A Chapel Road in Ramsgate, Pie Factory Music (one of Thanet's 'action zones') is an organisation set up to provide free music and related arts workshops for young people across East Kent, particularly those youth who find themselves detached from society. Established in 2001, Pie Factory Music aims to build skills that increase employability, particularly targeting young people who have 'fallen off the radar'. It is committed to the belief that music is a superb tool for motivation, inclusion and health in its broadest sense and is dedicated to using that tool effectively and flexibly in the East Kent community (www.piefactorymusic.com).

USA

Genuine Voices, Boston

Founded in 2002 by Juri Panda Jones (now known as Juri Ify Love) as a non-profit, charitable organisation with material support and encouragement from Berklee College of Music, the mission of Genuine Voices is to teach music to at-risk inner-city youths, especially those in juvenile detention centres, as a means of building their creativity and increasing their resilience. One such centre was Brighton Treatment Center, Boston. Juri believes that by fostering young people's musical abilities and skills she can assist youths in their ability to make positive life decisions (www.genuinevoices.com).

AS220, Providence

Broad Street Studios is an offshoot of AS220 which stands for Arts Space (number) 220 Empire Street, Providence. AS220 is a non-profit community arts space in downtown Providence whose mission is to provide an unjuried and uncensored forum for the arts. Broad Street Studios, located at 790 Broad Street, Providence, was founded in 2001 to focus on issues such as welfare/poverty, hip hop activism, arts and culture, racial justice, prisons and criminal justice.

Broad Street Studios is a local arts, culture and politics incubator. It includes White, Latina/o, African-American/Black youth aged 13 to 21 years in a range of arts/music projects and programs. Young artists produce a bi-monthly youth magazine, and have access to a recording studio and artist studios to create, market and produce their own small businesses in the arts. Many of the youth come from under-resourced communities and work closely with youth at local juvenile prisons. They orchestrate monthly open mic performances and host monthly dinners dubbed Food for Thought (www.as220.org/broadst).

Notes

1 Music is Youth and Youth is Music

1. The names used in this book are real names when the contributors requested this. In a few cases the names have been changed to pseudonyms.
2. UK garage (also known as UKG or simply 'garage') refers to several different varieties of modern electronic dance music generally connected to the evolution of house in the United Kingdom from the early to mid-1990s. It evolved from house music in the UK in the mid-1990s and by the late 1990s the scene settled upon the term UK garage. This style is now frequently combined with other forms of music like hip hop, rap and R&B, all broadly filed under the description 'urban music'.
3. While local members of the academic team in each country (see page vii) were responsible for their particular research sites, the chief investigators travelled and worked in each site between 2003 and 2005 for a period of time so as to alleviate as much inconsistency of method as possible. Between 2007 and 2011, the two authors of this book revisited and recontacted all of the youth and the mentors at each site.
4. Many of the young people themselves talked about this aspect of music copyright and IP very early on as they were concerned about their music lyrics or mixes being available to others on the project website. While they acknowledged the importance and need for sharing their resources and the ideal of 'the creative commons' they were also anxious to protect their own creative output and artistic integrity.
5. www.intomedia.org.uk/STEP.
6. http://www.guardian.co.uk/theobserver/2011/mar/13/letters-arts-spending-cuts, accessed 30 March 2011.
7. The original source of this information, following discussion with some of the youth workers in the UK, was a very informative Wiki article online (http://en.wikipedia.org./wiki/Big_Society, with the text made available under the Creative Commons Attribution-ShareAlike Licence, accessed 12 August 2010).
8. The two authors of this book are clearly not the only people who have contributed to the shaping and development of this project. See notes 13 and 15 for more details concerning the collaborations and publications.
9. During 2009, Juri Panda Jones, director of the charity and not-for-profit organisation Genuine Voices (www.genuinevoices.com), legally changed her name to Juri Ify Love for personal reasons. See the appendix for more information about the various CBOs with which we worked.
10. Between 2003 and 2006 we undertook most of our fieldwork in Boston at the Brighton Treatment Center. This has now closed and the new institution, which has replaced it, is called the Eliot Short-Term Treatment Center. ESTT serves twenty male adolescents between the ages of 13 and 22 who have been committed to the Department of Youth Services. Residents at ESTT have been recommended to complete a treatment program within a specific time assignment.

The average length of stay is between five and six months. Residents at ESTT attend school daily, and participate in clinical groups, recreational activities and individual counselling.
11. At time of writing, many of the researchers are inevitably now in new positions and places including Dr Shane Homan who is now Senor Lecturer at Monash University, Melbourne, Victoria, Australia; Professor Andy Bennett and Dr Sarah Baker, Griffith University, Queensland, Australia; Dr Bruce Cohen, Auckland University, New Zealand.
12. The full cast of this project including all the invaluable members of the research and administrative team over the years has been listed in the acknowledgements.
13. In her earlier work Geraldine Bloustien (2000, 2002, 2003a, 2003b) had worked with many young people from the Weekend Arts College (WAC) with the support of Celia Greenwood, Director, and Julian Sefton Green, Education Director, of the North London Arts College. The college runs a number of highly successful credited programs for young people who are antipathetic towards schooling, unsuccessful or have 'dropped out' early from formal secondary education.
14. Since 2009, Henry Jenkins has been the Provost's Professor of Communication, Journalism, and Cinematic Arts at the University of Southern California.
15. Many members of the original research team have already published from our project, either singularly or collectively. See, particularly, Baker (2007); Baker, Bennett and Homan (2009); Baker and Cohen (2008); Cohen (2008); Cohen and Baker (2007); Baker and Homan (2007). As the two people who originally conceived of the proposal, Bloustien and Peters decided to take a longer publishing timeframe and provide an in-depth overview of the whole project working with the youth and their adult mentors/trainers and organisational staff.
16. Our definition of 'youth' soon became extended to include young people up to the age of 27. In most countries we discovered this was inscribed into policy concerning activities and programs for young people and seemed to be in recognition of the stretching of the category of adolescence. The term 'disadvantage' was also extended to include both material and psychological difficulties. So, as Geraldine Bloustien had discovered in much of her earlier work (2002, 2003b), there were many young people who were financially secure through parental income but who suffered from other forms of social discrimination, disaffection or exclusion. The notion of youth being socially or culturally 'at risk' of not being able to achieve their full potential seemed to be particularly useful to us as a way of exploring young people's issues.
17. See http://www.acys.info/journal/issues/v26-n4-2007/not_children for Sheila Allison's most recent discussion about the complex definitions of youth and adolescence.
18. The fact that the team were able to reference a twentieth-century Russian artist in this way obviously implies that there was a level of sophistication and education in the group. As detailed in the following chapters, it is clear that one of Carclew's main aims and achievements is to bring together diverse groups of young people from across the city, from a range of socio-economic backgrounds and degrees of cultural capital.
19. Although the project was funded for three years, the study continued after that date as many of the young participants and the organisations wanted to continue the relationship and share their information about their current events and successes. In 2009 complementary follow-up research site visits were made to Newcastle, NSW, London and Berlin to undertake final discussions with the

participants and their mentors and to see what changes had occurred in the CBOs due to the 2008 financial downturn. The financial crisis of 2007–9 has been called the most serious financial crisis since the Great Depression (Pendery, 2009). Its global effects involve the failure of major businesses, declines in consumer wealth, substantial financial debts incurred by governments, and a significant decline in economic activity (see Wood, 2009).

20. Websites unfortunately come and go. However, in 2010 Immune still exists as a very successful band. One of the current websites linked to the band provides the following information:

> This is another great newcastle based band. Immune includes vocalist/guitarist Elliott Lewis, bassist Matt Walker, Drummer Cameron Overend and Lead Guitarist James Overend. Immune Started in 2003, and have been rocking ever since. Immune have been rocking the stages of Newcastle, and leaving the audience wanting more. Immune are a modern/alternative rock style and are very similar to Silverchair, which is really ironic considering Silverchair is a Newcastle band to. These Boys are truely talented, i really love there lyrics. my favourite song would have to be Fallen hero, it is really catchy and FANTAS-TIC lyrics (Fighting to feel Get closer know kneel I wish I had helped you But I wasn't there) (spelling as in the original, http://immune4jinn.tripod.com/id14.html, accessed 3 July 2010).

21. See www.wac.co.uk for more information.

2 Reflections on Theory and Method

1. Rowland has changed his 'professional' name several times over the past seven years, as have many of the young people in our research. His most recent 'stage name' is DJ Roland Samuel without the 'w'.
2. The names of DJ Roland's respondents are pseudonyms as they were not officially participating in this project and so no permission had been sought.
3. Unfortunately, we met Yitz Jordan in Australia towards the end of this project but he was interested in the aims of Playing for Life. He also expressed interest in keeping in contact and introducing us to his own communities of Orthodox Jewish musicians.
4. Accessed 12 August 2010.
5. The political districts Cohen refers to here had been amalgamated from the 23 districts into 12 new ones. Cohen looked at six political districts in his overview.
6. This paragraph was reproduced with the kind permission of Bruce Cohen and Ashgate Publishing.
7. One of the dangers of too narrow a construction is that the young people almost have to prove themselves to be 'underdogs' so that any youth showing initiative and demonstrating successful and effective survival strategies would automatically have to be excluded!
8. This is often resolved by the final text being converged into one narrative where the voice of the researcher incorporates and submerges the views of the respondents in a desire for coherence.
9. While many researchers perhaps would argue that they *are* treating the cultures they are studying as 'fluid, dynamic and experiential', in reality the pressures of deadlines and funding to finalise data collection, complete a project and publish

limit the amount of time in the field and tends to lead to self-fulfilling hypotheses concerning the findings. The authors' longitudinal approach and deliberately open expectations about the youth and their community resources in this project meant that we had to qualify and amend our findings several times over the long research period.

10. There still seems to be some difference of opinion about how much video footage was taken by the young people. For example, Cohen and Baker state in their 2007 publication that two of the young people, Tuesday (DJ Lady Lick) and Monique (DJ Topsy) only used the cameras once each 'in both cases to record a brief autobiographical account' (2007, n.p.). In fact this was not so as both young women produced several tapes of footage taken by themselves and others over the whole research period (2003–6) as well as some additional material later. (Some youth have continued to send material to us to the present day.) Furthermore, as explained in the main text below, many of the young people including Tuesday and Monique used still and video digital footage unsolicited as reflective tools to monitor their improvement and developing technical skills and also publish their own events and distribute on social networking sites.

11. There were many early television shows or social experiments that attempted to portray ordinary people as celebrities in 'unscripted' situations. Here we offer a few key examples, such as Allen Funt's 1948 *Candid Camera* in the US (Candid Camera, n.d.), with other shows quickly following, often using formats such as game shows, competitions and practical jokes that incorporated the audience members themselves as part of the show's 'talent'. Early American radio shows such as *Nightwatch* (night_watch.vintageradioshows.com/) from 1954 to 1955, which audio-recorded the ordinary daily routines of California police officers, and *You Asked For It* (1950–9), in which viewer requests dictated content, also introduced the notion of 'participatory media'. Michael Apted and Paul Almond's groundbreaking British series *Seven Up!* (Granada, 1964) interviewed a number of seven-year-old children from diverse class backgrounds, their responses juxtaposed for dramatic, political and comic effect. Later programs, such as the Dutch series *Nummer 28* (originally screened in 1991), began the device of recording the dramatic conflict that results from putting strangers in a room and seeing what happens. They also pioneered the overt use of soundtrack music and direct-to-camera 'diaries' or 'confessional' segments. As will be shown in the main text below, it is fascinating that this use of ambient, background music was one that all of the young participants incorporated in their own direct-to-camera extracts.

12. More information concerning the Don Snowdon Program can be found at http://www.uoguelph.ca/~snowden/about.html.

13. Because of these attributes PV has been acclaimed as being potentially one of the most effective tools to engage and mobilise the marginalised and disaffected both in the developed, post-industrial countries and in Third World societies. New developments with mobile technologies, such as cell-phone cameras and Web 2 technologies, have allowed this strategy to be more economically viable, to reach more people and offer even more opportunities for implementation of change and sustainable development (see Atton, 2007; Ashley et al., 2009; Willett, 2009a).

14. The first one, which was called *Mirror*, by Gordon Hencher, is still accessible on the BBC website.

15. The website, www.playingforlife.org.au, was active from 2003 to 2009. Many of the images in this book are taken from photographs and videos that were on the website.

16. Of course we have absolutely no control over what the youth place on their own social networking sites – nor should we – but we often seemed more aware than the youth about who else would be able to access these pages and could view them negatively.
17. The 'fly-on-the-wall' documentary portrayed the lives of Noeline Baker and Laurie Donaher from the Sydney waterside suburb of Sylvania Waters over a six-month period. The show focused on the couple's new-found wealth and materialistic lifestyle and also used tight editing to ruthlessly portray the entrenched interpersonal conflicts that lay beneath the surface. The couple's unwed status, Noeline's drinking problem, Laurie's racism, their materialism and the family's routine domestic disputes, all became the subject of gossip and debate in the Australian and British media.
18. The *7.30 Report* current affairs program examined the ethical issues of fly-on-the-wall documentaries. The inevitable naivety and gullibility of non-professional participants often means that the publicly broadcast or screened result is viewed as a 'breach of trust'.
19. It is important to stress again that the use of the word 'staged' points to the fact that we never understood the young people's self-portrayal on camera whether intimately confessional or extremely flamboyant to be somehow an 'authentic portrayal'. Rather it is an attempt at serious play (Schechner, 1993) or mimetic excess (Taussig, 1993) – an attempt to simultaneously play with, negotiate and constitute aspects of their self image (see Bloustien, 2003b for more examples of this use of cameras).
20. Tuesday had been a participant in Bloustien's previous research (2003b) and was still keen to contribute to Playing for Life, which focused far more on her music-making. She introduced us to her wider networks and showed us how she had been developing her music skills and realising her ambitions.
21. The 'Peachey Belt' is a local description for an amalgam of materially deprived council areas that included Playford, Elizabeth and Salisbury – see Chapters 4 and 5.

3 'Everyone Wants to be a DJ'

1. Tuesday is referring to 'God is a DJ' by Pink. Released 26 January 2004, recorded 2003. Label Arista, writer(s) Pink, Jonathan Davis, Billy Mann.
2. Arguably one of the earliest phenomenological accounts of acquiring musical skills is David Sudnow's (1978) self-reflective narration in which he describes learning to become a jazz improviser. Several other more recent studies of the relationship between embodiment and music learning have been written since, as in John Sloboda's (1988) edited collection, Benson (2003), Green (2008a, 2008b) and Clarke and Davidson's (1998) study, as well as Sudnow's own revised narrative in 2001. The authors decided to focus less on the phenomenological description here in this account of our project. Rather we trained our analytic lens on the ways in which the young people *themselves* discussed their own bodily engagement with their music, acquiring their skills and gaining authenticity through learning to master particular motor skills and bodily actions and emulate their musical mentors and idols. Like Sudnow, the youth all learnt to acquire the skills of listening, motor control, fluency and posture. Possibly, more important to note here is that *all* of the youth in our study saw their mastering of skills being more a question of learning how to be an accepted part of their experiential community

rather than just gaining individual expertise. A competent public performance and public recognition was essential, as explained in more detail in the main text.
3. The original research project (1987–9) was funded by the Gulbenkian Foundation to investigate young people's cultural activities in relation to media (radio, TV, magazines, film and so on).
4. A 'found' object, in this context, indicates the use of an object that was not designed for an artistic purpose but for another purpose completely, or it can be a natural object. These objects are discovered by the artist or musician to be capable of being employed in an artistic way, and are designated as 'found' to distinguish them from purposely created items used in the art forms.
5. The previous Palais website has disappeared with the venue. The new website, http://www.theloft.org.au/ does not have the bios of the Breakers.
6. Giddens' comments should be qualified, however, for a distinction needs to be made here between everyday life and media images and discourses. After all, obesity is one of the biggest health issues facing the Western world. Thank you to Larry Grossberg for pointing this out in personal correspondence (2011).
7. Monique was not alone among both men and women who would refer to a woman's perceived lack of common sense or intelligence as being a 'blonde' moment. It refers, of course, to the stereotypical perception of blonde-haired women which has two aspects: that blonde hair in women has historically and almost universally been considered attractive and desirable and secondly, that a blonde woman is often seen as relying on her good looks rather than her intelligence. This has become a popular culture derogatory stereotype so that the physical trait of hair colour in women indicates intelligence (or lack thereof).
8. More on the strangely 'reversed' argot of youth in the text below!
9. Also see the more famous single, with different but equally emotive lyrics, a hip hop and dance song with the same title 'God is a DJ' by Faithless, released on 24 August 1998. The single reached number six in the United Kingdom and also reached number one on the Billboard Hot Dance Club Play chart for one week in September 1998.
10. Recognising that the nature of 'raving' has changed over the last ten tears, Landau is extending the notion of 'raving' to describe a wide range of psychedelic and ecstatic dance events including all-night dancing, electronic music and clubbing (2004, p. 122).
11. For more ideas on the importance of social capital see Smith (2009).
12. http://www.novafm.com.au/nova919/video_the-funkoars-rap-with-tyson-the-15-year-old-rapper_106238, accessed 2 September 2010.

4 Creating Spaces

1. The term 'wigger', also referred to as 'wigga', 'whigger', 'whigga' or 'wegro', means someone who is 'acting black'. It is a pejorative word used for a white person who emulates mannerisms, slang and fashions associated with African-American culture, particularly in relation to hip hop culture and British grime/garage scene. The word brings together the word 'white' together with the derogatory term 'nigger'. It is often considered to be offensive because of its reference to 'nigger' and also for its deliberate questioning of what might be considered 'authentic', particularly in hip hop. See Gilroy (1991); Maxwell and Bambrick (1994); Mitchell (1996); Zuberi (2001); Connor (2003); and Kitwana (2005) for fascinating debates around this topic.

2. This distinction may or may not have been how the youth themselves understood their identity for many may have been second or third generation. On the other hand, because of religious and other cultural divisions, many of the youth who saw themselves as coming from a migrant background wanted to heighten and celebrate this difference through their dress, language, customs and music taste.
3. Drums, like most percussion instruments, used to be considered male instruments requiring particular power and strength and inappropriate for women. However, increasingly more and more young women are learning the instrument, as both a serious and recreational pastime. Several women have become successful professional drummers, including Cindy Blackman (Lenny Kravitz), Meg White (The White Stripes), Torrance Castellano (The Donnas) and Samantha Maloney (Hole), 'proving not only that gender is no longer relevant when it comes to playing the instrument, but also that "hitting like a girl" is no longer the insult it used to be' ('Drumming girls', 2003). Karin Woodley, of course, noted the importance of drumming for girls too in her classes for traditional drumming for Trinidadian youth at the Tabernacle.
4. While we are speaking here of Australian Aboriginal girls in urban settings, we do of course recognise that girls are more vulnerable and have less access to education, support systems and health than their male counterparts in countries around the globe. The problem is obviously more acute in developing countries where poverty is greatest and women have been historically marginalised.

   The social exclusion of girls has consequences at the country level. Even when national economies grow, excluded groups are left behind. Social isolation and relative economic deprivation are associated with poorer mental health, especially among females, and can further reduce the ability of excluded individuals to be productive members of society (Patel and Kleinman, 2003). As the gap between the poor and non-poor increases, poverty becomes deeper and more intractable (Hallman and Roca, 2007).
5. We visited Statthaus Böcklerpark five times over the period of the fieldwork and recorded several interviews with Wolfgang and his colleagues. The interviews, as in many of the Berlin youth centres and clubs, were conducted in a mixture of English and German. The German sections were translated by Bruce Cohen, Jessica Terruhn and Anna Steigemann. In July 2010 we learnt that the centre had been suddenly closed down. See the end of this chapter for more details.
6. The name 'crab' seems self-explanatory since it is performed when all of the DJ's fingers are curled making the hand look like a crab. One account from popular DJ history records that the crab scratch was invented by DJ Qbert as a variation on DJ Excel's 'twiddle'. Another account of the move's origin comes from Qbert himself. He argues that he and Mix Master Mike had just returned from Beirut, Lebanon where they had been served crepes one night after a show. When people in Beirut pronounced the word 'crepe' like 'cccccreb' Qbert said he used the same word to name the 'cccccreb' scratch which everyone now pronounces as the crab. The flare scratch was discovered/invented by DJ Flare and further developed most famously by DJ Qbert. The discovery and development of the flare scratch was instrumental in elevating this art form to the level of speed and technical scratching that is common today (http://www.cs.ubc.ca/~tbeamish/djtaxonomy/scratching.html. Information was originally sourced by Julie, 6 December 2004, and was later accessed online 10 March 2010).
7. This fascinating blurring of childhood and adult worlds that the 'Transformers quilt' suggests was one we found in many homes – note the photo that heads

this chapter where a stuffed toy rubs shoulders quite comfortably with the vinyl record stacks, sophisticated recording equipment and mixing decks of Mario's adult aspirations.
8. The further links of this article cover the biographies and attitudes of some of the youth hanging out at Alex: Energy, Melanie, Kevin, Speedo, Borste, Makke, Marcel, Flashy, Nicki.
9. Clearly, CBOs like Shep's Da Klinic, which is very much grassroots, do not have such a rationale or mission statement behind them. Yet even Shep will use such official discourse when speaking to potential government or educational sponsors or clients. See Chapter 6.
10. Even places of worship were never open to all, however well intentioned, but rather were accessible to those willing to accept a particular doctrine or set of beliefs. The Tabernacle (Photo 4.5), originally known as The Talbot Tabernacle, was founded as an evangelical Christian church in 1869 by the former barrister Gordon Furlong to serve as a 'non-sectarian Church of Christ'.
11. Indent was founded at the 1996 Drug Summit. One of the many outcomes of the summit was the development of a Youth Entertainment Pilot Project (YEP) to promote developments in government policy relating to the staging of under 18s and all ages events and drug and alcohol-free entertainment. Music NSW held a forum at the Powerhouse Museum on 27 November 1999 that brought together 120 young people from around NSW who were actively involved in youth events. The discussion at the forum led ultimately to the formation of the first Indent strategy. The strategy was well received and Indent was officially engaged with an initial financial commitment of $750,000 over three years ($250,000 a year). The name Indent comes from the words INDependent ENTertainment. Indent works directly with young people to empower them and help raise awareness of their needs, connecting them with support organisations in their community, providing opportunities, training and valuable experience and involving them in a range of tasks such as booking venues, liaising with police, managing security, organising public liability insurance, advertising and promotion (information from the Indent website, accessed 23 July 2010, http://www.indent.net.au/about/).
12. Genuine Voices runs or formerly ran programs in the following facilities: the Judge Connelly Youth Center – a 'hardware-secure long-term treatment' for the Department of Youth Services, Metro Region of Boston; Metro Youth Service Center; Boys and Girls Club Dorchester; and Skagit Valley YMCAs. See http://genuinevoices.com/ for more information.
13. The main instruments such as guitars, keyboards, the CD player, microphones, computer equipment and djembes (skin-covered hand drums) were kept locked in a cabinet in the library/meeting room between lessons.

5 Money Matters: Government Policy, Funding and Youth Music

1. The National Foundation for Youth Music (Youth Music) was founded by DCMS in 1999 to encourage innovative ideas and, as a complement to the Department for Education and Employment's (DfES) Standards Fund initiative, to extend access to music-making for young people. Youth Music is a delegate distributor of lottery money for Arts Council England, and also raises funds from other sources. In addition to its role in attracting and distributing funds to achieve its objectives,

it also acts as a national advocate to raise the profile of music education activities for young people. Working as an independent body, but in collaboration with others, including central government agencies, Youth Music champions the cause of young people's music making through a range of programs, including Youth Music Action Zones, Open Programs, Partnership Programs and Special Initiatives.
2. Triple J is the Australian Broadcasting Commission's youth radio and television station.
3. *Unearthed* is the name of a Triple J project to find and 'dig up' hidden musical talent in regional Australia. In its first stage *Unearthed* visited each region of Australia where Triple J had a transmitter, which was 41 regions in all. Beginning with the more rural areas it eventually also covered the capital cities. The second stage lasted from 2002 to 2005, where *Unearthed* visited each state only once but then featured *Unearthed* live music clips on *Rage*, Fly TV, ABC Local Radio and Radio National, providing important exposure for the young music artists. In 2006 the format became a more internet-driven competition, where the artists are now required to upload their music in MP3 format to be judged.

6 Becoming Phat: Youth, Music and Micro-Enterprise

1. Possibly inspired by the recent spate of reality TV programs that are based on singing or dancing performance (such as *X Factor* or the Australian, American and British *Idol* series) and the popularity of karaoke, Rockaoke offers the opportunity for audience members to sing publicly accompanied by a live band. As it is a competition (prizes are awarded to the best entertainer) most participants prepare for the night well ahead by selecting a song they know well from a provided list of classic rock, pop and country and memorising the lyrics. Each participant joins the live band on stage for 3 or 4 minutes with the onus being on the individual singer to perform and to entertain an audience. No autocues are used but lyric sheets are provided. Some bands only focus on performing Rockaoke sessions knowing it is a lucrative form of performance for them and an opportunity to have their music and style recognised widely.
2. Steffan 'Mr Wiggles' Clemente is a member of both the Rock Steady Crew and the Electric Boogal; hip hop dancer Hokuto 'Hok' Konishi is a member of both Quest Crew and Lux Aeterna dance company; Kate Prince, choreographer on *So You Think You Can Dance* (UK) is the founder and director of Zoo Nation. See Asante (2008), Chang (2005) and Kugelberg (2007).
3. Shep had said the same to me in direct communication several times but this particular statement is taken from a media interview, posted on Catapult website (http://www.abc.net.au/catapult/stories/s1260352.htm, accessed 12 February 2006). Catapult is the Australian Broadcasting Corporation's website to disseminate news about creative enterprise especially by young people. It also aims to serve as a forum and discussion board where young entrepreneurs can communicate and network.
4. See juripop.com for more information about Juri.
5. Sting, born Gordon Matthew Thomas Sumner (2 October 1951) is an English musician, singer-songwriter, activist, actor and philanthropist. His work was recognised by induction into the Songwriters Hall of Fame. In 2004, Sting was also awarded the British honour of Order of the British Empire (OBE). Before becoming a solo act, Sting was the principal songwriter, lead singer and bassist of the rock band The Police (http://www.sting.com/, accessed 5 November 2010).

6. Taken from field notes and personal correspondence. Some of Tuesday's story appears in Bloustien (2003b).
7. Tuesday here in the email repeated the mantra which had headed her profile page. It is obviously something that she considers to be significant.
8. Accessed May 2004.
9. Accessed 13 March 2006.
10. See www.junkcentral.com for more information about RGIT and other related projects.

7 Taking Flight: Creative Cultures and Beyond

1. The whole rap is available on the Genuine Voices website, under the audio title 'Smooth' (http://www.genuinevoices.com/audiovideo).
2. The names of the youth in detention or residential care are pseudonyms to protect confidentiality, in accordance with the legal and ethical requirements of the government departments.
3. Darren Henley, who joined the radio station in 1992, has worked closely with music educators, ministers and civil servants as Chairman of the Music Manifesto Partnership and Advocacy Group, and as Chairman of the Tune In Legacy Group. He also sat on the Conservative Party's Independent Review of Creative Industries (Department for Education).
4. In July 2010, Prime Minister David Cameron launched the coalition government's 'The Big Society', promoted as the flagship UK government policy. The idea is centred on giving voluntary groups and communities power to run public services, transferring power from the state to individuals. The response has been both negative and positive from all sides of the political spectrum, although the main concern expressed by media commentators seems to be the vagueness of the policy. See Beard (2010).
5. In February 2009, the Office for Standards in Education, Children's Services and Skills (Ofsted) published a report entitled *Making More of Music* based principally on evidence from inspections of music in a range of schools in England between 2005 and 2008.
6. We had already learnt about the key role of Youth Music as a major funding and advisory body during our investigation of CBOs in the UK (see Chapter 5 for more background information). The organisation was established in 1999 to address a major deficit in music provision for children and young people. It has been instrumental in driving change in the landscape of musical opportunity for young people over the past decade and is still a leading advocate for the advancement and greater funding of music education. See Youth Music (2009).
7. Green Day is an American punk rock band formed in 1987 and still very active today.
8. Alexis lives on a small wooden boat at Lady Gertrude South Dock Marina within a small community. Having moved from a home on land to the boat on water originally to save money, Alexis noted that in such environments the real meaning of community can flourish and develop.
9. The SOS Bus was set up in April 2001, building on an earlier Home Safe and Sound project. The catalyst was the deaths of two young men who both drowned after separate nights out in the city. The scheme used a 55-foot Mercedes bus built in 1980 from Berlin (Briscoe, 2009).
10. http://www.facebook.com/group.php?gid=7705051159&v=info.

11. The Paul Hamlyn Foundation funded a large-scale research project in Britain entitled Musical Futures, which began in 2003. The researchers engaged in the study described 'informal pedagogy' as the methodology of teaching and learning used by pop musicians in their music-making. It advocated a similar model to be used in school music education. We have similarly described the ways in which the youth in our project transferred and shared knowledge.
12. From the TINA 2005 website, http://www.thisisnotart.org/Program/Festivals Projects/Strike/tabid/93/Default.aspx, accessed 29 September 2005. This Is Not Art (TINA) began in 1998 as the National Young Writers Festival and the National Student Media Conference in Newcastle, New South Wales. Supported by and organised from the Octapod Association, these two events take place in the week after the Newcastle Fringe Festival. The TINA festival now takes place every year and it is still regarded by the youth at the Loft as an important forum for them to perform, observe the best in their field and measure their skills against others.

References

Abdelhadi, A. (2004) 'Surviving Siege, Closure and Curfew: The Story of a Radio Station', *Journal of Palestinian Studies*, 34(1): 51–67.
Adler, P. A. and Adler, P. (1987) *Membership Roles in Field Research* (Beverley Hills, CA: Sage).
Adoranti, K. (2009) 'Newcastle Loft Could be Lost', *Newcastle Star*, 6 May, http://www.newcastlestar.com.au/news/local/news/general/newcastle-loft-could-be-lost/1504765.aspx [accessed 5 August 2010].
Allison, S. (1999) 'How Young and Old are Youth?', *Youth Studies Australia*, 18(3): 2.
Appadurai, A. (1996) *Modernity at Large: Cultural Dimensions of Globalization* (Minneapolis: University of Minnesota Press).
Ardener, S. (ed.) (1993) *Women and Space: Ground Rules and Social Maps* (Oxford: Berg).
Arnett, J. and Tanner, J. (eds) (2005) *Emerging Adulthood in America: Coming of Age in the 21st Century* (Washington: American Psychological Association).
Asante, Jr, M. K. (2008) *It's Bigger Than Hip Hop: The Rise of the Post-Hip-Hop Generation* (New York: St Martin's Press).
Asch, T. (1992) 'The Ethics of Ethnographic Film Making', in P. Crawford and D. Turton (eds), *Film as Ethnography* (Manchester: Manchester University Press).
Ashley, H., Corbett, J., Garside, B. and Rambaldi, G. (2009) 'Change at Hand: Web 2.0 for Development', *Participatory Learning and Action*, 59(1): 8–20.
Atay, T. (2010) '"Ethnicity within Ethnicity" Among the Turkish-Speaking Immigrants in London', *Insight Turkey*, 12(1): 123–38.
Attali, J. (1985) *Noise: The Political Economy of Music*, trans B. Massumi (Minneapolis: University of Minnesota Press).
Atton, C. (2007) 'A Brief History: The Web and Interactive Media', in K. Cover, T. Dowmunt and A. Fountain (eds), *The Alternative Media Handbook* (London: Routledge).
Back, L. (1988) 'Coughing Up Fire: Sound Systems in South East London', *New Formations*, 5: 141–53.
Baker, S. (2001) 'Rock On, Baby! Pre-teen Girls and Popular Music', *Continuum: Journal of Media and Cultural Studies*, 15(3): 359–71.
Baker, S. (2007) 'Young People and Community Radio in the Northern Region of Adelaide, South Australia', *Popular Music and Society*, 30(5): 575–90.
Baker, S. and Cohen, B. (2008) 'From Snuggling and Snogging to Sampling and Scratching: Girls' (non-) Participation in Community-Based Music Activities', *Youth & Society*, 30(3): 316–39.
Baker, S. and Homan, S. (2007) 'Rap, Recidivism and the Creative Self: A Popular Music Programme for Young Offenders in Detention', *Journal of Youth Studies*, 10(4): 459–76.
Baker, S., Bennett, A. and Homan, S. (2009) 'Cultural Precincts, Creative Spaces: Giving the Local a Musical Spin?', *Space and Culture*, 12(2): 148–65.
Balint, A. (2010) 'Piracy Goes Kosher', *Index on Censorship*, 39(2): 112–16.
Banks, M. (2001) *Visual Methods in Social Research* (London: Sage).

Barthes, R. (1977) *Image, Music, Text* (New York: Hill and Wang).
Bateson, G. (1982 [1972]) *Steps to an Ecology of the Mind: Collected Essays in Anthropology, Psychiatry, Evolution, and Epistemology* (New York: Ballantine).
Battaglia, D. (ed.) (1995) *The Rhetorics of Self-Making* (Berkeley: University of California Press).
Battaglia, D. (1999) 'Toward an Ethics of the Open Subject: Writing Culture in Good Conscience', in H. Moore (ed.), *Anthropological Theory Today* (Cambridge: Polity Press).
Bauman, Z. (1998) *Work, Consumerism and the New Poor* (Buckingham: Open University Press).
Baumeister, R. F. (1986) *Identity, Cultural Change and the Struggle for Self* (New York: Oxford University Press).
Beard, M. ('Cassandra') (2010) 'Big Society: Cassandra Speaks', *The Times*, 19 July.
Beattie, K. (2004) *Documentary Screens: Non-fiction Film and Television* (Basingstoke and New York: Palgrave Macmillan).
Beaujot, R. and Kerr, J. (2007) *Emerging Youth Transition Patterns in Canada: Opportunities and Risks*, discussion paper (Ottawa: Policy Research Initiative).
Benjamin, W. (1978) *Reflections* (New York: Harcourt, Brace, Jovanovich).
Bennett, A. (1997) 'Bhangra in Newcastle: Music, Ethnic Identity and the Role of Local Knowledge', *Innovation: The European Journal of the Social Sciences*, 10(1): 107–16.
Bennett, A. (1998) 'The Frankfurt Rockmobil: A New Insight into the Significance of Music Making for Young People', *Youth and Policy*, 60: 16–29.
Bennett, A. (1999) 'Subcultures or Neo-Tribes? Rethinking the Relationship between Youth, Style and Musical Taste', *Sociology*, 33(3): 599–617.
Bennett, A. (2000) *Popular Music and Youth Culture: Music, Identity and Place* (Basingstoke: Macmillan).
Bennett, A. (2001) *Cultures of Popular Music* (Buckingham: Open University Press).
Bennett, A. (2008) 'Popular Music, Media and the Narrativisation of Place', in G. Bloustien, M. Peters and S. Luckman (eds), *Sonic Synergies: Music, Technology, Community and Identity* (Aldershot: Ashgate).
Benson, B. E. (2003) *The Improvisation of Musical Dialogue: A Phenomenology of Music* (Cambridge: Cambridge University Press).
Bentley, T. (2002 [1998]) *Learning Beyond the Classroom: Education for a Changing World* (London: DEMOS/Routledge).
Berger, J. and Heath, C. (2008) 'Who Drives Divergence? Identity Signalling, Outgroup Dissimilarity and the Abandonment of Cultural Tastes', *Journal of Personality and Social Psychology*, 5(3): 593–607.
Bessant, J. and Hil, R. (1997) *Youth Crime and the Media: Media Representations of and Reactions to Young People in Relation to Law and Order* (Hobart: Australian Clearinghouse for Youth Studies).
Best, S. and Kellner, D. (2003) 'Contemporary Youth and the Postmodern Adventure', *Review of Education, Pedagogy/Cultural Studies*, 25(2): 75–93.
Bey, H. (1991 [1985]) *T.A.Z.: The Temporary Autonomous Zone, Ontological Anarchy, Poetic Terrorism* (Brooklyn: Autonomedia).
Bianchini, F. (1995) 'Night Cultures, Night Economies', *Planning Practice*, 10(2): 121–6.
Bloustien, G. (1996) 'Striking Poses: Teenage Girls, Video Cams and the Exploration of Cultural Space', *Youth Studies Australia*, 15(3): 26–32.
Bloustien, G. (1998) 'It's Different to a Mirror 'cos it Talks to You', in S. Howard (ed.), *Wired Up: Young People and Electronic Media* (London: Falmer Press).

Bloustien, G. (1999) 'The Consequences of Being a Gift', *The Australian Journal of Anthropology*, 10(1): 77–93.
Bloustien, G. (2000) 'Why Mary Loves Reggae and Grace Adores Violent Femmes: Family, Fandom, Fantasy and Forays into Popular Taste', in T. Mitchell, P. Doyle and B. Johnson (eds), *Changing Sounds: Proceedings from IASPM – The International Association for the Study of Popular Music 10th International Conference, 9–13 July 1999* (Sydney: Faculty of Humanities and Social Sciences, University of Technology).
Bloustien, G. (2002) 'Ceci n'est pas une Jeune Fille: Videocams, Representation and Othering in the Lives of Teenage Girls', in H. Jenkins, J. Shattuc and T. McPherson (eds), *Hop on Pop: The Politics and Pleasures of Popular Culture* (Durham and London: Duke University Press).
Bloustien, G. (ed.) (2003a) *Envisioning Ethnography: Exploring the Meanings of the Visual in Research* (New York and London: Berghahn Journals).
Bloustien, G. (2003b) *Girl Making: A Cross-Cultural Ethnography of Growing up Female* (New York: Berghahn Books).
Bloustien, G. (2004a) 'Buffy Night at The Seven Stars: A "Subcultural" Happening at the "Glocal" Level', in A. Bennett and K. Harris (eds), *After Subculture: Critical Studies in Contemporary Youth Culture* (Basingstoke: Palgrave Macmillan).
Bloustien, G. (2004b) 'Still Picking Children from the Trees: Reimagining Woodstock in Twenty-First-Century Australia', in A. Bennett (ed.), *Remembering Woodstock* (Aldershot: Ashgate).
Bloustien, G. (2008) 'Up the Down Staircase: Grassroots Entrepreneurship in Young People's Music Practices', in G. Bloustien, M. Peters and S. Luckman (eds), *Sonic Synergies: Music, Technology, Community, Identity* (Aldershot: Ashgate).
Bloustien, G. and Peters, M. (2003) 'Playing For Life: New Approaches to Researching Youth and their Music Practices', *Youth Studies Australia*, 22(2): 32–9.
Bloustien, G. and Wood, D. (forthcoming) 'Can I Borrow Your Face for a Minute?', *Body and Society*.
Bloustien, G., Peters, M. and Luckman, S. (eds) (2008) *Sonic Synergies: Music, Technology, Community, Identity* (Aldershot: Ashgate).
Bolton, M. (2006) *The Isle of Thanet: Its History, People and Buildings* (Bolton, UK: Jane Black).
Bordo, S. (1993) *Unbearable Weight: Feminism, Western Culture and the Body* (Berkeley, CA: University of California Press).
Bourdieu, P. (1977) *Outline of a Theory of Practice* (Cambridge: Cambridge University Press).
Bourdieu, P. (1982) *Ce Que Parler Veut Dire: L'économie des Échanges Linquistiques* (Paris: Arthème Fayard).
Bourdieu, P. (1984) *Distinction: A Social Critique of the Judgement of Taste* (Cambridge, MA: Harvard University Press).
Bourdieu, P. (1986) 'The Forms of Capital', in J. G. Richardson (ed.), *Handbook for Theory and Research for the Sociology of Education* (New York: Greenwood Press).
Bourdieu, P. (1989) 'Social Space and Symbolic Power', *Sociological Theory*, 7: 14–24.
Bourdieu, P. (1990) *In Other Words* (Cambridge: Polity Press).
Bourdieu, P. (1991) *Language and Symbolic Power* (London: Sage).
Bourdieu, P. (1992) *The Logic of Practice* (Cambridge: Polity Press).
Bourdieu, P. (1993) *Sociology in Question* (London: Sage).
Bourdieu, P. (1998) *Practical Reason: On the Theory of Action* (Cambridge: Polity Press).
Bourdieu, P. (1999) *The Weight of the World: Social Suffering in Contemporary Society* (Oxford: Polity Press).

Bourdieu, P. and Wacquant, L. (1992) *An Invitation to Reflexive Sociology* (Chicago: University of Chicago Press).
Boyte, H. and Evans, S. (1992) *Free Spaces: The Sources of Democratic Change in America* (Chicago: University of Chicago Press).
Brewster, B. and Broughton, F. (2000) *Last Night a DJ Saved My Life: The History of the Disc Jockey* (New York: Grove Press).
Briscoe, K. (2009) 'On a Mission to help Norfolk's Youngsters', *Eastern Daily Press*, 7 November, p. 25, http://www.open247.org.uk/about-open/press-releases [accessed 21 November 2010].
Bruner, I. I. and Gordon, C. (1990) 'Music, Mood and Marketing', *Journal of Marketing*, 54(4): 94–104.
Bruns, A. (2008) *Blogs, Wikipedia, Second Life and Beyond: From Production to Produsage* (New York: Peter Lang).
Bryson, B. (1996) 'Anything but Heavy Metal: Symbolic Exclusion and Musical Dislikes', *American Sociological Review*, 61: 884–99.
Buckingham, D. (2000) *After the Death of Childhood: Growing Up in the Age of Electronic Media* (London: Polity Press).
Buckingham, D. and McFarlane, A. (2001) *A Digitally Driven Curriculum?* (London: IPPR).
Buckingham, D. and Scanlon, M. (2003) *Education, Entertainment and Learning in the Home* (Buckingham: Open University Press).
Buckingham, D. and Sefton-Green, J. (1994) *Cultural Studies goes to School: Reading and Teaching Popular Media* (London: Taylor & Francis).
Buckingham, D. and Willet, R. (eds) (2009) *Video Cultures: Media Technology and Everyday Creativity* (Basingstoke: Palgrave Macmillan).
Buckingham, D., Pini, M. and Willett, R. (2009) '"Take Back The Tube!" The Discursive Construction of Amateur Film and Video Making', in D. Buckingham and R. Willett (eds), *Video Cultures: Media Technology and Everyday Creativity* (Basingstoke: Palgrave Macmillan).
Burawoy, M. (2003) 'Revisits: An Outline of a Theory of Reflexive Ethnography', *American Sociological Review*, 68(5): 645–79.
Burgess, J. and Hartley, J. (2005) 'Digital Storytelling: New Literacy, New Audiences', paper presented at *MiT4: The Work of Stories, 4th Media in Transition Conference*, MIT, Cambridge, MA, May.
Burt, K. (2009) 'The Kids are Alright', *The Independent Life*, 23 November, http://www.open247.org.uk/media/dContent/mediaCentre/About-OPEN/News-Articles/11.23.09---independant---the-kids-are-alright.pdf [accessed 30 July 2010].
Bynner, J. (2005) 'Rethinking the Youth Phase of the Life-Course: The Case for Emerging Adulthood?', *Journal of Youth Studies*, 8(4): 367–84.
Cabinet Office, UK (2010) *Building the Big Society*, http://www.cabinetoffice.gov.uk/media/407789/building-big-society.pdf [accessed 12 August 2010].
Candid Camera (n.d.) *About Candid Camera: Allen Funt 1914–1999*, http://www.candidcamera.com/cc2/cc2e.html [accessed 4 December 2009].
Caputo, T. (1999) *Hearing the Voices of Youth: A Review of Research and Consultation Documents. Final Report* (Ottawa: Division of Childhood and Adolescence, Public Health Agency of Canada).
Caputo, V. (1995) 'Anthropology's Silent "Others"', in H. Wulff and V. Amit-Talai (eds), *Youth Cultures* (London: Routledge).
Carpentier, N. (2003) 'The BBC's Video Nation as a Participatory Media Practice: Signifying Everyday Life, Cultural Diversity and Participation in an Online Community', *International Journal of Cultural Studies*, 6: 425–47.

Chang, J. (2005) *Can't Stop Won't Stop: A History of the Hip-Hop Generation* (New York: St Martin's Press).
Chapman, R. (1990) 'The 1960s Pirates: A Comparative Analysis of Radio London and Radio Caroline', *Popular Music*, 9(2): 165–78.
Chatterton, P. and Hollands, R. (2002) 'Theorising Urban Playscapes: Producing, Regulating and Consuming Youthful Nightlife City Spaces', *Urban Studies*, 39(1): 95–116.
Childress, H. (2004) 'Teenagers, Territory and the Appropriation of Space', *Childhood*, 11(2): 195–205.
Chisholm, L. (2006) 'European Youth Research: Development, Debates, Demands', *New Directions for Child and Adolescent Development*, 113: 11–21.
Christie, E. and Bloustien, G. (2010) 'I-Cyborg: Disability, Affect and Public Pedagogy', *CDIS: Discourse: Studies in the Cultural Politics of Education*, 31(3): 483–98.
Cialdini, R. B., Borden, R. J., Thorne, A., Walker, M. R., Freeman, S. and Sloan, L. R. (1976) 'Basking in Reflected Glory: Three (Football) Field Studies', *Journal of Personality and Social Psychology*, 34: 366–75.
Cicchelli, V. and Martin, C. (2004) 'Young Adults in France: Becoming Adult in the Context of Increased Autonomy and Dependency', *Journal of Comparative Family Studies*, 35(4): 615–26.
City of Playford (2002) *Strategic Plan* (South Australia: City of Playford).
Clark, J., Dyson, A., Meagher, N., Robson, E. and Wootten, M. (2001a) 'Involving Young People in Research: The Issues', in J. Clark, A. Dyson, N. Meagher, E. Robson and M. Wootten (eds), *Young People as Researchers* (Leicester: Youth Work Press).
Clark, J., Dyson, A., Meagher, N., Robson, E. and Wootten, M. (eds) (2001b) *Young People as Researchers* (Leicester: Youth Work Press).
Clark, W. (2007) 'Delayed Transitions of Young Adults', *Canadian Social Trends*, no. 84, catalogue no. 11-008-XPE.
Clarke, E. F. and Davidson, J. W. (1998) 'The Body in Performance', in W. Thomas (ed.), *Composition-Performance-Reception* (Aldershot: Ashgate).
Cohen, B. (2007) 'Education, Work and Identity: Young Turkish Migrants in Germany and Young Pakistani Migrants in England', in T. Geisen and C. Riegel (eds), *Jugend, Partizipation und Migration: Orientierungen im Kontext von Integration und Ausgrenzung* (Wiesbaden: VS Verlag).
Cohen, B. (2008) 'Ethnic and Social Differences in Music Behaviour in a Fragmented Berlin', in G. Bloustien, M. Peters and S. Luckman (eds), *Sonic Synergies: Music, Technology, Community, Identity* (Aldershot: Ashgate).
Cohen, B. and Baker, S. (2007) 'DJ Pathways: Becoming a DJ in Adelaide and London', *Altitude*, 8, http://thealtitudejournal.org/2007/12/03/volume-8-popular-music-practices-formations-and-change-australian-perspectives-2007/ [accessed 20 May 2010].
Cohen, S. (1991) *Rock Culture in Liverpool* (Oxford: Clarendon Press).
Cohen, S. (1994) 'Identity, Place and the "Liverpool Sound"', in M. Stokes (ed.), *Ethnicity, Identity and Music: The Musical Construction of Place* (Oxford: Berg).
Coleman, R. (2008) 'The Becoming of Bodies: Girls, Media Effects, and Body Image', *Feminist Media Studies*, 8(2): 63–79.
Coles, B. (2006) 'Holistic and Joined-Up Youth Policy Thinking and Practice in the UK', paper presented at PRI Seminar on Canadian and International Perspectives on Youth Policy and Research, Ottawa, December.
Comedia (1991) *Out of Hours: A Study of Economic Social and Cultural Life in Twelve Town Centres in the UK* (Stroud: Comedia Consultancy).

Connell, J. and Gibson, C. (2003) *Sound Tracks: Popular Music, Identity and Place* (London: Routledge).
Connor, B. (2003) 'Good Buddha and Tzu: Middle-Class Wiggers from the Underside', *Youth Studies Australia*, 22(2): 48–53.
Cook, N. (2003) 'Music as Performance', in M. Clayton, T. Herbert and R. Middleton (eds), *The Cultural Study of Music: A Critical Introduction* (London and New York: Routledge).
Coote, A. (2010) 'Cameron's "Big Society" Will Leave the Poor and Powerless Behind', *Guardian Newspaper*, 19 July, http://www.guardian.co.uk/commentisfree/2010/july19/big-society-cameron-equal-opp [accessed 25 September 2010].
Corness, G. (2008) 'The Musical Experience Through the Lens of Embodiment', *Leonardo Music Journal*, 18: 21–4.
Crane, P. (1999) 'Young People and Public Space: Developing Inclusive Policy and Practice', *Scottish Youth Issues Journal*, 1(2): 105–24.
Cranpanzano, V. (1986) 'Hermes' Dilemma: The Masking of Subversion in Ethnographic Description', in J. Clifford and G. E. Marcus (eds), *Writing Culture: The Poetics and Politics of Ethnography* (Berkeley: University of California Press).
Crawford, A. and Flint, J. (2009) 'Urban Safety, Anti-Social Behaviour and the Night-Time Economy', *Criminology and Criminal Justice*, 9(4): 403–13.
Cross, B. (1993) *It's Not About a Salary: Rap, Race and Resistance in Los Angeles* (London: Verso).
Crossley, N. (2011) *Towards Relational Sociology* (London and New York: Routledge).
Crowe, D. (2003) 'Objectivity, Photography, and Ethnography', *Cultural Studies ⇔ Critical Methodologies*, 3(4): 470–85.
Csordas, T. (1994) *Embodiment and Experience* (Cambridge: Cambridge University Press).
Dacre, R. (2010) 'Our Story: About Open', Open Youth Trust website, http://www.open247.org.uk/about-open/our-story [accessed 21 November 2010].
'David Cameron Launches Tories' "Big Society" Plan' (2010) *BBC online*, 19 July, http://www.bbc.co.uk/news/uk-10680062 [accessed 12 August 2010].
Dawson, G. (1994) *Soldier Heroes: British Adventure, Empire and the Imagining of Masculinities* (London and New York: Routledge).
De Frantz, T. (2001) *Dancing Many Drums: Excavations in African-American Dance* (Madison: University of Wisconsin Press).
De Frantz, T. (2004) *Dancing Revelations: Alvin Ailey's Embodiment of African American Culture* (Oxford: Oxford University Press).
de Laine, M. (2000) *Fieldwork, Participation and Practice: Ethics and Dilemmas in Qualitative Research* (London: Sage).
Delamont, S. (2009) 'The Only Honest Thing: Autoethnography, Reflexivity and Small Crises in Fieldwork', *Ethnography and Education*, 4(1): 51–63.
Delaney, K., Prodigalidad, M. and Sanders, J. (2002) 'Young People and Public Space', Workshop presented at NCOSS 'Scales of Justice' Conference, Sydney, 24 July.
Deleuze, G. and Guattari, F. (2004) *A Thousand Plateaus: Capitalism and Schizophrenia* (London: Continuum).
Delgado, M. (2004) *Social Youth Entrepreneurship: The Potential for Youth and Community Transformation* (Westport, CT: Praeger).
DeNora, T. (2000) *Music in Everyday Life* (Cambridge: Cambridge University Press).
Department for Education (UK) (2010) *Education Secretary Michael Grove Announces Review of Music Education*, press notice, 24 September, http://www.education.gov.uk/

inthenews/pressnotices/a0064925/education-secretary-michael-gove-announces-review-of-music-education [accessed 24 November 2010].
Deutsch, E. (1993) 'The Concept of the Body', in T. Kasulis (ed.), *Self as Body in Asian Theory and Practice* (New York: State University of New York Press).
Dimitriadis, G. (2000) '"Making History Go" at a Local Community Centre: Popular Media and the Construction of Historical Knowledge Among African-American Youth', *Theory and Research in Social Education*, 28: 40–64.
Dimitriadis, G. (2001) *Performing Identity/Performing Culture: Hip Hop as Text, Pedagogy and Lived Practice* (New York: Peter Lang).
Dimitriadis, G. and Weis, L. (2001) 'Imagining Possibilities With and For Contemporary Youth: (Re)Writing and (Re)Visioning Education Today', *Qualitative Research*, 1: 223–40.
Doward, J. and Hinsliff, G. (2004) 'British Hostility to Muslims "Could Trigger Riots"', *The Observer*, 30 May, http://www.guardian.co.uk/uk/2004/may/30/race.religion [accessed 15 September 2010].
Dowmunt, T. (ed.) (1993) *Channels of Resistance: Global Television and Local Empowerment* (London: BFI Publishing with Channel 4).
Draper, P. (2007) 'Music Two-Point-Zero: How Participatory Culture is Re-claiming Knowledge, Power and Value Systems from the Inside Out', http://www.29.griffith.edu.au/radioimersd/images/stories/draper_091007_twilight_lecture.pdf [accessed 20 November 2007].
Dreilinger, D. (2010) 'Music for Life', *Berklee News*, 13 July.
'Drumming girls' trend supported by drum industry' (2003) *Pro-Music-News*, http://pro-music-news.com/html/09/e30918dr.htm [accessed 24 June 2010].
Dunbar-Hall, P. and Gibson, C. (2004) *Deadly Sounds, Deadly Places: Contemporary Aboriginal Music in Australia* (Sydney: University of NSW Press).
Duncan, N. (1996) 'Renegotiating Gender and Sexuality in Public and Private Spaces', in N. Duncan (ed.), *Bodyspace: Destabilising Geographies of Gender and Sexuality* (London: Routledge).
Dutton, K. R. (1995) *The Perfectible Body: The Western Ideal of Male Physical Development* (New York: Continuum).
Edwards, V. (2003) 'Youth Message in the Air', *News Review Messenger*, 10 December, 1(4).
European Group for Integrated Social Research (EGRIS) (2001) 'Misleading Trajectories: Transition Dilemmas of Young Adults in Europe', *Journal of Youth Studies*, 4(1): 101–18.
Evans, K. and Furlong, A. (1997) 'Metaphors of Youth Transitions: Niches, Pathways, Trajectories and Navigations', in J. Bynner, L. Chisholm and A. Furlong (eds), *Youth, Citizenship and Social Change in a European Context* (Aldershot: Avebury).
'Facing the Music in Cunnamulla' (2001) *7.30 Report*, Australian Broadcasting Corporation website, 22 January, http://www.abc.net.au/7.30/stories/s236397.htm [accessed 4 December 2009].
Fangen, K. (2007) 'Breaking Up the Different Constituting Parts of Ethnicity: The Case of Young Somalis in Norway', *Acta Sociologica*, 50: 401–14.
Featherstone, M. (2010) 'Body, Image and Affect in Consumer Culture', *Body and Society*, 16: 193–221.
Featherstone, M., Hepworth, M. and Turner, B. (eds) (1991) *The Body: Social Process and Cultural Theory* (London: Sage).
Ferrell, J. (2001) 'Free Radio: Caught Between Community Service and Criminalized Activity, Pirate Microbroadcasters are Challenging Authority', *Alternatives Journal*, 27(2): 10–15.

Fine, M. and Weis, L. (1998) *The Unknown City: Lives of Poor and Working-Class Young Adults* (New York: Beacon).
Fine, M. and Weis, L. (2000) *Construction Sites: Excavating Race, Class and Gender Among Urban Youth* (New York: Teachers College Press).
Fine, M., Weis, L., Centrie, C. and Roberts, R. (2000) 'Educating Beyond the Borders of Schooling', *Anthropology and Education Quarterly*, 31: 131–51.
Finnegan, R. (1998) *Tales of the City: A Study of Narrative and Urban Life* (Cambridge and New York: Cambridge University Press).
Finney, J. (2003) 'From Resentment to Enchantment: What a Class of Thirteen Year Olds and Their Music Teacher Tell us About a Musical Education', *International Journal of Education and the Arts*, 4(6): 1–23.
Fisher, J. (2002) 'Tattooing the Body: Marking Culture', *Body and Society*, 8(4): 91–107.
Flew, T., Ching, G., Stafford, A. and Tacchi, J. (2001) *Music Industry Development and Brisbane's Future as a Creative City* (Brisbane: Creative Industries Research and Applications Centre, QUT).
Florida, R. (2002) *The Rise of the Creative Class* (New York: Basic Books).
Fornäs, J. (1992) 'Otherness in Youth Culture', in C. Palmgren, K. Lovgren and G. Bolin (eds), *Ethnicity in Youth Culture* (Stockholm: Unit of Youth Culture Research, Stockholm University).
Fornäs, J., Lindberg, U. and Sernhede, O. (1995) *In Garageland: Rock, Youth, and Modernity* (London: Routledge).
Franke, S. (2010) *Current Realities and Emerging Issues Facing Youth in Canada* (Ottawa: Policy Research Initiative), http://www.policyresearch.gc.ca/page.asp?pagenm=2010-0017_01 [accessed 23 May 2010].
Freiberg, A. and Mahrad, C. (1982) *FDJ: Der Sozialistische Jugendverband der DDR* (Opladen: Westdeutscher Verlag).
Frisby, T. (1989) 'Soviet Youth Culture', in J. Riordan (ed.), *Soviet Youth Culture* (Bloomington and Indianapolis: Indiana University Press).
Frith, S. (1992) 'The Cultural Study of Popular Music', in L. Grossberg, C. Nelson and P. Treichler (eds), *Cultural Studies* (London: Routledge).
Frith, S. (1996) *Performing Rites* (Cambridge, MA: Harvard University Press).
Galligan, A. (2001) *Creativity, Culture, Education and Workforce* (Arlington, VA: Center for Arts and Culture).
Gardner, K. and Shukur, A. (1994) ' "I'm Bengali, I'm Asian, and I'm Living Here": The Changing Identities of British Bengalis', in R. Ballard (ed.), *Desh Pardesh: The South Asian Presence in Britain* (London: Hurst).
Gartman, D. (1991) 'Culture as Class Symbolization or Mass Reification: A Critique of Bourdieu's *Distinction*', *American Journal of Sociology*, 97(2): 421–47.
Gelder, K. (2005) *The Subcultures Reader*, 2nd edn. (London and New York: Routledge).
Gerth, H. H. and Wright-Mills, C. (1974 [1948]) *From Max Weber: Essays in Sociology* (London: Routledge & Kegan Paul).
Gibson, C. (2001) 'Appropriating the Means of Production: Dance Music Industries and Contested Digital Space', in G. St John (ed.), *FreeNRG: Notes from the Edge of the Dance Floor* (Melbourne: Common Ground).
Giddens, A. (1991) *Modernity and Self-Identity: Self and Society in the Late Modern Age* (Cambridge: Polity Press).
Gill, R. (2008) 'Empowerment/Sexism: Figuring Female Sexual Agency in Contemporary Advertising', *Feminism and Psychology*, 18(1): 35–60.
Gilpin, D. R., Palazzolo, E. and Brody, N. (2010) 'Socially Mediated Authenticity', *Journal of Communication Management*, 14(3): 258–78.

Gilroy, P. (1991) 'Sounds Authentic: Black Music, Ethnicity, and the Challenge of the Changing Same', *Black Music Research Journal*, 11(2): 1–36.
Giroux, H. (1982) 'Power and Resistance in the New Sociology of Education: Beyond Theories of Social and Cultural Reproduction', *Curriculum Perspectives*, 2(3): 1–13.
Goffman, E. (1956) *The Presentation of Self in Everyday Life* (New York: Doubleday).
Goffman, E. (1963) *Stigma: Notes on the Management of Spoiled Identity* (Englewood Cliffs: Prentice-Hall).
Goffman, E. (1970) *Strategic Interaction* (Oxford: Blackwell).
Gorder, K. L. (1980) 'Understanding School Knowledge: A Critical Appraisal of Basil Bernstein and Pierre Bourdieu', *Educational Theory*, 30(4): 335–46.
Gould, E. (2009) 'Music Education Desire(ing): Language, Literacy, and Lieder', *Philosophy of Music Education Review*, 17(1): 41–54.
Green, L. (2001) *How Popular Musicians Learn: A Way Ahead For Popular Music Education* (Aldershot: Ashgate).
Green, L. (2006) 'Popular Music Education in and for Itself, and for "Other" Music: Current Research in the Classroom', *International Journal of Music Education* (24 August): 101–18.
Green, L. (2008a) *Music, Informal Learning and the School: A New Classroom Pedagogy* (Aldershot: Ashgate).
Green, L. (2008b) *Music on Deaf Ears: Musical Meaning, Ideology and Education*, 2nd edn. (Bury St Edmunds: Abramis).
Gregory, D. (1986) 'Spatial Structure', in R. J. Johnston, D. Gregory, G. Pratt and M. Watts (eds), *The Dictionary of Human Geography*, 2nd edn. (Oxford: Blackwell).
Gregory, D. and Urry, J. (1985) *Social Relations and Spatial Structures* (London: Macmillan).
Grossberg, L. (1984) 'Another Boring Day in Paradise: Rock and Roll and the Empowerment of Everyday Life', *Popular Music*, 4: 225–60.
Grossberg, L. (2005) *Caught in the Crossfire: Kids, Politics, and America's Future* (Boulder and London: Paradigm Publishers).
Grossberg, L., Wartella, E., Whitney, C. D. and Macgregor Wise, J. (2006) *Media Making: Mass Media in a Popular Culture*, 2nd edn. (California: Sage Publications).
Grosz, E. (1995) *Space, Time and Perversion: Essays on the Politics of Bodies* (New York: Routledge).
Grosz, E. (1999) *Becomings: Explorations in Time, Memory, and Future* (Ithaca, NY: Cornell University Press).
Hager, L. (2008) 'Reform or Enrichment: Policy Mandates and Program Goals in Community Youth Arts', *Community Arts Network Reading Room*, http://www.communityarts.net/readingroom/archivefiles/2008/11/reform_or_enric.php [accessed 30 June 2009].
Hallman, K. and Roca, E. (2007) *Reducing the Social Exclusion of Girls* (New York: Population Council), http://www.popcouncil.org/pdfs/TABriefs/PGY_Brief27_SocialExclusion.pdf [accessed 23 May 2010].
Handelman, D. (1990) *Models and Mirrors: Towards an Anthology of Public Events* (Cambridge: Cambridge University Press).
Handelman, D. and Shulman, D. (1997) *God Inside Out: Nulliva's Game of Dice* (New York: Oxford University Press).
Hannerz, U. (1996) *Transnational Connections, Culture, People, Places* (London: Routledge).
Hardman, C. (1973) 'Can There be an Anthropology of Children?', *Journal of the Anthropological Society of Oxford*, 4(1): 85–99.

Hargreaves, I. (1999) 'The Ethical Boundaries of Reporting', in M. Ungersma (ed.), *Reporters and the Reported: The 1999 Vauxhall Lectures on Contemporary Issues in British Journalism* (Cardiff: Centre for Journalism Studies).

Harris, M. (2009) 'Newcastle City Council Gives the Loft a Reprieve', *Newcastle Herald*, 26 June, http://www.theherald.com.au/news/local/news/general/newcastle-city-council-gives-the-loft-a-reprieve/1551280.aspx [accessed 25 July 2010].

Hartley, J. (ed.) (2005) *Creative Industries* (Oxford: Blackwell).

Hartley, J. (2009) *The Uses of Digital Literacy* (Brisbane: Queensland University Press).

Hastrup, K. (1992) 'Writing Ethnography: State of the Art', in J. Okley and H. Callaway (eds), *Anthropology and Autobiography*, 29th edn. (London: Routledge).

Häußermann, H. (1997) 'Social Transformation of Urban Space in Berlin since 1990', in O. Kalltorp, I. Elander, O. Ericsson and M. Franzén (eds), *Cities in Transformation – Transformation in Cities: Social and Symbolic Change of Urban Space* (Aldershot: Avebury).

Häußermann, H. and Kapphan, A. (2001) *Berlin: From Divided to Fragmented City* (Berlin: Humboldt-Universität).

Hawkey, K. (1997) 'Roles, Responsibilities and Relationships in Mentoring', *Journal of Teacher Education*, 48: 325–35.

Hays, T. (1998) *Mentorship: The Construction of Meaning of the Relationship in the Training of Musicians* (Armidale: University of New England Press).

Heath, S. B. (2001) 'Three's Not a Crowd: Plans, Roles, and Focus in the Arts', *Educational Researcher*, 30(7): 10.

Heath, S. B. (2005) 'Strategic Thinking, Learning Environments, and Real Roles: Suggestions for Future Work', *Human Development*, 48: 350–5.

Heath, S. B. and McLaughlin, M. W. (eds) (1993) *Identity and Inner City Youth: Beyond Ethnicity and Gender* (New York: Teachers College Press).

Heath, S. B. and Roach, A. (1999) 'Imaginative Actuality', in E. Fiske (ed.), *Champions of Change: The Impact of the Arts on Learning* (Washington, DC: President's Committee on the Arts and Humanities).

Heath, S. B. and Smyth, L. (2000) *ArtShow* (Washington, DC: Partners for Livable Communities).

Heath, S. B., Soep, E. and Roach, A. (1998) 'Living the Arts Through Language-Learning: A Report on Community-Based Youth Organizations', *Americans for the Arts*, 2(7): 1–20.

Hebdige, D. (1979) *Subculture: The Meaning of Style* (London: Methuen).

Hebdige, D. (1988) *Hiding in the Light: On Images and Things* (London: Comedia).

Heyward, P. and Crane, P. (1998) *Out and About: In or Out? Better Outcomes from Young People's Use of Public and Community Space in the City of Brisbane* (Brisbane: Brisbane City Council).

Hickey Moody, A. (2009) *Unimaginable Bodies: Intellectual Disability, Performance and Becomings* (Rotterdam, NL: Sense Publishers).

Homan, S. (1999) 'Displaced Rhythms: Evicting Rock and Roll', in G. Bloustien (ed.), *Musical Visions* (Adelaide: Wakefield Press).

Homan, S. (2002a) 'Access All Eras: Careers, Creativity and the Tribute Band', *Perfect Beat: The Pacific Journal of Research into Contemporary Music and Popular Culture*, 5(4): 45–59.

Homan, S. (2002b) 'Cultural Industry or Social Problem? The Case of Australian Live Music', *Media International Australia, incorporating Culture and Policy*, 102: 88–100.

Homan, S. (2003) *The Mayor's a Square: Live Music and Law and Order in Sydney* (Newtown: Local Consumption Publishers).

Honneth, A. (1986) 'The Fragmented World of Symbolic Forms: Reflections on Pierre Bourdieu's Sociology of Culture', *Theory, Culture and Society*, 3: 55–66.

hooks, b. (1991) *Yearning: Race, Gender and Cultural Politics* (London: Turnaround Press).

Hopkins, P. (2007) '"Blue Squares", "Proper" Muslims and Transnational Networks: Narratives of National and Religious Identities Amongst Young Muslim Men Living in Scotland', *Ethnicities*, 7(1): 61–81.

Hudson, R. (1995) 'Making Music Work? Alternative Regeneration Strategies in a Deindustrialised Locality: The Case of Derwentside', *Transactions: Institute of British Geographers*, 20(4): 460–73.

Hudson, R. (2006) 'Regions and Place: Music, Identity and Place', *Progress in Human Geography*, 30(5): 626–34.

Huq, R. (2006) *Beyond Subculture: Pop, Youth and Identity in a Postcolonial World* (London: Routledge).

Hutnyk, J. and Sharma, S. (2000) 'Music and Politics: An Introduction', *Theory, Culture and Society*, 17: 55–63.

Hutson, S. R. (2000) 'The Rave: Spiritual Healing in Modern Western Subcultures', *Anthropology Quarterly*, 73(1): 35–49.

Jackson, L. A., Sullivan, L. A., Harnish, R. and Hodge, C. N. (1996) 'Achieving Positive Social Identity: Social Mobility, Social Creativity and Permeability of Group Boundaries', *Journal of Personality and Social Psychology*, 70: 241–54.

Jacobson, Y. and Luzzatto, D. (2004) 'Israeli Youth Body Adornments: Between Protest and Conformity', *Young*, 12: 155–74.

Jaggar, A. and Bordo, S. (eds) (1989) *Gender/Body/Knowledge: Feminist Reconstructions of Being and Knowing* (New Brunswick: Rutgers University Press).

Jayne, M. (2004) 'Culture That Works? Creative Industries Development in a Working-Class City', *Capital and Class*, 84: 199–210.

Jenkins, H. (2001) 'Culture Goes Global', *Technology Review* (July/August): 89.

Jenkins, H. (2003) preface to G. Bloustien (2003) *Girl Making* (Oxford: Berghahn).

Jenkins, H. (2006a) *Convergence Culture: Where Old and New Media Collide* (New York: New York University Press).

Jenkins, H. (2006b) *Fans, Bloggers and Gamers* (New York: New York University Press).

Jenkins, H., Shattuc, J. and McPherson, T. (eds) (2002) *Hop on Pop: The Politics and Pleasures of Popular Culture* (Durham, NC: Duke University Press).

Jenkins, R. (1982) 'Pierre Bourdieu and the Reproduction of Determinism', *Sociology*, 16 (2 May): 270–81.

Jetten, J. and Spears, R. (2003) 'The Discursive Potential of Differences and Similarities: The Role of Intergroup Distinctiveness and Intergroup Differentiation', *European Review of Social Psychology*, 14: 203–41.

Jones, G. (2002) *The Youth Divide: Diverging Paths to Adulthood* (York: Joseph Rowntree Foundation).

Jones, M. R. (2008) *Skintight: An Anatomy of Cosmetic Surgery* (Oxford: Berg).

Jones, M. and Yamagata, E. P. (2000) *And Justice for Some* (Washington, DC: Building Blocks for Youth Initiative).

Juszkiewicz, J. (2000) *Youth Crime/Adult Time* (Washington, DC: Building Blocks for Youth Initiative).

Kaare, B. H. and Lundby, K. (2008) 'Mediatized Lives: Autobiography and Assumed Authenticity in Digital Story Telling', in K. Lundby (ed.), *Digital Storytelling, Mediatized Stories: Self Representations in New Media* (New York: Peter Lang).

Kahn-Harris, K. (2006) *Extreme Metal: Music and Culture for the Edge* (Oxford: Berg).

Kamler, B., Comber, B., O'Brien, J. and Dornbrack, J. (2000) 'Cross-Generational and Historical Interviewing: Stories of Literacy Teachers' Work', paper presented at AARE Conference, Sydney, December.

Ke, S.-C. (2000) 'The Emergence, Transformation and Disintegration of Alternative Radio in Taiwan: From Underground Radio to Community Radio', *Journal of Communication Inquiry*, 24(4): 412–29.

Kelly, P. (2000) 'The Dangerousness of Youth-at-Risk: The Possibilities of Surveillance and Intervention in Uncertain Times', *Journal of Adolescence*, 23: 463–76.

Kemppainen, P. (2009) 'Pirates and the New Public Service Radio Paradigm', *Radio Journal: International Studies in Broadcast & Audio Media*, 7(2): 123–34.

Kenway, J., Bullen, E. and Robb, S. (eds) (2004) *Innovation and Tradition: The Arts, Humanities, and the Knowledge Economy* (New York: Peter Lang).

Kim, J., De Dios, M., Caraballo, P., Arciniegas, M., Abdul-Matin, I. and Taha, K. (2002) *Future 500: Youth Organizing and Activism in the United States* (New Orleans: Subway and Elevated Press).

Kitwana, B. (2005) *Why White Kids Love Hip Hop: Wanksats, Wiggers, Wannabes and the New Reality of Race in America* (New York: Basic Civitas Books).

Knowles, J. G., Cole, A. L. and Presswood, C. S. (2008) *Through Preservice Teachers' Eyes: Exploring Field Experiences Through Narrative and Inquiry* (Halifax: Nova Scotia Backalong Books).

Koppelstädter, L. (2010) 'Generation Alex: Raver, Jumper, Punker and Skater', *Zitty Magazine*, 14 July, trans. A. Steigemann, http://www.zitty.de/magazin-berlin/61409/ [accessed 15 July 2010].

Kugelberg, J. (2007) *Born in the Bronx* (New York: Rizzoli International Publications).

Kusow, A. (2001 [1998]) 'Stigma and Social Identities: The Process of Identity Work Among Somali Immigrants in Canada', in M. S. Lilius (ed.), *Variations on the Theme of Somaliness* (Åbo: Centre For Continuing Education, Åbo Akademi University).

Landau, J. (2004) 'The Flesh of Raving: Merleau-Ponty and the Experience of Ecstasy', in G. St John (ed.), *Rave Culture and Religion* (London: Routledge).

Lash, S. and Urry, J. (1987) *The End of Organised Capitalism* (Cambridge: Polity Press).

Laski, M. (1961) *Ecstasy: A Study of Some Secular and Religious Experiences* (London: Cresset Press).

Laski, M. (1980) *Everyday Ecstasy* (London: Thames and Hudson).

Leadbeater, C. (1999) *Living on Thin Air: The New Economy* (London: Viking).

Leadbeater, C. (2002) *Up the Down Escalator: Why the Global Pessimists are Wrong* (London: Viking).

Leadbeater, C. and Oakley, K. (1999) *The Independents: Britain's New Cultural Entrepreneurs* (London: Demos).

LeFebvre, H. (1991) *The Production of Space* (Oxford: Blackwell).

Lerner, R. (1996) 'Editorial: Research on Adolescence: Then, Now, and Next', *Journal of Research on Adolescence*, 6(4): 365–75.

Lesko, N. (1988) 'The Curriculum of the Body: Lessons from a Catholic High School', in L. Roman, L. Christian-Smith and E. Ellsworth (eds), *Becoming Feminine: The Politics of Popular Culture* (London: Falmer Press).

Levin, H. J. (2010) *The Invisible Resource: Use and Regulation of the Radio Spectrum* (London: RFF Library Collection: Policy & Governance).

Lévi-Strauss, C. (1972 [1966]) *The Savage Mind* (London: Weidenfeld & Nicolson).

Lewin, P. and Williams, J. P. (2009) 'The Ideology and Practice of Authenticity in Punk Culture', in P. Vannini and J. Patrick Williams (eds), *Authenticity in Culture, Self, and Society* (Farnham, Surrey: Ashgate).

Lewis, C. (1996) 'Woman, Body, Space: Rio Carnival and the Politics of Performance', *Gender, Place and Culture*, 3(1): 23–42.

Liebau, E. (2010) 'The Development of the Concept of Arts Education in Germany: From *Kulturelle Bildung* to Arts Education', *UNESCO Today*, 1: 11–13.

Low, S. M. (2003) 'Embodied Space(s): Anthropological Theories of Body, Space and Culture', *Space and Culture*, 6(1): 9–18.

Low, S. M. and Lawrence-Zúñiga, D. (2002) *The Anthropology of Space and Place: Locating Culture* (London: Blackwell Publishing).

Luckman, S. (2008) '"Unalienated Labour" and Creative Industries: Situating Micro-Entrepreneurial Dance Music Subcultures in the New Economy', in G. Bloustien, M. Peters and S. Luckman (eds), *Sonic Synergies: Music, Identity, Technology and Community* (Aldershot: Ashgate).

Lykke, N. (2000) 'Are Cyborgs Queer: Biological Determinism and Feminist Theory in the Age of New Reproductive Technologies and Reprogenetics', paper presented at the 4th European Feminist Research Conference, Body Gender Subjectivity: Crossing Disciplinary and Institutional Borders, Bologna, 28 September–1 October.

Lynch, G. (2006) 'The Role of Popular Music in the Construction of Alternative Spiritual Identities and Ideologies', *Journal for the Scientific Study of Religion*, 45(4): 481–8.

Lynn, M. and Snyder, C. R. (2002) 'Uniqueness Seeking', in C. R. Snyder and S. J. Lopez (eds), *Handbook of Positive Psychology* (London: Oxford University Press).

Lyons, J. O. (1978) *The Invention of the Self* (Carbondale, IL: Southern Illinois University Press).

MacRae, R. (2007) '"Insider" and "Outsider" Issues in Youth Research', in P. Hodkinson and W. Dieke (eds), *Youth Cultures: Scenes, Subcultures and Tribes* (New York and London: Routledge).

Maffesolli, M. (1996 [1988]) *The Time of the Tribes: The Decline of Individualism in Mass Society* (London: Sage).

Mahmood, S. (2001) 'Feminist Theory, Embodiment and the Docile Agent: Some Reflections on Egyptian Islamic Revival', *Cultural Anthropology*, 16(2): 202–36.

Mahrad, C. (1977) 'Jugendpolitik in der DDR', in W. Waide and B. Hille (eds), *Jugend im Doppelten Deutcschland* (Opladen: Westdeutscher Verlag).

Malbon, B. (1999) *Clubbing, Dancing, Ecstasy and Vitality* (London: Routledge).

Malone, K. (2002) 'Street Life: Youth, Culture and Competing Uses of Public Space', *Environment and Urbanization*, 14(2): 157–68.

Marcus, G. (1980) 'The Ethnographic Subject as Ethnographer: A Neglected Dimension of Anthropological Research', *Rice University Studies*, 66: 55–6.

Marcus, G. and Fischer, M. (1986) 'Ethnography and Interpretive Anthropology', in G. Marcus and M. Fischer (eds), *Anthropology as Cultural Critique: An Experimental Moment in the Human Sciences* (Chicago: University of Chicago Press).

Marks, P. (2009) 'Net Gives Pirate Radio the Last Laugh', *New Scientist*, 202(2711): 20–2.

Martin, R. (1990) *Performance as a Political Act: The Embodied Self* (New York: Bergin and Garvey).

Mason, M. (2008) *The Pirate's Dilemma: How Youth Culture is Reinventing Capitalism* (New York: Free Press).

Massey, D. (1994) *Space, Place and Gender* (Cambridge: Polity Press).

Massumi, B. (2002) *Parables for the Virtual: Movement, Affect, Sensation* (Durham, NC: Duke University Press).

Matthews, H. (2001) 'Participatory Structures and the Youth of Today: Engaging Those who are Hardest to Reach', *Ethics, Place and Environment*, 4(2): 153–9.

Maxwell, I. and Bambrick, N. (1994) 'Discourses of Culture and Nationalism in Sydney Hip Hop', *Perfect Beat: The Journal of Research into Contemporary Music and Popular Culture*, 2(1): 1–19.
McCabe, K. (2007) 'Hill Top Hoods on Classics', *The Daily Telegraph*, 17 May, http://www.dailytelegraph.com.au/entertainment/music/hilltop-hoods-on-classics/story-e6frexl9-1111113555454 [accessed 20 June 2010].
McCarthy, C., Hudak, G., Miklaucic, S. and Saukko, P. (eds) (1999) *Sound Identities: Popular Music and the Cultural Politics of Education* (New York: Peter Lang).
McClary, S. (1994) 'Same as it Ever Was: Youth Culture and Music', in A. Ross and T. Rose (eds), *Microphone Fiends: Youth Music and Youth Culture* (New York: Routledge).
McEachern, C. (1998) 'A Mutual Interest? Ethnography in Anthropology and Cultural Studies', *The Australian Journal of Anthropology*, 9(3): 251–64.
McLaughlin, M. (2000) *Community Counts: How Youth Organisations Matter for Youth Development* (Washington, DC: Public Education Network).
McNamara, L. M. and Ballard, M. E. (1999) 'Resting Arousal, Sensation Seeking, and Music Preference', *Genetic, Social, and General Psychology Monographs*, 125: 229–36.
McRobbie, A. (1999) *In the Culture Society: Art, Fashion and Popular Music* (London and New York: Routledge).
McRobbie, A. (2002a) 'Clubs to Companies: Notes on the Decline of Political Culture in Speeded Up Creative Worlds', *Cultural Studies*, 16(4): 516–32.
McRobbie, A. (2002b) 'From Holloway to Hollywood: Happiness at Work in the New Cultural Economy', in P. Du Gay and M. Pryke (eds), *Cultural Economy: Cultural Analysis and Commercial Life* (London: Sage).
McSharry, M. (2009) *Schooled Bodies? Negotiating Adolescent Validation Through Press, Peers and Parents* (Stoke-on-Trent: Trentham Books).
Meadows, D. (2006) 'New Literacies for a Participatory Culture in the Digital Age', Community Media Association Festival & AGM, http://www.commedia.org.uk/a=bout-cma/cma-events/cma-festival-and-agm-2006/speeches/daniel-meadows-speech/.
Meyers, D. E. (2008) 'Life Span Engagement and the Question of Relevance: Challenges for Music Education Research in the Twenty-First Century', *Music Education Research*, 10(1): 1–14.
Miles, S. (2000) *Youth Lifestyles in a Changing World* (Buckingham: Open University Press).
Miller, T. (2009) 'From Creative To Cultural Industries', *Cultural Studies*, 23(1): 88–99.
Mitchell, B. A. (2006) *The Boomerang Age: Transitions to Adulthood in Families* (New Brunswick and London: Aldine Transaction).
Mitchell, C., Pithouse, K. and Moletsane, R. (2009) 'The Social Self in Self Study: Author Conversations', in K. Pithouse, C. Mitchell and R. Moletsane (eds), *Making Connections: Self Study and Social Action* (New York: Peter Lang).
Mitchell, T. (1996) *Popular Music and Local Identity* (London: Leicester University Press).
Mitchell, T. (ed.) (2001) *Global Noise: Rap and Hip Hop Outside of the USA* (Middletown, CT: Wesleyan University Press).
Moe, R. and Wilkie, C. (1997) *Changing Places: Rebuilding Community in the Age of Sprawl* (New York: Owl Publishing Company).
Moore, H. (1994) *A Passion for Difference: Essays in Anthropology and Gender* (Cambridge: Polity Press).
Morris, E. (2004) 'Creative Arts: A New Way Forward', *Allbusiness Magazine*, 6 January, http://www.allbusiness.com/retail-trade/miscellaneous-retail-retail-stores-not/4384560.

National Advisory Committee on Creative and Cultural Education (1999) *All Our Futures: Creativity, Culture and Education* (London: Secretaries of State).
Newburn, T., Shiner, M. and Young, T. (2005) *Dealing with Disaffection: Young People, Mentoring, and Social Inclusion* (Devon and Oregon: Willan Publishing).
Newcastle City Council (2000a) *Newcastle City Council Plan* (Newcastle: Newcastle City Council).
Newcastle City Council (2000b) *Newcastle Economic Development Strategy* (Newcastle: Newcastle City Council).
Newcastle City Council (2003) *Palais Royale Report: Commitment to Young People* (Newcastle: Newcastle City Council).
Nilan, P. (1992) 'Kazzies, DBTs, and Tryhards: Categorisations of Style in Adolescent Girls' Talk', *British Journal of Education*, 13(2): 201–14.
O'Brien, S. (2009) 'Save the Loft', *Green Left*, 2 May, http://www.greenleft.org.au/node/41577 [accessed 20 July 2010].
O'Connor, J. (1998) 'Popular Culture, Reflexivity and Urban Change', in J. Verwinjen and P. Lehtovuori (eds), *Creative Cities: Cultural Industries, Urban Development and the Information Society* (Helsinki: University of Art and Design).
Ofsted (2009) *Making More of Music: An Evaluation of Music in Schools 2005–08* (Manchester: Ofsted).
Okely, J. (1992) 'Anthropology and Autobiography: Participatory Experience and Embodied Knowledge', in J. Okely and H. Callaway (eds), *Anthropology and Autobiography* (London and New York: Routledge).
Ortbals, C. D. and Rincker, M. E. (2009) 'Fieldwork, Identities and Intersectionality: Negotiating Gender, Race, Class, Religion, Nationality and Age in the Research Field Abroad', *Political Science and Politics*, 42(2): 287–90.
Ozawa-De Silva, C. (2002) 'Beyond the Body/Mind? Japanese Contemporary Thinkers on Alternative Sociologies of the Body', *Body and Society*, 8(2): 21–38.
Pack, S. (2006) 'Social Thought and Commentary: How They See Me vs. How I See Them: The Ethnographic Self and the Personal Self', *Anthropological Quarterly*, 79(1): 105–22.
Parkin, F. (1979) *Marxism and Class Theory* (London: Taverstock).
Patel, V. and Kleinman, A. (2003) 'Poverty and Common Development Disorders in Developing Countries', *Bulletin of the World Health Organization*, 81: 609–15.
Pendery, D. (2009) 'Three Top Economists Agree 2009 Worst Financial Crisis Since Great Depression; Risks Increase if Right Steps are not Taken', *Reuters Business Wire*, 27 February, http://www.reuters.com/article/idUS193520+27-Feb-2009+BW20090227 [accessed 12 August 2010].
Peters, M. (1993) 'Playing With/For Power', paper presented at Issues in Australian Childhood Conference, QUT, Brisbane, September.
Peters, M. (1994a) 'Boys Whistle, Girls Sing: School Grounds', *Loisir et Société: Society and Leisure*, 17(1): 221–39.
Peters, M. (1994b) 'Embodied Play', paper presented at World Play Conference, University of Melbourne, Melbourne.
Peters, M. (2008) 'Risky Economies: Community-Based Organizations and the Music-Making Practices of Marginalized Youth', in G. Bloustien, M. Peters and S. Luckman (eds), *Sonic Synergies: Music, Technology, Community, Identity* (Aldershot: Ashgate).
Pilkington, H. (1994) *Russia's Youth and its Culture: A Nation's Constructors and its Constructed* (London: Routledge).
Pini, M. (2001) *Club Cultures and Female Subjectivity: The Move from Home to House* (New York: Palgrave Macmillan).

Pini, M. (2006) 'Girls on Film: Video Diaries as "Auto-Ethnographies"', paper presented at London Knowledge Lab for Media and Youth Cultures Seminar Series, London, May.

Pink, S. (2007) *Doing Visual Ethnography: Images, Media and Representation in Research* (London: Sage).

Pithouse, K., Mitchell, C. and Moletsane, R. (eds) (2009) *Making Connections: Self Study and Social Action* (New York: Peter Lang).

Pitts, S. E. (2001) Whose Aesthetics? Public, Professional and Pupil Perceptions of Music Education', *Research Studies in Music Education*, 17: 54–60.

Prime Minister's Office, UK (2010) 'Government Launches "Big Society" Programme', *Number10.gov.uk*, 18 May, http://www.number10.gov.uk/news/topstorynews/2010/05/big-society-50248 [accessed 12 August 2010].

Prince's Trust (2003) *Annual Report* (London: Prince's Trust).

Prosser, J. (ed.) (1998) *Image-Based Research: A Source Book for Qualitative Researchers* (London: Falmer Press).

Quarry, W. (1994) *The Fogo Process: An Experiment in Participatory Communication* (Guelph: University of Guelph).

Rabinow, P. (1977) *Reflections on Fieldwork in Morocco* (Berkeley: University of California Press).

Rabinow, P. (1988) 'Beyond Ethnography: Anthropology as Nominalism', *Cultural Anthropology*, 3: 355–64.

Rainwater, J. (1989) *Self Therapy* (London: Crucible).

Richard, B. and Kruger, H. (1998) 'Ravers' Paradise? German Youth Cultures in the 1990s', in T. Skelton and G. Valentine (eds), *Cool Places: Geographies of Youth Cultures* (London. Routledge).

Richards, C. (1998) *Teen Spirits: Music and Identity in Media Education* (London: University College London Press).

Riddell, M. (2010) 'It will Need More than Jam and Jerusalem to Create a Big Society', *The Daily Telegraph Online*, 19 July, http:/www.telegraph.co.uk/comment/columnists/maryridell/7899331/It-will-need-more-than-jam-and-Jerusalem-to-create-a-Big-Society.html [accessed 30 July 2010].

Rietveld, H. (1993) 'Living the Dream', in S. Redhead (ed.), *Rave Off: Politics and Deviance in Contemporary Youth Culture* (Aldershot and Brookfield: Ashgate).

Rifkin, J. (2000) *The Age of Access: How the Shift from Ownership to Access is Transforming Modern Life* (London: Penguin).

Riley, A. (2007) 'Why Gangs of Youths Buzz off When They Hear the Hum of a Mosquito', *Times Online*, 21 April, http://www.timesonline.co.uk/tol/news/uk/crime/article1680234.ece [accessed 24 May 2010].

Rivera, R. Z. (2003) *New York Ricans from the Hip Hop Zone* (New York: Palgrave Macmillan).

Roberts, M. (2006) 'From "Creative City" to "No-go Areas": The Expansion of the Night-Time Economy in British Town and City Centres', *Cities*, 23(5): 331–8.

Roberts, M., Turner, C., Osborn, G. and Greenfield, S. (2006) 'A Continental Ambience? Lessons in Managing Alcohol-Related Evening and Night-Time Entertainment from Four European Capitals', *Urban Studies*, 43(7): 1105–25.

Robertson, D. (2009) 'STABBINGS Vicious Attacks are Becoming Commonplace State on a Knife Edge as Violence Escalates', *The Advertiser*, 3 January: 45.

Robinson, G. (2009) 'Manly "Morons" Rampage was Racist: Academic', *Sydney Morning Herald*, 27 January, http://www.smh.com.au/news/national/manly-morons-racist-says-academic/2009/01/27/1232818417563.html [accessed 3 November 2010].

Rodin, J. (1992) 'Body Mania', *Psychology Today*, 25(1): 56–60.

Rose, M. (2007) 'Video Nation and Digital Storytelling: A BBC/Public Partnership in Content Creation', in K. Coyer, T. Dowmunt and A. Fountain (eds), *The Alternative Media Handbook* (London: Routledge).

Rose, S. (2010) 'Myplace: Putting the Youth Back in Youth Centre', *The Guardian*, 11 April, http://www.guardian.co.uk/artanddesign/2010/apr/11/myspace-youth-centres [accessed 30 May 2010].

Rosenbaum, L. (2005) 'Build the Perfect Body', *Men's Health*, 20(1): 116–22.

Ross, A. and Rose, T. (1994) *Microphone Fiends: Youth Music & Youth Culture* (New York: Routledge).

Rubin, J. (1970) *Do it: Scenarios of the Revolution* (New York: Ballantine Books).

Rushkoff, D. (2004) 'Foreword', in G. St John (ed.), *Rave Culture and Religion* (London and New York: Routledge).

Russell, L. (2005) 'It's a Question of Trust: Balancing the Relationship Between Students and Teachers in the Ethnographic Field', *Qualitative Research*, 5(2): 181–99.

Salavuo, M. (2006) 'Open and Informal Online Communities as Forums of Collaborative Musical Activities and Learning', *British Journal of Music Education*, 23(3): 253–71.

Salavuo, M. (2008) 'Social Media as an Opportunity for Pedagogical Change in Music Education', *Intellect: Journal of Music Education and Technology*, 1(2–3): 121–36.

Schechner, R. (1985) *Between Theatre and Anthropology* (Philadelphia: University of Pennsylvania Press).

Schechner, R. (1993) *The Future of Ritual* (London: Routledge).

Schneider, J. (2002) 'Reflexive/Diffractive Ethnography', *Cultural Studies ⇔ Critical Methodologies*, 2(4): 460–82.

Schratz, M. and Walker, R. (1995) *Research as Social Change: New Opportunities for Qualitative Research* (London and New York: Routledge).

Schultz, K. (2001) 'Stretching the Boundaries of Participatory Research: Insights from Conducting Research with Urban Adolescents', *Australian Educational Researcher*, 28(2): 1–28.

Schultz, K. and Hull, G. (2002) 'Locating Literacy Theory in Out-of-School Contexts', in G. Hull and K. Schultz (eds), *School's Out! Bridging Out-of-School Literacies with Classroom Practice* (New York: Teachers College Press).

Sciama, L. (1993) 'The Problem of Privacy in Mediterranean Anthropology', in S. Ardener (ed.), *Women and Space: Ground Rules and Social Maps* (Oxford: Berg).

Shepherd, J. and Wick, P. (1997) *Music and Cultural Theory* (Cambridge: Polity Press).

Shilling, C. (1993) *The Body and Social Theory* (London: Sage).

Shouse, E. (2005) 'Feeling, Emotion, Affect', *M/C Journal*, 8(6), http://journal.media-culture.org.au/0512/03-shouse.php [accessed 15 September 2010].

Shuman, M. H. (1998) *Going Local: Creating Self-Reliant Communities in a Global Age* (New York: Free Press).

Skeggs, B. (1997) *Formations of Class and Gender: Becoming Respectable* (London: Sage).

Sloboda, J. (ed.) (1988) *Generative Processes in Music: The Psychology of Performance, Improvisation, and Composition*. Oxford Science Publications (New York: Oxford University Press).

Smith, D. (1988) 'Femininity as Discourse', in L. Roman and L. Christian-Smith (eds), *Becoming Feminine: The Politics of Popular Culture* (London: Falmer Press).

Smith, F. M. (1998) 'Between East and West: Sites of Resistance in East German Youth Cultures', in T. Skelton and G. Valentine (eds), *Cool Places: Geographies of Youth Cultures* (London: Routledge).

Smith, M. K. (2009) 'Social Capital', *The Encyclopedia of Informal Education*, http://www.infed.org/biblio/social_capital.htm [accessed 21 October 2010].

Soja, E. W. (1989) *Postmodern Geographies: The Reassertion of Space into Critical Social Theory* (London: Verso).

Soja, E. W. (1996) *Third Space: Journeys to Los Angeles and Other Real-and-Imagined Places* (Cambridge, MA: Blackwell Publishers).

Soysal, L. (2001) 'Diversity of Experience, Experience of Diversity: Turkish Migrant Youth Culture in Berlin', *Cultural Dynamics*, 13(1): 5–28.

Spain, D. (1992) *Gendered Spaces* (Chapel Hill, NC: University of North Carolina Press).

Sparks, M. (2010) 'Centre is Open to all Possibilities', *Norwich Evening News*, 22 February, p. 14, http://www.open247.org.uk/media/dContent/mediaCentre/About-OPEN/2010/02.22.10---en---centre-is-open-to-all-possibilities.pdf [accessed 23 November 2010].

St John, G. (ed.) (2004) *Rave Culture and Religion* (London and New York: Routledge).

St John, G. (2009) *Technomad: Global Raving Counterculture* (London: Equinox).

Statistics Canada (1999) *Youth in Transition Survey* (Ottawa: Statistics Canada).

Statistics Canada (2001) *Youth in Transition Survey* (Ottawa: Statistics Canada).

Stein, A. (2004) 'Music, Mourning, and Consolation', *Journal of the American Psychoanalytic Association*, 52(3): 783–811.

Stokes, M. (ed.) (1994) *Ethnicity, Identity and Music: The Musical Construction of Place* (Oxford: Berg).

Strangelove, M. (2010) *Watching YouTube: Extraordinary Videos by Ordinary People* (Toronto: University of Toronto Press).

Sudnow, D. (1978) *Ways of the Hand: The Organization of Improvised Conduct* (Cambridge, MA: Harvard University Press).

Sudnow, D. (2001) *Ways of the Hand: A Rewritten Account* (Cambridge, MA: MIT Press).

Sullivan, A. (2002) 'Bourdieu and Education: How Useful is Bourdieu's Theory for Researchers?', *Netherlands Journal of Social Sciences*, 38(2): 144–66.

Suransky, P. V. (1982) *The Erosion of Childhood* (Chicago: University of Chicago Press).

Tait, G. (1995) 'Shaping the "At-Risk" Youth: Risk, Governmentality and the Finn Report', *Discourse*, 16(1): 123–34.

Tait, G. (2000) *Youth, Sex, and Government. Eruptions: New Thinking across the Disciplines* (New York: Peter Lang).

Taussig, M. (1987) *Shamanism, Colonialism and the Wild Man: A Study in Terror and Healing* (Chicago: University of Chicago Press).

Taussig, M. (1993) *Mimesis and Alterity* (New York: Routledge).

Tedlock, D. (1983) *The Spoken Word and the Work of Interpretation* (Philadelphia: University of Pennsylvania Press).

'The Big Society' (2010) *The Times*, 14 April, http://timesonline.co.uk/tol/comment/leading article/article7096805.ece [accessed 12 August 2010].

Thomas, C. and Bromley, R. (2000) 'City-Centre Revitalisation: Problems of Fragmentation and Fear in the Evening and Night-Time City', *Journal of Urban Studies*, 37(8): 1403–29.

Thornton, S. (1995) *Club Cultures: Music, Media and Subcultural Capital* (Cambridge: Polity Press).

Tranberg Hansen, K. (2004a) 'Dressing Dangerously: Miniskirts, Gender Relations, and Sexuality in Zambia', in Jean Allman (ed.), *Fashioning Africa: Power and the Politics of Dress* (Bloomington: Indiana University Press).

Tranberg Hansen, K. (2004b) 'The World in Dress: Anthropological Perspectives on Clothing, Fashion, and Culture', *Annual Review of Anthropology*, 33: 369–92.
Turner, B. S. (1996 [1984]) *The Body and Society: Explorations in Social Theory* (London: Sage).
Turner, T. (1991) 'The Social Dynamics of Visual Media in an Indigenous Society: The Cultural Meaning and the Personal Politics of Video Making in Kayapo Communities', *Visual Anthropology Review*, 7(2): 68–76.
Turner, T. (1992) 'Defiant Images: The Kayapo Appropriation of Video', *Anthropology Today*, 8(6): 5–16.
Turner, T. (1995) 'Representation, Collaboration and Mediation in Contemporary Ethnographic and Indigenous Media', *Visual Anthropology Review*, 11(2): 102–6.
Turner, V. (1969) *The Ritual Process: Structure and Anti-Structure* (Chicago: Aldine).
Turner, V. (1982) *From Ritual to Theatre: The Human Seriousness of Play* (New York: Performing Arts Journal Publications).
Väkevä, L. (2010) 'Garage Band or GarageBand®? Remixing Musical Futures', *British Journal of Music Education*, 27(1): 59–70.
Valentine, G. (2004) *Public Space and the Culture of Childhood* (Aldershot: Ashgate).
Wagner, R. (1975) *The Invention of Culture* (Chicago: University of Chicago Press).
Wall, T. (2006) 'Out on the Dance Floor: The Politics of Dancing on the Northern Soul Scene', *Popular Music*, 25(3): 431–45.
Wallace, R. (2009) 'Social Partnerships in Learning: Negotiating Disenfranchised Learner Identities', *US–China Education Review*, 6(6): 37–46.
Walser, R. (1993) *Running with the Devil: Power, Gender, and Madness in Heavy Metal Music* (Middletown, CT: Wesleyan University Press).
Walsh, C. (2008) 'The Mosquito: A Repellent Response', *Youth Justice*, 8(2): 122–33.
Wang, C. (1997) 'Photovoice: Concept, Methodology, and Use for Participatory Needs Assessment', *Health Education and Behavior*, 24(3): 369–87.
Waterkamp, D. (1989) 'Erziehung zur Identfikation mit dem Staat in der DDR', in B. Claußen (ed.), *Politische Sozialisation Jugendlicher in Ost und West* (Bonn: Bundeszentrale für Politische Bildung).
Weitz, J. (1996) *Coming Up Taller: Arts and Humanities Programs for Children and Youth at Risk* (Darby, PA: Diane Publishing Company).
Wenger, E. (1998) *Communities of Practice: Learning, Meaning and Identity* (Cambridge: Cambridge University Press).
Werbner, P. (1996) 'Fun Spaces: On Identity and Social Empowerment among British Pakistanis', *Theory, Culture and Society*, 13(4): 53–79.
Westerlund, H. (2006) 'Garage Rock Bands: A Future Model for Developing Musical Expertise?' *International Journal of Music Education*, 24: 119–25.
Wexler, P. (1983) 'Movement, Class and Education', in L. Barton and S. Walker (eds), *Race, Class and Education* (London: Croom-Helm).
Wexler, P. (1992) *Becoming Somebody: Toward a Social Psychology of School* (London: Falmer Press).
White, R. (1990) *No Space of Their Own: Young People and Social Control in Australia* (New York: Cambridge University Press).
White, S. and Kenyon, P. (2000) *Enterprise-Based Youth Employment Policies, Strategies and Programmes* (Geneva: ILO).
Whiteley, S., Bennett, A. and Hawkins, S. (eds) (2004) *Music, Space and Place: Popular Music and Cultural Identity* (Aldershot and Burlington: Ashgate).

Willett, R. (2009a) 'Always On: Camera Phones, Video Production and Identity', in D. Buckingham and R. Willet (eds), *Video Cultures: Media Technology and Everyday Creativity* (Basingstoke: Palgrave Macmillan).
Willett, R. (2009b) 'In the Frame: Mapping Camcorder Cultures', in D. Buckingham and R. Willett (eds), *Video Cultures: Media Technology and Everyday Creativity* (London: Routledge).
Williams, C. (2001) 'Does It Really Matter? Young People and Popular Music', *Popular Music*, 20(2): 223–42.
Williams, K. (2009) 'Youth Stand Ground Over the Loft', *Newcastle Herald*, 15 June, http://www.theherald.com.au/news/local/news/general/youth-stand-ground-over-the-loft/1540204.aspx?order=1 [accessed 26 July 2010].
Williams, R. (1980) 'Advertising: The Magic System', in R. Williams (ed.), *Problems in Materialism and Culture* (London: Verso).
Willis, P. (1990) *Common Culture* (Buckingham: Open University Press).
Willis, P. (1998) 'Notes on Common Culture: Towards a Grounded Aesthetics', *European Journal of Cultural Studies*, 1(2): 163–76.
Willis, P., Jones, S., Canaan, J. and Hurd, G. (1993) *Common Culture: Symbolic Work at Play in the Everyday Cultures of the Young* (Milton Keynes: Open University Press).
Wilson, D., Rose, J. and Colvin, E. (2009) 'Marginalized Youth, Surveillance and Public Space', *Australian Policy Online*, http://www.apo.org.au/[accessed 24 June 2010].
Wilson, H. (2005) 'If it Takes a Village to Raise a Child, How Many Children Does it Take to Raise a Village?', *Community Youth Development Journal* (23 February): 95–8.
Winlow, S. and Hall, S. (2005) *Violent Night: Urban Leisure and Contemporary Culture* (Oxford: Berg).
Wood, D. (2009) 'Financial Crisis: Four Take Aways from Istanbul', *The Huffington Post*, 5 October, http://www.huffingtonpost.com/barry-d-wood/financial-crisis-four-tak_b_309402.html [accessed 16 November 2010].
Wright, R. (2008) 'Kicking the Habitus: Power, Culture and Pedagogy in the Secondary School Music Curriculum', *Music Education Research*, 10(3): 389–402.
Wulff, H. (1995) 'Introducing Youth Culture in its Own Right: The State of the Art and New Possibilities', in H. Wulff and V. Amit-Talai (eds), *Youth Cultures: A Cross-Cultural Perspective* (London: Routledge).
Youth Music (2009) 'Ofsted Publish Report on Music in Schools', *Youth Music Blog*, 4 February, http://www.youthmusic.org.uk/news/ofsted-publish-report-on-music-in-schools.html [accessed 25 November 2010].
Youth at Risk (2010) *Youth at Risk*, http://www.youthatrisk.org.uk [accessed 6 October 2010].
Yuasa, Y. (1987) *The Body: Toward an Eastern Mind–Body Theory* (New York: State University of New York Press).
Zeitlyn, D. and Fischer, M. (2003) *Visual Anthropology in the Digital Mirror: Computer-Assisted Visual Anthropology* (Canterbury: University of Kent).
Zuberi, N. (2001) 'Black Whole Styles: Sounds, Technology and Diaspora Aesthetics', in N. Zuberi (ed.), *Sounds English: Transnational Popular Music* (Chicago: University of Illinois Press).
Zukin, S. (1991) *Landscapes of Power: From Detroit to Disney World* (Berkeley: University of California Press).

Index

Adam (Henry)   32, 79–80, 125, 135, 153
Adelaide, South Australia   2, 23, 27–30, 77, 92, 99, 194–203, 216, 257–8
AKarts   34, 168, 188, 242, 244, 256, 261
Alexis (Johnson)   34, 168–71, 188–9, 204, 242–6, 261
Alicia (Woodrow)   2, 28, 199, 219–20, 222–4, 226, 228, 253
Alleins e.V.   156, 178, 260
AS220   182–7, 204–5, 255–6, 262
authenticity   12, 17, 32, 47–9, 60, 68, 84–5, 90–1, 93, 101–4, 106–8, 111, 117–18, 221
auto-video-ethnography   6–7, 10, 20, 22, 26
  see also ethnography
Azza (Aaron John Hainsworth)   32–3, 79–80, 124, 135–6, 150, 153

Barney (Langford)   151–3, 156
bedrooms   71–4, 81, 123–4, 127, 135–40, 206, 221
Ben (Moss)   199–201
Berlin, Germany   23, 37–8, 52–5, 95, 128–33, 142–3, 156–8, 167, 174–9, 247, 252–4, 258–60
Boston, USA   38–9, 162–4, 179–82, 261–2
Bourdieu, Pierre   7, 14, 16, 44–6, 51, 57, 84, 87, 91, 93–4, 102–3, 116, 127, 134, 140, 149
breakdancing   32, 78–9, 89, 105–6, 109, 130, 176
Bret (pseudonym)   92–3, 100, 196–7
Brighton Treatment Center   12–13, 61–2, 67, 89, 121, 139, 162–4, 179–82, 187, 204, 235–6, 240–1, 249, 262

Café Lietz   94–5, 176–8, 254, 259
capital, social/cultural   19, 48–9, 84, 90–1, 102–3, 106, 111, 114, 116, 182, 218
Carclew Youth Arts Centre   27–8, 77–8, 147, 198–202, 257

censorship   67–8, 70, 121, 196, 198
clothing   71, 85, 87, 93, 95–102, 104–7, 114, 210, 216
community-based organisations   5, 8, 21–3, 27–39, 55, 128, 142, 144–58, 161–2, 165–89, 191–205, 227, 237, 254–6, 257–62
Crossley, Nick   45, 47

Da Klinic   29–30, 87–8, 104–5, 109, 118–21, 161–3, 202–4, 220, 225–8, 251, 257
Dave (DJ Maths/Dave Watson)   32, 78, 94, 105, 109
DJing   29–30, 48, 71–4, 83–4, 86, 109–15, 118, 137–9, 213, 215, 220–2, 225, 231
Duncan, Nancy   127, 140

employment
  day jobs   2, 49, 58, 74, 179, 212, 221–2, 227
  in music/the arts   72, 84, 184, 206–7, 216–19, 226–7, 229, 255
  pathways to   166, 168–9, 172–3, 185–6, 188–9, 191, 203, 218, 232, 242, 249, 255
ethnic minorities   8, 32–3, 35, 53, 97, 115, 128, 131–3, 142, 156, 167, 175–6, 178–9, 258–61
ethnography   6–7, 16, 55, 57, 60–1, 63–5, 70
event management   27–8, 31, 77–8, 199–203, 219, 221–2, 237, 253

Facebook
  see social networking
female dancers   109, 129–30
female musicians   37, 95–100, 128–9, 141–2, 178
funding   36, 76, 121, 153, 159, 161, 168–70, 173–4, 176, 179–80, 183,

187–9, 196–8, 200–1, 203–5, 227, 238, 245–6
funding cuts   9–10, 146, 157, 163, 171, 174, 177, 254, 256

garage music   2, 50, 251
Garth (Linsenmeier)   100
Genuine Voices   12–13, 38, 62, 67, 121, 123, 162–4, 179–82, 204, 233–4, 236, 240–1, 261–2
Giddens, Anthony   45, 91
girls
  see female musicians; female dancers; space and gender
Goffman, Erving   102, 133
government policies   168, 172, 174, 179, 203
  Australia   153–6, 174, 190–4
  Germany   157, 174–5
  UK   8–10, 159, 166–8, 170, 172–4, 188, 238–40, 246, 256
graffiti   80, 150–1, 251, 254
group identity   85, 87, 90, 93, 101–2, 104, 106–7, 117, 141, 179

habitus   44, 46, 93, 135
hip hop   12, 21, 29–30, 32–3, 49–50, 79–80, 85, 88, 94, 104, 110, 118, 120–1, 124, 132, 142, 162, 176, 186, 216, 220, 226–7, 250–1

Juri (Juri Ify Love/Juri Panda Jones)   12, 38–9, 62, 67, 89, 121–2, 162–4, 179–82, 187, 204, 220, 227, 234, 236, 240, 249, 261–2

Kandinsky Sessions   27–8, 77–8, 198–202, 257
Karin (Woodley)   34, 115, 147, 189
Katie (Williams)   34, 206–11, 253
Kent, UK   35–7, 158–9, 161, 170–1, 261
Kyle (DJ D'Andrea/Kyle D'Andrea)   30, 43, 48, 71–3, 101–2, 109–10, 137, 140

language   118–21
  see also censorship
Leadbeater, Charles   217–18, 255
Lilly (Buvka)   29, 194–8

local government/councils   22–3, 28, 35, 146–7, 150, 154–5, 157–8, 161, 167, 172, 189–98, 251, 254, 256
Loft, the   151–6, 194, 254, 258
London, UK   2, 8, 33–4, 208–11, 213–15, 221, 261

Magda (Albrecht)   37, 95–6, 176, 252
marginalisation   4–5, 18, 21–2, 57–9, 81, 140, 143, 145, 166–7, 173–5, 180, 184, 195, 243–4, 246, 250–1, 257–8, 261
Maxim   131–3
McRobbie, Angela   207, 217
mentoring   69, 73, 108–11, 114, 168–9, 188–9, 198–9, 201–2, 204–5, 218, 236–7, 242–4, 248, 250, 252
methodology   5–8, 10–13, 15, 16, 55–6, 60–3, 67
  co-researchers   5–7, 10–11, 22, 63, 70
  'objectivity'   60, 64
  recruitment   23, 26–7, 57
  see also auto-video-ethnography, ethnography, video
Michael (Trower)   29, 92–3, 196
Michelle (Mitolo)   28, 200, 219, 222, 224
Mike (Fagg)   36–7, 158–9, 161, 241–2
'mimetic excess'   15, 44, 95, 150
mobile phones   13, 58, 67, 70, 72
Monique (Gilbert)   99–100, 196–7

Newcastle, New South Wales   23, 31–3, 124–5, 150–6, 190–4, 251, 254, 258

Open youth venue   159–61, 246

Palais Royale Youth Venue   31–3, 80, 88, 124–5, 149–53, 156, 191–4, 251, 254, 258
participatory media/video
  see video
Patterns in Static   2, 219–20, 222–4, 253
Pie Factory Music   35–7, 158–9, 161, 170–2, 234, 241, 255, 261
place: influence on music   53, 124–6, 153

play/'serious play'   5, 13–15, 17, 41, 44, 46, 48, 51–2, 56, 70, 84, 86, 124, 126, 133–4, 141, 144, 149, 153, 161, 234–5, 236, 238, 240
practising skills   48, 74, 78–9, 108–10, 135–9, 220–2, 229, 248–9, 252
Prince's Trust   168–9, 187–9, 204, 242
'producers'   3, 65
promotion (of events/bands)   28, 81, 136, 200–1, 215, 222–6
Providence, Rhode Island, USA   182–7, 255–6, 262

radio   29, 49–50, 67, 74–7, 89, 92, 99–100, 116, 119–21, 136, 192, 194–8, 213–15, 220, 253
  pirate radio   229–32
raves   71, 111–14, 225
Rowland (DJ Roland Samuel)   1–2, 12, 34, 49–50, 67, 89, 103–4, 169, 188–9, 204, 207, 213–15, 220, 225, 227, 231–2, 242, 249

Saul (Standerwick)   32–3, 117, 206, 251
school
  curriculum   8, 157, 174, 238–40, 248
  dropping out   3, 18, 157, 174
  hours   175, 177, 254
self-making   17, 42, 44, 47–8, 51–2, 60, 90–1, 108, 126, 141, 217–18, 221, 235
Shep (DJ Shep/Adrian Shepherd)   29–30, 62, 87, 104–5, 109–11, 119–21, 163, 202–3, 216–20, 225–8, 251, 257
skateboarding   151–2
social networking sites   2, 13, 24, 47, 49–50, 62, 68, 72–3, 77, 89, 91, 105, 121, 154–5, 207, 211, 213–15, 219, 222, 246–7, 249–53
social praxeology   7, 16, 44, 46

space
  and gender   95, 128–31, 141–2, 144, 178, 185–6, 209
  and power relations   5, 126–9, 133–4, 139–40, 144, 147–9, 158
  private   5, 73–4, 123–4, 126–7, 135–41, 144, 149, 161
  public   5, 71, 124–5, 131, 139–50, 156–61, 190–1, 236–7, 243, 254
surveillance   142–5

Tabernacle, the   34, 148, 189, 261
Taussig, Michael   14–15, 221
Thornton, Sarah   102–3, 217
Totally Stressed   37, 95–6, 252
training   8, 19, 78–9, 89, 99, 109, 151, 162–4, 204–5, 212, 237, 240–1, 248
Tuesday (DJ Lady Lick/Tuesday Benfield)   xi, 34, 48, 62, 74, 83–4, 138, 140, 215, 219–22, 227, 230–1

Vanessa (Cussack)   74–6, 99–100
Vicci (Marsh)   77–8, 199, 202
video   7, 10, 13–15, 47, 56–7, 61–3, 65–75, 77–81, 136–8, 140, 214, 250, 252
  participatory video   65–8

website: Playing for Life   6, 67–70, 220
Weekend Arts College   33, 148, 212
Wexler, Philip   91–2, 220
Will (Zahra)   92, 136, 196–7, 253
Willis, Paul   86–7
workshops   29, 31–2, 36, 69, 80, 109, 119, 151–2, 163, 168, 220, 225, 227, 237, 241

Yitzchak (Jordan/Y-Love)   50–1
youth, definition   24–6
Youth Revolutions   29, 67, 74–7, 92, 99–100, 121, 136, 139, 162, 194–8, 204, 253, 257–8